The Political Economy of Indonesia's Economic Development, Volume I

Sangaralingam Ramesh

The Political Economy of Indonesia's Economic Development, Volume I

The Dawn of Civilisation to a New Order Era: 2000BC to 1998AD

palgrave
macmillan

Sangaralingam Ramesh
University of Oxford and University
College London
London, UK

ISBN 978-3-031-94349-2 ISBN 978-3-031-94350-8 (eBook)
https://doi.org/10.1007/978-3-031-94350-8

This Palgrave Macmillan imprint is published by the registered company Springer Nature Switzerland AG
The registered company address is: Gewerbestrasse 11, 6330 Cham, Switzerland

For my father and my mother,
Nallathamby Sangaralingam and Pathmarani Sangaralingam
Inuvil and Karinagar, Ceylon.

Preface

The story of Indonesia's economic development is one of resilience, adaptation, and transformation. Spanning over four millennia, the trajectory of this archipelagic nation's political economy is intertwined with its diverse geography, rich cultural heritage, and dynamic interactions with the global economy. From the earliest signs of civilization to the consolidation of a modern nation-state, Indonesia has navigated the tides of history with ingenuity and determination, crafting a unique narrative that continues to evolve.

This first volume of *The Political Economy of Indonesia's Economic Development: 2000 BC to 2024 AD*, titled *The Dawn of Civilisation to a New Order Era: 2000 BC to 1998 AD*, embarks on an ambitious journey to explore the foundational phases of Indonesia's economic and political history. By delving into ancient trade networks, the rise and fall of powerful kingdoms, the influences of colonialism, and the emergence of the New Order, this volume seeks to contextualize the forces that have shaped Indonesia's economic and political landscape over millennia. The roots of Indonesia's political economy stretch deep into prehistory. Archaeological evidence reveals thriving trade networks as early as 2000 BC, connecting the islands to mainland Asia and beyond. These early interactions fostered cultural exchanges, technological advancements, and the development of agricultural and maritime economies that would underpin Indonesia's growth for centuries to come. The advent of Hindu-Buddhist kingdoms, the spread of Islam, and the establishment of vast maritime empires such as Srivijaya and Majapahit further illustrate the adaptability and ingenuity of Indonesia's societies in responding to internal and external challenges. The colonial era marked a significant turning point, as European powers sought to exploit the archipelago's abundant resources. Under Dutch colonial rule, Indonesia's economic systems were reoriented to serve global markets, prioritizing exports of spices, sugar, coffee, and rubber. This extractive model, while fostering infrastructure development and global integration, entrenched deep economic and social inequalities that persisted well into the twentieth century. The struggles for independence during the mid-twentieth century were as much about reclaiming political sovereignty as they were about economic self-determination.

The New Order era (1966–1998) under President Suharto marked another critical juncture in Indonesia's political economy. Characterized by centralized governance and a focus on industrialization, this period witnessed remarkable economic growth but also gave rise to systemic corruption and environmental degradation. The policies of this era laid the groundwork for modern Indonesia's economic structure, shaping its industries, trade relationships, and political institutions in profound ways. This volume endeavours to present a comprehensive narrative of these transformative periods, drawing on a multidisciplinary approach that incorporates history, economics, sociology, and political science. By analysing the interplay between political structures, economic systems, and societal change, it aims to illuminate the forces that have driven Indonesia's development and the challenges it has faced along the way.

Writing this preface is an opportunity to reflect on the complexities and contradictions inherent in the study of Indonesia's political economy. It is a reminder of the nation's ability to navigate upheaval and innovation while maintaining a sense of continuity and identity. As Indonesia moves forward in the twenty-first century, this historical perspective offers valuable insights into its ongoing journey towards inclusive and sustainable development. This work would not have been possible without the contributions of scholars, historians, and analysts who have dedicated themselves to understanding Indonesia's past and present. Their research, coupled with the lived experiences of countless Indonesians, forms the foundation of this narrative. I am deeply grateful for their insights and inspiration. I invite readers to embark on this exploration of Indonesia's political and economic evolution, with the hope that it will deepen appreciation for the nation's rich history and its enduring quest for prosperity and justice. It is my sincere belief that understanding Indonesia's past is essential to navigating its future and the need to eradicate poor governance and corruption in order to optimize economic development, and I am honoured to share this journey with you.

Oxford, UK Sangaralingam Ramesh

Acknowledgements

I would like to thank Wyndham Hacket Pain, Senior Editor (Economics) at Palgrave Macmillan for his ongoing support in the time it has taken for this book to be written. Furthermore, I would like to thank my former Indonesian classmates from SOAS, Alex Margaronis, Dr E. Pantja Pramudya, and Professor Aloysius Brata of the Atma Jaya Yogyakarta University for giving me the inspiration to write these volumes on the economic development of their country. Finally, I would like to thank the production team at Palgrave Macmillan for their support in the transformation of the manuscript into the published book.

Contents

PART I

Ancient Foundations

CHAPTER 1

Introduction

Understanding Indonesia's Political Economy: A Historical Perspective

Indonesia's political economy reflects a complex historical evolution, shaped by millennia of trade, colonization, independence struggles, and authoritarian governance. Its strategic position in global trade routes positioned early kingdoms like Srivijaya and Majapahit as vital maritime trading hubs, laying the foundations for economic and cultural exchange.[1] The Dutch colonial period further entrenched Indonesia's integration into global markets through exploitative systems like the Cultivation System, which prioritized European economic interests at the expense of local development.[2] Post-independence, Sukarno's Guided Democracy era sought to assert economic sovereignty through nationalization, though mismanagement and political polarization hampered growth.[3] The transition from Sukarno's Guided Democracy era to the New Order regime under Suharto marked a pivot to market-oriented

[1] Wolters, O. W. (1999) History, Culture and Region in Southeast Asian Perspectives. Ithaca, NY: Cornell University Press.

[2] Boomgaard, P. (1990) Children of the Colonial State: Population Growth and Economic Development in Java 1795–1880. Amsterdam: Free University Press.

[3] Anderson, B. R. O'G. (1990) Language and Power: Exploring Political Cultures in Indonesia. Ithaca, NY: Cornell University Press.

S. Ramesh, *The Political Economy of Indonesia's Economic Development, Volume I*, https://doi.org/10.1007/978-3-031-94350-8_1

reforms, attracting foreign investment and fostering industrialization, but also embedding crony capitalism and corruption.[4] This volume provides a detailed examination of these transformative periods, emphasizing the persistent challenges of economic inequality, regional disparities, and governance weaknesses, while also highlighting Indonesia's resilience and adaptive capacity in navigating its path to becoming one of Southeast Asia's largest emerging economies. As the world's fourth most populous country, with an estimated 277 million people as of 2024.[5] Furthermore, Indonesia is a diverse archipelago of over 17,000 islands, home to more than 300 ethnic groups and a rich linguistic and cultural heritage.[6] The nation's religious composition is predominantly Muslim, with approximately 87% of its population adhering to Islam, making it the largest Muslim-majority country globally[7] alongside significant Christian, Hindu, and Buddhist minorities. Moreover, Indonesia's economic strength is underpinned by its vast natural resources, including significant reserves of coal, palm oil, natural gas, and nickel—critical for global supply chains and the green energy transition.[8] The country plays a central role in ASEAN, both politically and economically, accounting for nearly 40% of the region's GDP.[9] As a member of the G20, Indonesia has positioned itself as a key player in the global economy, balancing its export-driven industries with an expanding domestic market.[10] Despite facing challenges such as economic inequality, environmental degradation, and shifting geopolitical landscapes, Indonesia's ability to adapt to global economic trends

[4] Booth, A. (1998) The Indonesian Economy in the Nineteenth and Twentieth Centuries: A History of Missed Opportunities. London: Macmillan.

[5] World Bank (2024) World Development Indicators: Indonesia. Washington, DC: World Bank.

[6] Ricklefs, M. C. (2008) A History of Modern Indonesia since c. 1200. 4th edn. Basingstoke: Palgrave Macmillan.

[7] Fealy, G. and White, S. (2008) Expressing Islam: Religious Life and Politics in Indonesia. Singapore: ISEAS Publishing.

[8] Purnomo, H. and Anand, A. (2022) 'Indonesia's Natural Resources and the Green Energy Transition: Opportunities and Challenges', Journal of Southeast Asian Economies, 39(1), pp. 45–62.

[9] ASEANSecretariat (2023) ASEAN Key Figs. 2023. Jakarta: ASEAN Secretariat.

[10] Hill, H. (2018) Indonesia's Economy in the New World: Globalisation and its Implications. Singapore: ISEAS Publishing.

and policy shifts has solidified its place as a rising economic power in both Southeast Asia and the broader world economy."

The Dawn of Civilization and Early Economic Foundations

Trade and Agricultural Beginnings (2000 BC–1 AD)

Indonesia's strategic geographic position made it a crucial node in ancient maritime trade routes. The archipelago's early role in maritime trade between Southeast Asia and South Asia from 1000 BC to 1 AD fostered economic interactions with Indian merchants, who exchanged textiles and metalwork for Indonesia's spices and forest products.[11] Chinese records from the Han Dynasty further highlight the archipelago's importance as a transit point in the Maritime Silk Road, enhancing Indonesia's economic influence across Asia.[12] The early kingdoms of Srivijaya (seventh-thirteenth century) and Majapahit (thirteenth-sixteenth century) capitalized on this strategic position by controlling key maritime routes, particularly the Strait of Malacca, thereby generating wealth through trade tariffs and fostering cultural exchanges with India and China.[13] Srivijaya's economic dominance was reinforced by its role as a centre of Mahayana Buddhism, attracting pilgrims and scholars whose presence stimulated local economies through increased demand for goods and services.[14] Agriculture also played a pivotal role, with early Indonesian societies adopting wet-rice cultivation as early as 2000 BC. The construction of irrigation systems, including canals and terraces, allowed for efficient water management, enabling sustained agricultural productivity that supported population growth and the development of complex

[11] Wolters, O. W. (1999) History, Culture and Region in Southeast Asian Perspectives. Ithaca, NY: Cornell University Press.

[12] Ricklefs, M. C. (2008) A History of Modern Indonesia Since c.1200. 4th edn. Stanford, CA: Stanford University Press.

[13] Wolters, O. W. (1999) History, Culture and Region in Southeast Asian Perspectives. Ithaca, NY: Cornell University Press.

[14] Boomgaard, P. (1990) Children of the Colonial State: Population Growth and Economic Development in Java, 1795–1880. Amsterdam: Free University Press.

societies.[15] Archaeological findings indicate the domestication of taro, yam, and bananas alongside rice, reflecting early agricultural diversification that laid the economic foundations for later state formation.[16] Hindu-Buddhist influences further shaped the economic landscape, introducing caste-based economic structures, temple economies, and merchant guilds. Indian cultural exchanges via maritime trade facilitated the adoption of Sanskrit for administration and the construction of monumental architecture like Borobudur, signifying economic wealth and political authority.[17]

The Impact of Colonialism on Indonesia's Economy

Dutch Colonial Rule and Economic Reorientation (1600 s-1942)

The arrival of the Dutch East India Company (VOC) in the 1600 s reshaped Indonesia's economy through monopolistic control over the spice trade, disrupting indigenous trade networks and marginalizing local merchants.[18] The Preanger System in Java forced farmers to grow cash crops like coffee under exploitative conditions, reducing subsistence farming and leading to food insecurity.[19] The Cultivation System (1830s-1870s) intensified this exploitation by mandating farmers to allocate land and labour to export crops such as sugar and coffee, leading to widespread poverty and famine, particularly in Java during the 1840s.[20] Legal frameworks like the Agrarian Law of 1870 facilitated European land

[15] Boomgaard, P. (1990) Children of the Colonial State: Population Growth and Economic Development in Java, 1795–1880. Amsterdam: Free University Press.

[16] Ricklefs, M. C. (2008) A History of Modern Indonesia Since c.1200. 4th edn. Stanford, CA: Stanford University Press.

[17] Wolters, O. W. (1999) History, Culture and Region in Southeast Asian Perspectives. Ithaca, NY: Cornell University Press.

[18] Booth, A. (1998) The Indonesian Economy in the Nineteenth and Twentieth Centuries: A History of Missed Opportunities. London: Macmillan.

[19] Ricklefs, M. C. (2008) A History of Modern Indonesia Since c.1200. 4th edn. Stanford, CA: Stanford University Press.

[20] Booth, A. (1998) The Indonesian Economy in the Nineteenth and Twentieth Centuries: A History of Missed Opportunities. London: Macmillan.

leases, dispossessing local farmers and entrenching economic inequality.[21] Infrastructure developments, such as railways and ports, were designed to facilitate resource extraction rather than promote local development.[22]

The Economic Impact of Japanese Occupation (1942–1945)

Japanese rule prioritized resource extraction for its war effort, requisitioning food and raw materials, which led to widespread famine, particularly in Java where over 2.4 million people died of starvation.[23] The romusha system conscripted millions of Indonesians into forced labour, dismantling traditional agricultural systems and exacerbating rural poverty.[24] The economic devastation caused by Japanese policies weakened Dutch colonial structures, fostering nationalist sentiments and setting the stage for Indonesia's independence in 1945.[25]

Post-Independence Economic Struggles (1945–1965)

Sukarno's Guided Democracy and Economic Nationalism

After gaining independence, Indonesia's economy faced severe challenges such as hyperinflation, inadequate infrastructure, and political fragmentation. Sukarno's Guided Democracy (1959–1965) sought to address these through state control and economic nationalism. The nationalization of 246 Dutch-owned enterprises, including key industries like oil, rubber, and tin, aimed to sever colonial economic ties and promote self-reliance.[26] However, operational inefficiencies, due to insufficient managerial expertise, led to declining productivity and corruption,

[21] Ricklefs, M. C. (2008) A History of Modern Indonesia Since c.1200. 4th edn. Stanford, CA: Stanford University Press.

[22] Wolters, O. W. (1999) History, Culture and Region in Southeast Asian Perspectives. Ithaca, NY: Cornell University Press.

[23] Booth, A. (1998) The Indonesian Economy in the Nineteenth and Twentieth Centuries: A History of Missed Opportunities. London: Macmillan.

[24] Ricklefs, M. C. (2008) A History of Modern Indonesia Since c.1200. 4th edn. Stanford, CA: Stanford University Press.

[25] Wolters, O. W. (1999) History, Culture and Region in Southeast Asian Perspectives. Ithaca, NY: Cornell University Press.

[26] Booth, A. (1998) The Indonesian Economy in the Nineteenth and Twentieth Centuries: A History of Missed Opportunities. London: Macmillan.

notably within Pertamina, the state oil company. Import substitution policies, designed to reduce foreign dependency, struggled due to bureaucratic inefficiency and widespread corruption.[27] Sukarno's interventionist economic model, characterized by state-led industrialization and excessive money printing, resulted in hyperinflation exceeding 600% annually by 1965.[28] The government's reliance on foreign debt, particularly from the Soviet Union and China in exchange for raw materials, further strained the economy due to inefficient barter trade agreements.[29] By the early 1960s, Indonesia's economic stagnation was marked by food shortages and declining industrial output. The focus on grand infrastructure projects, such as Monas and Hotel Indonesia, drained public finances without yielding economic returns.[30] Regional disparities grew as resource-rich provinces felt marginalized by Jakarta's centralized control over revenues, contributing to local unrest.[31] Ultimately, these economic challenges fuelled widespread dissatisfaction, setting the stage for political upheaval and the eventual transition to Suharto's New Order regime in 1966.

The New Order Era (1966–1998) and Economic Transformation

Suharto's Market-Oriented Reforms

The New Order regime under Suharto marked a significant departure from Sukarno's autarkic and nationalistic economic policies, embracing market-oriented reforms and economic liberalization. Suharto's consolidation of power in 1966 allowed for the implementation of pragmatic economic strategies aimed at stabilizing the economy, which had been

[27] Lindblad, J.T. (2008) Bridges to New Business: The Economic Decolonization of Indonesia. Leiden: KITLV Press.

[28] Feith, H. (1962) The Decline of Constitutional Democracy in Indonesia. Ithaca, NY: Cornell University Press.

[29] Kahin, G. M. (1952) Nationalism and Revolution in Indonesia. Ithaca, NY: Cornell University Press.

[30] Ricklefs, M. C. (2008) A History of Modern Indonesia Since c.1200. 4th edn. Stanford, CA: Stanford University Press.

[31] Reid, A. (1974) The Indonesian National Revolution, 1945–1950. Hawthorn, VIC: Longman Australia.

plagued by hyperinflation and declining production during the final years of Sukarno's rule.[32] Central to these reforms was the so-called Berkeley Mafia, a group of Western-trained Indonesian economists who designed and implemented policies that emphasized fiscal discipline, monetary stability, and a more open economy.[33] These technocrats, influenced by neoclassical economic theories, played a critical role in curbing inflation, stabilizing the rupiah, and attracting foreign investment, particularly through the liberalization of foreign direct investment laws.[34]

The oil boom of the 1970s provided a crucial financial cushion that enabled the New Order government to fund large-scale infrastructure projects, expand education access, and improve health services.[35] Revenues from oil exports allowed Indonesia to reduce its dependence on foreign aid temporarily and finance ambitious development plans, including the Trans-Sumatra and Trans-Java highways, extensive irrigation networks, and rural electrification programs.[36] However, the country's heavy reliance on oil exports also made it vulnerable to external shocks, as evidenced by the economic challenges that followed the global oil price collapse in the early 1980s. In response, the government embarked on a series of structural adjustments, including the deregulation of key sectors, reduction of tariffs, and privatization of state-owned enterprises.[37]

A cornerstone of the New Order's economic success was the Green Revolution, which significantly boosted agricultural productivity, particularly rice production, through extensive investments in irrigation, high-yield seed varieties, fertilizers, and rural infrastructure.[38] These agricultural reforms not only improved food security but also contributed to rural development and poverty reduction, though they were not without environmental and social costs, including deforestation and

[32] Hill, H. (1996). The Indonesian Economy since 1966: SoutheastAsia's Emerging Giant. Cambridge University Press.

[33] Robison, R. (1986). Indonesia: The rise of capital. Allen & Unwin.

[34] MacIntyre, A. (1991). Business and politics in Indonesia. Allen & Unwin.

[35] Booth, A. (1998). The Indonesian economy in the nineteenth and twentieth centuries: A history of missed opportunities. Macmillan.

[36] Ricklefs, M. C. (2008). A history of modern Indonesia since c.1200. Palgrave Macmillan.

[37] Thee, K. W. (2012). Indonesia's Economy since Independence. Institute of Southeast Asian Studies.

[38] Elson, R. E. (2009). The idea of Indonesia: A history. Cambridge University Press.

increased rural inequality.[39] The New Order era laid the groundwork for Indonesia's integration into the global economy, but its development model also entrenched patronage politics, corruption, and authoritarian control, factors that would contribute to its eventual downfall during the 1997–1998Asian Financial Crisis.[40] Nonetheless, the economic transformation achieved during Suharto's rule remains a defining chapter in Indonesia's modern economic development.

Economic Growth and Its Discontents

The New Order era witnessed impressive economic growth, with Indonesia's GDP expanding at an average annual rate of around 7% between 1967 and 1997, driven by export-oriented industrialization, foreign investment, and state-led infrastructure development.[41] However, this economic success was accompanied by systemic corruption, nepotism, and crony capitalism, which became hallmarks of Suharto's regime. Suharto's family and close associates, including powerful conglomerates like the Salim Group, controlled vast swathes of the economy, from banking and manufacturing to infrastructure and natural resources.[42] State contracts, monopolies, and licences were frequently awarded based on political connections rather than merit, inflating costs and stifling competition.[43]

While the capital city Jakarta and other urban centres experienced rapid development with modern infrastructure, shopping malls, and high-rise buildings, rural areas were often left behind. Despite agricultural reforms under the Green Revolution, many rural communities, especially in resource-rich but politically marginalized provinces such as Aceh and Papua, felt excluded from the nation's economic prosperity. The exploitation of natural resources in these regions, including oil, gas, and

[39] Lucas, A., & Warren, C. (2013). Land for the People: The State and Agrarian Conflict in Indonesia. Ohio University Press.

[40] Schwarz, A. (1999). A nation in waiting: Indonesia's search for stability. Allen & Unwin.

[41] Hill, H. (1996). The Indonesian economy since 1966: SoutheastAsia's emerging giant. Cambridge University Press.

[42] Robison, R. (1986). Indonesia: The rise of capital. Allen & Unwin.

[43] McLeod, R. H. (2000). Suharto's Indonesia: A better class of corruption. Agenda: A Journal of Policy Analysis and Reform, 7(2), 99–112.

minerals, fuelled local grievances as revenues largely benefited Jakarta-based elites, while environmental degradation and displacement affected local populations.'[44,45] The disparity between urban and rural development, along with the regime's repressive political tactics, contributed to growing resentment and regional unrest. In Aceh, dissatisfaction over economic exploitation and human rights abuses culminated in the resurgence of separatist movements led by the Free Aceh Movement (GAM).[46] Similarly, in Papua, the extraction of natural resources by state-owned enterprises and foreign companies, such as Freeport-McMoRan's Grasberg mine, intensified calls for independence.[47] Furthermore, Suharto's economic policies prioritized short-term growth and political stability over long-term institutional development. The patronage system ensured that wealth remained concentrated within a narrow elite, with little effort to build transparent and accountable governance structures. This created economic vulnerabilities that became starkly evident during the 1997 Asian Financial Crisis when Indonesia's crony-capitalist system collapsed under the weight of unsustainable debt and capital flight.[48] Despite these challenges, the New Order era laid the foundation for Indonesia's integration into the global economy. However, the economic disparities, entrenched corruption, and regional discontent left a complex legacy that would shape Indonesia's post-Suharto economic and political landscape.[49]

[44] Ricklefs, M. C. (2008). A history of modern Indonesia since c.1200. Palgrave Macmillan.

[45] Aspinall, E. (2007). The construction of grievance: Natural resources and identity in a separatist conflict. Journal of Conflict Resolution, 51(6), 950–972.

[46] Aspinall, E. (2009). Islam and nation: Separatist rebellion in Aceh, Indonesia. Stanford University Press.

[47] Leith, D. (2002). The Politics of Power: Freeport in Suharto's Indonesia. University of Hawaii Contemporary Southeast Asia, 24(1), 33–58.

[48] MacIntyre, A. (2003). The power of institutions: Political architecture and governance. Cornell University Press.

[49] Schwarz, A. (1999). A nation in waiting: Indonesia's search for stability. Allen & Unwin.

The 1997 Asian Financial Crisis and Suharto's Downfall

The 1997 Asian Financial Crisis laid bare Indonesia's economic vulnerabilities, including its overreliance on short-term foreign debt, weak financial institutions, and a crony-capitalist system that prioritized political connections over financial prudence.[50] As the crisis unfolded, the rupiah depreciated by over 80% against the US dollar, leading to severe liquidity shortages, widespread corporate defaults, and the near collapse of the banking sector.[51] The sudden reversal of foreign capital inflows exposed the fragile underpinnings of Indonesia's rapid growth during the New Order era.[52] In response, the Indonesian government sought assistance from the International Monetary Fund (IMF), which provided a bailout package worth approximately $43 billion. However, the IMF's stringent austerity measures—such as subsidy cuts on essential goods, tight monetary policies, and structural reforms aimed at dismantling monopolies—exacerbated economic hardship for ordinary Indonesians, leading to soaring inflation, rising unemployment, and increasing poverty levels.[53] The removal of fuel and food subsidies, in particular, triggered widespread public anger, as prices of basic commodities skyrocketed.[54] Public discontent, which had been simmering under Suharto's authoritarian rule, erupted into mass protests across the country, particularly in Jakarta, Yogyakarta, and Surabaya. Students, labour unions, and civil society groups, already disillusioned with the regime's endemic corruption and nepotism, mobilized in large numbers, demanding political reform and Suharto's resignation.[55] The violent crackdown on demonstrators,

[50] Hill, H. (1999). The Indonesian Economy in Crisis: Causes, Consequences, and Lessons. Institute of Southeast Asian Studies.

[51] McLeod, R. H. (1998). Indonesia: Financial Fragility and the IMF Intervention. Southeast Asian Affairs, 1998, 113–133.

[52] MacIntyre, A. (1999). Political Institutions and the Economic Crisis in SoutheastAsia. Asian Survey, 39(4), 647–668.

[53] Soesastro, H., & Basri, M. C. (1998). The IMF and Indonesia: Economic Reform and Restructuring. The Indonesian Quarterly, 26(2), 113–128.

[54] Sharma, S. D. (2003). The Asian Financial Crisis: Crisis, Reform and Recovery. Manchester University Press.

[55] Aspinall, E. (2005). Opposing Suharto: Compromise, Resistance, and Regime Change in Indonesia. Stanford University Press.

including the Trisakti University shootings in May 1998, further fuelled anti-government sentiments.[56] Amid mounting pressure from the public, political elites, and even the military, Suharto was left with little choice but to step down. On May 21, 1998, after 32 years in power, Suharto resigned, marking the end of the New Order era and ushering in a period of political transition known as the Reformasi era.[57] His departure also signalled the beginning of structural economic reforms, including the restructuring of the banking sector, efforts to tackle corruption, and the decentralization of political power.[58] The crisis highlighted the perils of Indonesia's economic model under Suharto—rapid growth fuelled by foreign debt, state monopolies controlled by politically connected elites, and an underregulated financial system. It also underscored the importance of institutional reforms, which would shape Indonesia's post-New Order economic and political trajectory.[59]

Conclusion: Lessons from Indonesia's Economic History

Indonesia's economic development reveals a complex interplay of geography, politics, and global economic forces that have shaped its developmental trajectory over millennia. From the ancient trade networks of Srivijaya and Majapahit to the exploitative systems of Dutch colonial rule and the post-independence struggles under Sukarno, Indonesia's economy has been defined by both remarkable resilience and persistent structural challenges. One of the most significant lessons from Indonesia's economic past is the enduring impact of colonial exploitation. Dutch policies, particularly the Cultivation System, reoriented Indonesia's economy towards the production of cash crops for European markets at the expense

[56] Lane, M. (2019). Decentralization and Its Discontents: An Essay on Class, Political Agency and National Perspective in Indonesian Politics. ISEAS–YusofIshak Institute.

[57] Ricklefs, M. C. (2008). A History of Modern Indonesia since c.1200. Palgrave Macmillan.

[58] Hadiz, V. R., & Robison, R. (2004). Reorganizing Power in Indonesia: The Politics of Oligarchy in an Age of Markets. Routledge.

[59] Rosser, A. (2002). The Politics of Economic Liberalization in Indonesia: State, Market and Power. Routledge.

of local development.[60] The legacy of this extractive economy is evident in the persistent economic inequalities and underdevelopment in rural and outer island regions, which continue to lag behind urban centres like Jakarta. The post-independence period under Sukarno highlighted the challenges of balancing economic nationalism with pragmatic governance. While the nationalization of Dutch enterprises aimed to assert economic sovereignty, the lack of institutional capacity and managerial expertise led to inefficiencies and corruption.[61] Sukarno's focus on grandiose infrastructure projects and reliance on foreign aid, particularly from the Soviet Union and China, exacerbated economic vulnerabilities, culminating in hyperinflation and economic stagnation by the mid-1960s.[62]

The New Order era under Suharto marked a critical shift towards market-oriented reforms and economic liberalization. The involvement of the Berkeley Mafia brought about fiscal discipline, monetary stability, and an open-door policy for foreign investment, driving rapid economic growth.[63] However, this growth was accompanied by systemic corruption, nepotism, and crony capitalism. Suharto's regime prioritized short-term economic gains and political stability over long-term institutional development, leading to a fragile economic system heavily reliant on external debt and vulnerable to global shocks.[64] The 1997 Asian Financial Crisis exposed these vulnerabilities, with the collapse of the rupiah, widespread corporate defaults, and a near-complete breakdown of the financial system. The IMF-imposed austerity measures, while necessary for macroeconomic stabilization, exacerbated social and economic hardships, leading to mass protests and the eventual fall of Suharto.[65] The crisis underscored the dangers of an over-leveraged economy, weak regulatory frameworks, and the absence of transparent governance.

[60] Boomgaard, P. (1990) Children of the Colonial State: Population Growth and Economic Development in Java 1795–1880. Amsterdam: Free University Press.

[61] Feith, H. (1962). The Decline of Constitutional Democracy in Indonesia. Ithaca, NY: Cornell University Press.

[62] Hill, H. (1996) The Indonesian Economy since 1966: SoutheastAsia's Emerging Giant. Cambridge University Press.

[63] Robison, R. (1986) Indonesia: The rise of capital. Allen & Unwin.

[64] McLeod, R. H. (2000) 'Suharto's Indonesia: A better class of corruption', Agenda: A Journal of Policy Analysis and Reform, 7(2), pp. 99–112.

[65] MacIntyre, A. (1999) 'Political Institutions and the Economic Crisis in SoutheastAsia', Asian Survey, 39(4), pp. 647–668.

Key Lessons for Future Economic Policy

Strengthening Institutional Capacity: Future governments must prioritize the development of robust institutions that ensure transparency, accountability, and the rule of law. Indonesia's political economy remains dominated by oligarchic interests, which stifles competition and innovation. Institutional reforms are crucial for breaking this cycle.[66] The specific institutional reforms which are needed are as follows.

Judicial Reform

Indonesia's judiciary has long been plagued by corruption and political interference.[67] Reforms should focus on ensuring judicial independence, improving the appointment process for judges, and establishing strict anti-corruption measures within the legal system. A transparent and fair judiciary is essential for enforcing contracts, protecting property rights, and ensuring the rule of law.

Anti-Corruption Measures

Strengthening the Corruption Eradication Commission (KPK), which has faced political pushback in recent years, is vital for economic reforms to be successful in generating long-term sustainable economic growth.[68] Legislative reforms should enhance the KPK's powers to investigate and prosecute high-level corruption, particularly within state-owned enterprises and government procurement processes.

Decentralization and Local Governance

While decentralization aimed to empower local governments, it has often led to localized corruption and inefficiency.[69] Institutional reforms should include mechanisms for financial oversight of local budgets, transparent allocation of resources, and community participation in decision-making processes to ensure that decentralization benefits all regions equitably.

[66] Hadiz, V. R. and Robison, R. (2004) Reorganizing Power in Indonesia: The Politics of Oligarchy in an Age of Markets. Routledge.

[67] McLeod, R. H. (2000) 'Suharto's Indonesia: A better class of corruption', Agenda: A Journal of Policy Analysis and Reform, 7(2), pp. 99–112.

[68] Hadiz, V. R. and Robison, R. (2004) Reorganizing Power in Indonesia: The Politics of Oligarchy in an Age of Markets. Routledge.

[69] Lane, M. (2019). Decentralization and Its Discontents: An Essay on Class, Political Agency and National Perspective in Indonesian Politics. ISEAS–YusofIshak Institute.

Regulatory and Bureaucratic Reforms

Indonesia's regulatory environment is often criticized for being cumbersome and opaque, deterring investment.[70] Simplifying business licensing processes, reducing bureaucratic red tape, and ensuring that regulatory bodies operate independently and transparently are critical steps for fostering a more competitive business environment.

Strengthening Financial Regulation

The 1997 Asian Financial Crisis highlighted the weaknesses in Indonesia's financial regulatory framework.[71] Reforms should include stricter oversight of banking practices, enhanced risk management protocols, and the establishment of an independent financial regulatory authority to prevent future economic crises.

Public Sector Governance

Enhancing the efficiency and accountability of the public sector is essential. This can be achieved through performance-based management systems, digitalization of government services to reduce human intervention and corruption, and comprehensive training programs for civil servants to improve competence and service delivery.[72]

Land and Resource Management

Clear and enforceable land rights are crucial for both economic development and social stability, especially in rural areas.[73] Reforms should focus on modernizing land registration systems, protecting indigenous land rights, and ensuring transparent and equitable resource management practices to avoid conflicts and ensure sustainable development.

Reforms are also needed in other areas of Indonesia's economy.

Diversifying the Economy: Indonesia's heavy reliance on natural resources has made it susceptible to commodity price fluctuations. Investment in manufacturing, technology, and services can reduce this dependency and promote sustainable growth.[74]

[70] Hill, H. (2018). Indonesia's Economy in the New World: Globalisation and its Implications. Singapore: ISEAS Publishing.

[71] Sharma, S. D. (2003). The Asian Financial Crisis: Crisis, Reform and Recovery. Manchester University Press.

[72] Thee, K. W. (2012). Indonesia's Economy since Independence. Institute of Southeast Asian Studies.

[73] Lucas, A., & Warren, C. (2013). Land for the People: The State and Agrarian Conflict in Indonesia. Ohio University Press.

[74] Thee, K. W. (2012). Indonesia's Economy since Independence. Institute of Southeast Asian Studies.

Addressing Regional Inequality: The economic marginalization of resource-rich provinces like Aceh and Papua has fuelled social unrest and separatist movements.[75] Decentralization policies must be accompanied by equitable distribution of resources and development initiatives that empower local communities.

Promoting Human Capital Development: Education and skill development are critical for fostering innovation and enhancing productivity. The success of the Green Revolution demonstrated how investments in agricultural technology transformed rural economies.[76] Similar investments in education and vocational training can drive future economic growth.

Ensuring Sustainable Development: Indonesia's vast natural resources, including coal, palm oil, and nickel, present both opportunities and challenges, particularly in the context of the global green energy transition.[77] Policies that promote sustainable resource management and environmental protection are essential for long-term prosperity.

Enhancing Financial Regulation: The financial collapse during the Asian Financial Crisis highlighted the need for robust regulatory frameworks. Strengthening financial oversight and ensuring prudent fiscal policies can safeguard against future economic shocks.[78]

Pathway to Becoming a Global Economic Power: Indonesia's potential to become an economic superpower lies in its demographic dividend, strategic geographic position, and abundant natural resources. However, realizing this potential requires decisive policy actions that address historical economic shortcomings. Future governments must focus on fostering inclusive growth, reducing corruption, investing in infrastructure and human capital, and integrating into global value chains

[75] Aspinall, E. (2009) Islam and nation: Separatist rebellion in Aceh, Indonesia. Stanford University Press.

[76] Elson, R. E. (2009) The idea of Indonesia: A history. Cambridge University Press.

[77] Purnomo, H. and Anand, A. (2022) 'Indonesia's Natural Resources and the Green Energy Transition: Opportunities and Challenges', Journal of Southeast Asian Economies, 39(1), pp. 45–62.

[78] Sharma, S. D. (2003) The Asian Financial Crisis: Crisis, Reform and Recovery. Manchester University Press.

through innovation and technology. Indonesia's history is one of adaptation and resilience.[79] By learning from past mistakes and leveraging its strengths, Indonesia can chart a path towards sustainable and inclusive economic development, ultimately positioning itself as a leading global economic power.

References

Anderson, B. R. O'G. (1990) *Language and Power: Exploring Political Cultures in Indonesia.* Ithaca, NY: Cornell University Press.

ASEAN Secretariat (2023) ASEAN Key Figures 2023. Jakarta: ASEAN Secretariat.

Aspinall, E. (2005). Opposing Suharto: Compromise, Resistance, and Regime Change in Indonesia. Stanford University Press.

Aspinall, E. (2007). The construction of grievance: Natural resources and identity in a separatist conflict. Journal of Conflict Resolution, 51(6), 950-972.

Aspinall, E. (2009). Islam and nation: Separatist rebellion in Aceh, Indonesia. Stanford University Press.

Boomgaard, P. (1990) *Children of the Colonial State: Population Growth and Economic Development in Java 1795-1880.* Amsterdam: Free University Press.

Booth, A. (1998) *The Indonesian Economy in the Nineteenth and Twentieth Centuries: A History of Missed Opportunities.* London: Macmillan.

Elson, R. E. (2009). The idea of Indonesia: A history. Cambridge University Press.

Fealy, G. and White, S. (2008) Expressing Islam: Religious Life and Politics in Indonesia. Singapore: ISEAS Publishing.

Feith, H. (1962) The Decline of Constitutional Democracy in Indonesia. Ithaca, NY: Cornell University Press.

Hadiz, V. R., & Robison, R. (2004). Reorganizing Power in Indonesia: The Politics of Oligarchy in an Age of Markets. Routledge.

Hill, H. (1996). The Indonesian Economy since 1966: Southeast Asia's Emerging Giant. Cambridge University Press.

Hill, H. (1999). The Indonesian Economy in Crisis: Causes, Consequences, and Lessons. Institute of Southeast Asian Studies.

Hill, H. (2018) Indonesia's Economy in the New World: Globalisation and its Implications. Singapore: ISEAS Publishing.

Kahin, G. M. (1952) Nationalism and Revolution in Indonesia. Ithaca, NY: Cornell University Press.

[79] Ricklefs, M. C. (2008) A History of Modern Indonesia since c.1200. 4th edn. Stanford, CA: Stanford University Press.

Lane, M. (2019). Decentralization and Its Discontents: An Essay on Class, Political Agency and National Perspective in Indonesian Politics. ISEAS—Yusof Ishak Institute.

Leith, D. (2002). The Politics of Power: Freeport in Suharto's Indonesia. University of Hawaii Contemporary Southeast Asia, 24(1), 33-58.

Lindblad, J.T. (2008) Bridges to New Business: The Economic Decolonization of Indonesia. Leiden: KITLV Press.

Lucas, A., & Warren, C. (2013). Land for the People: The State and Agrarian Conflict in Indonesia. Ohio University Press.

MacIntyre, A. (1991). Business and politics in Indonesia. Allen & Unwin.

MacIntyre, A. (1999). Political Institutions and the Economic Crisis in Southeast Asia. Asian Survey, 39(4), 647-668.

MacIntyre, A. (2003). The power of institutions: Political architecture and governance. Cornell University Press.

McLeod, R. H. (1998). Indonesia: Financial Fragility and the IMF Intervention. Southeast Asian Affairs, 1998, 113-133.

McLeod, R. H. (2000). Suharto's Indonesia: A better class of corruption. Agenda: A Journal of Policy Analysis and Reform, 7(2), 99–112.

Purnomo, H. and Anand, A. (2022) 'Indonesia's Natural Resources and the Green Energy Transition: Opportunities and Challenges', Journal of Southeast Asian Economies, 39(1), pp. 45-62.

Reid, A. (1974) The Indonesian National Revolution, 1945–1950. Hawthorn, VIC: Longman Australia.

Ricklefs, M. C. (2008) A History of Modern Indonesia Since c.1200. 4th edn. Stanford, CA: Stanford University Press.

Robison, R. (1986). Indonesia: The rise of capital. Allen & Unwin.

Rosser, A. (2002). The Politics of Economic Liberalization in Indonesia: State, Market and Power. Routledge.

Schwarz, A. (1999). A nation in waiting: Indonesia's search for stability. Allen & Unwin.

Sharma, S. D. (2003). The Asian Financial Crisis: Crisis, Reform and Recovery. Manchester University Press.

Soesastro, H., & Basri, M. C. (1998). The IMF and Indonesia: Economic Reform and Restructuring. The Indonesian Quarterly, 26(2), 113-128.

Thee, K. W. (2012). Indonesia's Economy since Independence. Institute of Southeast Asian Studies.

Wolters, O. W. (1999) *History, Culture and Region in Southeast Asian Perspectives*. Ithaca, NY: Cornell University Press.

World Bank (2024) World Development Indicators: Indonesia. Washington, DC: World Bank.

CHAPTER 2

The Dawn of Civilization (2000 BC–1 AD)

Introduction

Overview of Early Human Settlement

There are two main theories which seeks to explain how Homo Sapiens prevailed as the dominant hominin species whilst the others died out and became extinct.[1] The first of the theories is the multi-regional model which stipulates that Homo Sapiens emerged as the dominant global hominin species as a result of spontaneous evolution from Homo Erectus to Homo Sapiens simultaneously in multiple locations. On the other hand, the 'out of Africa' or 'replacement theory' suggests that Homo Sapiens moving out of Africa gradually replaced archaic Homo Sapiens and other hominin species at a global level at different times. However, no matter which of the two theories is accepted as being the most appropriate for explaining how Homo Sapiens populated the planet and became the dominant species, there is little doubt as to the cradle of their emergence being Africa. Moreover, it is also evident that it took time for Homo Sapiens to evolve in Africa as well as to supersede Homo Erectus as the pre-dominant hominin species there. The protruded forehead and strong, denser jawbone structure of Homo Erectus was not

[1] Widianto, H. and Noerwidi, S. (2023), The emergence and distribution of early modern human in Indonesia. L'Anthropologie, 127(3), p. 103161.

S. Ramesh, *The Political Economy of Indonesia's Economic Development, Volume I*, https://doi.org/10.1007/978-3-031-94350-8_2

evident in Homo Sapiens. This is due to the differences in the dietary intake of the two species. Homo Erectus, although familiar with fire, tended to eat raw vegetation and raw meat and so required a strong jawbone structure to chew and break down the plant and meat into smaller pieces in order to facilitate more efficient digestion. On the other hand, Homo Sapiens tended to eat plant and meat which had been cooked and was therefore softer, needing less chewing, as it entered the digestive tract. The need for a dense, robust jawbone structure resulted in Homo Erectus having a long and low skull. This resulted in Homo Erectus having less brain capacity than Homo Sapiens whose skull was rounded with a more elevated skull 'roof 'than that of Homo Erectus, allowing for a larger brain capacity.[2] This larger brain capacity ensured that Homo Sapiens was a more intelligent and innovative hominin species than Homo Erectus. Homo Sapiens may have been more efficient with regards to gathering and protecting food supplies. It may also have been able to communicate more effectively allowing for a stronger community structure which would have resulted in better care of infants, children, pregnant women and the elderly. Better communication would also have resulted in greater cooperation amongst individuals with regards to the defence of the community. In contrast, amongst the Homo Erectus population food gathering would have been less efficient, as would have been communication between individuals and the nurturing of the young. The result would have been a decline in the Homo Erectus population and an increase in the Homo Sapien population. An even global distribution of this effect would have meant that the Homo Erectus global population was falling and being supplanted by a rising population of Homo Sapiens. Archaeological sites such as Skhul and Qafzeh in Israel illustrates the presence of anatomically modern humans, Homo Sapiens, out of Africa. Remains at the site at Skhul site are dated to be between 100,000 and 130,000 years while remains at the Qafzeh site are dated to be between 90,000 and 120,000 years. However, other Homo Sapien remains found at Misliya Cave in Israel have been dated to be between 177,000 and 194,000 years old.[3] This would suggest that Homo Sapiens

[2] Ibid.

[3] Widianto, H. and Noerwidi, S. (2023), The emergence and distribution of early modern human in Indonesia. L'Anthropologie, 127(3), p. 103161.

had begun to leave Africa much earlier than had been thought.[4] Moreover, by 40,000 years ago Homo Sapiens had spread across all of the world's continents.[5] Cro-Magnon Man was the direct descendant of modern Europeans and inhabited Europe until the end of the last ice age 10,000 years ago at the start of the Holocene period.[6] Although, Cro-Magnon Man had the features of modern Homo Sapiens it could be that its genetic makeup still constituted some elements of Homo Erectus from the late Pleistocene period. The remains of Homo Erectus Pekinensis has also been found in China. Although, the earliest archaic Homo Sapien remains found in China has been Liujiang Man, carbon dated to be about 35,000 years old.[7] The cranium of Liujiang Man exhibited a combination of East Asian and Australomelanesian features.[8] Although, it is likely to have been present in China and East Asia as far back as 139,000 years ago[9] with a presence of over 153,000 years not being an impossibility.[10] In any case, it is likely that Liujiang Man is the earliest form of archaic hominin in East Asia.[11] However, it is likely that South-East Asia including Indonesia did not experience a Homo Sapien presence until the second half of the late Pleistocene, between 63,000 years and 11,700 years ago. This period

[4] Hershkovitz, I., Weber, G.W., Quam, R., Duval, M., Gru¨ n, R., Kinsley, L., Ayalon, A., Bar-Matthews, M., Valladas, H., Mercier, N., Arsuaga, J.L., Martino´ n-Torres, M., Bermudez de Castro, J.M., Fornai, C., Martın-Frances, L., Rachel Sarig, R., May, H., Krenn, V.A., Slon, V., Rodrıguez, L., Garcıa, R., Lorenzo, C., Carretero, J.M., Frumkin, A., Shahack-Gross, R., Bar-Yosef Mayer, D.E., Cui, Y., Wu, X., Peled, N., Groman-Yaroslavski, I., Weissbrod, L., Yeshurun, R., Tsatskin, A., Zaidner, Y., Weinstein-Evron, M. (2018), The earliest modern humans outside Africa. Science 359 (6374), 456–459, http://dx.doi.org/10.1126/science.aap8369.

[5] Bellwood, Ardelean, C.F., Becerra-Valdivia, L., et al. (2020), Evidence of human occupation in Mexico around the Last Glacial Maximum. Nature 584 (7819), 87–92.

[6] Widianto, H. and Noerwidi, S. (2023), The emergence and distribution of early modern human in Indonesia. L'Anthropologie, 127(3), p. 103161.

[7] Coon, C.S. (1962), The Origin of Races. Borzoi Book, New York.

[8] Ibid.

[9] Shen, G., Wang, W., Wang, Q., Zhao, J., Collerson, K., Zhou, C., Tobias, P. (2002), U-Series dating of Liujiang hominid site in Guangxi, Southern China. Journal of human Evolution 43 (6), 817–829.

[10] Widianto, H. and Noerwidi, S. (2023), The emergence and distribution of early modern human in Indonesia. L'Anthropologie, 127(3), p. 103161.

[11] Ibid.

of time is important for the study of human evolution because it encompasses the time during which Homo Sapiens spread out of Africa into the other parts of the world. The second half of the late Pleistocene was also a period of time during which large mammal species exhibited significant changes in not only geographical distribution but also in the size of their populations. The earliest form of archaic Homo Sapiens in Indonesia is considered to be Wajak Man whose fossilised remains have been found in Tulungagung, East Java. Wajak Man of East Java is comparable to other specimens found at sites in Thailand, Malaysia as well as the Philippines[12]; and has been carbon dated to be between 40,000 and 6500 years old.[13] The other sites are Moh Khiew, Thailand, Niah, Sarawak, Malaysia and Tabon, Palawan, Philippines. The Niah cave complex in Malaysia is a huge place with several entrances and it has been a site of human occupation from between 40,000 to 2000 years.[14] The skull and intra-cranial fragments of a young female adult have been found at the western entrance to the Niah cave complex. The Niah 'deep' skull is considered to be evidence of the earliest human occupation of South-East Asia, carbon dated to be at least 39,000 years old.[15] Although, its actual age is subject to debate amongst scholars.[16] The Niah skull has a vertical forehead, a face that is broad and short with the roof of the skull not being very thick at all.[17] The Niah skull shares many features of Tasmanian and Australian aborigines as do the skull fragments found at Wajak and Tabon.[18] The Niah supra-orbital torus and the canine fossae are not very well developed and

[12] Bellwood, P. (1997), Prehistory of the Indo-Malaysian Archipelago. University of Hawaii Press, Honolulu, Hawaii384p.

[13] Koenigswald, G.H.R. von. (1956), The geological age of Wadjak Man from Java. Proceedings of the Koninklijke Nederlandsch Akademie van Wetenschappen (PKNAW), Serie B 59 (5), 455–457.

[14] Widianto, H. and Noerwidi, S. (2023), The emergence and distribution of early modern human in Indonesia. L'Anthropologie, 127(3), p. 103161.

[15] Majid, Z. (1982), The West Mouth, Niah, in the Prehistory of SoutheastAsia. Sarawak Museum Journal 31 (52) [Special monograph no 3].

[16] Kennedy, K.A. (1977), The deep skull of Niah: An assessment of twenty years of speculation concerning its evolutionary significance. Asian Perspectives, 20(1), pp. 32–50.

[17] Widianto, H. and Noerwidi, S. (2023), The emergence and distribution of early modern human in Indonesia. L'Anthropologie, 127(3), p. 103161.

[18] Durband, A.C. and Westaway, M.C. (2013), Perspectives on the origins of modern Australians. The Origins of Modern Humans: Biology Reconsidered, pp. 123–150.

the palatines are distinct from those of Wajak Man.[19] With regards to the latter, the fragments associated with two skulls were found in East Java, one of a female and one of a male. Both skulls resemble the skulls of Australoid Aborigines, although the Wajak skull capacity is by far bigger. The Wajak female has a capacity of 1550 cm while that of the Wajak male has a capacity of 1650 cm. The male and the female Wajak skulls differ in this way. Nevertheless, both skulls are long and thick with large teeth and strong mandibles.[20] The Wajak male skull is broad but flat in shape. Both the male and the female skulls exhibit no canine fossae, and the facial features of both skulls are flat in shape. The features of the Wajak skulls in comparison to the skulls of other Homo Sapien races has been the subject of debate. On the one hand, some assert that the Wajak skulls exhibit primarily Australomelanesoid[21] features, others assert that the skulls also exhibit Mongoloid features.[22] However, the Wajak skulls are also similar to those found in Polynesia and Micronesia because the tuberculum precondylus is present in both sets of skulls. The tuberculum precondylus also known as the precondylar tubercle is a small bony prominence located on the underside of the occipital bone of the skull, near the occipital condyles. It is thought that the main function of the tuberculum precondylus is as a point of attachment for ligaments or muscles involved in the stabilisation of the skull and the cervical spine. Others have also noticed similarities between the skulls of Wajak Man and those of Australian in origin particularly in the context of the flatter nature of the face as well as with regards to its dimensions.[23] Ancient human skulls found at Keilor in Australia also bear similarities with the features of the

[19] Widianto, H. and Noerwidi, S. (2023), The emergence and distribution of early modern human in Indonesia. L'Anthropologie, 127(3), p. 103161.

[20] Widianto, H. and Noerwidi, S. (2023), The emergence and distribution of early modern human in Indonesia. L'Anthropologie, 127(3), p. 103161.

[21] Dubois E. (1921), De proto-Australische Fossiele Mensch van Wadjak (Java), Koninklijke Nederindsch Akademie van Wetenschappen te Amsterdam, Verslag an de gewone Vergaderingen der Wis-, en Natuurkundige Afdeeling, 29, pp. 88–105.

[22] Jacob, T. (1977), Evolution of man in SoutheastAsia", Berkala Ilmu Kedokteran,. J Med Sci IX (4), 175–186.

[23] Weidenreich, F. (1945), The Keilor Skull: a Wadjak Skull from SoutheastAustralia, American Journal of Physical Anthropology 3, 21–33.

skulls of Wajak Man[24] as they also do with the Lujiang skull.[25] The similarities between the features of the skulls of archaic Homo Sapiens in Java, China and on the Australian continent suggests a strong genetic link between the peoples populating Asia in the late Pleistocene period.[26]

Another hominin species was discovered in Indonesia in 2003 at Liang Bua, Flores Island. The specimen was aptly named Flores Man and due to its small stature quickly caught the imagination of the media who nicknamed it as the 'Hobbit.' The hominin was alive in the area around the end of the Pleistocene; and its fossilised remains indicates features of both Homo Sapiens as well as those of Homo Erectus.[27] However, the features of the latter were so prominent in Flores Man that it has been dubbed as a smaller version of Homo Erectus.[28] Another fossilised hominin discovery from the Late Pleistocene in Sumatra, Lida Ajar Man, suggests that the rain forest environment was also widely inhabited by early modern humans whose remains have been dated to be between 73,000 and 63,000 years old.[29] It is thought that Homo Sapiens arrived on Java Island at around the time of the last interglacial maximum.[30] The last interglacial maximum, commonly referred to as the Eemian Interglacial, occurred approximately 125,000 years ago. This period is well-documented in paleoclimatology and is significant for understanding Earth's natural climate cycles and their impact on

[24] Coon, C.S. (1962), The Origin of Races. Borzoi Book, New York.

[25] Widianto, H. and Noerwidi, S. (2023), The emergence and distribution of early modern human in Indonesia. L'Anthropologie, 127(3), p. 103161.

[26] Ibid.

[27] Widianto, H. (2004), Siapakah Dia, Homo floresiensis?, Kompas Edisi 5, 52.

[28] Zeitoun, V., Barriel, V., Widianto, H. (2016), Phylogenetic analysis of the calvaria of Homo floresiensis species. Palevol 15 (5), 555–568, http://dx.doi.org/10.1016/j.crpv.2015.12.002.

[29] Noerwidi, S., Vialet, A., Widianto, H., Kurniawan, I., Zaim, J., Suriyanto, R.A., Joordens, J., Lorenzo, C., Simanjuntak, T., Se´mah, F. (2020), Exploring the diversity of fossil hominin dental patterns in the western Indonesian archipelago during the Quaternary by Geometric Morphometric Analysis. Application on second upper and lower molars. L'anthropologie 124 (5), 102791.

[30] Widianto, H. and Noerwidi, S. (2023), The emergence and distribution of early modern human in Indonesia. L'Anthropologie, 127(3), p. 103161.

global environments.[31] The Eemian Interglacial, occurring approximately 125,000 to 115,000 years ago, was characterized by global temperatures that were 1–2 °C warmer than present, significantly reduced polar ice, and sea levels 6–9 meters higher than today. During this period, the Arctic was ice-free in summer, and forests extended into regions now dominated by tundra. The Eemian climate was stable, fostering the expansion of warm-adapted species across Europe and North America.[32,33] During the Eemian Interglacial, approximately 125,000 to 115,000 years ago, Homo sapiens migrated into Southeast Asia, including the Indonesian archipelago, as part of their broader dispersal out of Africa. This migration was facilitated by a combination of environmental and geographic factors prevalent during this period. Homo sapiens likely travelled from Africa through the Arabian Peninsula and South Asia, eventually reaching Southeast Asia.[34] During the Eemian, lower sea levels compared to today exposed land bridges, such as the Sunda Shelf, which connected mainland Southeast Asia with the islands of Sumatra, Java, and Borneo, making it easier for populations to move into the Indonesian region.[35] These land connections, combined with the warm and resource-rich environments, supported early human settlement in the area. The ecological conditions during the Eemian Interglacial were favourable, with tropical rainforests and abundant fauna providing essential resources for Homo sapiens.[36] These conditions likely encouraged the establishment of early human communities in Indonesia, where they could thrive in a tropical

[31] Schellenberger, A., et al. (2010), Comparing Last Interglacial Climate and Sea-Level Estimates from Proxy Data and Climate Models, Climate of the Past, 6(4), 447–457. https://doi.org/10.5194/cp-6-447-2010.

[32] Dutton, A., & Lambeck, K. (2012), Ice Volume and Sea Level During the Last Interglacial, Science, 337(6091), 216–219. https://doi.org/10.1126/science.1205749.

[33] Masson-Delmotte, V., Schulz, M., Abe-Ouchi, A., et al. (2013), Information from Paleoclimate Archives, In: Climate Change 2013: The Physical Science Basis. Contribution of Working Group I to the Fifth Assessment Report of the Intergovernmental Panel on Climate Change. Cambridge University Press.

[34] Mellars, P., Gori, K. C., Carr, M., Soares, P. A., & Richards, M. B. (2013), Genetic and archaeological perspectives on the initial modern human colonization of southern Asia. Proceedings of the National Academy of Sciences, 110(26), 10699–10704.

[35] Bird, M. I., & Taylor, D. (2015), Deep-sea and terrestrial records of climate change IN Handbook of Sea-Level Research (pp. 431–444). Wiley.

[36] Storm, P., de Vos, J., Aziz, F., & Kosumi, E. (2005), WajakMan: An Indonesian early modern human? Homo: Journal of Comparative Human Biology, 55(1), 45–72.

climate. Archaeological evidence, such as the fossil remains found at Wajak in Java, dating to around 37,000 to 28,000 years ago, indicates that Homo sapiens had settled in Indonesia by this time.[37] Although these fossils are from a slightly later period, they suggest that the migration into the region occurred during or shortly after the Eemian Interglacial. This reflects the understanding that fossil evidence found in Southeast Asia, particularly in Indonesia, can be dated to a period after the Eemian Interglacial (125,000 to 115,000 years ago), yet these fossils imply an earlier migration event. The Wajak fossils found in Java, Indonesia, are dated to approximately 37,000 to 28,000 years ago, which is well after the Eemian Interglacial.[38] However, the presence of these fossils indicates that Homo sapiens had already reached and established themselves in the region by this time. Given the geographical and environmental conditions during the Eemian, including the presence of land bridges such as the Sunda Shelf and favourable climate conditions.[39] It is plausible that the initial migration of Homo sapiens into Southeast Asia and Indonesia occurred during or shortly after the Eemian Interglacial. The timing of these fossils suggests that the ancestors of the populations found in Wajak migrated during a period when lower sea levels and more temperate conditions facilitated movement across the region. The relatively later dating of these fossils does not preclude an earlier migration; rather, it suggests that these populations had been present in the region for several tens of thousands of years, potentially migrating during the Eemian or immediately following it when conditions were still conducive to human dispersal.[40] The hypothesis that Homo sapiens potentially migrated into Southeast Asia, including Indonesia, during the Eemian Interglacial or immediately following it, is supported by a combination of genetic, archaeological, and paleoenvironmental evidence. Genetic studies suggest that modern human populations in Southeast Asia and Australasia share a deep ancestry, indicating an early

[37] Ibid.

[38] Storm, P., de Vos, J., Aziz, F., & Kosumi, E. (2005), WajakMan: An Indonesian early modern human? Homo: Journal of Comparative Human Biology, 55(1), 45–72.

[39] Bird, M. I., & Taylor, D. (2015), Deep-sea and terrestrial records of climate change IN Handbook of Sea-Level Research (pp. 431–444). Wiley.

[40] Mellars, P., Gori, K. C., Carr, M., Soares, P. A., & Richards, M. B. (2013), Genetic and archaeological perspectives on the initial modern human colonization of southern Asia. Proceedings of the National Academy of Sciences, 110(26), 10699–10704.

dispersal event from Africa through southern Asia. Research on mitochondrial DNA and Y-chromosome data points to a migration route known as the "Southern Dispersal," which likely occurred during a period of favourable climatic conditions, such as the Eemian Interglacial.[41] These studies propose that the warm and stable climate during the Eemian could have facilitated human migration through the coastal routes of South Asia, eventually leading to settlements in Southeast Asia. Archaeological findings, including stone tools and fossil remains in Southeast Asia, support the theory of early human migration during or shortly after the Eemian. The presence of Homo sapiens fossils in regions like Niah Cave in Borneo, which are dated to around 45,000 years ago, suggests that humans had already established themselves in Southeast Asia during the Late Pleistocene.[42] These early settlements could have been the result of migrations initiated during the Eemian or immediately after, when sea levels were low, and land bridges facilitated movement into the region. Paleoenvironmental reconstructions indicate that the Eemian Interglacial was characterized by a warm and stable climate, with reduced ice cover and higher sea levels than during glacial periods. However, following the Eemian, the transition to cooler and drier conditions may have triggered further human dispersal as populations sought new, resource-rich environments.[43] The Sunda Shelf, which was periodically exposed due to fluctuating sea levels, would have provided a pathway for migration into the Indonesian archipelago. The Sunda Shelf refers to a vast continental shelf in Southeast Asia that extends from the Malay Peninsula and Sumatra to Borneo and Java. During periods of lower sea levels, such as during glacial periods, substantial portions of the Sunda Shelf were exposed, creating land bridges that connected these landmasses. This geographical feature has played a crucial role in human migration, ecological diversity, and the distribution of flora and fauna in the region. The

[41] Soares, P. A., et al. (2012). The Expansion of mtDNA Haplogroup L3 within and out of Africa. Molecular Biology and Evolution, 29(3), 915–927. https://doi.org/10.1093/molbev/msr245.

[42] Barker, G., et al. (2007), The 'human revolution' in lowland tropical SoutheastAsia: the antiquity and behaviour of anatomically modern humans at Niah Cave (Sarawak, Borneo). Journal of Human Evolution, 52(3), 243–261. https://doi.org/10.1016/j.jhevol.2006.08.011.

[43] Tzedakis, P. C., et al. (2003), Climate and Vegetation in SoutheastEurope during the Last Interglacial. Quaternary Science Reviews, 22(15–17), 1449–1461. https://doi.org/10.1016/S0277-3791(03)00138-2.

Sunda Shelf is part of the larger Sunda Plate and is one of the world's largest submerged continental shelves. It is shallow, with depths less than 100 meters. The shelf was fully or partially exposed during several periods of the Pleistocene, especially during the Last Glacial Maximum (approximately 20,000 years ago), when sea levels were significantly lower than today.[44] These lower sea levels connected mainland Southeast Asia with the islands of Sumatra, Java, and Borneo, forming a continuous landmass that significantly influenced migration and biodiversity. The exposure of the Sunda Shelf during glacial periods created land bridges that facilitated the migration of early Homo sapiens and other species from the Asian mainland to the Indonesian archipelago. This movement was particularly significant during periods of favourable climatic conditions, such as the Eemian Interglacial, when humans could move more easily across the region.[45] The Sunda Shelf thus served as a crucial corridor for the dispersal of human populations, as well as for the exchange of cultural and technological innovations. The exposure and subsequent submersion of the Sunda Shelf have had profound effects on the distribution of species in Southeast Asia. The land bridges that formed during glacial periods allowed for the migration and mixing of terrestrial species, contributing to the region's rich biodiversity. Conversely, the rising sea levels that followed these periods isolated populations, leading to speciation and the development of unique ecosystems on the islands of the Indonesian archipelago.[46] The Sunda Shelf is a critical geographic and geological feature that has influenced human migration, ecological patterns, and the evolutionary history of Southeast Asia. Its periodic exposure during the Pleistocene provided a land bridge that connected the Asian mainland with the Indonesian islands, facilitating the movement of early humans and contributing to the region's biodiversity.

[44] Voris, H. K. (2000). Maps of Pleistocene Sea Levels in SoutheastAsia: Shorelines, River Systems and Time Durations. Journal of Biogeography, 27(5), 1153–1167. https://doi.org/10.1046/j.1365-2699.2000.00489.x.

[45] Bird, M. I., & Taylor, D. (2015), Deep-sea and terrestrial records of climate change IN Handbook of Sea-Level Research (pp. 431–444). Wiley.

[46] Woodruff, D. S. (2010), Biogeography and conservation in SoutheastAsia: a gradual shift eastward? Frontiers of Biogeography, 2(1), 5–16. https://doi.org/10.21425/F5FBG10121.

Importance of Archaeological Studies in Understanding Prehistoric Indonesia

Archaeological studies play a crucial role in uncovering the rich prehistoric past of Indonesia, providing insights into human evolution, migration patterns, cultural developments, and environmental changes over millennia. The Indonesian archipelago, with its complex geography and history, has been a focal point for understanding early human dispersal, adaptation, and innovation in Southeast Asia. Indonesia's archaeological sites have been pivotal in tracing the migration and evolution of early humans. Fossils such as those from Java Man (Homo erectus) have provided evidence of early human presence in the region, dating back over a million years.[47] These findings have challenged the traditional "Out of Africa" hypothesis by suggesting that Southeast Asia was a significant region for human evolution. Furthermore, the discovery of Homo floresiensis on the island of Flores has introduced a new dimension to our understanding of human diversity and adaptability.[48] Archaeological research has also revealed the development of early cultures and technologies in prehistoric Indonesia. Stone tools found in various sites across the archipelago indicate the technological advancements of early human populations, such as the use of hand axes and other implements for hunting and gathering.[49] The transition from hunter-gatherer societies to more complex agricultural communities is evidenced by the remains of early farming practices and settlement structures, particularly in the eastern islands.[50] Indonesia's diverse environments, from tropical rainforests to volcanic landscapes, have shaped human adaptation and interaction with the natural world. Archaeological studies have shown how early populations adapted to these varied environments, developing unique survival strategies. For example, the use of fire and domestication of plants and animals were crucial for sustaining communities in the

[47] Swisher, C. C., et al. (1994). Age of the earliest known hominids in Java, Indonesia. Science, 263(5150), 1118–1121. https://doi.org/10.1126/science.8108729.

[48] Brown, P., et al. (2004). A new small-bodied hominin from the Late Pleistoceneof Flores, Indonesia. Nature, 431(7012), 1055–1061. https://doi.org/10.1038/nature02999.

[49] Van Heekeren, H. R. (1957). The Stone Age of Indonesia. Martinus Nijhoff.

[50] Bellwood, P. (2007). First Farmers: The Origins of Agricultural Societies. Blackwell Publishing.

challenging landscapes of Indonesia.[51] Additionally, the study of ancient pollen and charcoal records has provided insights into how these early populations managed and altered their environments.[52] The strategic location of Indonesia within the maritime networks of Southeast Asia has been highlighted through archaeological findings. The archipelago served as a crossroads for cultural exchange, as evidenced by the spread of Neolithic pottery and other artifacts across the islands.[53] These exchanges were not only technological but also involved the spread of languages, beliefs, and social practices, shaping the diverse cultural landscape of Indonesia.[54] The significance of Indonesian archaeology extends beyond regional boundaries, contributing to the broader understanding of global prehistory. For instance, the study of rock art in Sulawesi has provided some of the earliest evidence of symbolic behaviour in humans, dating back over 40,000 years.[55] This challenges the notion that such complex behaviour emerged solely in Europe and emphasizes the global nature of early human creativity and expression. Moreover, archaeological studies in Indonesia have played a vital role in the conservation and protection of cultural heritage. By documenting and analyzing ancient sites, archaeologists have helped preserve Indonesia's rich prehistoric legacy for future generations.[56] This is particularly important in a rapidly developing country where modern infrastructure projects can threaten ancient sites. In summary, it can be said that archaeological studies are indispensable for understanding prehistoric Indonesia. They provide a window into the early human occupation, cultural development, and environmental

[51] Golson, J. (1977). No room at the top: agricultural intensification in the New Guinea Highlands IN Allen, J., Golson, J., & Jones, R. (Eds.), Sunda and Sahul: Prehistoric Studies in SoutheastAsia, Melanesia and Australia (pp. 601–638). Academic Press.

[52] Hunt, C. O., & Rabett, R. J. (2014). Holocene landscapes in SoutheastAsia: context for early human adaptation and settlement. Journal of Archaeological Science, 51, 12–23. https://doi.org/10.1016/j.jas.2012.09.031.

[53] Spriggs, M. (2011), Archaeology and the Austronesian expansion: Where are we now? Antiquity, 85(328), 510–528. https://doi.org/10.1017/S0003598X00067910.

[54] Bellwood, P. (1997), Prehistory of the Indo-Malaysian Archipelago. University of Hawai'i Press.

[55] Aubert, M., et al. (2014), Pleistocene cave art from Sulawesi,Indonesia. Nature, 514(7521), 223–227. https://doi.org/10.1038/nature13422.

[56] Pannell, S. (2006), Reconciling nature and culture in a global context? Lessons from the World Heritage List. Australasian Journal of Environmental Management, 13(1), 36–45. https://doi.org/10.1080/14486563.2006.9725110.

adaptation in the region. The discoveries made through these studies have not only deepened our knowledge of Indonesia's past but have also contributed to the global narrative of human history. As archaeological techniques and technologies continue to advance, future research in Indonesia will undoubtedly uncover even more about the rich tapestry of human life in this part of the world.

Early Human Inhabitants

Migration and Settlement Patterns

Southeast Asia and Indonesia represent a critical region for understanding early human migration and settlement patterns, serving as a bridge between the Asian mainland and the Pacific Islands. The migration of Homo sapiens into this area has been shaped by a combination of geographic, environmental, and cultural factors that have contributed to the region's rich archaeological record. This essay explores the migration and settlement patterns of early humans in Southeast Asia and Indonesia, highlighting key findings and theories supported by recent archaeological and genetic research.

Southeast Asia, including Indonesia, is characterized by its complex geography, comprising a vast archipelago with thousands of islands. The region's topography has been heavily influenced by tectonic activity, creating a diverse landscape of mountains, forests, and coastlines. During the Pleistocene epoch, fluctuating sea levels exposed vast land bridges such as the Sunda Shelf, which connected the Asian mainland with the islands of Sumatra, Java, and Borneo.[57] These land connections provided pathways for the migration of Homo sapiens and other species into the region. The climatic conditions during the Pleistocene also played a crucial role in shaping migration patterns. Periods of glaciation led to lower sea levels, exposing additional land and facilitating the movement of populations. Conversely, interglacial periods, such as the Eemian Interglacial, resulted in higher sea levels, isolating populations on islands and contributing to the development of unique cultures and subspecies.[58]

[57] Bellwood, P. (2007), First Islanders: Prehistory and Human Migration in Island SoutheastAsia. Journal of Southeast Asian Archaeology.

[58] O'Connor, S., & Bulbeck, D. (2012), Homo sapiens in Island SoutheastAsia: Current Perspectives and Future Directions. Asian Perspectives.

The combination of these geographic and environmental factors created a dynamic landscape that both enabled and constrained human migration and settlement.

The migration of Homo sapiens into Southeast Asia is believed to have occurred in several waves, beginning around 70,000 years ago during the "Southern Dispersal"out of Africa. This migration route likely took early humans along the southern coastlines of Asia, through the Arabian Peninsula, India, and eventually into Southeast Asia.[59] The exposed Sunda Shelf provided a land corridor for these early migrants, allowing them to reach the Indonesian archipelago. Archaeological evidence supports the presence of early Homo sapiens in Southeast Asia by at least 50,000 years ago. Sites such as Niah Cave in Borneo and Tabon Cave in the Philippines have yielded human remains and artifacts that date to this period, indicating that early humans had successfully adapted to the tropical environments of the region.[60] These early populations likely relied on a combination of hunting, gathering, and coastal foraging, as evidenced by the presence of stone tools, shell middens, and animal remains at these sites. The movement of Homo sapiens into Indonesia specifically is supported by the discovery of the Wajak fossils in Java, which date to around 37,000 to 28,000 years ago.[61]These fossils suggest that early humans had reached and settled in Indonesia by this time, possibly during or shortly after the Eemian Interglacial, when environmental conditions were favourable for migration. The genetic evidence further supports this timeline, with mitochondrial DNA studies indicating a deep ancestry for modern Indonesian populations that dates back to these early migrations.[62] The Sunda and Sahul Shelves, which were periodically exposed during periods of lower

[59] Soares, P. A., et al. (2012), The Expansion of mtDNA Haplogroup L3 within and out of Africa. Molecular Biology and Evolution, 29(3), 915–927. https://doi.org/10.1093/molbev/msr245.

[60] Barker, G., et al. (2007), The 'human revolution' in lowland tropical SoutheastAsia: the antiquity and behaviour of anatomically modern humans at Niah Cave (Sarawak, Borneo). Journal of Human Evolution, 52(3), 243–261. https://doi.org/10.1016/j.jhevol.2006.08.011.

[61] Storm, P., de Vos, J., Aziz, F., & Kosumi, E. (2005), WajakMan: An Indonesian early modern human? Homo: Journal of Comparative Human Biology, 55(1), 45–72. https://doi.org/10.1016/j.jhevol.2006.08.011.

[62] Bellwood, P. (2007), First Islanders: Prehistory and Human Migration in Island SoutheastAsia. Journal of Southeast Asian Archaeology.

sea levels, played a critical role in the migration and settlement of Southeast Asia and Indonesia. The Sunda Shelf connected the Asian mainland with the islands of Sumatra, Java, and Borneo, while the Sahul Shelf connected Australia with New Guinea and parts of eastern Indonesia.[63] These land bridges facilitated the movement of Homo sapiens and other species across the region, contributing to the spread of human populations and the exchange of cultural practices. The exposure of the Sunda Shelf during the Last Glacial Maximum (approximately 20,000 years ago) created a vast, interconnected landmass that allowed for the movement of human populations across Southeast Asia and into Indonesia. This period of land exposure likely facilitated the migration of new populations into the region, as well as the spread of technologies such as pottery and agriculture.[64] The subsequent rise in sea levels following the glacial period isolated populations on the islands of the Indonesian archipelago, leading to the development of distinct cultures and languages. The Sahul Shelf, although less extensive than the Sunda Shelf, played a similarly key role in the migration of early humans into Australasia. The colonization of Australia and New Guinea is believed to have occurred around 50,000 years ago, with early human populations crossing the narrow sea channels that separated the Sahul landmass from the islands of eastern Indonesia.[65] This migration represents one of the earliest known instances of oceanic voyaging and demonstrates the adaptability and technological innovation of early Homo sapiens. The archaeological record in Southeast Asia and Indonesia reveals the development of a diverse range of cultures and technologies, shaped by the region's unique geography and environmental conditions. The transition from hunter-gatherer societies to more complex agricultural communities is evidenced by the remains of early

[63] Bird, M. I., Taylor, D., & Hunt, C. (2005), Palaeoenvironments of insular SoutheastAsia during the Last Glacial Period: a savanna corridor in Sundaland? Quaternary Science Reviews, 24(20–21), 2228–2242. https://doi.org/10.1016/j.quascirev.2005.04.004.

[64] Bellwood, P. (2007), First Islanders: Prehistory and Human Migration in Island SoutheastAsia. Journal of Southeast Asian Archaeology.

[65] O'Connor, S., & Bulbeck, D. (2012), Homo sapiens in Island SoutheastAsia: Current Perspectives and Future Directions. Asian Perspectives.

farming practices and settlement structures in the region.[66] These developments were likely influenced by both internal innovation and external contact with other cultures, as Southeast Asia has long been a crossroads for trade and migration.

One of the most significant cultural developments in prehistoric Southeast Asia was the introduction of Neolithic pottery and agriculture, which began around 4000 years ago. This period saw the spread of rice cultivation, animal domestication, and permanent settlements across the region, leading to the rise of more complex societies.[67] The spread of these technologies is believed to have been facilitated by the migration of Austronesian-speaking populations from Taiwan and southern China into Southeast Asia and Indonesia.[68] These migrations brought new technologies and social practices that fundamentally transformed the region's cultural landscape.

The development of maritime networks also played a crucial role in the exchange of cultural practices and the spread of modern technologies. The islands of Indonesia, situated at the intersection of major trade routes, became key hubs for the exchange of goods and ideas between the Asian mainland and the Pacific Islands.[69] This interaction is evidenced by the presence of imported pottery, metal tools, and other artifacts at archaeological sites throughout the region. These maritime networks facilitated not only the spread of material culture but also the exchange of religious beliefs, languages, and social practices, contributing to the rich cultural diversity of Southeast Asia and Indonesia.

The ability of early human populations to adapt to the diverse and often challenging environments of Southeast Asia and Indonesia is a key theme in the region's prehistoric archaeology. The tropical rainforests, volcanic landscapes, and coastal ecosystems of the region required different survival strategies, and archaeological evidence suggests that early humans developed a range of technologies and practices to thrive

[66] Bellwood, P. (2007), First Islanders: Prehistory and Human Migration in Island SoutheastAsia. Journal of Southeast Asian Archaeology.

[67] Spriggs, M. (2011), Archaeology and the Austronesian expansion: Where are we now? Antiquity, 85(328), 510–528. https://doi.org/10.1017/S0003598X00067910.

[68] Bellwood, P. (2007), First Islanders: Prehistory and Human Migration in Island SoutheastAsia. Journal of Southeast Asian Archaeology.

[69] Ibid.

in these environments.[70] One example of this adaptation is the use of fire for forest management and hunting. Charcoal and pollen records from various sites in Indonesia indicate that early humans used fire to clear land for hunting and for agriculture.[71] This practice would have allowed them to create more open environments that were easier to navigate and provided better opportunities for hunting game. The use of fire also suggests a level of environmental management and control that reflects the adaptability and ingenuity of early human populations. Another example is the development of watercraft and seafaring skills. The presence of human populations on islands such as Flores, Timor, and Sulawesi, which have never been connected to the mainland by land bridges, indicates that early Homo sapiens developed the ability to cross significant sea barriers.[72] The construction and use of boats for fishing, trade, and migration would have been crucial for the settlement of the Indonesian archipelago and the spread of human populations across the region.

The environmental changes that occurred in Southeast Asia and Indonesia during the Holocene, following the end of the Last Glacial Maximum, had a significant impact on human populations. The rise in sea levels led to the flooding of the Sunda and Sahul Shelves, isolating populations on the newly formed islands and leading to the development of distinct cultures and languages.[73] These changes also forced human populations to adapt to new environments, leading to innovations in agriculture, fishing, and other subsistence strategies. The volcanic activity that is characteristic of the Indonesian archipelago also played a role in shaping human settlement patterns. The eruption of Mount Toba around 74,000 years ago, one of the largest volcanic eruptions in Earth's

[70] Golson, J. (1977), No room at the top: agricultural intensification in the New Guinea Highlands. In Allen, J., Golson, J., & Jones, R. (Eds.), Sunda and Sahul: Prehistoric Studies in SoutheastAsia, Melanesia and Australia (pp. 601–638). Academic Press.

[71] Hunt, C. O., & Rabett, R. J. (2014), Holocene landscapes in SoutheastAsia: context for early human adaptation and settlement. Journal of Archaeological Science, 51, 12–23. https://doi.org/10.1016/j.jas.2012.09.031.

[72] O'Connor, S., & Bulbeck, D. (2012), Homo sapiens in Island SoutheastAsia: Current Perspectives and Future Directions. Asian Perspectives.

[73] Bird, M. I., Taylor, D., & Hunt, C. (2005), Palaeoenvironments of insular SoutheastAsia during the Last Glacial Period: a savanna corridor in Sundaland? Quaternary Science Reviews, 24(20–21), 2228–2242. https://doi.org/10.1016/j.quascirev.2005.04.004.

history, had a profound impact on the region's climate and ecosystems.[74] The resulting "volcanic winter" would have drastically reduced temperatures and disrupted food sources, forcing human populations to adapt or migrate to more favourable environments. Archaeological evidence suggests that some populations may have migrated southward to escape the effects of the eruption, contributing to the spread of Homo sapiens into new areas of Southeast Asia and Indonesia.[75]

In recent years, genetic studies have provided valuable insights into the migration and settlement patterns of early humans in Southeast Asia and Indonesia. The analysis of mitochondrial DNA, Y-chromosome data, and autosomal markers has helped to trace the ancestry of modern populations in the region and has shed light on the timing and routes of early human migrations.[76] One of the key findings from genetic studies is the identification of a deep ancestry shared by modern populations in Southeast Asia, Papua New Guinea, and Australia. This genetic connection supports the theory of an early migration of Homo sapiens into the region during the "Southern Dispersal"out of Africa.[77] The genetic evidence also suggests that these early populations remained relatively isolated from later migrations, leading to the development of distinct genetic lineages in different parts of the region.[78] Genetic studies have also provided evidence for the migration of Austronesian-speaking populations from Taiwan and southern China into Southeast Asia and Indonesia. These migrations, which began around 4000 years ago, brought new technologies, languages, and cultural practices that had a lasting impact on the region.[79] The genetic markers associated with these migrations can still be

[74] Oppenheimer, S. (2002), Eden in the East: The Drowned Continent of SoutheastAsia. Orion Publishing.

[75] Ibid.

[76] Soares, P. A., et al. (2012), The Expansion of mtDNA Haplogroup L3 within and out of Africa. Molecular Biology and Evolution, 29(3), 915–927. https://doi.org/10.1093/molbev/msr245.

[77] O'Connor, S., & Bulbeck, D. (2012), Homo sapiens in Island SoutheastAsia: Current Perspectives and Future Directions. Asian Perspectives.

[78] Soares, P. A., et al. (2012), The Expansion of mtDNA Haplogroup L3 within and out of Africa. Molecular Biology and Evolution, 29(3), 915–927. https://doi.org/10.1093/molbev/msr245.

[79] Bellwood, P. (2007), First Islanders: Prehistory and Human Migration in Island SoutheastAsia. Journal of Southeast Asian Archaeology.

found in modern populations throughout Southeast Asia and the Pacific Islands, highlighting the enduring influence of these early movements on the region's cultural landscape. Archaeological evidence continues to play a crucial role in understanding the migration and settlement patterns of early humans in Southeast Asia and Indonesia. Advances in modern research techniques, such as radiocarbon dating, stratigraphy, and isotope analysis, have allowed archaeologists to build more detailed chronologies and to reconstruct past environments with greater accuracy.[80] These techniques have provided new insights into the timing of human migrations, the development of early cultures, and the interactions between different populations. For example, the use of radiocarbon dating has helped to establish a timeline for the colonization of the Indonesian archipelago, confirming the presence of Homo sapiens in the region by at least 50,000 years ago.[81] Stratigraphic analysis has revealed the layers of occupation at key archaeological sites, providing evidence of continuous human habitation and the development of new technologies over time.[82] Isotope analysis of human remains has provided information on the diets and subsistence strategies of early populations, shedding light on how they adapted to the diverse environments of Southeast Asia and Indonesia.[83] The use of ancient DNA (aDNA) analysis is also emerging as a powerful tool for understanding the genetic relationships between early human populations in Southeast Asia and Indonesia. Although the region's tropical climate poses challenges for the preservation of DNA, advances in extraction and sequencing techniques have made it possible to obtain genetic material from ancient remains.[84] This has the potential to

[80] Spriggs, M. (2011), Archaeology and the Austronesian expansion: Where are we now? Antiquity, 85(328), 510–528. https://doi.org/10.1017/S0003598X00067910.

[81] Barker, G., et al. (2007), The 'human revolution' in lowland tropical SoutheastAsia: the antiquity and behaviour of anatomically modern humans at Niah Cave (Sarawak, Borneo). Journal of Human Evolution, 52(3), 243–261. https://doi.org/10.1016/j.jhevol.2006.08.011.

[82] Spriggs, M. (2011), Archaeology and the Austronesian expansion: Where are we now? Antiquity, 85(328), 510–528. https://doi.org/10.1017/S0003598X00067910.

[83] Hunt, C. O., & Rabett, R. J. (2014), Holocene landscapes in SoutheastAsia: context for early human adaptation and settlement. Journal of Archaeological Science, 51, 12–23. https://doi.org/10.1016/j.jas.2012.09.031.

[84] Soares, P. A., et al. (2012), The Expansion of mtDNA Haplogroup L3 within and out of Africa. Molecular Biology and Evolution, 29(3), 915–927. https://doi.org/10.1093/molbev/msr245.

provide new insights into the migration patterns, population interactions, and genetic diversity of early humans in the region.

As archaeological research in Southeast Asia and Indonesia continues to advance, new discoveries and techniques will undoubtedly shed further light on the migration and settlement patterns of early humans in the region. The integration of genetic data with archaeological and environmental evidence will provide a more comprehensive understanding of the complex interactions that shaped the prehistoric landscape of Southeast Asia and Indonesia. Future research is likely to focus on several key areas, including the timing and routes of early migrations, the development of maritime technologies, and the impact of environmental changes on human populations. The continued exploration of archaeological sites, both on land and underwater, will also be crucial for uncovering new evidence of early human activity in the region. The study of prehistoric Southeast Asia and Indonesia not only provides insights into the history of the region but also contributes to the broader understanding of human evolution and migration. By examining the ways in which early humans adapted to and interacted with their environments, archaeologists can gain a deeper understanding of the processes that have shaped human history across the globe. In conclusion, the migration and settlement patterns of early humans in Southeast Asia and Indonesia were shaped by a combination of geographic, environmental, and cultural factors. The region's complex geography, including the Sunda and Sahul Shelves, played a critical role in facilitating the movement of populations and the exchange of cultural practices. Archaeological and genetic evidence supports the presence of Homo sapiens in Southeast Asia by at least 50,000 years ago, with subsequent migrations contributing to the region's rich cultural diversity. The development of early cultures in Southeast Asia and Indonesia was influenced by both internal innovation and external contact, with the spread of Neolithic pottery, agriculture, and maritime technologies playing a key role in shaping the region's prehistoric landscape. The ability of early human populations to adapt to the diverse environments of Southeast Asia and Indonesia is evidenced by their use of fire, development of watercraft, and responses to environmental changes such as volcanic eruptions. As research in the region continues to advance, new discoveries and techniques will undoubtedly enhance our understanding of the migration and settlement patterns of early humans in Southeast Asia and Indonesia. This research not only contributes to the history of the region but also to the broader understanding of human evolution and the global patterns of migration that have shaped our species.

The Austronesian Expansion

The Austronesian expansion is one of the most significant prehistoric migration events, involving the spread of Austronesian-speaking peoples from Taiwan across the Pacific and Indian Oceans. This migration, which began around 5000 years ago, had profound cultural, linguistic, and genetic impacts across Southeast Asia, including the Indonesian archipelago. The Austronesian expansion is believed to have originated in Taiwan, where Austronesian-speaking peoples began migrating southward around 3000 BCE.[85] These early migrants travelled through the Philippines and the Indonesian archipelago, utilizing their advanced seafaring skills and knowledge of the maritime environment to navigate across vast oceanic distances. The expansion into the Indonesian archipelago marked a critical phase in this migration, as the region served as a staging ground for further movements into the Pacific and Indian Oceans.[86] Archaeological evidence supports the spread of Austronesian-speaking peoples through the Indonesian archipelago, characterized by the introduction of Neolithic technologies such as pottery, agriculture, and animal domestication.[87] These technological advancements facilitated the establishment of permanent settlements and the development of complex societies across the region. Linguistic evidence further corroborates this migration, as Austronesian languages are widely spoken across Indonesia and the broader Southeast Asian region.[88] Genetic studies have provided additional insights into the Austronesian expansion, revealing a deep genetic connection between populations in Taiwan, the Philippines,

[85] Bellwood, P. (1997), Prehistory of the Indo-Malaysian Archipelago. Honolulu: University of Hawai'i Press.

[86] Spriggs, M. (2011), Archaeology and the Austronesian Expansion: Where are We Now? Antiquity, 85(328), 510–528.

[87] Bellwood, P. (1997), Prehistory of the Indo-Malaysian Archipelago. Honolulu: University of Hawai'i Press.

[88] Pawley, A. (2002), The Austronesian Dispersal: Languages, Technologies, People. Annual Review of Anthropology, 31(1), 443–470.

Indonesia, and the Pacific Islands.[89] These studies indicate that the migration involved not only the movement of people but also the exchange of genetic material, leading to the diverse genetic landscape observed in the region today. The distribution of Austronesian-speaking populations and their genetic markers across the Indonesian archipelago supports the theory of a rapid and widespread dispersal facilitated by maritime technology.[90] The Austronesian expansion had significant cultural and social impacts on the populations of the Indonesian archipelago. The introduction of modern technologies, social practices, and belief systems transformed the region's cultural landscape. For example, the spread of rice cultivation and the domestication of animals like pigs and chickens were central to the development of agricultural societies in Indonesia.[91] Additionally, the Austronesian-speaking migrants established trade networks and maritime connections that linked the Indonesian archipelago with other parts of Southeast Asia and the Pacific.[92]

The success of the Austronesian expansion is often attributed to the development of sophisticated maritime technology, including the construction of outrigger canoes and advanced navigation techniques. These innovations allowed Austronesian-speaking peoples to travel across open ocean waters and colonize distant islands.[93] The ability to undertake long-distance voyages was crucial for the expansion from the Indonesian archipelago to other parts of Southeast Asia and Oceania. The Austronesian expansion from the Indonesian archipelago represents a pivotal chapter in the prehistory of Southeast Asia and the Pacific. This migration, driven by advances in maritime technology and agricultural practices, facilitated the widespread dispersal of Austronesian-speaking peoples across a vast geographic area. The Austronesians developed sophisticated

[89] Soares, P., Trejaut, J. A., Rito, T., Cavadas, B., Hill, C., Eng, K. K., ... & Macaulay, V. A. (2011). Ancient Voyaging and Polynesian Origins: Evidence from Mitochondrial DNA Lineages. Nature, 467(7317), 206–210.

[90] Bellwood, P. (1997), Prehistory of the Indo-Malaysian Archipelago. Honolulu: University of Hawai'i Press.

[91] Spriggs, M. (2011). Archaeology and the Austronesian Expansion: Where are We Now? Antiquity, 85(328), 510–528.

[92] Kirch, P. V. (2017), On the Road of the Winds: An Archaeological History of the PacificIslands before European Contact. University of California Press.

[93] Anderson, A. (2009). The Global Origins and Development of Seafaring. Cambridge Archaeological Journal, 19(1), 79–84.

outrigger canoes, which provided essential stability for oceanic navigation, and the use of crab-claw sails, which enhanced their ability to travel long distances. They also mastered navigation techniques using stars, ocean swells, and wind patterns.[94] The archaeological, linguistic, and genetic evidence collectively highlights the significance of this expansion in shaping the cultural and demographic landscape of the region.

Agricultural Developments

Early Farming Techniques and Crops

The development of early farming techniques and the domestication of crops in Indonesia and Southeast Asia played a crucial role in shaping the region's cultural and ecological landscape. This report examines the origins and practices of early agriculture in the region, focusing on the types of crops cultivated and the techniques employed by early farmers.

The transition from hunting and gathering to agriculture in Southeast Asia and Indonesia was a gradual process that began during the Holocene epoch, around 10,000 years ago. Early farming communities employed a variety of techniques adapted to the diverse environments of the region. These techniques included swidden (slash-and-burn) agriculture, wet-rice cultivation, and the use of raised fields and irrigation systems.[95] Swidden agriculture, which involved clearing forested areas through burning and cultivating crops in the nutrient-rich ash, was widely practiced in the hilly and forested areas of Southeast Asia, particularly in Indonesia. This technique allowed early farmers to cultivate a variety of crops in areas with poor soil fertility, although it required the periodic movement of agricultural plots to maintain soil productivity.[96] Wet-rice cultivation which eventually became the dominant form of agriculture in lowland areas, involved the construction of paddy fields that could be flooded to support the growth of rice. This method of farming was particularly effective in

[94] Kirch, P. V. (2017), On the Road of the Winds: An Archaeological History of the PacificIslands before European Contact. University of California Press.

[95] Denham, T., & Donohue, M. (2009), Pre-Austronesian Dispersal of Agriculture and Associated Language in Island SoutheastAsia and the Western Pacific. Current Anthropology, 50(3), 379–391.

[96] Paz, V. (2002). Island SoutheastAsia: Spread or Friction Zone? Asian Perspectives, 41(1), 64–89.

the fertile river valleys and floodplains of the region.[97] A diverse range of crops was cultivated in early Southeast Asia and Indonesia, many of which were domesticated in the region before the arrival of Austronesian-speaking peoples. These crops included taro (Colocasia esculenta), yam (Dioscorea spp.), banana (Musa spp.), and sugarcane (Saccharum officinarum).[98] Taro and yam were among the first crops to be domesticated in the region, and they were cultivated using techniques that took advantage of the region's wet and humid conditions. These root crops were essential staples for early farming communities, providing reliable sources of calories and nutrition.[99]

Bananas and sugarcane, both of which are thought to have been domesticated in Southeast Asia, played significant roles in the agricultural systems of early Southeast Asian societies. Bananas, in particular, were highly valued for their fruit and were likely propagated through vegetative means, as they do not produce viable seeds[100] Sugarcane, another vegetatively propagated crop, was used not only for its sweet juice but also for making alcoholic beverages and as a source of fuel.[101] The introduction of rice (Oryza sativa) cultivation into Southeast Asia marked a significant shift in agricultural practices. Rice, believed to have been domesticated in the Yangtze River Valley of China, spread into Southeast Asia and Indonesia around 4000 years ago.[102] Wet-rice cultivation, in particular, led to the establishment of more permanent and densely populated agricultural communities, as the crop provided high yields that could support

[97] Barker, G. (2006), The Agricultural Revolution in Prehistory: Why Did Foragers Become Farmers? Oxford University Press.

[98] Denham, T., & Donohue, M. (2009), Pre-Austronesian Dispersal of Agriculture and Associated Language in Island SoutheastAsia and the Western Pacific. Current Anthropology, 50(3), 379–391.

[99] Barker, G. (2006), The Agricultural Revolution in Prehistory: Why Did Foragers Become Farmers? Oxford University Press.

[100] Paz, V. (2002), Island SoutheastAsia: Spread or Friction Zone? Asian Perspectives, 41(1), 64–89.

[101] Fuller, D. Q., Sato, Y.-I., Castillo, C., Qin, L., Weisskopf, A. R., & Kingwell-Banham, E. (2010), Consilience of Genetics and Archaeobotany in the Study of Rice Domestication and Spread in Asia. Proceedings of the National Academy of Sciences, 107(25), 10767–10774.

[102] Bellwood, P. (1997), Prehistory of the Indo-Malaysian Archipelago. Honolulu: University of Hawai'i Press.

larger populations.[103] The adoption of agriculture in Southeast Asia and Indonesia had profound effects on the development of societies in the region. The ability to produce surplus food allowed for the growth of more complex social structures, including the rise of chiefdoms and early states.[104] Agricultural surplus also facilitated trade, both within the region and with neighbouring areas, as surplus crops could be exchanged for other goods and resources.[105] The diversity of crops cultivated in the region reflects the adaptability and innovation of early Southeast Asian farmers. Their ability to develop agricultural systems suited to the varied environments of the region laid the foundation for the rich agricultural traditions that continue to be a central part of Southeast Asian and Indonesian cultures today.

Early farming techniques and the domestication of crops in Southeast Asia and Indonesia were instrumental in shaping the region's cultural and ecological history. The use of swidden agriculture, wet-rice cultivation, and the domestication of a diverse array of crops enabled early farmers to thrive in the region's challenging environments. These agricultural practices not only supported the development of complex societies but also laid the groundwork for the continued agricultural productivity of Southeast Asia and Indonesia.

Wet-Rice Cultivation

Wet-rice cultivation, also known as paddy rice farming, is one of the most significant agricultural practices in Southeast Asia and Indonesia. This report explores the origins, development, and impact of wet-rice cultivation in the region, highlighting key archaeological, historical, and ecological findings. The practice of wet-rice farming has shaped the cultural, social, and economic landscapes of Southeast Asia and continues to be a cornerstone of agriculture in the region. The origins of wet-rice cultivation in Southeast Asia can be traced back to around 4000 years ago, during the Neolithic period. Archaeological evidence suggests that the practice was introduced from the Yangtze River Valley in China,

[103] Spriggs, M. (2011), Archaeology and the Austronesian Expansion: Where are We Now? Antiquity, 85(328), 510–528.

[104] Ibid.

[105] Barker, G. (2006), The Agricultural Revolution in Prehistory: Why Did Foragers Become Farmers? Oxford University Press.

where rice was first domesticated.[106] The spread of rice cultivation into Southeast Asia is closely linked to the migration of Austronesian-speaking peoples, who brought with them not only rice but also other agricultural practices and technologies.[107]

Early wet-rice farming in Southeast Asia likely began in the lowland areas with access to abundant water sources, such as river valleys and deltas. The fertile floodplains of the Mekong, Chao Phraya, and Red River deltas provided ideal conditions for the cultivation of rice, which requires standing water for much of its growth cycle. The construction of irrigation systems, including canals, dikes, and terraces, allowed early farmers to control water levels and extend rice cultivation to a broader range of environments.[108] Archaeobotanical studies have provided crucial insights into the development of wet-rice cultivation in Southeast Asia. Analysis of plant remains from archaeological sites has revealed a gradual shift from a diverse array of crops to a more specialized focus on rice, reflecting the increasing importance of this staple crop.[109] The standardization of rice cultivation practices, including the selection of high-yielding varieties and the development of more efficient planting and harvesting techniques, contributed to the widespread adoption of wet-rice farming across the region.[110] The development of wet-rice cultivation also involved significant innovations in land management. The use of ploughing, transplanting seedlings, and constructing paddy fields were crucial for maximizing productivity and ensuring a stable food supply.[111] These practices required a coordinated effort among farming communities, leading

[106] Fuller, D.Q. & Qin, L. (2009), Water management and labour in the origins and dispersal of Asian rice. World Archaeology, 41(1), pp. 88–111.

[107] Glover, I. (1984), SoutheastAsia and the diffusion of rice cultivation. In D.G. Baker, I.C. Glover, & G. Philip (Eds.), The origins and spread of agriculture and pastoralism in Eurasia (pp. 413–424). Duckworth.

[108] Rigg, J. (2013), Rural Development in SoutheastAsia: Dispossession, Accumulation and Persistence. Cambridge University Press.

[109] Fuller, D.Q. & Qin, L. (2009), Water management and labour in the origins and dispersal of Asian rice. World Archaeology, 41(1), pp. 88–111.

[110] Barker, G. (2006), The Agricultural Revolution in Prehistory: Why Did Foragers Become Farmers? Oxford University Press.

[111] Glover, I. (1984), SoutheastAsia and the diffusion of rice cultivation. In D.G. Baker, I.C. Glover, & G. Philip (Eds.), The origins and spread of agriculture and pastoralism in Eurasia (pp. 413–424). Duckworth.

to the establishment of complex social structures and cooperative labour systems.[112]

The expansion of wet-rice cultivation had a profound impact on the environment of Southeast Asia and Indonesia. The transformation of natural landscapes into cultivated fields led to changes in local ecosystems, including the alteration of watercourses and the loss of natural vegetation.[113] The reliance on irrigation also introduced new challenges, such as the need for constant maintenance of water management systems and the risk of soil degradation due to salinization and nutrient depletion.[114] However, wet-rice cultivation also brought ecological benefits. The creation of paddy fields provided habitats for a variety of aquatic species, contributing to local biodiversity. Additionally, the practice of rotating rice with other crops, such as legumes, helped to maintain soil fertility and reduce the spread of pests and diseases.[115]

Wet-rice cultivation has played a central role in the socio-economic development of Southeast Asia and Indonesia. The ability to produce surplus rice enabled the growth of larger, more complex societies and the rise of early states and kingdoms.[116] Rice became a symbol of wealth and power, with control over rice production and distribution closely tied to political authority.

Culturally, rice is deeply embedded in the traditions and rituals of Southeast Asian societies. It is not only a staple food but also holds symbolic significance in religious and ceremonial practices. Festivals celebrating the rice harvest, such as the Balinese "Galungan" and the Thai

[112] Leach, E.R. (1999), Culture and Communication: The Logic by which Symbols are Connected. Cambridge University Press.

[113] Rigg, J. (2013), Rural Development in SoutheastAsia: Dispossession, Accumulation and Persistence. Cambridge University Press.

[114] Van Liere, W.J., 1980. Traditional Water Management in the Lower Mekong Basin. In A. T. Grove (Ed.), Water, Land and Man: A Synthesis of Hydrology, Geomorphology and Socio-Economic Geography (pp. 55–78). Routledge.

[115] Barker, G. (2006), The Agricultural Revolution in Prehistory: Why Did Foragers Become Farmers? Oxford University Press.

[116] Leach, E.R. (1999), Culture and Communication: The Logic by which Symbols are Connected. Cambridge University Press.

"Loy Krathong," reflect the importance of rice in the cultural identity of the region.[117]

Wet-rice cultivation has been a defining feature of agriculture in Southeast Asia and Indonesia for thousands of years. Its origins in the region are intricately linked to the spread of Austronesian-speaking peoples and the adoption of new agricultural practices. The development of wet-rice farming has had far-reaching ecological, economic, and cultural impacts, shaping the landscapes and societies of Southeast Asia. As both a food source and a cultural symbol, rice continues to play a significant role in the lives of millions of people across the region.

Trade and Early Societies

Maritime Trade Networks

The maritime trade networks connecting Indonesia, South Asia, East Asia, and Southeast Asia from 5000 BC to 700 AD were instrumental in shaping the cultural, economic, and political landscapes of these regions. These networks facilitated the exchange of goods, ideas, and technologies, leading to the development of complex societies and the spread of major cultural influences, such as those from India and China, throughout Southeast Asia and beyond. Maritime trade in the region dates back to as early as 5000 BC, with the movement of goods such as obsidian, pottery, and shell ornaments between island communities in Indonesia and the mainland of Southeast Asia. The early trade was primarily regional, focusing on the exchange of raw materials and craft goods among neighbouring communities.[118] These networks laid the foundation for more extensive trade as maritime technology improved, and seafaring skills developed.

By 3000 BC, the Austronesian-speaking peoples had begun their expansive migration across the islands of Southeast Asia, bringing with

[117] Bowen, J.R. (1995), Prayers to the Spirit of a Rice Paddy: Religion and Agrarian Ritual in Central Java. In Asian Visions of Authority: Religion and the Modern States of Eastand SoutheastAsia (pp. 227–254). University of California Press.

[118] Bellina, B. & Glover, I.C. (2004), The Archaeology of Early Contact with India and the Mediterranean World, from the Fourth Century BC to the Fourth Century AD. In I.C. Glover & P. Bellwood (Eds.), SoutheastAsia: From Prehistory to History (pp. 68–89). Routledge.

them advanced maritime technology, such as outrigger canoes and navigational techniques that allowed them to traverse vast ocean distances.[119] This migration facilitated the spread of agricultural practices, languages, and cultural practices across the region, further enhancing the interconnectedness of Southeast Asian communities. The period between 1000 BC and 1 AD saw significant developments in maritime trade between Southeast Asia, including Indonesia, and South Asia. The growing demand for luxury goods, such as spices, aromatics, and precious stones, fuelled the expansion of trade networks across the Bay of Bengal and the Indian Ocean.[120] Southeast Asian traders began to establish regular contact with Indian merchants, who brought goods such as textiles, metalwork, and beads in exchange for the region's valuable spices and forest products. This period also witnessed the first signs of Indian cultural influence in Southeast Asia, particularly in the form of religious ideas, art, and architecture. Indian traders and religious missionaries introduced elements of Hinduism and Buddhism, which were gradually adopted by local rulers and integrated into indigenous belief systems.[121] The establishment of these cultural ties laid the groundwork for the later spread of Indianized kingdoms in Southeast Asia.

The first centuries AD marked the expansion of Southeast Asian trade networks to include East Asia, particularly China. The Han Dynasty (206 BC–220 AD) in China began to establish maritime connections with Southeast Asia, driven by the Chinese demand for luxury goods such as pearls, spices, and exotic animals.[122] Chinese records from this period describe the trade routes that connected China with the kingdoms of Southeast Asia, including the exchange of goods and tribute. The development of the Maritime Silk Road during this period further integrated Southeast Asia into the broader trade networks of East Asia. The Maritime

[119] Kirch, P.V. (2017), On the Road of the Winds: An Archaeological History of the PacificIslands before European Contact. Revised Edition. University of California Press.

[120] Bellina, B. & Glover, I.C. (2004), The Archaeology of Early Contact with India and the Mediterranean World, from the Fourth Century BC to the Fourth Century AD. In I.C. Glover & P. Bellwood (Eds.), SoutheastAsia: From Prehistory to History (pp. 68–89). Routledge.

[121] Ibid.

[122] Manguin, P.-Y. (1993), Pre-Aryan and Pre-Indian Influences in SoutheastAsia: A Study of the Lower and Central Mekong Basin. In H. P. Ray & J. F. Salles (Eds.), Tradition and Archaeology: Early Maritime Contacts in the Indian Ocean (pp. 135–164). Manohar.

Silk Road was a network of sea routes that facilitated the exchange of goods between China, Southeast Asia, South Asia, and the Mediterranean world.[123] Southeast Asia, including the Indonesian archipelago, played a crucial role as a transit point for goods moving between these regions. The increasing presence of Chinese goods, such as silk and ceramics, in Southeast Asian archaeological sites from this period reflects the growing importance of maritime trade with East Asia.[124]

By the fifth century AD, the Indonesian archipelago had become a major hub for maritime trade, with several key port polities emerging as centres of commerce and culture. These port polities, such as Srivijaya in Sumatra and Tarumanagara in West Java, controlled strategic points along the trade routes that connected the Indian Ocean with the South China Sea.[125] Their power and wealth were largely derived from their ability to facilitate and tax the flow of goods through their ports. The rise of Srivijaya as a dominant maritime power in the seventh century AD is particularly significant. Srivijaya controlled the Strait of Malacca, one of the most important maritime chokepoints in the world, which allowed it to dominate trade between the Indian Ocean and the South China Sea[126] The kingdom's strategic location and control over the regional trade network enabled it to exert influence over much of Southeast Asia, spreading Indian cultural influences, particularly Buddhism, throughout the region. The influence of Indian culture, facilitated by maritime trade, is evident in the widespread adoption of Indian scripts, languages, religious practices, and art forms in Southeast Asia during this period.[127] The region's ruling elites, in particular, embraced these elements as a means

[123] Liu, X. (2010), The Silk Road in World History. Oxford University Press.

[124] Wade, G. (2009), The Pre-Modern EastAsian Maritime Realm: An Overview of European-Language Sources. In D. W. Kang, G. Wade, & K. Choy (Eds.), EastAsian Maritime History (pp. 13–54). Brill.

[125] Manguin, P.-Y. (1993), Pre-Aryan and Pre-Indian Influences in SoutheastAsia: A Study of the Lower and Central Mekong Basin. In H. P. Ray & J. F. Salles (Eds.), Tradition and Archaeology: Early Maritime Contacts in the Indian Ocean (pp. 135–164). Manohar.

[126] Wolters, O.W. (1967), Early Indonesian Commerce: A Study of the Origins of Srivijaya. Cornell University Press.

[127] Bellina, B. & Glover, I.C. (2004), The Archaeology of Early Contact with India and the Mediterranean World, from the Fourth Century BC to the Fourth Century AD. In I.C. Glover & P. Bellwood (Eds.), SoutheastAsia: From Prehistory to History (pp. 68–89). Routledge.

of legitimizing their power and connecting themselves to the prestigious Indian cultural sphere.

From 5000 BC to 700 AD, the maritime trade networks between Indonesia, South Asia, East Asia, and Southeast Asia were instrumental in shaping the development of the region. These networks facilitated not only the exchange of goods but also the flow of ideas, technologies, and cultural practices, leading to the rise of complex societies and the spread of major religious and cultural influences. The strategic location of the Indonesian archipelago and its role as a hub for maritime trade helped to position Southeast Asia as a crucial player in the broader networks of global commerce during this period.

Formation of Early Societies

The formation of societies in Indonesia and Southeast Asia was a complex process shaped by environmental factors, migration patterns, technological innovations, and cultural exchanges. This analysis focuses on evaluating the key developments in the formation of early societies in this region, drawing on archaeological, historical, and anthropological evidence. The earliest societies in Indonesia and Southeast Asia were formed by communities of hunter-gatherers who began to settle in the region over 40,000 years ago. These early inhabitants adapted to a variety of environments, from the tropical rainforests of Sumatra and Borneo to the coastal and riverine areas of the Indonesian archipelago. The region's diverse ecosystems provided abundant resources, allowing these communities to establish semi-permanent settlements.[128] The transition to agricultural societies began around 4000 to 5000 years ago with the introduction of rice cultivation and the domestication of other crops. The development of wet-rice agriculture, in particular, allowed for more stable food production and led to the establishment of larger, more permanent settlements. These early agricultural societies laid the foundation for the development of complex social structures.[129]

A significant factor in the formation of societies in Indonesia and Southeast Asia was the migration of Austronesian-speaking peoples from

[128] Bellwood, P. & Nitihaminoto, G. (1993), The Buidane Culture of the Talaud Islands, North Eastern Indonesia. Asian Perspectives, 32(1), pp. 73–97.

[129] Glover, I.C. (2006), SoutheastAsia: From Prehistory to History. Routledge.

Taiwan around 4000 years ago. These migrants brought with them advanced maritime technology, agricultural practices, and social organization. As they settled in the Indonesian archipelago and the broader Southeast Asian region, they interacted with indigenous populations, leading to the exchange of cultural practices and the formation of new social groups.[130] The Austronesian migration played a crucial role in shaping the linguistic and cultural landscape of Southeast Asia. The spread of Austronesian languages and cultural practices is evident in the archaeological record, particularly in the distribution of pottery styles, agricultural tools, and burial practices.[131] The integration of Austronesian migrants with local populations led to the formation of early chiefdoms and proto states, which were characterized by hierarchical social structures and the centralization of power.[132] The formation of complex societies in Southeast Asia and Indonesia was marked by the emergence of chiefdoms and early states around 2000 years ago. These societies were often cantered around strategic locations, such as river valleys, coastal areas, and trade routes. The control of agricultural production, trade, and religious practices allowed local leaders to consolidate power and establish more centralized political structures.[133]

One of the earliest and most significant examples of state formation in the region is the kingdom of Funan, which emerged in the Mekong Delta around the first century AD. Funan was a key centre for trade between India and China, and its rulers adopted Indian cultural and religious practices, including Hinduism and Buddhism. The adoption of Indian culture and the development of trade networks were crucial in the formation of early states in Southeast Asia.[134] The formation of societies in Southeast Asia and Indonesia was also heavily influenced by cultural exchanges

[130] Bellwood, P. & Nitihaminoto, G. (1993), The Buidane Culture of the Talaud Islands, North Eastern Indonesia. Asian Perspectives, 32(1), pp. 73–97.

[131] Chao, C. (2008), Pottery, Stratigraphy, and Seafaring in the Lapita Complex: The Field Seasons of 2005–2007. Journal of the Indo-Pacific Prehistory Association, 28(3), pp. 213–226.

[132] Spriggs, M. (2011), Archaeology and the Austronesian Expansion: Where are We Now? Antiquity, 85(328), pp. 510–528.

[133] Chao, C. (2008), Pottery, Stratigraphy, and Seafaring in the Lapita Complex: The Field Seasons of 2005–2007. Journal of the Indo-Pacific Prehistory Association, 28(3), pp. 213–226.

[134] Bellina, B. & Glover, I.C. (2004), The Archaeology of Early Contact with India and the Mediterranean World, from the Fourth Century BC to the Fourth Century

with neighbouring regions, particularly India and China. The introduction of Indian religions, such as Hinduism and Buddhism, had a profound impact on the social and political structures of the region. Indian religious ideas were often adopted by local rulers to legitimize their authority and reinforce social hierarchies.[135] The spread of Buddhism in particular played a significant role in the formation of societies in the Indonesian archipelago. The kingdom of Srivijaya, which emerged in Sumatra around the seventh century AD, became a major centre of Buddhist learning and pilgrimage. Srivijaya's control over key maritime trade routes allowed it to exert influence over much of Southeast Asia, spreading both Buddhism and its own political and cultural influence across the region.[136] The development of trade networks was another key factor in the formation of societies in Indonesia and Southeast Asia. The region's strategic location between the Indian Ocean and the South China Sea made it a crucial hub for maritime trade. The exchange of goods, such as spices, textiles, and metals, facilitated the growth of early urban centres and the accumulation of wealth, which in turn supported the development of more complex social structures.[137]

The rise of trade also led to increased interaction between diverse cultural groups, contributing to the region's rich cultural diversity. The integration of various ethnic groups and the blending of indigenous and foreign cultural practices played a central role in the formation of distinct regional identities within Southeast Asia.[138] (Wolters, 1982). The formation of societies in Indonesia and Southeast Asia was a dynamic process influenced by a range of factors, including environmental adaptation, migration, cultural exchange, and economic development. The

AD. In I.C. Glover & P. Bellwood (Eds.), SoutheastAsia: From Prehistory to History (pp. 68–89). Routledge.

[135] Mabbett, I.W. & Chandler, D.P. (1995), The Khmers. Blackwell Publishers.

[136] Manguin, P.-Y. (1993), Pre-Aryan and Pre-Indian Influences in SoutheastAsia: A Study of the Lower and Central Mekong Basin. In H. P. Ray & J. F. Salles (Eds.), Tradition and Archaeology: Early Maritime Contacts in the Indian Ocean (pp. 135–164). Manohar.

[137] Manguin, P.-Y. (1993), Pre-Aryan and Pre-Indian Influences in SoutheastAsia: A Study of the Lower and Central Mekong Basin. In H. P. Ray & J. F. Salles (Eds.), Tradition and Archaeology: Early Maritime Contacts in the Indian Ocean (pp. 135–164). Manohar.

[138] Wolters, O.W. (1982), History, Culture, and Region in Southeast Asian Perspectives. SEAP Publications.

region's early societies were characterized by their ability to adapt to diverse environments, integrate modern technologies and cultural practices, and establish complex social and political structures. The legacy of these early societies continues to shape the cultural and social landscape of Southeast Asia and Indonesia today, in the following ways:

a) **Religious Practices**: The enduring influence of Hinduism and Buddhism is evident in the religious practices of Bali, Indonesia, and Thailand, where rituals, festivals, and temple architecture are deeply rooted in these early religions.[139]
b) **Language and Scripts**: Sanskrit and other Indian languages have influenced Southeast Asian languages, such as Javanese and Balinese scripts, which are derived from ancient Indian scripts[140]
c) **Agricultural Practices**: The wet-rice cultivation systems, introduced during early societal developments, remain fundamental to the region's agriculture, particularly in Indonesia and Vietnam.[141]
d) **Architectural Styles**: The architectural heritage of early societies is seen in the iconic temples like Borobudur and Prambanan in Indonesia, which continue to be significant cultural landmarks.[142]
e) **Social and Political Structures**: The hierarchical political systems established by early kingdoms such as Srivijaya continue to influence governance and social structures in modern Southeast Asia.[143]

[139] Geertz, C. (1973), The Interpretation of Cultures. Basic Books.

[140] Gonda, J. (1973), Sanskritin Indonesia. International Academy of Indian Culture.

[141] Barker, G. (2006), The Agricultural Revolution in Prehistory: Why Did Foragers Become Farmers? Oxford University Press.

[142] Soekmono, R. (1976), Chandi Borobudur: A Monument of Mankind. Assen: Van Gorcum.

[143] Wolters, O.W. (1982), History, Culture, and Region in Southeast Asian Perspectives. SEAP Publications.

Cultural and Technological Advances

Pottery and Metallurgy

The emergence and development of pottery and metallurgy in Indonesia and Southeast Asia represent significant milestones in the region's prehistoric and early historic periods. These technological advancements were instrumental in shaping the cultural, economic, and social landscapes of the region. This section explores the origins, evolution, and impact of pottery and metallurgy in Southeast Asia, with a particular focus on Indonesia, drawing on a range of academic sources. Pottery production in Southeast Asia dates back to the Neolithic period, around 4000–3000 BCE, when early communities began to settle and develop agricultural practices. The earliest pottery in the region was typically handmade and characterized by simple forms and decorations. These early vessels were primarily used for cooking, storage, and ritual purposes.[144] The introduction of pottery allowed for the better storage of surplus food, which supported the development of more complex societies. In Indonesia, evidence of early pottery has been found in several archaeological sites, including the islands of Sulawesi and Java. The pottery from these sites shares similarities with pottery from mainland Southeast Asia, suggesting a diffusion of ceramic technology across the region. The spread of pottery-making techniques was facilitated by the migration of Austronesian-speaking peoples, who carried their technological knowledge as they settled in various parts of Southeast Asia.[145]

The development of pottery in Southeast Asia is strongly associated with the rise of sedentary agricultural communities. The production of pottery became more sophisticated over time, with the introduction of the potter's wheel and the development of more complex firing techniques. These advancements allowed for the production of more durable and aesthetically pleasing ceramics, which became an important aspect of social and cultural expression.[146] The development of metallurgy in Southeast Asia marks a significant technological advancement that began

[144] Higham, C. (2002) Early Cultures of Mainland SoutheastAsia. Art Media Resources.

[145] Bellwood, P. (2007), Prehistory of the Indo-Malaysian Archipelago. 3rd edition. ANU E Press.

[146] Bulbeck, D. (1996), The Bronze-Iron Age of South Sulawesi,Indonesia: Mortuary Traditions, Metallurgy and Trade. In N. Barnard (Ed.), Ancient Chinese and SoutheastAsian Bronze Age Cultures (pp. 353–370). Taipei: SMC Publishing Inc.

around 1500 BCE. The earliest evidence of metalworking in the region is associated with the production of bronze, an alloy of copper and tin. Bronze artifacts, including tools, weapons, and ornaments, have been found at various archaeological sites across Southeast Asia, indicating that the technology spread rapidly throughout the region.[147] In Indonesia, the Bronze Age is characterized by the production of intricate bronze drums, known as Dong Son drums, which are believed to have originated from northern Vietnam and spread across the region through trade and cultural exchange. These drums were used in ritual contexts and as symbols of power and prestige. The distribution of Dong Son drums across Indonesia highlights the region's participation in a broader network of trade and cultural exchange during the Bronze Age.[148]

The transition from the Bronze Age to the Iron Age in Southeast Asia occurred around 500 BCE. Ironworking technology, which was introduced from the Indian subcontinent, allowed for the production of more durable tools and weapons. The adoption of iron technology had a profound impact on the social and economic structures of Southeast Asian societies, enabling more efficient agriculture, warfare, and construction.[149] The development of metallurgy in Southeast Asia is closely linked to the rise of complex societies and the establishment of early states. The control of metal resources and the production of metal goods became central to the power and authority of ruling elites. Metal artifacts, particularly those made of bronze and iron, were often used as status symbols and in religious rituals, reinforcing social hierarchies and cultural practices.[150] In Indonesia, the production of bronze and iron artifacts is associated with the development of early polities, such as the kingdom of Srivijaya in Sumatra. The control of metal production and trade routes contributed to the wealth and power of these early states. The spread of metallurgy

[147] Ibid.

[148] Higham, C. (2002), Early Cultures of Mainland SoutheastAsia. Art Media Resources.

[149] Bulbeck, D. (1996), The Bronze-Iron Age of South Sulawesi,Indonesia: Mortuary Traditions, Metallurgy and Trade. In N. Barnard (Ed.), Ancient Chinese and SoutheastAsian Bronze Age Cultures (pp. 353–370). Taipei: SMC Publishing Inc.

[150] Bellina, B. & Glover, I.C. (2004), The Archaeology of Early Contact with India and the Mediterranean World, from the Fourth Century BC to the Fourth Century AD. In I.C. Glover & P. Bellwood (Eds.), SoutheastAsia: From Prehistory to History (pp. 68–89). Routledge.

also facilitated the exchange of ideas and technologies between Southeast Asia and neighbouring regions, including South Asia and China.[151]

The development of pottery and metallurgy in Southeast Asia cannot be understood without considering the region's role in long-distance trade networks. From the first millennium BCE, Southeast Asia became an important hub in the trade of luxury goods, including metals and ceramics. The demand for these goods stimulated the production of high-quality pottery and metal artifacts, which were traded across the region and beyond.[152] The production of glass beads, for instance, involved sophisticated techniques that were likely influenced by Indian and Chinese technologies. These beads, often used as trade items and in ritual contexts, have been found in numerous archaeological sites in Indonesia, reflecting the region's active participation in early global trade networks.[153] The integration of Southeast Asia into these networks facilitated the exchange of technological knowledge, contributing to the development of local pottery and metallurgical traditions.

The emergence and development of pottery and metallurgy in Indonesia and Southeast Asia were pivotal in the region's cultural and technological evolution. Pottery, which began in the Neolithic period, supported the growth of agricultural societies and facilitated the storage and distribution of food. Metallurgy, which developed during the Bronze Age and expanded during the Iron Age, played a critical role in the rise of complex societies and early states. The interaction between local innovations and external influences through trade and migration significantly shaped the development of these technologies, leaving a lasting impact on the region's history.

[151] Dussubieux, L. & Gratuze, B. (2007), Circulation of Glass and Other Precious Materials in SoutheastAsia. In J. Miksic (Ed.), Earthenware in SoutheastAsia: Proceedings of the Singapore Symposium on Southeast Asian Archaeology 2006 (pp. 91–112). Singapore: Singapore University Press.

[152] Manguin, P.-Y. (1993), Pre-Aryan and Pre-Indian Influences in SoutheastAsia: A Study of the Lower and Central Mekong Basin. In H. P. Ray & J. F. Salles (Eds.), Tradition and Archaeology: Early Maritime Contacts in the Indian Ocean (pp. 135–164). Manohar.

[153] Dussubieux, L. & Gratuze, B. (2007), Circulation of Glass and Other Precious Materials in SoutheastAsia. In J. Miksic (Ed.), Earthenware in SoutheastAsia: Proceedings of the Singapore Symposium on Southeast Asian Archaeology 2006 (pp. 91–112). Singapore: Singapore University Press.

Megalithic Traditions

The megalithic traditions of Indonesia and Southeast Asia represent one of the most intriguing aspects of the region's prehistoric and early historic periods. These traditions, characterized by the construction of large stone structures for ceremonial, funerary, and social purposes, have left an indelible mark on the cultural landscape of the region. This report explores the origins, development, and significance of megalithic traditions in Indonesia and Southeast Asia, drawing on archaeological evidence and scholarly analysis. Megalithic traditions in Southeast Asia began to emerge during the Neolithic period, around 2500 BCE. These traditions involved the erection of large stone monuments, including menhirs (standing stones), dolmens (stone tables), and stone alignments, often associated with burial practices and ancestor worship.[154] The widespread distribution of megalithic sites across the region, from Sumatra and Java in Indonesia to mainland Southeast Asia, indicates the importance of these structures in the social and religious life of early communities.

The origins of Southeast Asian megalithic traditions are complex and involved multiple influences. Some scholars suggest that these traditions may have been indigenous developments, arising independently in different regions in response to local social and environmental conditions.[155]. Others propose that the megalithic practices in Southeast Asia were influenced by contacts with South Asia and other regions where megalithic cultures were also prominent.[156]

As megalithic traditions spread throughout Southeast Asia, they developed distinct regional characteristics. In Indonesia, for example, the island of Nias is renowned for its elaborate megalithic structures, including large stone statues and ceremonial platforms. These structures are often associated with the power and status of local chiefs, who commissioned their

[154] Bellwood, P. (1988), Archaeological Research in SoutheastAsia: A Brief Overview. Asian Perspectives, 27(2), pp. 107–115.

[155] Spriggs, M. (1993), The Lapita Cultural Complex: Origins, Distribution, Contemporaries and Successors. Journal of Pacific Archaeology, 4(1), pp. 19–24.

[156] Bellwood, P. (1988), Archaeological Research in SoutheastAsia: A Brief Overview. Asian Perspectives, 27(2), pp. 107–115.

construction to demonstrate their authority and to honour their ancestors.[157] The practice of building megalithic monuments in Nias continues to this day, reflecting the deep cultural significance of these structures. In other parts of Indonesia, such as Sulawesi and the Lesser Sunda Islands, megalithic traditions took on different forms. In Sulawesi, the Toraja people are known for their megalithic burial sites, where large stone tombs and effigies are erected to honor the dead. These practices are closely tied to the Toraja's belief in the afterlife and the importance of maintaining strong ties with the ancestors.[158] The diversity of megalithic traditions in Indonesia highlights the adaptability of these practices to different cultural and environmental contexts. In mainland Southeast Asia, megalithic traditions were also widespread, particularly in regions such as the Malay Peninsula and Thailand. In these areas, megalithic structures often took the form of burial mounds or stone circles, which were used for both ceremonial and funerary purposes. The construction of these monuments was typically a communal effort, reflecting the social cohesion of early agricultural communities.[159] The similarities between Southeast Asian and South Asian megalithic practices have led some researchers to explore possible cultural connections between these regions, although the exact nature of these links remains a subject of debate.

The construction of megalithic monuments in Southeast Asia was intricately linked to the development of social hierarchies and the centralization of power. The ability to mobilize labour and resources for the construction of large stone structures was a key indicator of social status and political authority. In many cases, megalithic monuments served as symbols of the power and prestige of local elites, who used these structures to legitimize their rule and to reinforce social inequalities.[160]. The role of megalithic monuments in ancestor worship and ritual activities

[157] Effert, R.(2003), Royal Authority and Tribal Chiefs: The Politics of Megalithic Monuments in SoutheastAsia. Bijdragen tot de Taal-, Land- en Volkenkunde, 159(2), pp. 281–310.

[158] Adams, K.M. (2010), Art as Politics: Re-Crafting Identities, Tourism, and Power in Tana Toraja, Indonesia. University of Hawaii Press.

[159] Spriggs, M. (1993), The Lapita Cultural Complex: Origins, Distribution, Contemporaries and Successors. Journal of Pacific Archaeology, 4(1), pp. 19–24.

[160] Adams, K.M. (2010), Art as Politics: Re-Crafting Identities, Tourism, and Power in Tana Toraja, Indonesia. University of Hawaii Press.

also played a crucial role in maintaining social cohesion. By honouring the ancestors and reinforcing communal ties through shared rituals, megalithic traditions helped to strengthen the social fabric of early Southeast Asian societies. The emphasis on ancestor worship in megalithic traditions is evident in the continued importance of these practices in some contemporary Southeast Asian cultures, where megalithic structures are still used in ritual contexts.[161] The megalithic traditions of Southeast Asia and Indonesia have left a lasting legacy on the region's cultural landscape. These monuments are not only important archaeological sites but also continue to play a significant role in the cultural identity of the communities that maintain them. The ongoing use of megalithic structures in rituals and ceremonies, particularly in Indonesia, underscores the enduring significance of these traditions in contemporary society.[162] The study of megalithic traditions also provides valuable insights into the social and cultural dynamics of prehistoric Southeast Asia. The construction and use of megalithic monuments reflect the complex interplay between social organization, religious beliefs, and environmental factors. By examining these structures, researchers can gain a better understanding of the ways in which early Southeast Asian societies adapted to their environments and developed distinctive cultural practices.[163]

The emergence and development of megalithic traditions in Indonesia and Southeast Asia represent a significant aspect of the region's prehistoric and early historic periods. These traditions, characterized by the construction of large stone monuments for ceremonial, funerary, and social purposes, played a significant role in the social and cultural life of early Southeast Asian societies. The diversity of megalithic practices across the region reflects the adaptability of these traditions to diverse cultural and environmental contexts, while their continued significance in contemporary society highlights their enduring cultural importance.

[161] Spriggs, M. (1993), The Lapita Cultural Complex: Origins, Distribution, Contemporaries and Successors. Journal of Pacific Archaeology, 4(1), pp. 19–24.

[162] Bellwood, P. (1988), Archaeological Research in SoutheastAsia: A Brief Overview. Asian Perspectives, 27(2), pp. 107–115.

[163] Effert, R. (2003), Royal Authority and Tribal Chiefs: The Politics of Megalithic Monuments in SoutheastAsia. Bijdragen tot de Taal-, Land- en Volkenkunde, 159(2), pp. 281–310.

Influence of External Cultures

Indian Influence and Early Hindu-Buddhist Presence

The spread of Indian cultural and religious influences across Southeast Asia, including Indonesia, marks one of the most significant periods in the region's history. This process, often referred to as "Indianization," began around the first few centuries CE and led to the establishment of Hindu-Buddhist kingdoms and the integration of Indian religious, artistic, and political practices into Southeast Asian societies. This section examines the origins, development, and impact of Indian influences and the early Hindu-Buddhist presence in Indonesia and Southeast Asia.

The early influence of Indian culture in Southeast Asia can be traced back to the rise of maritime trade routes across the Indian Ocean, which facilitated the exchange of goods, ideas, and religious practices between the Indian subcontinent and Southeast Asia. By the first century CE, Southeast Asian ports had become integral parts of the maritime trade networks linking India, China, and the Mediterranean world.[164] These networks not only brought goods like spices, textiles, and precious stones but also carried Indian cultural and religious influences to the shores of Southeast Asia. Indian traders, priests, and adventurers played a key role in transmitting Indian cultural practices to Southeast Asia. The adoption of Indian religious and cultural norms by local rulers was likely motivated by the prestige and authority that these practices conferred, which were seen as enhancing the legitimacy and power of their rule.[165] Over time, this cultural exchange led to the establishment of Hindu and Buddhist kingdoms throughout the region. The first Hindu-Buddhist states in Southeast Asia began to emerge around the fourth century CE, with the establishment of the Funan kingdom in what is now southern Vietnam and Cambodia. Funan was heavily influenced by Indian culture, as evidenced by its adoption of Sanskrit as the language of administration and its use of Indian-style coinage, art, and architecture.[166] The

[164] Manguin, P.-Y. (2010), Southeast Asian Kingdoms and the Maritime Silk Road: New Evidence from Archaeology and Art History. In A. Schottenhammer (Ed.), The Emporium of the World: Maritime Quanzhou, 1000–1400 (pp. 241–262). Brill.

[165] Kulke, H. (1990), Indian Colonies, Indianization or Cultural Convergence? Reflections on the Changing Image of India's Role in South-EastAsia. In H. Kulke (Ed.), The State and the Statecraft in Early South-East Asia (pp. 232–246). Brill.

[166] Ibid.

kingdom's rulers embraced Hinduism and Buddhism, building temples dedicated to Hindu deities and the Buddha, which became centres of religious and political power. In Indonesia, the earliest evidence of Indian influence dates to the fourth century CE, with the establishment of the Tarumanagara kingdom in West Java. Inscriptions from this period, written in Sanskrit and using the Pallava script, indicate the presence of Hindu religious practices and the worship of Vishnu and Shiva.[167] The spread of Buddhism in Indonesia is also evidenced by the construction of stupas and the presence of Buddhist inscriptions, particularly in Central Java. The Srivijaya kingdom, which emerged in the seventh century CE in Sumatra, became a major centre of Buddhist learning and maritime trade. Srivijaya's strategic location along the Strait of Malacca allowed it to control trade between the Indian Ocean and the South China Sea, and the kingdom played a crucial role in the spread of Buddhism across Southeast Asia.[168] The Srivijaya rulers patronized Buddhist institutions and scholars, attracting pilgrims and monks from across the region, including China and India.[169]

The process of Indianization in Southeast Asia involved the selective adoption and adaptation of Indian cultural practices by local elites. Rather than a wholesale adoption of Indian culture, Southeast Asian rulers integrated Indian religious concepts, political ideologies, and artistic styles into their own cultural frameworks, creating a unique blend of Indian and indigenous elements.[170]

One of the most significant aspects of this cultural integration was the adaptation of the Indian concept of kingship, which linked the ruler's authority to divine sanction. Southeast Asian rulers adopted titles such as "devaraja" (god-king) and constructed monumental temples that symbolized their divine connection, such as the Prambanan temple complex in

[167] Manguin, P.-Y. (2010), Southeast Asian Kingdoms and the Maritime Silk Road: New Evidence from Archaeology and Art History. In A. Schottenhammer (Ed.), The Emporium of the World: Maritime Quanzhou, 1000–1400 (pp. 241–262). Brill.

[168] Wolters, O.W. (1999), History, Culture, and Region in Southeast Asian Perspectives. SEAP Publications.

[169] Manguin, P.-Y. (2010), Southeast Asian Kingdoms and the Maritime Silk Road: New Evidence from Archaeology and Art History. In A. Schottenhammer (Ed.), The Emporium of the World: Maritime Quanzhou, 1000–1400 (pp. 241–262). Brill.

[170] Kulke, H. (1990), Indian Colonies, Indianization or Cultural Convergence? Reflections on the Changing Image of India's Role in South-EastAsia. In H. Kulke (Ed.), The State and the Statecraft in Early South-East Asia (pp. 232–246). Brill.

Central Java and the Angkor Wat temple in Cambodia.[171] These temples served not only as religious centres but also as political symbols, reinforcing the ruler's authority and the unity of the state. The integration of Hindu and Buddhist religious practices also led to the development of syncretic traditions in Southeast Asia. In Java, for example, Hindu and Buddhist elements were often combined in the construction of temples and in religious ceremonies, reflecting the flexibility and adaptability of religious practices in the region.[172] This syncretism allowed for the coexistence of different religious traditions and contributed to the rich cultural diversity of Southeast Asia. Indian influences had a profound impact on the art and architecture of Southeast Asia, particularly in the construction of religious monuments and the development of artistic styles. The spread of Indian artistic traditions can be seen in the adoption of Indian iconography, such as the depiction of Hindu gods and goddesses in temple carvings and sculptures.[173] The influence of Indian temple architecture is also evident in the construction of monumental structures such as the Borobudur and Prambanan temples in Indonesia, which are among the most significant examples of Indian-inspired architecture in Southeast Asia.[174]

These temples were not merely places of worship but also served as centres of learning and cultural exchange, where scholars and artists from different regions came together to share ideas and techniques. The integration of Indian artistic styles with local traditions led to the creation of a distinct Southeast Asian artistic heritage, characterized by its intricate carvings, elaborate sculptures, and grand architectural designs.[175] By the fourteenth and fifteenth centuries, the influence of Hinduism and Buddhism in Southeast Asia began to decline, as the region witnessed

[171] Cœdès, G. (1968), The Indianized States of SoutheastAsia. University of Hawaii Press.

[172] Miksic, J.N. (2011), Southeast Asian Ceramics: New Light on Old Pottery. Southeast Asian Ceramic Society.

[173] Miksic, J.N. (2011), Southeast Asian Ceramics: New Light on Old Pottery. Southeast Asian Ceramic Society.

[174] Cœdès, G. (1968), The Indianized States of SoutheastAsia. University of Hawaii Press.

[175] Manguin, P.-Y. (2010), Southeast Asian Kingdoms and the Maritime Silk Road: New Evidence from Archaeology and Art History. In A. Schottenhammer (Ed.), The Emporium of the World: Maritime Quanzhou, 1000–1400 (pp. 241–262). Brill.

the rise of Islam, particularly in the Malay Peninsula and Indonesia. However, the legacy of Hindu-Buddhist states continued to shape the cultural and religious landscape of Southeast Asia long after their decline. The temples, inscriptions, and art left behind by these states remain as enduring symbols of the region's rich cultural heritage.[176] In modern Indonesia, for instance, Hinduism remains a major religion in Bali, where the traditions and practices of the ancient Hindu-Buddhist kingdoms are still observed. The continued importance of these traditions in contemporary Southeast Asian societies highlights the lasting impact of Indian influences on the region's cultural identity.[177]

The Indian influences and the early Hindu-Buddhist presence in Indonesia and Southeast Asia were pivotal in shaping the region's historical development. The process of Indianization, facilitated by maritime trade and cultural exchange, led to the emergence of Hindu-Buddhist kingdoms that integrated Indian religious, political, and artistic traditions into their own cultural frameworks. The legacy of these early states is evident in the region's monumental architecture, religious practices, and cultural diversity, which continue to influence Southeast Asia today.

The Spread of Religions and Art Forms

The spread of religions and art forms in Indonesia and Southeast Asia was a profound process that significantly shaped the cultural, social, and political landscapes of the region. From the early centuries CE, the region saw the introduction and development of Hinduism, Buddhism, and later Islam, each leaving a lasting impact on the region's artistic and architectural heritage. This report examines the spread of these religions and their associated art forms, drawing on a range of scholarly sources. The introduction of Hinduism and Buddhism to Southeast Asia, including Indonesia, began around the early centuries CE, primarily through the medium of trade and cultural exchange with the Indian subcontinent.[178] Indian traders, priests, and scholars brought with them religious texts,

[176] Wolters, O.W. (1999), History, Culture, and Region in Southeast Asian Perspectives. SEAP Publications.

[177] Miksic, J.N. (2011), Southeast Asian Ceramics: New Light on Old Pottery. Southeast Asian Ceramic Society.

[178] Bosch, F.D.K. (1961), The Golden Germ: An Introduction to Indian Symbolism. Mouton.

rituals, and iconography that gradually integrated into the local cultures of Southeast Asia.

Hinduism and Buddhism were embraced by the local elites, who saw in these religions a means to legitimize their rule and enhance their cultural prestige.[179] This adoption of Indian religions was not merely passive; local rulers and societies actively engaged with these religious traditions, interpreting and integrating them in ways that were compatible with indigenous beliefs and practices.[180]

The spread of Hinduism and Buddhism in Southeast Asia was accompanied by the introduction of Indian art forms, which were adapted and localized to fit the cultural contexts of the region. The most significant manifestation of this is seen in the region's religious architecture, particularly in the construction of temples and monuments. One of the most prominent examples of Hindu art in Southeast Asia is the Prambanan temple complex in Central Java, Indonesia, which dates to the ninth century CE. This complex, dedicated to the Hindu Trimurti (Brahma, Vishnu, and Shiva), reflects the classical Indian temple architecture with its towering spires and intricate stone carvings.[181] The Prambanan complex is a testament to the spread of Hindu religious art and its adaptation in the Southeast Asian context, where it was integrated with local styles and materials. Buddhist art also found a prominent place in Southeast Asia, with the Borobudur temple in Central Java serving as one of the most significant examples. Constructed in the eighth-ninth centuries CE, Borobudur is a massive stupa that incorporates Indian Buddhist iconography, such as the Buddha images and narrative reliefs depicting the life of the Buddha.[182] However, Borobudur also reflects the local Javanese cultural influences, seen in the syncretic mix of Hindu and indigenous elements within its architecture and iconography.[183]

From the thirteenth century onwards, Islam began to spread across Southeast Asia, particularly through the activities of Muslim traders and

[179] Wolters, O.W. (1967), Early Indonesian Commerce: A Study of the Origins of Srīvijaya. Cornell University Press.

[180] Ibid.

[181] Bosch, F.D.K. (1961), The Golden Germ: An Introduction to Indian Symbolism. Mouton.

[182] Woodward, M. (1997), Java, Indonesiaand Islam. Springer.

[183] Bosch, F.D.K. (1961), The Golden Germ: An Introduction to Indian Symbolism. Mouton.

missionaries from South Asia and the Middle East. The arrival of Islam marked a new phase in the region's religious and artistic history. Unlike Hinduism and Buddhism, Islam did not emphasize figural representation in religious art due to its aniconic traditions.[184] Instead, Islamic art in Southeast Asia developed around geometric patterns, calligraphy, and the architectural embellishment of mosques. One of the key examples of Islamic architectural influence is the Great Mosque of Demak in Java, Indonesia, which was built in the fifteenth century. The mosque's design reflects a blend of Javanese architectural traditions with Islamic elements, particularly in its tiered roof structure and the use of carved wooden panels with intricate geometric and floral patterns.[185] This integration of local and Islamic art forms demonstrates the adaptability and creativity with which Southeast Asian societies incorporated new religious influences. The spread of different religions in Southeast Asia did not result in the complete displacement of earlier traditions; rather, it led to a complex process of syncretism, where different religious and cultural elements were blended to create unique artistic forms. This syncretism is particularly evident in the way Southeast Asian societies integrated Hindu, Buddhist, and indigenous motifs within their religious art.[186] For instance, in Bali, Hinduism was combined with local animist traditions to create a distinct form of Balinese Hinduism, which is reflected in the region's temple architecture and ritual arts. Balinese temples, such as Pura Besakih, incorporate elements of Hindu cosmology, such as the Mount Meru axis, with indigenous ancestor worship practices.[187] The rich tradition of Balinese dance and shadow puppetry (wayang kulit) also reflects this syncretic heritage, where Hindu epics like the Ramayana are performed within a distinctly Balinese cultural framework. While the spread of Hinduism, Buddhism, and Islam introduced new religious and artistic forms to Southeast Asia, these were not static or uniform across the region. Instead, they underwent continuous transformation as they

[184] Wade, G. (2009), The Origins and Roles of Islamic Maritime Structures in SoutheastAsia. Institute of Southeast Asian Studies.

[185] Azra, A. (2006), The Origins of Islamic Reformism in SoutheastAsia: Networks of Malay-Indonesian and Middle Eastern 'Ulamā' in the Seventeenth and Eighteenth Centuries. Allen & Unwin.

[186] Wolters, O.W. (1967), Early Indonesian Commerce: A Study of the Origins of Śrīvijaya. Cornell University Press.

[187] Geertz, C. (1973), The Interpretation of Cultures: Selected Essays. Basic Books.

interacted with local cultures and adapted to new social and political contexts.[188] This dynamic process of cultural exchange and adaptation is a key characteristic of Southeast Asian religious art, where change and continuity coexist in complex ways. In contemporary times, the artistic traditions associated with these religions continue to play a significant role in Southeast Asian cultural life. The preservation and revival of traditional art forms, such as Balinese dance and Javanese batik, are not just cultural artifacts but living traditions that connect modern societies with their historical and religious heritage.[189]

The spread of religions and art forms in Indonesia and Southeast Asia was a multifaceted process that significantly influenced the region's cultural development. The introduction of Hinduism, Buddhism, and later Islam brought new religious ideas and artistic traditions, which were creatively integrated into local cultures. The result was a rich and diverse artistic heritage that continues to define the cultural identity of Southeast Asia today. The enduring legacy of these religious and artistic traditions is a testament to the region's historical openness to cultural exchange and its capacity for artistic innovation.

Conclusion

The early civilizations of Indonesia played a pivotal role in shaping the region's cultural, social, and technological landscapes. From the migration and settlement patterns of Homo sapiens during the Pleistocene to the Austronesian expansion, the development of agricultural techniques, and the emergence of complex societies, these key developments highlight Indonesia's importance in prehistoric times.

One of the most significant aspects of early Indonesian civilization is the role of the region as a migration hub. The exposure of the Sunda Shelf during glacial periods provided a land bridge that facilitated the movement of populations into the Indonesian archipelago, leading to the establishment of early human settlements. These migrations, influenced by environmental factors such as fluctuating sea levels and volcanic activity, laid the foundation for the diverse and rich cultural tapestry of the region. The transition from hunter-gatherer societies to agricultural

[188] Miksic, J. and Goh, G.Y. (2017), Ancient SoutheastAsia. Routledge.

[189] Ibid.

communities marked another critical development in early Indonesian civilization. The introduction of wet-rice cultivation and the domestication of various crops, including taro, yam, and bananas, supported the growth of more permanent and complex societies. These agricultural advancements not only sustained larger populations but also allowed for the rise of social hierarchies and the establishment of early states.

The influence of external cultures, particularly from India, was instrumental in shaping the religious and artistic traditions of Indonesia. The spread of Hinduism and Buddhism through maritime trade routes led to the development of syncretic traditions that blended Indian religious concepts with indigenous practices. This cultural exchange resulted in the construction of monumental religious structures such as the Prambanan and Borobudur temples, which continue to be central to Indonesia's cultural heritage.

Reflecting on the legacy of these prehistoric societies, it is clear that the foundations laid by early Indonesian civilizations continue to influence the region today. The adaptability and resilience of these societies in the face of environmental changes and cultural exchanges are evident in the enduring traditions, religious practices, and social structures that define modern Indonesia. The rich archaeological record of the region not only provides valuable insights into the past but also underscores the importance of preserving this heritage for future generations.

References

Adams, K.M. (2010), Art as Politics: Re-Crafting Identities, Tourism, and Power in Tana Toraja, Indonesia. University of Hawaii Press.

Anderson, A. (2009). The Global Origins and Development of Seafaring. Cambridge Archaeological Journal, 19(1), 79–84.

Aubert, M., et al. (2014), Pleistocene cave art from Sulawesi, Indonesia. *Nature*, 514(7521), 223–227. https://doi.org/10.1038/nature13422.

Azra, A. (2006), The Origins of Islamic Reformism in Southeast Asia: Networks of Malay-Indonesian and Middle Eastern 'Ulamā' in the Seventeenth and Eighteenth Centuries. Allen & Unwin.

Barker, G. (2006), The Agricultural Revolution in Prehistory: Why Did Foragers Become Farmers? Oxford University Press.

Barker, G., et al. (2007), The 'human revolution' in lowland tropical Southeast Asia: the antiquity and behaviour of anatomically modern humans at Niah Cave (Sarawak, Borneo). Journal of Human Evolution, 52(3), 243–261. https://doi.org/10.1016/j.jhevol.2006.08.011.

Bellina, B. & Glover, I.C. (2004), The Archaeology of Early Contact with India and the Mediterranean World, from the Fourth Century BC to the Fourth Century AD. In I.C. Glover & P. Bellwood (Eds.), Southeast Asia: From Prehistory to History (pp. 68–89). Routledge.

Bellwood, P. & Nitihaminoto, G. (1993), The Buidane Culture of the Talaud Islands, North Eastern Indonesia. Asian Perspectives, 32(1), pp. 73–97.

Bellwood, P. (1988), Archaeological Research in Southeast Asia: A Brief Overview. Asian Perspectives, 27(2), pp. 107–115.

Bellwood, P. (1997), Prehistory of the Indo-Malaysian Archipelago. University of Hawaii Press, Honolulu, Hawaii384p.

Bellwood, P. (2007). First Farmers: The Origins of Agricultural Societies. Blackwell Publishing.

Bellwood, P. (2007), First Islanders: Prehistory and Human Migration in Island Southeast Asia. Journal of Southeast Asian Archaeology.

Bellwood, Ardelean, C.F., Becerra-Valdivia, L., et al. (2020), Evidence of human occupation in Mexico around the Last Glacial Maximum. Nature 584 (7819), 87–92.

Bird, M. I., Taylor, D., & Hunt, C. (2005), Palaeoenvironments of insular Southeast Asia during the Last Glacial Period: a savanna corridor in Sundaland? Quaternary Science Reviews, 2.4(20–21), 2228–2242. https://doi.org/10.1016/j.quascirev.2005.04.004.

Bird, M. I., & Taylor, D. (2015), Deep-sea and terrestrial records of climate change IN Handbook of Sea-Level Research (pp. 431–444). Wiley.

Bosch, F.D.K. (1961), The Golden Germ: An Introduction to Indian Symbolism. Mouton.

Bowen, J.R. (1995), Prayers to the Spirit of a Rice Paddy: Religion and Agrarian Ritual in Central Java. In Asian Visions of Authority: Religion and the Modern States of East and Southeast Asia (pp. 227–254). University of California Press.

Brown, P., et al. (2004). A new small-bodied hominin from the Late Pleistocene of Flores, Indonesia. Nature, 431(7012), 1055–1061. https://doi.org/10.1038/nature02999.

Bulbeck, D. (1996), The Bronze-Iron Age of South Sulawesi, Indonesia: Mortuary Traditions, Metallurgy and Trade. In

Barnard, N. (Ed.), Ancient Chinese and Southeast Asian Bronze Age Cultures (pp. 353–370). Taipei: SMC Publishing Inc.

Chao, C. (2008), Pottery, Stratigraphy, and Seafaring in the Lapita Complex: The Field Seasons of 2005–2007. Journal of the Indo-Pacific Prehistory Association, 28(3), pp. 213–226.

Cœdès, G. (1968), The Indianized States of Southeast Asia. University of Hawaii Press.

Coon, C.S. (1962), The Origin of Races. Borzoi Book, New York.

Denham, T., & Donohue, M. (2009), Pre-Austronesian Dispersal of Agriculture and Associated Language in Island Southeast Asia and the Western Pacific. Current Anthropology, 50(3), 379–391.

Dubois E. (1921), De proto-Australische Fossiele Mensch van Wadjak (Java), Koninklijke Nederindsch Akademie van Wetenschappen te Amsterdam, Verslag an de gewone Vergaderingen der Wis-, en Natuurkundige Afdeeling, 29, pp. 88–105.

Durband, A.C. and Westaway, M.C. (2013), Perspectives on the origins of modern Australians. The Origins of Modern Humans: Biology Reconsidered, pp. 123–150.

Dussubieux, L. & Gratuze, B. (2007), Circulation of Glass and Other Precious Materials in Southeast Asia. In J. Miksic (Ed.), Earthenware in Southeast Asia: Proceedings of the Singapore Symposium on Southeast Asian Archaeology 2006 (pp. 91–112). Singapore: Singapore University Press.

Dutton, A., & Lambeck, K. (2012), Ice Volume and Sea Level During the Last Interglacial, *Science*, 337(6091), 216–219. https://doi.org/10.1126/science.1205749.

Effert, R. (2003), Royal Authority and Tribal Chiefs: The Politics of Megalithic Monuments in Southeast Asia. Bijdragen tot de Taal-, Land- en Volkenkunde, 159(2), pp. 281–310.

Fuller, D.Q. & Qin, L. (2009), Water management and labour in the origins and dispersal of Asian rice. World Archaeology, 41(1), pp. 88–111.

Fuller, D. Q., Sato, Y.-I., Castillo, C., Qin, L., Weisskopf, A. R., & Kingwell-Banham, E. (2010), Consilience of Genetics and Archaeobotany in the Study of Rice Domestication and Spread in Asia. Proceedings of the National Academy of Sciences, 107(25), 10767–10774.

Geertz, C. (1973), The Interpretation of Cultures. Basic Books.

Glover, I. (1984), Southeast Asia and the diffusion of rice cultivation. In D.G. Baker, I.C. Glover, & G. Philip (Eds.), The origins and spread of agriculture and pastoralism in Eurasia (pp. 413–424). Duckworth.

Glover, I.C. (2006), Southeast Asia: From Prehistory to History. Routledge.

Golson, J. (1977). No room at the top: agricultural intensification in the New Guinea Highlands IN Allen, J., Golson, J., & Jones, R. (Eds.), Sunda and Sahul: Prehistoric Studies in Southeast Asia, Melanesia and Australia (pp. 601–638). Academic Press.

Gonda, J. (1973), Sanskrit in Indonesia. International Academy of Indian Culture.

Hershkovitz, I., Weber, G.W., Quam, R., Duval, M., Gru¨ n, R., Kinsley, L., Ayalon, A., Bar-Matthews, M., Valladas, H., Mercier, N., Arsuaga, J.L., Martino´ n-Torres, M., Bermudez de Castro, J.M., Fornai, C., Martın-Frances, L., Rachel Sarig, R., May, H., Krenn, V.A., Slon, V., Rodrıguez, L., Garcıa, R., Lorenzo, C., Carretero, J.M., Frumkin, A., Shahack-Gross,

R., Bar-Yosef Mayer, D.E., Cui, Y., Wu, X., Peled, N., Groman-Yaroslavski, I., Weissbrod, L., Yeshurun, R., Tsatskin, A., Zaidner, Y., Weinstein-Evron, M. (2018), The earliest modern humans outside Africa. Science 359 (6374), 456–459, https://doi.org/10.1126/science.aap8369.

Higham, C. (2002) Early Cultures of Mainland Southeast Asia. Art Media Resources.

Hunt, C. O., & Rabett, R. J. (2014). Holocene landscapes in Southeast Asia: context for early human adaptation and settlement. Journal of Archaeological Science, 51, 12–23. https://doi.org/10.1016/j.jas.2012.09.031

Jacob, T. (1977), Evolution of man in Southeast Asia'', Berkala Ilmu Kedokteran,. J Med Sci IX (4), 175–186.

Kennedy, K.A. (1977), The deep skull of Niah: An assessment of twenty years of speculation concerning its evolutionary significance. Asian Perspectives, 20(1), pp. 32–50.

Kirch, P. V. (2017), On the Road of the Winds: An Archaeological History of the Pacific Islands before European Contact. University of California Press.

Koenigswald, G.H.R. von. (1956), The geological age of Wadjak Man from Java. Proceedings of the Koninklijke Nederlandsch Akademie van Wetenschappen (PKNAW), Serie B 59 (5), 455–457.

Kulke, H. (1990), Indian Colonies, Indianization or Cultural Convergence? Reflections on the Changing Image of India's Role in South-East Asia. In H. Kulke (Ed.), The State and the Statecraft in Early South-East Asia (pp. 232–246). Brill.

Leach, E.R. (1999), Culture and Communication: The Logic by which Symbols are Connected. Cambridge University Press.

Liu, X. (2010), The Silk Road in World History. Oxford University Press.

Mabbett, I.W. & Chandler, D.P. (1995), The Khmers. Blackwell Publishers.

Majid, Z. (1982), The West Mouth, Niah, in the Prehistory of Southeast Asia. Sarawak Museum Journal 31 (52) [Special monograph no 3].

Manguin, P.-Y. (1993), Pre-Aryan and Pre-Indian Influences in Southeast Asia: A Study of the Lower and Central Mekong Basin. In H. P. Ray & J. F. Salles (Eds.), Tradition and Archaeology: Early Maritime Contacts in the Indian Ocean (pp. 135–164). Manohar.

Manguin, P.-Y. (2010), Southeast Asian Kingdoms and the Maritime Silk Road: New Evidence from Archaeology and Art History. In A. Schottenhammer (Ed.), The Emporium of the World: Maritime Quanzhou, 1000–1400 (pp. 241–262). Brill.

Masson-Delmotte, V., Schulz, M., Abe-Ouchi, A., et al. (2013), Information from Paleoclimate Archives, In: Climate Change 2013: The Physical Science Basis. Contribution of Working Group I to the Fifth Assessment Report of the Intergovernmental Panel on Climate Change. Cambridge University Press.

Mellars, P., Gori, K. C., Carr, M., Soares, P. A., & Richards, M. B. (2013), Genetic and archaeological perspectives on the initial modern human colonization of southern Asia. Proceedings of the National Academy of Sciences, 110(26), 10699–10704.

Miksic, J.N. (2011), Southeast Asian Ceramics: New Light on Old Pottery. Southeast Asian Ceramic Society.

Miksic, J. and Goh, G.Y. (2017), Ancient Southeast Asia. Routledge.

Noerwidi, S., Vialet, A., Widianto, H., Kurniawan, I., Zaim, J., Suriyanto, R.A., Joordens, J., Lorenzo, C., Simanjuntak, T., Se´mah, F. (2020), Exploring the diversity of fossil hominin dental patterns in the western Indonesian archipelago during the Quaternary by Geometric Morphometric Analysis. Application on second upper and lower molars. L'anthropologie 124 (5), 102791.

Shen, G., Wang, W., Wang, Q., Zhao, J., Collerson, K., Zhou, C., Tobias, P. (2002), U-Series dating of Liujiang hominid site in Guangxi, Southern China. Journal of human Evolution 43 (6), 817–829.

O'Connor, S., & Bulbeck, D. (2012), Homo sapiens in Island Southeast Asia: Current Perspectives and Future Directions. Asian Perspectives.

Oppenheimer, S. (2002), Eden in the East: The Drowned Continent of Southeast Asia. Orion Publishing.

Pannell, S. (2006), Reconciling nature and culture in a global context? Lessons from the World Heritage List. Australasian Journal of Environmental Management, 13(1), 36–45. https://doi.org/10.1080/14486563.2006.9725110.

Pawley, A. (2002), The Austronesian Dispersal: Languages, Technologies, People. Annual Review of Anthropology, 31(1), 443–470.

Paz, V. (2002). Island Southeast Asia: Spread or Friction Zone? Asian Perspectives, 41(1), 64–89.

Rigg, J. (2013), Rural Development in Southeast Asia: Dispossession, Accumulation and Persistence. Cambridge University Press.

Schellenberger, A., et al. (2010), Comparing Last Interglacial Climate and Sea-Level Estimates from Proxy Data and Climate Models, Climate of the Past, 6(4), 447–457. https://doi.org/10.5194/cp-6-447-2010.

Soares, P., Trejaut, J. A., Rito, T., Cavadas, B., Hill, C., Eng, K. K., ... & Macaulay, V. A. (2011). Ancient Voyaging and Polynesian Origins: Evidence from Mitochondrial DNA Lineages. Nature, 467(7317), 206–210.

Soares, P. A., et al. (2012), The Expansion of mtDNA Haplogroup L3 within and out of Africa. Molecular Biology and Evolution, 29(3), 915–927. https://doi.org/10.1093/molbev/msr245.

Soekmono, R. (1976), Chandi Borobudur: A Monument of Mankind. Assen: Van Gorcum.

Spriggs, M. (1993), The Lapita Cultural Complex: Origins, Distribution, Contemporaries and Successors. Journal of Pacific Archaeology, 4(1), pp. 19–24.

Spriggs, M. (2011), Archaeology and the Austronesian expansion: Where are we now? Antiquity, 85(328), 510–528. https://doi.org/10.1017/S0003598X00067910.

Storm, P., de Vos, J., Aziz, F., & Kosumi, E. (2005), Wajak Man: An Indonesian early modern human? Homo: Journal of Comparative Human Biology, 55(1), 45–72.

Swisher, C. C., et al. (1994). Age of the earliest known hominids in Java, Indonesia. Science, 263(5150), 1118–1121. https://doi.org/10.1126/science.8108729

Tzedakis, P. C., et al. (2003), Climate and Vegetation in Southeast Europe during the Last Interglacial. Quaternary Science Reviews, 22(15–17), 1449–1461. https://doi.org/10.1016/S0277-3791(03)00138-2.

Van Heekeren, H. R. (1957). The Stone Age of Indonesia. Martinus Nijhoff.

Van Liere, W.J., 1980. Traditional Water Management in the Lower Mekong Basin. In A. T. Grove (Ed.), Water, Land and Man: A Synthesis of Hydrology, Geomorphology and Socio-Economic Geography (pp. 55–78). Routledge.

Voris, H. K. (2000). Maps of Pleistocene Sea Levels in Southeast Asia: Shorelines, River Systems and Time Durations. Journal of Biogeography, 27(5), 1153–1167. https://doi.org/10.1046/j.1365-2699.2000.00489.x

Wade, G., 2009. The Pre-Modern East Asian Maritime Realm: An Overview of European-Language Sources. In D. W. Kang, G. Wade, & K. Choy (Eds.), East Asian Maritime History (pp. 13–54). Brill.

Wade, G. (2009), The Pre-Modern East Asian Maritime Realm: An Overview of European-Language Sources. In D. W. Kang, G. Wade, & K. Choy (Eds.), East Asian Maritime History (pp. 13–54). Brill.

Weidenreich, F. (1945), The Keilor Skull: a Wadjak Skull from Southeast Australia, American Journal of Physical Anthropology 3, 21–33.

Widianto, H. (2004), Siapakah Dia, Homo floresiensis?, Kompas Edisi 5, 52.

Widianto, H. and Noerwidi, S. (2023), The emergence and distribution of early modern human in

Indonesia. L'Anthropologie, 127(3), p. 103161.

Wolters, O.W. (1967), Early Indonesian Commerce: A Study of the Origins of Srivijaya. Cornell University Press.

Wolters, O.W. (1999), History, Culture, and Region in Southeast Asian Perspectives. SEAP Publications.

Zeitoun, V., Barriel, V., Widianto, H. (2016), Phylogenetic analysis of the calvaria of Homo floresiensis species. Palevol 15 (5), 555–568, https://doi.org/10.1016/j.crpv.2015.12.002.

CHAPTER 3

Trade and Kingdoms (1 AD–1500 AD)

Introduction

The period from 1 to 1500 AD marks a transformative era in the history of Indonesia and Southeast Asia, characterized by the extensive development of maritime trade networks and the rise of influential kingdoms. During this time, the Indonesian archipelago became a central hub in global trade routes that connected the Indian Ocean to the South China Sea. The strategic location of Indonesia facilitated the exchange of goods, ideas, and cultures, leading to significant sociopolitical developments across the region. Trade was the lifeblood of these early kingdoms, driving economic prosperity and enabling the accumulation of wealth and power. The interaction between local societies and foreign traders from India, China, the Arab world, and later, European powers, profoundly shaped the cultural and religious landscape of Indonesia. The spread of Hinduism and Buddhism through trade links led to the establishment of Indianized kingdoms such as Srivijaya and Majapahit, which played pivotal roles in the political and cultural development of Southeast Asia.[1,2] Trade and the rise of kingdoms in Indonesia were intricately linked, with commerce

[1] Reid, A. (1988), SoutheastAsia in the Age of Commerce, 1450–1680: Volume One, The Lands below the Winds. Yale University Press.

[2] Hall, K.R. (2011), A History of Early SoutheastAsia: Maritime Trade and Societal Development, 100–1500. Rowman & Littlefield Publishers.

S. Ramesh, *The Political Economy of Indonesia's Economic Development, Volume I*, https://doi.org/10.1007/978-3-031-94350-8_3

acting as a catalyst for state formation and the consolidation of political power. The wealth generated from trade allowed rulers to build sophisticated administrative structures, commission monumental architecture, and patronize religious institutions. These developments, in turn, reinforced the rulers' authority and legitimacy. The strategic control of trade routes, such as the Strait of Malacca, enabled kingdoms like Srivijaya to dominate regional trade and exert influence over vast territories. The rise of such powerful states facilitated the spread of cultural and religious practices, including Hinduism, Buddhism, and later Islam, throughout the Indonesian archipelago. This period also saw the flourishing of art, literature, and architecture, influenced by both local traditions and foreign interactions.[3,4]

This chapter aims to explore the intricate relationship between trade and the rise of kingdoms in Indonesia from 1 to 1500 AD. It will examine how maritime trade networks contributed to the formation and expansion of early Indonesian polities, focusing on key kingdoms such as Srivijaya and Majapahit. The chapter will also analyse the role of trade in facilitating cultural and religious exchanges, particularly the spread of Hinduism, Buddhism, and Islam. Additionally, the chapter will consider the socio-economic impacts of trade on Indonesian society, including the development of urban centres and the evolution of social hierarchies. By drawing on a range of scholarly sources, the chapter will provide a comprehensive overview of how trade shaped the political, cultural, and economic landscape of Indonesia during this crucial period.

Early Maritime Trade Routes (1 AD–500 AD)

The establishment of maritime trade routes across the Indonesian archipelago was a critical development during the first five centuries AD. These routes emerged as vital conduits for the exchange of goods, ideas, and cultural practices between the islands of Indonesia and other parts of Southeast Asia, South Asia, and beyond. The geographic position of the Indonesian archipelago, straddling key maritime passages between the

[3] Ibid.

[4] Reid, A. (1988), SoutheastAsia in the Age of Commerce, 1450–1680: Volume One, The Lands below the Winds. Yale University Press.

Indian Ocean and the South China Sea, made it an essential hub in the broader network of trade routes that connected the East and the West.[5] Indigenous seafarers in the region developed advanced navigational skills and shipbuilding techniques, enabling them to establish regular trade connections both within the archipelago and with distant lands. The strategic location of Indonesian ports, such as those in Sumatra and Java, facilitated their rise as significant centres of trade and cultural exchange. The Indonesian archipelago became a melting pot of various cultures and a focal point for the spread of religious, artistic, and technological innovations.[6] The interaction between Indonesian traders and their Indian and Chinese counterparts played a significant role in shaping the economic and cultural landscape of the region. Indian traders, in particular, brought with them not only goods but also religious and cultural practices that deeply influenced the societies of the Indonesian archipelago. The introduction of Hinduism and Buddhism through these interactions led to the establishment of Indianized kingdoms such as Srivijaya and Tarumanagara.[7] Chinese traders were also active in the region, with early Chinese records indicating regular trade missions to Southeast Asia from as early as the Han Dynasty. The exchange of silk, ceramics, and other luxury goods for Southeast Asian spices, resins, and forest products was a cornerstone of the trade relationship between China and the Indonesian archipelago. These interactions fostered a rich cultural exchange, with Chinese art, architecture, and political ideas leaving a lasting impact on the region.[8]

The spice trade was central to the economic activities of the Indonesian archipelago during this period. The region was renowned for its production of valuable spices, such as cloves, nutmeg, and mace, which were highly sought after in international markets. These spices were not only used for culinary purposes but also for medicinal and religious practices, making them some of the most valuable commodities in global

[5] Wolters, O.W. (1967), Early Indonesian Commerce: A Study of the Origins of Srīvijaya. Cornell University Press.

[6] Bellina, B. and Glover, I. (2004), SoutheastAsia: From Prehistory to History. Routledge.

[7] Manguin, P.-Y. (2010), Early trading polities of SoutheastAsia: Their markets and the Indian Oceantrade network. Journal of Southeast Asian Studies.

[8] Wolters, O.W. (1967), Early Indonesian Commerce: A Study of the Origins of Srīvijaya. Cornell University Press.

trade.[9] The high demand for spices attracted traders from across the world, including India, China, and later, the Arab world. The lucrative spice trade led to the growth of powerful trading states in the Indonesian archipelago, such as Srivijaya, which controlled the production and distribution of these goods. The wealth generated from the spice trade facilitated the rise of these states and enabled them to exert influence over regional trade networks.[10] The extensive trade networks that developed across the Indonesian archipelago had profound effects on the region's social and political structures. The wealth generated from trade enabled the rise of powerful kingdoms and the establishment of complex hierarchical societies. Rulers of these kingdoms leveraged their control over trade routes and valuable resources to consolidate power and legitimize their rule. The accumulation of wealth also led to the patronage of religious institutions, the construction of monumental architecture, and the flourishing of arts and culture.[11] Furthermore, the interaction with foreign traders and cultures led to significant changes in the social fabric of Indonesian societies. The introduction of new religious ideas, such as Hinduism and Buddhism, played a crucial role in the development of state ideologies and administrative systems. The influence of Indian political models, combined with local traditions, resulted in the formation of unique syncretic cultures that characterized the kingdoms of early Indonesia.[12]

The Rise of Early Kingdoms (1 AD–700 AD)

The formation of early Indonesian polities from 1 to 700 AD was a dynamic process driven by the interaction between indigenous traditions and external influences. These early states were often cantered around

[9] Bellina, B. and Glover, I. (2004), SoutheastAsia: From Prehistory to History. Routledge.

[10] Manguin, P.-Y. (2010), Early trading polities of SoutheastAsia: Their markets and the Indian Oceantrade network. Journal of Southeast Asian Studies.

[11] Wolters, O.W. (1967), Early Indonesian Commerce: A Study of the Origins of Srīvijaya. Cornell University Press.

[12] Bellina, B. and Glover, I. (2004), SoutheastAsia: From Prehistory to History. Routledge.

strategic locations, such as river valleys and coastal areas, which facilitated control over trade routes and resources. Local leaders, who initially held power based on their control of agricultural production and ritual authority, began to centralize political structures as they engaged more with external traders and adopted modern technologies.[13] The rise of these polities was marked by the development of more complex social hierarchies and the emergence of ruling dynasties. This period also saw the establishment of urban centres, where trade, administration, and religious practices were concentrated. The increasing importance of trade led to the growth of port cities, which became hubs for both economic and cultural exchange.[14] The introduction of Hinduism and Buddhism, collectively referred to as Indianization, had a profound impact on the political and cultural landscapes of early Indonesian kingdoms. Indianization began as early as the first century AD, driven by trade interactions with South Asia, where Indian traders and religious figures introduced these religions to Southeast Asia. Local rulers quickly adopted Hindu and Buddhist practices, seeing in them powerful tools for legitimizing their authority and organizing their states.[15] Hinduism and Buddhism provided the ideological frameworks for the development of more sophisticated forms of governance, including the concept of divine kingship, where rulers were seen as incarnations of gods or as their representatives on earth. These religions also brought with them new forms of art, architecture, and literature, which were used to convey religious messages and to glorify the rulers who commissioned them. The influence of Indian culture is evident in the early inscriptions, temple architecture, and sculpture found throughout Indonesia.[16] The kingdoms of Funan, Tarumanagara, and Srivijaya are among the most significant early states in Southeast Asia, each playing a crucial role in the region's history. Funan (first– Century AD), located in the Mekong Delta region, Funan is considered one of the earliest Indianized kingdoms in Southeast Asia. It was a major centre of trade, connecting the maritime routes of the Indian Ocean with the South China Sea. Funan's rulers adopted Hinduism and

[13] Cœdès, G. (1968), The Indianized States of SoutheastAsia. Australian National University Press.

[14] Kulke, H. (1990), A History of India. Routledge.

[15] Ibid.

[16] Bosch, F.D.K. (1961), The Golden Germ: An Introduction to Indian Symbolism. Mouton.

later Buddhism, constructing temples and commissioning inscriptions in Sanskrit that reflect the kingdom's integration into the Indian cultural sphere.[17] Tarumanagara (fourth—seventh Century AD): Located in West Java, Tarumanagara is one of the earliest Hindu-Buddhist kingdoms in Indonesia. The kingdom is known for its Sanskrit inscriptions and its early adoption of Hinduism, particularly the worship of Vishnu. These inscriptions, such as those at Ciaruteun and Tugu, highlight the influence of Indian political and religious concepts on the kingdom's rulers.[18] Srivijaya (seventh–thirteenth Century AD): Srivijaya, based in Sumatra, was a powerful maritime empire that controlled the Strait of Malacca, a crucial chokepoint in the region's trade routes. Srivijaya was a major centre for Mahayana Buddhism, attracting pilgrims and scholars from across Asia. The kingdom's wealth from trade allowed it to exert influence over vast territories, and its rulers used Buddhism to enhance their political legitimacy.[19]

The rise of these early kingdoms brought about significant cultural and political developments in Indonesia and Southeast Asia. Indianization played a key role in shaping the cultural identity of the region, introducing new religious concepts, artistic styles, and literary traditions. This period saw the construction of monumental architecture, including temples and stupas that symbolized both religious devotion and royal power.[20] Politically, the adoption of Indian models of governance and the concept of divine kingship helped to centralize authority and legitimize the rule of kings. The rulers of these early kingdoms were seen as the upholders of dharma (cosmic order), and they used this religious authority to maintain social and political stability. This period also witnessed the codification of laws and the establishment of bureaucratic institutions that would influence the governance of later Southeast Asian states.[21] The cultural and political innovations of this era laid the foundations for the later development of more complex and centralized states in the region, such as

[17] Cœdès, G. (1968), The Indianized States of SoutheastAsia. Australian National University Press.

[18] Kulke, H. (1990), A History of India. Routledge.

[19] Bosch, F.D.K. (1961), The Golden Germ: An Introduction to Indian Symbolism. Mouton.

[20] Ibid.

[21] Kulke, H. (1990), A History of India. Routledge.

the Khmer Empire and the Majapahit Kingdom. The legacy of these early kingdoms can still be seen today in the rich cultural and religious traditions of Indonesia and Southeast Asia.

These sections provide a comprehensive examination of the rise of early kingdoms in Indonesia and Southeast Asia, focusing on the formation of polities, the impact of Indianization, key kingdoms, and the cultural and political developments of the era. The scholarly sources offer a robust foundation for understanding the complexities of this transformative period in Southeast Asian history.

Srivijaya: A Maritime Empire (Seventh–Thirteenth Century)

The Srivijaya empire, which emerged in the seventh century, played a pivotal role in Southeast Asian trade due to its strategic location along major maritime routes. Srivijaya's control of key ports on Sumatra and its dominance over the Strait of Malacca allowed it to serve as a central hub for the exchange of goods between the Indian Ocean and the South China Sea. This positioning made Srivijaya a crucial player in the international trade networks that connected China, India, the Middle East, and the broader Southeast Asian region.[22] Srivijaya's importance in regional trade was further enhanced by its ability to facilitate and control the flow of valuable commodities, such as spices, resins, and luxury goods, which were in high demand across Asia and beyond. The empire's wealth and power were derived from the tariffs and tribute it imposed on the ships passing through its controlled waters. This not only boosted Srivijaya's economy but also allowed it to maintain a strong navy, which was essential for protecting its interests and ensuring the security of trade routes.[23] Srivijaya's control over the Strait of Malacca was central to its dominance in Southeast Asia. The Strait of Malacca, one of the most important maritime chokepoints in the world, served as the main conduit for trade between the East and West. By controlling this narrow passage, Srivijaya could regulate the flow of goods, impose tolls, and collect tribute

[22] Wolters, O.W. (1999), History, Culture, and Region in Southeast Asian Perspectives. Institute of Southeast Asian Studies.

[23] Christie, J.W. (1995), States without Cities: Demographic Trends in Early Java. Indonesia, 60, pp. 23–40.

from passing ships, thereby ensuring its economic prosperity and political influence.[24]

Srivijaya's dominance over the Strait also allowed it to exert influence over other regional trade networks, including those in the South China Sea and the Bay of Bengal. The empire's strategic alliances and vassal relationships with other kingdoms in Southeast Asia further expanded its reach, enabling Srivijaya to become a central node in the regional trade system. This control not only enhanced Srivijaya's wealth but also positioned it as a key intermediary between the major civilizations of Asia, including India and China.[25]

Beyond its economic power, Srivijaya was a significant center of Buddhist learning and religious activity. The empire was a major patron of Mahayana Buddhism and played a key role in the spread of Buddhism throughout Southeast Asia. Srivijaya's rulers supported the construction of monasteries and stupas, and the empire became a pilgrimage site for Buddhists from across Asia, including China and India. The famous Chinese monk Yijing, who visited Srivijaya in the seventh century, documented its importance as a center of Buddhist scholarship and practice.[26] The cultural influence of Srivijaya extended to the arts, literature, and architecture. The empire's support for Buddhist institutions fostered a flourishing of religious art, including stone carvings, bronze sculptures, and manuscript production. These cultural contributions not only enriched Srivijaya but also had a lasting impact on the broader region, influencing the development of Buddhist art and architecture in neighbouring kingdoms, such as Angkor in Cambodia and Pagan in Burma.[27]

The decline of Srivijaya began in the eleventh century, precipitated by several factors, including internal strife, the rise of rival powers, and shifting trade routes. One of the critical blows to Srivijaya's dominance came from the Chola Dynasty of South India, which launched a series of naval expeditions against Srivijaya in the early eleventh century. These attacks weakened Srivijaya's control over the Strait of Malacca and

[24] Wolters, O.W. (1999), History, Culture, and Region in Southeast Asian Perspectives. Institute of Southeast Asian Studies.

[25] Miksic, J. (2011), Singapore and the Silk Road of the Sea, 1300–1800. NUS Press.

[26] Christie, J.W. (1995), States without Cities: Demographic Trends in Early Java. Indonesia, 60, pp. 23–40.

[27] Miksic, J. (2011), Singapore and the Silk Road of the Sea, 1300–1800. NUS Press.

diminished its influence in the region.[28] As Srivijaya's power waned, its territories were gradually absorbed by emerging kingdoms, such as the Javanese kingdom of Majapahit. Despite its decline, Srivijaya's legacy endured in the cultural and religious life of Southeast Asia. The empire's role in the spread of Buddhism and its contributions to art and architecture left a lasting imprint on the region's cultural heritage. Moreover, the model of a maritime-based, trade-oriented empire established by Srivijaya influenced the political and economic strategies of subsequent Southeast Asian states.[29]

The Emergence of the Majapahit Kingdom (Thirteenth–Fifteenth Century)

The Majapahit Kingdom, which emerged in the late thirteenth century, is renowned for its extensive territorial expansion and consolidation of power across Southeast Asia. Founded by Raden Wijaya in 1293 after the decline of the Singhasari kingdom, Majapahit quickly established itself as a dominant force in the region. Under the leadership of Gajah Mada, the kingdom's military commander and prime minister, Majapahit pursued an aggressive policy of expansion, aiming to bring the entire archipelago under its control.[30] Gajah Mada's famous oath, the *Sumpah Palapa*, signified his commitment to unifying the Nusantara (the Indonesian archipelago) under Majapahit rule. Through a series of military campaigns and strategic alliances, Majapahit expanded its influence over Java, Sumatra, the Malay Peninsula, Borneo, and parts of the Philippines. This territorial expansion was not only a display of military prowess but also a means of securing control over vital trade routes and resources, which were crucial for maintaining the kingdom's power.[31]

Trade played a crucial role in the economy of the Majapahit Kingdom and significantly influenced its interactions with other states in Southeast

[28] Wolters, O.W. (1999), History, Culture, and Region in Southeast Asian Perspectives. Institute of Southeast Asian Studies.

[29] Miksic, J. (2011), Singapore and the Silk Road of the Sea, 1300–1800. NUS Press.

[30] Pigeaud, T.G.T. (1960), Java in the fourteenth Century: A Study in Cultural History. The Hague: Martinus Nijhoff.

[31] Robson, S.O. (1995), Desawarnana (Nagarakrtágama) by Mpu Prapanca. Leiden: KITLV Press.

Asia. The kingdom's strategic location along key maritime trade routes allowed it to control the flow of goods, including spices, textiles, precious metals, and ceramics, between the Indian Ocean and the South China Sea. Majapahit's ports became important centres of commerce, attracting traders from across Asia and facilitating the exchange of goods and ideas.[32] Majapahit's dominance in regional trade was further reinforced by its extensive network of tributary states, which paid tribute in the form of goods and resources. This system not only enriched the kingdom but also helped to establish Majapahit as a major political and economic power in Southeast Asia. The prosperity generated by trade enabled the kingdom to finance its military campaigns, build monumental architecture, and support a flourishing cultural life. Moreover, Majapahit's trade connections facilitated cultural exchanges that introduced new artistic and religious ideas to the region.[33] The Majapahit era is often regarded as a golden age of Javanese culture, marked by significant achievements in art, literature, and architecture. The Majapahit era, spanning from the late thirteenth to the early sixteenth century, is frequently hailed as a golden age of Javanese culture, characterized by flourishing artistic, literary, and architectural achievements. This period witnessed significant developments in art, where relief sculptures and terracotta artworks adorned the many temples and buildings constructed during this time. A notable example is the intricate carvings found at the Candi Panataran, which depict scenes from popular Hindu epics such as the Ramayana and Mahabharata.[34] In literature, the era is marked by the composition of the "Nagarakretagama," a Javanese epic poem written in 1365 by the poet Mpu Prapanca. This poem provides not only a detailed account of King Hayam Wuruk's reign but also offers insights into the cultural, religious, and social aspects of Majapahit society.[35] Furthermore, the "Tantu Pagelaran" and the "Pararaton" are other significant literary works from this period that combine mythology, history, and moral instruction,

[32] Munoz, P.M. (2006), Early Kingdoms of the Indonesian Archipelago and the Malay Peninsula. Editions Didier Millet.

[33] Pigeaud, T.G.T. (1960), Java in the fourteenth Century: A Study in Cultural History. The Hague: Martinus Nijhoff.

[34] Kempers, A.J. (1991), Monumental Bali: Introduction to Balinese Archaeology & Guide to the Monuments. Periplus Editions.

[35] Robson, S.O. (1995), Desawarnana (Nagarakrtagama) by Mpu Prapanca. Leiden: KITLV Press.

reflecting the philosophical depth and narrative complexity of Javanese culture during the Majapahit era.[36] Architecturally, the Majapahit era is distinguished by the construction of monumental temple complexes and water gardens, which exhibit a blend of Hindu and Buddhist influences. The Trowulan site, believed to be the capital of the Majapahit Kingdom, features remnants of royal palaces, ceremonial pools, and impressive gateways, demonstrating advanced engineering and artistic skills.[37] These structures were not only places of worship but also served as centres of cultural gatherings and state functions, showcasing the intricate relationship between architecture and the sociopolitical fabric of Majapahit.

The kingdom's wealth, derived from trade and tribute, allowed for the patronage of the arts, leading to the creation of some of Indonesia's most iconic cultural artifacts. The economic prosperity of the Majapahit Kingdom, fuelled by extensive trade networks and tribute from vassal states, facilitated a vibrant patronage of the arts. This wealth enabled the commissioning of iconic cultural artifacts that continue to define Indonesian heritage today. A key example of this artistic patronage is the construction of the majestic temple complex at Candi Sukuh, which showcases distinctive thematic reliefs and sculptures that blend Hindu mythology with indigenous cultural motifs.[38] The Majapahit era is also renowned for its unique batik and textile production, which flourished under royal sponsorship. These textiles were not only significant for their intricate designs and the complexity of their production techniques but also served as important ceremonial and trade items, reflecting the kingdom's socio-economic dynamics.[39] The batik designs from this period are characterized by their detailed geometric and floral patterns, which have been passed down through generations and remain a staple of Indonesian craft. Moreover, the era saw significant advancements in metalwork, particularly in the creation of bronze and gold artifacts. The discovery of various ritualistic and decorative items in regions once

[36] Kumar, A. (2019), Javanese Literature in Surakarta Manuscripts. Cornell University Press.

[37] Jordaan, R. (1996), The Mystery of the MajapahitKingdom. Asian Studies Review.

[38] Kieven, L. (2013), Following the Cap-Figure in Majapahit Temple Reliefs: A New Look at the Religious Function of EastJavanese Temples. Brill.

[39] Napier, A.D. (1988), The Age of Batik: The Art and Craft of Batik in Asia. SoutheastAsia Publications.

under Majapahit influence, such as the famed Wonoboyo hoard, illustrates the elevated level of artisanry and aesthetic sensibility of the time. These items, including jewellery, coins, and ceremonial weapons, underscore the sophisticated metallurgical skills and the aesthetic values of the Majapahit artisans.[40] Majapahit's artistic achievements are particularly evident in its temple architecture, which reflects a synthesis of indigenous Javanese and Indian influences.[41] One of the most remarkable examples of Majapahit architecture is the Candi Panataran, a temple complex in East Java that served as a religious and cultural centre. The temples built during this period are characterized by their intricate stone carvings, which depict scenes from Hindu epics such as the Ramayana and Mahabharata, as well as local legends. These temples not only served religious functions but also symbolized the kingdom's power and divine mandate.[42] In addition to architecture, the Majapahit era saw the flourishing of literature, with the production of important texts such as the *Nagarakretagama*, a Javanese eulogy that provides valuable insights into the kingdom's history and culture. The period also witnessed advancements in the decorative arts, including metalwork, ceramics, and sculpture. The legacy of Majapahit's artistic and cultural achievements continues to influence Indonesian art and culture to this day.[43] The enduring impact of the Majapahit Kingdom on contemporary Indonesian art and culture is profound, resonating in various forms of artistic expression and cultural practices. Scholarly insights[44] underscores this ongoing influence, suggesting a direct lineage from the historical achievements of the Majapahit era to modern Indonesian cultural expressions. One significant area where Majapahit's legacy is evident is in traditional Javanese and Balinese art. The kingdom was known for its exquisite relief sculptures and architecture, examples of which can be seen in the remnants of temples such as Candi Sukuh and Candi Cetho. These

[40] Miksic, J. (1990), Old Javanese Gold: The Hunter Thompson Collection at Yale. Yale University Press.

[41] Pigeaud, T.G.T. (1960), Java in the fourteenth Century: A Study in Cultural History. The Hague: Martinus Nijhoff.

[42] Munoz, P.M. (2006), Early Kingdoms of the Indonesian Archipelago and the Malay Peninsula. Editions Didier Millet.

[43] Robson, S.O. (1995), Desawarnana (Nagarakrtagama) by Mpu Prapanca. Leiden: KITLV Press.

[44] Ibid.

sites display a distinct style that blends Hindu and Buddhist motifs with indigenous aesthetics—elements that continue to appear in contemporary Indonesian sculpture and temple architecture.[45] Majapahit's contribution to literature, particularly through works like the "Nagarakretagama" by Mpu Prapanca, has helped shape the Javanese and Balinese literary traditions. This epic poem not only provides a historical account of the kingdom's rulers but also offers insights into the social and cultural norms of the time. Such literary works have been a source of inspiration for modern Indonesian writers and playwrights, who draw on their themes and styles.[46] The influence of Majapahit also extends to cultural practices, especially in ceremonies and religious rituals. Many contemporary Hindu rituals in Bali, for instance, trace their origins back to practices popular during the Majapahit period. This includes the Galungan festival, which celebrates the victory of dharma over adharma, reflecting the Hindu philosophy that was prevalent in Majapahit society.[47] In the Balinese Hindu tradition, particularly during the Galungan festival, the concepts of dharma and adharma are vividly illustrated, embodying the eternal conflict between good and evil. Dharma, as expounded in Hindu scriptures, represents righteousness, duty, and the moral law that governs individual conduct and sustains the universe. It is the path of right action and ethical behaviour that every individual is expected to follow.[48] On the other hand, adharma denotes the absence or violation of this moral law, encompassing all forms of injustice, falsehood, and immoral acts that disrupt societal harmony and personal integrity.[49] The Galungan festival, which marks the victory of dharma over adharma, is a celebration of this moral victory, reinforcing the belief that adherence to dharma leads to order and prosperity, while succumbing to adharma results in chaos and suffering. This festival thus serves as a cultural reaffirmation of these guiding principles, reminding adherents of the importance of righteousness in maintaining balance in the world. Furthermore, the architectural

[45] Kieven, L. (2013), Following the Cap-Figure in Majapahit Temple Reliefs: A New Look at the Religious Function of EastJavanese Temples. Brill.

[46] Kumar, A. (2019), Javanese Literature in Surakarta Manuscripts. Cornell University Press.

[47] Schoppert, P. (1997), Bali: Cultural Tourism and Touristic Culture. Archipelago Press.

[48] Michaels, A. (2004), Hinduism. Past and present. Princeton University Press.

[49] Rodrigues, H. (2006), Introducing Hinduism. Routledge.

legacy of Majapahit is visible in the layout and design of modern Balinese temples and palaces. The use of red brick and split gates (candi bentar), as well as specific temple orientations, are derived from architectural styles that were popularized during the Majapahit era. These elements are considered quintessential in traditional Balinese architecture today.[50]

Trade Networks and International Relations (Seventh–Fifteenth Century)

The period between the seventh and fifteenth centuries was marked by extensive interaction between Southeast Asia, particularly Indonesia, and the major civilizations of China, India, and the Islamic world. These interactions were driven by the region's strategic position along key maritime trade routes, making it a focal point for international commerce and cultural exchange. The Indonesian archipelago, with its abundant resources and strategic location, became a nexus where the economic and cultural currents of these great civilizations converged.[51] Interaction with China intensified during the Tang and Song dynasties when Chinese traders and diplomats established regular maritime routes connecting the South China Sea with the Indian Ocean. Chinese records from this period document the presence of Southeast Asian envoys at the Chinese court, indicating the diplomatic and commercial exchanges that took place. During the Tang and Song dynasties, Chinese historical records, such as the *Old Book of Tang* and *New Book of Tang*, meticulously documented the interactions between China and Southeast Asia. These records include detailed accounts of diplomatic missions, where envoys from Southeast Asian kingdoms, such as Srivijaya, visited the Chinese imperial court. Such visits were not merely ceremonial; they were crucial for establishing and maintaining trade relationships and political alliances.[52] The presence of

[50] Davison, J. (2003), Balinese Architecture: Towards an Encyclopedia. Tuttle Publishing.

[51] Reid, A. (1993), SoutheastAsia in the Age of Commerce, 1450–1680: Volume Two, Expansion and Crisis. Yale University Press.

[52] Wang, G. (1998), China and the Chinese Overseas. Times Academic Press.

these envoys at the Chinese court highlights the importance of Southeast Asia in the maritime silk route and reflects the complex web of diplomatic and commercial exchanges that characterized the period. Through these interactions, Southeast Asian states not only secured economic benefits but also gained prestige and legitimacy, both domestically and in the broader region. Moreover, these records provide invaluable insights into the nature of early international relations in East and Southeast Asia, illustrating the diplomatic strategies and the mutual benefits derived from these historical interactions.[53] The trade relationship with China was mutually beneficial: Southeast Asia exported spices, resins, and precious woods to China, while importing silk, ceramics, and metal goods.[54] The influence of Chinese culture in Indonesia is evident in the adoption of certain artistic styles, ceramics, and even elements of statecraft, particularly in the coastal polities that engaged most directly with Chinese traders.[55]

India's influence on Indonesia was even more profound, particularly in the realms of religion, art, and governance. From the early centuries CE, Indian traders, priests, and scholars travelled to Southeast Asia, bringing with them Hinduism and Buddhism, which were adopted by local rulers as state religions. This Indianization of Southeast Asia is most evident in the Indian-inspired architecture, Sanskrit inscriptions, and the adoption of Indian legal codes and political ideas in early Southeast Asian states.[56] The Chola Dynasty's naval expeditions in the eleventh century further strengthened the commercial and cultural ties between India and Southeast Asia, facilitating a flow of goods, ideas, and religious influences across the Indian Ocean.[57] The Chola Dynasty's naval expeditions in the eleventh century were instrumental in enhancing the commercial and cultural ties between India and Southeast Asia, catalysing a significant exchange of goods, ideas, and religious influences across the Indian Ocean. Here are examples underpinned by academic sources:

[53] Ptak, R. (1998), China's Seaborne Trade with South and SoutheastAsia (1200–1750). Ashgate.

[54] Wade, G. (2009), The Asian Seas: Trade, Travel, and Visions of the Other (1400–1750). Ashgate.

[55] Ibid.

[56] Majumdar, R.C. (1986), History of SoutheastAsia. McMillan.

[57] Kulke, H. (1990), A History of India. Routledge.

Goods:

- **Spices and Natural Resources:** Southeast Asia, rich in natural resources, exported spices like cloves and nutmeg to India. In return, Southeast Asia imported Indian textiles and finished goods, which were highly valued in the region.[58]
- **Ceramics and Precious Metals:** Indian ceramics and precious metals, including gold and silver, were traded extensively, influencing local craftsmanship and jewellery designs in Southeast Asia.[59]

Ideas:

- **Architectural Innovations:** Indian architectural styles significantly influenced Southeast Asian temple and palace designs, introducing features such as the stepped pyramid that became prevalent in places like Java and Bali.[60]
- **Political and Administrative Concepts:** The Indian varna system and concepts of kingship were adopted by Southeast Asian polities, shaping their governance structures and statecraft philosophies.[61]

Religious Influences:

- **Spread of Hinduism and Buddhism:** The Cholas, fervent patrons of Hinduism and Buddhism, facilitated the spread of these religions through their maritime activities. Temples built in the Chola architectural style can still be found across Southeast Asia, and these serve as centres for religious practices and rituals.[62]

[58] Hall, K.R. (2011), A History of Early SoutheastAsia: Maritime Trade and Societal Development, 100–1500. Rowman & Littlefield.

[59] Miksic, J. (1995), Old Javanese Gold: The Hunter Thompson Collection at Yale. Yale University Press.

[60] Acri, A. (2017), Esoteric Buddhism in Mediaeval Maritime Asia: Networks of Masters, Texts, Icons. ISEAS—Yusof. Ishak Institute.

[61] Kulke, H. (1990), A History of India. Routledge.

[62] Steinberg, D.J., et al. (1987), In Search of SoutheastAsia: A Modern History. University of Hawaii Press.

- **Religious Art and Iconography:** The religious art of India, including depictions of Hindu gods and Buddhist icons, influenced the artistic expressions in Southeast Asia, leading to a fusion of artistic styles seen in local sculptures and paintings.[63]

Interaction with the Islamic world began to intensify from the thirteenth century onwards, driven by the expansion of Islamic trade networks across the Indian Ocean. Arab and Persian merchants played a significant role in introducing Islam to the Indonesian archipelago, particularly in port cities that were key nodes in the international trade network.[64] The spread of Islam in Indonesia was closely linked to these commercial interactions, as Muslim traders established mosques and communities in coastal towns, laying the groundwork for the gradual Islamization of the region.[65]

The Silk Road, both the overland and maritime routes, played a crucial role in the development of trade networks between Indonesia and the wider world from the seventh to the fifteenth century. The maritime Silk Road, in particular, was instrumental in linking the Indonesian archipelago to the vast trade networks that spanned from the Mediterranean to East Asia. This network facilitated the exchange of goods, ideas, and cultures across thousands of miles of ocean, with Southeast Asia serving as a key transit point.[66] The maritime Silk Road enabled the movement of high-value goods such as spices, silk, porcelain, and precious metals. Indonesia, particularly the islands of Java and Sumatra, was renowned for its production of spices, which were in high demand across Asia and Europe. The control of these trade routes was crucial for the wealth and power of Indonesian states such as Srivijaya and later Majapahit, which became dominant players in the regional economy by

[63] Guy, J. (1998), Oriental Trade Ceramics in South-EastAsia, Ninth to Sixteenth Centuries: With a Catalogue of Chinese, Vietnamese and Thai Wares in Australian Collections. Oxford University Press.

[64] Lombard, D. (1990), Le carrefour javanais. Essai d'histoire globale (The Javanese Crossroads: Towards a Global History). Éditions de l'École des hautes études en sciences sociales.

[65] Ricklefs, M.C. (2006), A History of Modern Indonesia Since c.1200. Palgrave Macmillan.

[66] Wade, G. (2009), The Asian Seas: Trade, Travel, and Visions of the Other (1400–1750). Ashgate.

regulating the flow of goods through their ports.[67] These trade routes were not only conduits for material goods but also for the spread of religions, technologies, and cultural practices, making the maritime Silk Road a significant factor in the cultural and political development of Indonesia.[68] The maritime trade routes also connected Indonesia to the Islamic world, with Muslim merchants from the Middle East and South Asia playing a pivotal role in the region's economy. As Islam spread along these trade routes, it gradually became the dominant religion in many parts of Indonesia, particularly in key trading cities such as Aceh, Malacca, and Demak. The maritime Silk Road thus served as both a commercial highway and a channel for the dissemination of Islamic culture and religion across Southeast Asia.[69]

The spread of Islam in Indonesia was deeply intertwined with the region's trade networks, which connected it to the broader Islamic world. From the thirteenth century onwards, the arrival of Muslim traders from the Middle East, India, and China played a crucial role in the gradual Islamization of the Indonesian archipelago. These traders, who were often also missionaries, established Muslim communities in key port cities, where they built mosques, established schools, and spread Islamic teachings.[70] The appeal of Islam in Indonesia was partly due to its association with the prosperous and influential Muslim trading networks. Conversion to Islam was often motivated by the desire to integrate more fully into these networks, which offered economic benefits and social mobility. The adoption of Islam by local rulers further accelerated its spread, as it became associated with political power and legitimacy. The conversion of the rulers of Aceh, Demak, and Malacca to Islam in the fifteenth century marked a turning point in the Islamization of the region, leading to the establishment of Islamic sultanates that played a dominant role

[67] Manguin, P.-Y. (2010), Early trading polities of SoutheastAsia: Their markets and the Indian Oceantrade network. Journal of Southeast Asian Studies.

[68] Reid, A. (1993), SoutheastAsia in the Age of Commerce, 1450–1680: Volume Two, Expansion and Crisis. Yale University Press.

[69] Hall, K.R. (2011), A History of Early SoutheastAsia: Maritime Trade and Societal Development, 100–1500. Rowman & Littlefield.

[70] Laffan, M. (2011), The Makings of Indonesian Islam: Orientalism and the Narration of a Sufi Past. Princeton University Press.

in Indonesian politics and society.[71] Islam in Indonesia also took on a distinct character, shaped by the region's pre-existing cultural and religious traditions. The spread of Islam was often syncretic, blending Islamic teachings with local customs and beliefs. This syncretism is evident in the various forms of Islamic practice in Indonesia, from the Sufi traditions that emphasize mysticism and personal piety, to the influence of pre-Islamic Hindu-Buddhist practices in Javanese Islam[72] The role of trade in spreading Islam in Indonesia underscores the importance of economic networks in facilitating not only the exchange of goods but also the transmission of religious and cultural ideas.[73]

The Spread of Islam and the Formation of Islamic Sultanates (Thirteenth–Fifteenth Century)

The spread of Islam in Southeast Asia during the thirteenth to fifteenth centuries was largely facilitated by the region's extensive trade networks, which connected the Indonesian archipelago to the broader Islamic world. Muslim traders from the Arabian Peninsula, Persia, India, and China began arriving in Southeast Asia as early as the seventh century, but it was during the thirteenth century that Islam began to establish a more significant foothold, primarily through the influence of these traders and the Sufi missionaries who accompanied them.[74] Trade routes served as conduits not only for goods but also for religious and cultural exchanges. Muslim merchants settled in key port cities, such as Samudra Pasai in Sumatra, Malacca in the Malay Peninsula, and Gresik in Java, where they established small but influential communities. These traders brought with them not just commodities like spices and textiles, but also their religious

[71] Ricklefs, M.C. (2006), A History of Modern Indonesia Since c.1200. Palgrave Macmillan.

[72] Azra, A. (2004), The Origins of Islamic Reformism in SoutheastAsia: Networks of Malay-Indonesian and Middle Eastern 'Ulamā' in the Seventeenth and Eighteenth Centuries. Allen & Unwin.

[73] Lombard, D. (1990), Le carrefour javanais. Essai d'histoire globale (The Javanese Crossroads: Towards a Global History). Éditions de l'École des hautes études en sciences sociales.

[74] Ricklefs, M.C. (2006), A History of Modern Indonesia Since c.1200. Palgrave Macmillan.

beliefs and practices. Over time, these communities grew in size and influence, serving as important nodes in the spread of Islam throughout the region.[75]

Sufi missionaries played a particularly crucial role in the spread of Islam in Southeast Asia. Sufism, with its emphasis on mysticism, personal piety, and a direct, emotional connection to God, resonated with the local populations, who were already familiar with similar spiritual traditions within Hinduism and Buddhism. The Sufi approach to Islam was adaptable and accommodating, allowing for the integration of pre-Islamic beliefs and practices into the new religious framework. This syncretic form of Islam was more easily accepted by the local population, as it did not demand a complete rejection of their existing cultural and religious identities.[76]

Sufi missionaries, often associated with specific Sufi orders (tariqas), travelled widely across the Indonesian archipelago, establishing lodges (zawiyas) and schools (madrasas) that became centres of Islamic learning. They used local languages and cultural symbols to convey Islamic teachings, making the religion more accessible to the masses. The spread of Islam through these means was largely peaceful, with conversions often motivated by the desire to join the prosperous and cosmopolitan Muslim trading networks, which offered both economic opportunities and social mobility.[77] The establishment of Islamic sultanates in Sumatra, Java, and the Malay Peninsula from the thirteenth to the fifteenth centuries marked a significant shift in the political and religious landscape of Southeast Asia. These sultanates emerged as powerful regional entities, often taking over the roles of earlier Hindu-Buddhist kingdoms and leveraging their strategic locations along vital trade routes to gain economic and political power. In Sumatra, the Sultanate of Samudra Pasai became the first major Islamic state in Southeast Asia, founded in the late thirteenth century. It quickly established itself as a key player in the Indian Ocean trade,

[75] Azra, A. (2006), The Origins of Islamic Reformism in SoutheastAsia: Networks of Malay-Indonesian and Middle Eastern 'Ulamā' in the Seventeenth and Eighteenth Centuries. Allen & Unwin.

[76] Johns, A.H. (1995), Sufism in SoutheastAsia: Reflections and Reconsiderations. Journal of Southeast Asian Studies.

[77] Azra, A. (2006), The Origins of Islamic Reformism in SoutheastAsia: Networks of Malay-Indonesian and Middle Eastern 'Ulamā' in the Seventeenth and Eighteenth Centuries. Allen & Unwin.

connecting the Malay Archipelago with the Middle East, South Asia, and China. Samudra Pasai's rulers adopted Islam as the state religion and became patrons of Islamic scholarship, attracting scholars from across the Muslim world. The sultanate's prosperity was closely tied to its control of the trade in spices and other valuable goods, which helped to spread Islam throughout the region as merchants and travellers passed through its ports.[78]

The Malay Peninsula saw the rise of the Sultanate of Malacca in the fifteenth century, which became one of the most important Islamic states in Southeast Asia. Malacca's strategic location on the narrow strait between Sumatra and the Malay Peninsula allowed it to dominate regional trade routes. The conversion of its ruler, Parameswara, to Islam marked the beginning of Malacca's transformation into a cosmopolitan Islamic centre. Under the rule of Sultan Mansur Shah (r. 1459–1477), Malacca reached its zenith, becoming a major hub for trade, culture, and Islamic learning. Malacca's influence extended across the region, and its model of governance, based on Islamic principles, was emulated by other emerging sultanates in the archipelago.[79]

In Java, the rise of Islamic sultanates began in earnest in the fifteenth century with the decline of the Majapahit Empire, a Hindu-Buddhist kingdom that had dominated the region for centuries. The Sultanate of Demak, founded by Raden Patah in the early sixteenth century, was the first major Islamic state in Java. Demak's rulers capitalized on the weakening of Majapahit and the growing appeal of Islam among Javanese elites to establish their authority. They promoted Islam as a unifying force and used it to legitimize their rule, building mosques, establishing Islamic courts, and fostering the growth of Islamic education.[80] These sultanates not only played a central role in the spread of Islam but also in the economic and political integration of Southeast Asia. By controlling key ports and trade routes, they facilitated the movement of goods, people, and ideas across the region, creating a network of Islamic states

[78] Johns, A.H. (1995), Sufism in SoutheastAsia: Reflections and Reconsiderations. Journal of Southeast Asian Studies.

[79] Azra, A. (2006), The Origins of Islamic Reformism in SoutheastAsia: Networks of Malay-Indonesian and Middle Eastern 'Ulamā' in the Seventeenth and Eighteenth Centuries. Allen & Unwin.

[80] Ricklefs, M.C. (2006), A History of Modern Indonesia Since c.1200. Palgrave Macmillan.

that shared a common religious and cultural identity. The rise of these sultanates marked the beginning of a new era in Southeast Asian history, where Islam became the dominant religious and political force, shaping the region's development for centuries to come.[81]

The transition from Hindu-Buddhist kingdoms to Islamic sultanates in Southeast Asia during the thirteenth to fifteenth centuries was a complex and gradual process influenced by a variety of factors, including trade, political changes, and the spread of Islamic teachings. This transformation was marked by the decline of major Hindu-Buddhist states such as the Majapahit Empire in Java and the Srivijaya Empire in Sumatra, and the rise of new Islamic powers that redefined the region's political and religious landscape.[82] In many cases, the conversion of local rulers to Islam was a strategic decision driven by the need to align with the powerful Muslim trading networks that dominated the Indian Ocean. These networks provided access to lucrative markets, valuable goods, and potential alliances with other Muslim rulers. The adoption of Islam by local elites was often followed by the establishment of Islamic institutions, such as mosques, madrasas, and Islamic courts, which gradually replaced the Hindu-Buddhist structures that had previously dominated the region.[83] The transition was also facilitated by the syncretic nature of Islam as it was practiced in Southeast Asia. Rather than completely displacing the existing Hindu-Buddhist traditions, Islam in this region often incorporated elements of these earlier beliefs. This syncretism is evident in the way Javanese Islam, for example, retained aspects of Hindu-Buddhist cosmology, rituals, and artistic expression, even as it embraced Islamic teachings. This blending of traditions allowed for a smoother transition and helped Islam to be more readily accepted by the local population.[84]

[81] Johns, A.H. (1995), Sufism in SoutheastAsia: Reflections and Reconsiderations. Journal of Southeast Asian Studies.

[82] Ricklefs, M.C. (2006), A History of Modern Indonesia Since c.1200. Palgrave Macmillan.

[83] Azra, A. (2006), The Origins of Islamic Reformism in SoutheastAsia: Networks of Malay-Indonesian and Middle Eastern 'Ulamā' in the Seventeenth and Eighteenth Centuries. Allen & Unwin.

[84] Johns, A.H. (1995), Sufism in SoutheastAsia: Reflections and Reconsiderations. Journal of Southeast Asian Studies.

The decline of Hindu-Buddhist states such as Majapahit during the late fifteenth century can be attributed to a confluence of internal conflicts, economic challenges, and the ascendancy of Islamic sultanates within the region. This transformation was not abrupt but evolved over several decades, influenced by both internal dynamics and external pressures:

Internal Conflicts: The Majapahit Empire, once a formidable power in Southeast Asia, began to experience significant internal strife following the death of King Hayam Wuruk in 1389. Succession disputes and regional rebellions weakened central authority, fragmenting the empire into multiple competing polities. This disintegration was exacerbated by the ambitious and often conflicting interests of court officials and regional leaders, leading to prolonged periods of instability and conflict.[85]

Economic Challenges: Concurrently, Majapahit faced substantial economic challenges. The empire's economy had heavily relied on trade, but it began to suffer as important trade routes shifted away from Java towards Malacca, a rising power that offered more efficient and secure trading conditions. This shift was driven in part by the strategic location of Malacca along the Strait, which allowed it to control the lucrative spice trade, previously dominated by Hindu-Buddhist states like Srivijaya and later Majapahit.[86]

Influence of Islamic Sultanates: The growing influence of Islamic sultanates also played a crucial role in the decline of Hindu-Buddhist kingdoms. As Islam spread through trade and the proselytizing efforts of Muslim traders and Sufi missionaries, regions such as Sumatra, the Malay Peninsula, and coastal Java saw the rise of Islamic sultanates. These new Islamic states, such as the Sultanate of Malacca and the Sultanate of Demak, were often more economically dynamic and politically stable compared to the fracturing Hindu-Buddhist states. The Islamic sultanates not only provided new centres of power but also facilitated the spread of Islam through strategic marriages, trade alliances, and military conquest,

[85] Ricklefs, M.C. (1993), War, Culture and Economy in Java, 1677–1726: Asian and European Imperialism in the Early Karatsuba Period. Sydney: Asian Studies Association of Australia.

[86] Reid, A. (1993), SoutheastAsia in the Age of Commerce 1450–1680, Volume Two: Expansion and Crisis. New Haven: Yale University Press.

further eroding the influence of Hindu-Buddhist rulers.[87] The rise of Islamic sultanates in Southeast Asia during the late fifteenth and early sixteenth centuries marked a significant shift in the region's political and religious landscape, as they became new centres of power and actively facilitated the spread of Islam. This process was multifaceted, involving strategic marriages, trade alliances, and military conquests that collectively helped to erode the influence of existing Hindu-Buddhist rulers.[88]

Strategic Marriages: One of the key strategies employed by Islamic sultanates to extend their influence was through strategic marriages. For example, the Sultanate of Malacca, under Sultan Mansur Shah (r. 1459–1477), forged alliances with other regional powers through marriage. Sultan Mansur Shah married the princess of Rokan and formed alliances with other regional rulers, integrating their realms under Islamic governance and facilitating the spread of Islam through familial ties (Reid, 1993). Sultan Mansur Shah's marriage to the Princess of Rokan is an exemplar of the strategic alliances formed by Southeast Asian sultans to expand their influence and consolidate power. The princess, Putri Rokan, hailed from a prominent ruling family in the region known today as Riau, a strategic area on the eastern coast of Sumatra. This marriage, occurring during Mansur Shah's reign from 1459 to 1477, was not just a union of two individuals but a calculated political manoeuvre to strengthen Malacca's geopolitical stance in the region.[89] Princess Putri Rokan was a member of the ruling family from Rokan, a region strategically located along the eastern coast of Sumatra, in what is today known as the Riau province. This area was significant due to its proximity to the crucial maritime route, the Strait of Malacca, which was a vital corridor for trade and cultural exchanges between various civilizations in Southeast Asia and beyond.[90]

[87] Andaya, B.W. (2001), To Live as Brothers: Southeast Sumatra in the Seventeenth and Eighteenth Centuries. University of Hawaii Press.

[88] Andaya, B.W. (2001), To Live as Brothers: SoutheastSumatra in the Seventeenth and Eighteenth Centuries. University of Hawaii Press.

[89] Reid, A. (1993), SoutheastAsia in the Age of Commerce 1450–1680, Volume Two: Expansion and Crisis. New Haven: Yale University Press.

[90] Andaya, B.W. (2001), To Live as Brothers: SoutheastSumatra in the Seventeenth and Eighteenth Centuries. University of Hawaii Press.

The religion of Princess Rokan and her family, prior to their engagement with Islamic sultanates like Malacca, would have been predominantly Hindu-Buddhist, which was the major religious tradition in Southeast Asia before the spread of Islam. The royal families of many such regions typically adhered to these religions, integrating local animist practices with Hindu-Buddhist rituals, which were central to the cultural and religious life of their kingdoms.[91]

By the time of Princess Rokan's marriage to Sultan Mansur Shah, Islam had begun making significant inroads into Southeast Asian maritime states, especially through trade connections and the strategic marriages of local rulers with Muslim royals or nobles. The union between Sultan Mansur Shah and Princess Rokan served as a catalyst for the further Islamization of her region, as these matrimonial alliances were often followed by the adoption of Islam by the local ruling elite. This adoption was strategic, allowing them to forge stronger bonds with the powerful and increasingly influential Islamic trading networks.[92] The Princess of Rokan's family realm, Rokan, became an important node in the spread of Islam, transitioning from its Hindu-Buddhist roots as the region was integrated into the broader Islamic world through both political alliances and economic incentives provided by the flourishing trade under Islamic governance.[93] The marriage brought substantial advantages to Malacca. It provided direct access to the crucial Strait of Malacca, enhancing the sultanate's control over one of Southeast Asia's most significant maritime trade routes. This control allowed the Sultanate of Malacca to flourish economically and emerge as a pivotal player in regional trade, facilitating the exchange of goods and the propagation of Islam across the Malay Archipelago.[94]

[91] Reid, A. (1993), SoutheastAsia in the Age of Commerce 1450–1680, Volume Two: Expansion and Crisis. New Haven: Yale University Press.

[92] Barrett, D.P. & Worden, R.L. (1995), Early SoutheastAsia: Selected Readings. Ithaca, NY: Cornell University Southeast Asia Program Publications.

[93] Andaya, B.W. (2001). The World of Maluku: Eastern Indonesia in the Early Modern Period. Honolulu: University of Hawaii Press.

[94] Ibid.

Furthermore, this alliance exemplified how matrimonial ties were used to establish and reinforce political alliances, which were crucial for the spread of Islamic governance. Through these unions, Malacca was able to exert influence over its neighbours, ensuring a cooperative relationship that stabilized the region under Islamic rule. These strategic marriages also facilitated cultural and religious integration, fostering an environment where Islamic teachings could spread more readily, contributing to the Islamization of the region.[95] By marrying into the local nobility, Sultan Mansur Shah ensured that Malacca was not seen as an external aggressor but as part of the regional political fabric. This acceptance was vital for the peaceful spread of Islam, as it reduced resistance to new religious practices introduced by the sultanate, helping to gradually transform the religious landscape of Southeast Asia from Hindu-Buddhist dominance to a predominantly Muslim region:

Trade Alliances: Trade alliances also played a crucial role in the spread of Islam. The Sultanate of Malacca, strategically located on the Malacca Strait, became a major commercial hub, engaging in trade with various Islamic regions and beyond. These economic relationships were often underpinned by mutual Islamic ties, which not only enhanced trade but also fostered a shared religious identity that encouraged the adoption of Islam by trading partners and their subjects.[96]

Military Conquests: Military conquest was another method through which Islamic sultanates expanded their influence. The Sultanate of Demak, for instance, played a pivotal role in the decline of the Hindu-Buddhist Majapahit Empire. By launching military campaigns against disintegrating Hindu-Buddhist states and supporting Islamic uprisings within these regions, Demak was able to convert significant territories to Islam, replacing Hindu-Buddhist rulers with Muslim leaders who aligned with the Sultanate's interests.[97] These strategies were not isolated

[95] Barrett, D.P. & Worden, R.L. (1995), Early SoutheastAsia: Selected Readings. Ithaca, NY: Cornell University Southeast Asia Program Publications.

[96] Hall, K.R. (2011), A History of Early SoutheastAsia: Maritime Trade and Societal Development, 100–1500. Lanham, MD: Rowman & Littlefield Publishers.

[97] Ricklefs, M.C. (2008), A History of Modern Indonesia Since c.1200. 4th edn. London: Palgrave Macmillan.

but interconnected, each reinforcing the spread of Islam while simultaneously diminishing the political, cultural, and religious influence of Hindu-Buddhist kingdoms in the region. This transition marked the end of the Hindu-Buddhist era in Southeast Asia and the beginning of a new Islamic chapter in the region's history, characterized by the rise of Islamic sultanates that played a central role in shaping the region's political, cultural, and religious development.[98]

The spread of Islam and the formation of Islamic sultanates in Southeast Asia from the thirteenth to fifteenth centuries brought about profound cultural and religious transformations across the region. These changes were not uniform but varied depending on local contexts, resulting in a rich tapestry of Islamic practices that were deeply intertwined with existing cultural traditions. One of the most significant transformations was in the religious landscape, where Islam gradually supplanted Hinduism and Buddhism as the dominant faith in many parts of Southeast Asia. This shift was marked by the construction of mosques, the establishment of Islamic schools (madrasas), and the spread of Islamic law (sharia) as the basis for governance and social organization. However, the adoption of Islam did not lead to the wholesale abandonment of pre-Islamic beliefs. Instead, many elements of Hindu-Buddhist and indigenous traditions were incorporated into local Islamic practices, resulting in a syncretic form of Islam that was uniquely Southeast Asian.[99] This syncretism is particularly evident in the cultural expressions of the region, such as architecture, literature, and art. In Java, for example, the influence of Hindu-Buddhist architecture is still visible in the design of early Islamic mosques, which often retained elements of earlier temple architecture, such as tiered roofs and intricate carvings. Similarly, Javanese shadow puppetry (wayang kulit), which has its roots in Hindu epics like the Ramayana and Mahabharata, continued to flourish under Islamic rule, with new stories and characters being introduced to reflect Islamic

[98] Ricklefs, M.C. (2006), Islamic States in Java 1500–1700: The Rise of Islamin SoutheastAsia. Honolulu: University of Hawaii Press.

[99] Azra, A. (2006), The Origins of Islamic Reformism in SoutheastAsia: Networks of Malay-Indonesian and Middle Eastern 'Ulama' in the Seventeenth and Eighteenth Centuries. Honolulu: University of Hawaii Press.

themes.[100] Literature and scholarship also underwent significant transformations during this period. The introduction of Arabic script and Islamic literary forms influenced local languages and literary traditions, leading to the development of a rich body of Islamic literature in languages such as Malay, Javanese, and Acehnese. Islamic scholars in Southeast Asia engaged in theological debates, produced religious texts, and established networks of learning that connected the region to the broader Muslim world. This intellectual activity helped to integrate Southeast Asia into the global Islamic community (ummah) and facilitated the exchange of ideas and knowledge across the region.[101] (Johns, 1995).

The spread of Islam also brought about changes in social and political structures. The concept of divine kingship, which had been central to Hindu-Buddhist governance, was replaced by the idea of the ruler as the protector of Islam and the enforcer of sharia law. This shift in political ideology was accompanied by changes in social organization, with Islamic principles influencing marriage customs, inheritance laws, and community life. However, these changes were not imposed uniformly, and local practices often persisted alongside Islamic norms, creating a dynamic and pluralistic society (Ricklefs, 2006). The cultural and religious transformations of this period laid the foundation for the development of a distinctive Southeast Asian Islam, characterized by its diversity, adaptability, and deep connections to local traditions. These transformations continue to shape the cultural and religious life of the region to this day, reflecting the enduring legacy of the Islamic sultanates and the rich interplay between global and local influences in Southeast Asia.[102]

[100] Ricklefs, M.C. (2006), Islamic States in Java 1500–1700: The Rise of Islamin SoutheastAsia. Honolulu: University of Hawaii Press.

[101] Johns, A.H. (1995), From Coastal Settlement to Islamic School and City: Islamization in Sumatra,the Malay Peninsula, and Java. In: Tarling, N. (ed.) The Cambridge History of SoutheastAsia: Volume One, Part One, From Early Times to c.1500. Cambridge: Cambridge University Press, pp. 190–229.

[102] Azra, A. (2006), The Origins of Islamic Reformism in SoutheastAsia: Networks of Malay-Indonesian and Middle Eastern 'Ulama' in the Seventeenth and Eighteenth Centuries. Honolulu: University of Hawaii Press.

Economic and Cultural Exchange

Trade has historically been a significant conduit for the diffusion of cultural practices, technologies, and ideas, profoundly shaping the art, architecture, and literature of Southeast Asia, including Indonesia. The flow of goods across trade networks brought with it not only material wealth but also intangible cultural assets that influenced local artistic expressions, architectural styles, and literary traditions. One of the most notable influences on Southeast Asian art and architecture came from India, facilitated by maritime trade routes. The Indianization of Southeast Asia began as early as the first century CE and continued through subsequent centuries, deeply impacting the region's culture. This cultural exchange is evident in the proliferation of Indian-style temples across the region, particularly in Java and Sumatra. Temples such as Borobudur and Prambanan in Java showcase the intricate carvings and architectural designs that draw heavily from Indian prototypes, particularly those associated with Hinduism and Buddhism.[103] These religious monuments were not merely replicas but were adapted to fit the local context, incorporating indigenous elements and materials, which created a unique architectural style that resonated with the local population.

Similarly, the art of Southeast Asia was influenced by foreign cultures, particularly through the introduction of Indian, Chinese, and later, Islamic motifs. This influence is seen in the iconography of religious sculptures, the motifs used in textiles, and the stylistic elements in metalwork and pottery. For instance, the depiction of Hindu deities in Javanese and Balinese sculpture shows a blend of Indian iconography with local artistic conventions, creating a distinct visual style that reflects the region's syncretic culture.[104] Literature also played a crucial role in cultural diffusion, with Indian epics like the Ramayana and Mahabharata becoming integral to Southeast Asian literary traditions. These texts were not only translated into local languages but were also reinterpreted to reflect local beliefs and social norms. The Javanese version of the Ramayana, for example, differs significantly from the Indian original, incorporating

[103] Kulke, H. (1999), A History of India. London: Routledge.

[104] Manguin, P.Y., Mani, A. & Wade, G. (2011), Early Interactions Between South and SoutheastAsia: Reflections on Cross-Cultural Exchange. Singapore: Institute of Southeast Asian Studies.

Javanese customs and moral lessons.[105] This literary exchange was facilitated by the scholarly exchanges that occurred as a result of trade, with manuscripts and texts being carried along the same routes as goods, leading to a rich intermingling of literary traditions across the region.

The process of cultural diffusion through trade in Southeast Asia not only introduced foreign elements into local traditions but also gave rise to syncretic cultural practices that combined indigenous and external influences. This syncretism is most evident in the religious, architectural, and artistic traditions of the region, where foreign concepts and styles were adapted and blended with local customs to create unique cultural expressions. In religion, the arrival of Hinduism and Buddhism via Indian traders and missionaries led to the development of a syncretic religious landscape in Southeast Asia. Indigenous animist beliefs were not displaced but rather incorporated into the new religions, creating a complex religious tapestry. For example, in Bali, the local Hinduism that developed is a blend of traditional Balinese animism with Hindu concepts imported from India. This has resulted in a unique form of worship that involves both the reverence of Hindu gods and the veneration of local spirits and ancestors.[106] Similarly, in Java, the integration of Islam with pre-existing Hindu-Buddhist and animist practices gave rise to a distinctly Javanese form of Islam, which includes the veneration of sacred sites and the incorporation of Hindu-Buddhist symbols in Islamic rituals.[107]

In architecture, the fusion of indigenous and foreign elements is evident in the construction of religious and royal buildings. The early temples of Java, such as those in the Dieng Plateau, reflect a blending of Indian architectural principles with local construction techniques and materials. This syncretism is also visible in the royal palaces (kraton) of Java, which combine Islamic architectural elements with pre-Islamic, Hindu-Buddhist designs, symbolizing the continuity and adaptation of

[105] Bellina, B. (2007), Cultural Exchange Between Indiaand SoutheastAsia: Production and Distribution of Hard Stone Ornaments (VIc BC—VIc AD). Paris: École Française d'Extrême-Orient.

[106] Manguin, P.Y., Mani, A. & Wade, G. (2011), Early Interactions Between South and SoutheastAsia: Reflections on Cross-Cultural Exchange. Singapore: Institute of Southeast Asian Studies.

[107] Ricklefs, M.C. (2006), Islamic States in Java 1500–1700: The Rise of Islamin SoutheastAsia. Honolulu: University of Hawaii Press.

local traditions in the face of external influences.[108] Artistic traditions in Southeast Asia also exhibit a syncretic nature, particularly in the visual arts and performing arts. The shadow puppet theatre (wayang kulit) of Java and Bali, for instance, is a product of cultural synthesis, where the stories of the Indian epics Ramayana and Mahabharata are performed using puppets that are designed in a style that is uniquely Southeast Asian. The narratives have been localized, with characters and themes that reflect the social and political context of the region.[109] Syncretism in literature is another example of this cultural blending. The adaptation of Indian epics into Southeast Asian contexts involved significant modifications to the original stories, incorporating local folklore, values, and social structures. The result was a body of literature that was both familiar and new, resonating with local audiences while introducing them to broader cultural narratives from across Asia.[110] These syncretic traditions were not static; they evolved over time as new influences arrived through ongoing trade and interaction. The ability of Southeast Asian societies to absorb and adapt foreign elements into their own cultural frameworks is a testament to the region's dynamic and pluralistic cultural identity, which continues to thrive today.

Decline of the Major Kingdoms (Fifteenth Century)

The fifteenth century marked a period of significant political transformation in Southeast Asia, characterized by the decline of major kingdoms such as Srivijaya and Majapahit and the rise of regional powers that led to the fragmentation of the Indonesian archipelago. This fragmentation was the result of a combination of internal and external factors, including the emergence of powerful regional states, shifts in trade routes, and the increasing influence of Islam in the region.

[108] Kulke, H. (1999), A History of India. London: Routledge.

[109] Bellina, B. (2007), Cultural Exchange Between Indiaand SoutheastAsia: Production and Distribution of Hard Stone Ornaments (VIc BC—VIc AD). Paris: École Française d'Extrême-Orient.

[110] Miksic, J.N. (1990), Old Javanese Gold: The Hunter Thompson Collection at the Yale University Art Gallery. New Haven, CT: Yale University Art Gallery.

One of the primary reasons for the decline of Srivijaya and Majapahit was the rise of new regional powers that began to challenge their dominance. In Sumatra, the weakening of Srivijaya, which had been a dominant maritime power for centuries, allowed for the emergence of new Islamic sultanates such as the Sultanate of Malacca. Malacca's strategic location on the Strait of Malacca enabled it to control one of the most important maritime trade routes in the world, attracting traders from across Asia and gradually eclipsing Srivijaya as the region's premier trading hub.[111] The success of Malacca, along with other emerging powers such as Aceh in northern Sumatra, contributed to the fragmentation of the archipelago, as these new states asserted their independence and competed for control of trade and resources. In Java, the Majapahit Empire, which had been the dominant power in the region since the thirteenth century, began to experience internal strife and a loss of central authority. The empire's decline was accelerated by the rise of local Islamic states, such as the Sultanate of Demak, which gradually took over the territory and influence of Majapahit.[112] The conversion of key Javanese elites to Islam and the spread of Islamic practices throughout the island further weakened Majapahit's hold over its vassal states, leading to the gradual disintegration of the empire into smaller, competing polities. The fragmentation of the archipelago was also influenced by shifting trade routes, which redirected economic activity away from traditional centres of power like Srivijaya and Majapahit. The increasing importance of the Malacca Strait as a trade corridor between the Indian Ocean and the South China Sea meant that coastal states with access to these routes became more powerful, while inland and less strategically located kingdoms declined.[113] The rise of these new regional powers, each with its own interests and alliances, led to a more fragmented political landscape in Southeast Asia, setting the stage for the region's subsequent history of competition and conflict among smaller states.

The arrival of European powers in Southeast Asia during the fifteenth century had a profound impact on the region's trade networks and the

[111] Andaya, B.W. & Andaya, L.Y. (1982), A History of Malaysia. London: Macmillan.

[112] Ricklefs, M.C. (2006), Islamic States in Java 1500–1700: The Rise of Islamin SoutheastAsia. Honolulu: University of Hawaii Press.

[113] Reid, A. (2015), A History of SoutheastAsia: Critical Crossroads. Chichester: Wiley Blackwell.

existing kingdoms, further contributing to the decline of major powers like Srivijaya and Majapahit. The Portuguese were the first Europeans to establish a significant presence in the region, followed by the Spanish, Dutch, and British. Their arrival marked the beginning of a new era in Southeast Asian history, characterized by increased competition for control of trade routes and the imposition of European colonial interests on the region's indigenous states. The Portuguese conquest of Malacca in 1511 was a turning point in Southeast Asian history. Malacca had been a thriving center of trade, serving as a crucial link between the Indian Ocean and the South China Sea. Its capture by the Portuguese not only disrupted the existing trade networks but also signalled the decline of indigenous powers like Srivijaya and Majapahit, which had relied heavily on their control of regional trade.[114] The Portuguese established a fortified trading post in Malacca, using it as a base to control the spice trade and to exert influence over other trading ports in the region. This shift in power significantly weakened the position of local rulers, who were unable to compete with the superior naval and military technology of the Europeans.[115] The Dutch and the British followed the Portuguese into Southeast Asia, further intensifying the competition for control of trade. The Dutch East India Company (VOC), in particular, played a crucial role in reshaping the political and economic landscape of the Indonesian archipelago. By establishing a monopoly over the spice trade and systematically undermining local rulers, the Dutch were able to assert control over large parts of the region, including the former territories of Majapahit.[116] The arrival of the Dutch and their subsequent colonization efforts led to the further fragmentation of the archipelago, as the VOC sought to weaken the power of indigenous states and to integrate them into their colonial empire. The impact of European colonization on Southeast Asia was not limited to the economic sphere. The introduction of Christianity, European legal systems, and new forms of governance also contributed to the cultural and social transformation of the region. Indigenous kingdoms that had once been powerful and independent were

[114] Andaya, B.W. & Andaya, L.Y. (1982), A History of Malaysia. London: Macmillan.

[115] Ricklefs, M.C. (2006), Islamic States in Java 1500–1700: The Rise of Islamin SoutheastAsia. Honolulu: University of Hawaii Press.

[116] Reid, A. (2015), A History of SoutheastAsia: Critical Crossroads. Chichester: Wiley Blackwell.

reduced to vassal states or were entirely absorbed into the colonial territories of the European powers. This period marked the end of the era of great indigenous kingdoms in Southeast Asia and the beginning of a long period of European domination, which would continue until the mid-twentieth century.[117] This evaluation provide a comprehensive analysis of the factors contributing to the decline of Srivijaya and Majapahit, emphasizing the rise of regional powers, the impact of European colonization, and the fragmentation of the Southeast Asian archipelago. The scholarly sources offer a robust foundation for understanding the complexities of this transformative period in the region's history.

Legacy of Indonesian Trade and Kingdoms (1 AD–1500 AD)

The period from 1 to 1500 AD was a transformative era in Indonesian history, characterized by the emergence and decline of powerful kingdoms such as Srivijaya and Majapahit, and the development of extensive trade networks. These historical dynamics left a profound legacy on Indonesian culture, religion, and society, shaping the archipelago's identity in ways that continue to resonate in modern Indonesia. One of the most significant cultural impacts of this period was the widespread diffusion and localization of Indian culture, particularly through the introduction of Hinduism and Buddhism. These religions were not only adopted by the ruling elites but also integrated into the daily lives of the local population, influencing art, architecture, literature, and social norms. Temples such as Borobudur and Prambanan stand as enduring symbols of this cultural synthesis, blending Indian architectural styles with local Javanese artistry.[118] These religious influences also extended to social structures, where the caste system, though not as rigid as in India, influenced social stratification in early Indonesian societies.[119] The arrival of Islam in the thirteenth century added another layer to Indonesia's cultural and religious mosaic. As Islam spread through trade routes and was embraced by

[117] Andaya, B.W. & Andaya, L.Y. (1982), A History of Malaysia. London: Macmillan.

[118] Lombard, D. (2000), Le carrefour javanais: Essai d'histoire globale. Paris: Éditions de l'EHESS.

[119] Heidhues, M.S. (2000), SoutheastAsia: A Concise History. London: Thames & Hudson.

local rulers, it gradually supplanted Hinduism and Buddhism, particularly in Java and Sumatra. However, the transition was not a complete replacement but rather a syncretic process where Islamic beliefs were blended with pre-existing Hindu-Buddhist and animist practices. This syncretic form of Islam, which persists in Indonesia today, is evident in the unique blend of religious rituals, architectural styles, and cultural practices found throughout the archipelago (Vickers, 2005). The development of this distinct Indonesian Islam has had a lasting impact on the nation's identity, positioning it as the largest Muslim-majority country in the world, yet one that retains a deep respect for its diverse cultural heritage. The social organization of Indonesian societies during this period was also heavily influenced by the trade networks and political structures established by these early kingdoms. The hierarchical nature of these societies, with a powerful ruling elite at the top, was mirrored in the governance structures of later Indonesian states. The importance of trade and the economic wealth it generated also laid the groundwork for a mercantile class that played a crucial role in the economic and political life of the region. This legacy of trade and hierarchical social organization can still be seen in modern Indonesia's regional diversity and the enduring influence of local elites in political and economic affairs.[120]

The early trade networks and kingdoms that flourished in Indonesia from 1 to 1500 AD have had a lasting influence on the development of modern Indonesia. These early states, such as Srivijaya and Majapahit, were not only powerful political entities but also centres of economic and cultural exchange that helped to shape the social and political landscape of the Indonesian archipelago.

One of the most enduring legacies of these early kingdoms is the concept of political unity across the archipelago. The Majapahit Empire, in particular, is often celebrated in Indonesian history as a precursor to the modern Indonesian state, with its influence extending over much of what is now Indonesia. The idea of a unified archipelago, or *Nusantara*, which was promoted by Majapahit, has been a powerful symbol in Indonesian nationalism and has influenced the country's modern territorial boundaries and national identity.[121] This legacy is reflected in the motto of

[120] Lombard, D. (2000), Le carrefour javanais: Essai d'histoire globale. Paris: Éditions de l'EHESS.

[121] Vickers, A. (2005), A History of Modern Indonesia. Cambridge: Cambridge University Press.

Indonesia, *Bhinneka Tunggal Ika* (Unity in Diversity), which emphasizes the unity of Indonesia despite its cultural and ethnic diversity—a concept rooted in the historical experience of Majapahit.

The early trade networks established by these kingdoms also laid the foundations for Indonesia's role as a major player in global trade. The strategic location of the Indonesian archipelago along the maritime trade routes between the Indian Ocean and the South China Sea made it a crucial link in the global economy. This role as a crossroads of trade has continued into the modern era, with Indonesia remaining a key player in the global economy due to its abundant natural resources and strategic location.[122] The legacy of these trade networks is also evident in the multiculturalism of modern Indonesia, as centuries of trade brought not only goods but also people, ideas, and cultures from across Asia and beyond.

The influence of early kingdoms on modern Indonesian governance is also significant. The hierarchical structures of these early states, with a strong central authority supported by local elites, have parallels in the modern Indonesian political system. The influence of local elites, or *adat* leaders, continues to play a role in regional governance and social organization, reflecting the enduring impact of these early kingdoms on Indonesian political culture.[123] Additionally, the legacy of Islamic sultanates that emerged in the wake of these early Hindu-Buddhist kingdoms has shaped Indonesia's modern identity as the world's largest Muslim-majority country, with Islamic institutions playing a central role in the nation's social and political life. The period from 1 to 1500 AD was one of profound significance for the Indonesian archipelago, laying the foundations for the cultural, religious, and political landscape that continues to define modern Indonesia. The rise and fall of powerful kingdoms such as Srivijaya and Majapahit, and the establishment of extensive trade networks, had far-reaching consequences that shaped the course of Indonesian history.

One of the key reflections on this period is the role of cultural and religious syncretism in shaping Indonesian identity. The ability of Indonesian societies to absorb and adapt foreign influences—whether from India,

[122] Heidhues, M.S. (2000), SoutheastAsia: A Concise History. London: Thames & Hudson.

[123] Lombard, D. (2000), Le carrefour javanais: Essai d'histoire globale. Paris: Éditions de l'EHESS.

China, or the Islamic world—while maintaining a strong sense of local identity, is one of the defining characteristics of the region's history. This syncretic process not only enriched Indonesian culture but also facilitated the spread of new ideas and technologies, making the archipelago a vibrant center of cultural exchange.[124] The blending of Hindu-Buddhist and Islamic traditions, in particular, created a unique cultural synthesis that continues to influence Indonesian art, architecture, and religious practices today. The historical significance of this period is also evident in the way it set the stage for the emergence of modern Indonesia. The concept of a unified archipelago, first promoted by the Majapahit Empire, has remained a powerful idea in Indonesian nationalism, influencing the country's territorial boundaries and national identity.[125] (Vickers, 2005). The legacy of trade and cultural exchange established during this period also laid the groundwork for Indonesia's role in the global economy, with the archipelago continuing to be a major hub of trade and cultural interaction in Southeast Asia. Moreover, the period from 1 to 1500 AD highlights the importance of adaptability and resilience in the face of change. The decline of Srivijaya and Majapahit and the rise of new powers such as Malacca and Demak demonstrate the dynamic nature of Indonesian history, where periods of decline were often followed by renewal and transformation. This resilience is a key theme in Indonesian history, reflecting the ability of its people to navigate and adapt to the challenges posed by both internal and external forces.[126]

In conclusion, the period from 1 to 1500 AD was a formative era in Indonesian history, characterized by the rise and fall of great kingdoms, the spread of religions, and the establishment of trade networks that connected the archipelago to the wider world. The legacies of this period—cultural syncretism, political unity, and economic interconnectedness—continue to shape the identity of modern Indonesia, making it a nation that is both deeply rooted in its history and dynamically engaged with the world. Indonesia's dynamic engagement with the world is reflected in how it continues to integrate its rich

[124] Lombard, D. (2000), Le carrefour javanais: Essai d'histoire globale. Paris: Éditions de l'EHESS.

[125] Vickers, A. (2005), A History of Modern Indonesia. Cambridge: Cambridge University Press.

[126] Heidhues, M.S. (2000), SoutheastAsia: A Concise History. London: Thames & Hudson.

historical legacies with contemporary global trends and challenges. The country's cultural syncretism, which emerged from the blending of Hindu-Buddhist, Islamic, and indigenous traditions, allows Indonesia to maintain a unique cultural identity while also being open to global cultural exchanges. This adaptability has enabled Indonesia to participate actively in global dialogues on culture, religion, and heritage, showcasing its diverse traditions on the world stage.

Politically, the concept of unity that dates back to the Majapahit Empire has evolved into a modern commitment to national cohesion and participation in international diplomacy. Indonesia's active role in organizations like the Association of Southeast Asian Nations (ASEAN) and the United Nations reflects its engagement with global governance and regional stability. Its history of unifying a vast archipelago with diverse cultures has informed its approach to international cooperation and conflict resolution. Economically, Indonesia's historical role as a hub of trade in Southeast Asia has continued into the present, with the country playing a significant role in global trade networks. Its strategic location and abundant natural resources make Indonesia a critical player in the global economy, particularly in industries such as palm oil, natural gas, and textiles. The legacy of economic interconnectedness has positioned Indonesia as a key emerging market that attracts foreign investment and engages in international trade, contributing to global economic dynamics. Overall, Indonesia's engagement with the world is a blend of maintaining its historical roots while actively participating in global cultural, political, and economic processes, ensuring its relevance and influence on the international stage.

Conclusion

The period between 1 and 1500 AD marked a transformative era in the Indonesian archipelago, characterized by the rise and fall of powerful kingdoms such as Srivijaya and Majapahit, and the establishment of extensive maritime trade networks that connected Indonesia to the broader Indian Ocean world. These early polities leveraged their strategic locations along vital trade routes to control the flow of goods, ideas, and cultural practices, thereby asserting their dominance over the region. The kingdoms of Srivijaya and Majapahit, in particular, became central hubs for trade, facilitating the exchange of valuable commodities such as spices, resins, and precious metals, which were in high demand across

Asia and beyond.[127,128] The wealth generated from trade not only strengthened these kingdoms' political power but also fuelled the development of sophisticated cultural and religious traditions, including the spread of Hinduism, Buddhism, and later Islam, which profoundly shaped Indonesian society.[129]

Throughout this period, the interplay between trade and state formation was a defining feature of Indonesian history. The control of strategic maritime routes enabled these early kingdoms to amass considerable wealth, which they used to build monumental architecture, patronize the arts, and establish religious institutions. The spread of Hindu-Buddhist culture through trade links led to the Indianization of the region, resulting in the construction of iconic temples like Borobudur and Prambanan, which blended Indian and local artistic elements.[130] Later, the arrival of Islam via trade routes introduced new religious and cultural practices that further enriched Indonesia's diverse cultural landscape. The period also saw the emergence of powerful regional sultanates, such as those in Aceh, Demak, and Malacca, which played a pivotal role in the spread of Islam across the archipelago and the establishment of Islamic political and social institutions.[131] Trade was the engine driving the political and cultural developments in early Indonesian history. The strategic control of maritime trade routes by kingdoms such as Srivijaya and Majapahit allowed these polities to dominate regional commerce and exert influence over vast territories. These trade networks facilitated not only the exchange of goods but also the flow of ideas, technologies, and cultural practices, which had a lasting impact on the social and political structures of the region. The interaction with traders from

[127] Reid, A. (1988), SoutheastAsia in the Age of Commerce, 1450–1680: Volume One, The Lands below the Winds. New Haven, CT: Yale University Press.

[128] Hall, K.R. (2011), A History of Early SoutheastAsia: Maritime Trade and Societal Development, 100–1500. Lanham, MD: Rowman & Littlefield Publishers.

[129] Vickers, A. (2005), A History of Modern Indonesia. Cambridge: Cambridge University Press.

[130] Heidhues, M.S. (2000), SoutheastAsia: A Concise History. London: Thames & Hudson.

[131] Lombard, D. (2000), Le carrefour javanais: Essai d'histoire globale. Paris: Éditions de l'EHESS.

India, China, the Middle East, and later Europe, introduced new religious, artistic, and intellectual traditions to the Indonesian archipelago, leading to the development of a rich and syncretic cultural heritage that combined indigenous elements with foreign influences.[132] The spread of Hinduism and Buddhism through these trade networks played a crucial role in the formation of early Indonesian polities, providing the ideological foundation for the centralization of power and the establishment of divine kingship. The adoption of these religions by local rulers helped to legitimize their authority and consolidate their control over their territories. Similarly, the spread of Islam from the thirteenth century onwards was closely linked to the region's trade networks, with Muslim traders and missionaries establishing Islamic communities in key port cities, which eventually led to the rise of Islamic sultanates.[133] These developments highlight the integral role of trade in shaping the political and cultural history of Indonesia, as it facilitated the exchange of ideas and practices that transformed the region's social fabric and contributed to the formation of the diverse and pluralistic society that characterizes modern Indonesia.

The study of early Indonesian history offers a wealth of opportunities for further research, particularly in the areas of trade, cultural exchange, and state formation. One promising avenue for future research is the exploration of the connections between Indonesia and other regions along the Indian Ocean trade routes, including South Asia, the Middle East, and East Africa. By examining the movement of goods, people, and ideas across these vast networks, scholars can gain a deeper understanding of how these interactions influenced the development of Indonesian societies and contributed to the region's cultural and religious diversity.[134,135] Another important area of research is the study of the syncretic cultural practices that emerged in Indonesia as a result

[132] Reid, A. (1988), SoutheastAsia in the Age of Commerce, 1450–1680: Volume One, The Lands below the Winds. New Haven, CT: Yale University Press.

[133] Hall, K.R. (2011), A History of Early SoutheastAsia: Maritime Trade and Societal Development, 100–1500. Lanham, MD: Rowman & Littlefield Publishers.

[134] Reid, A. (1988), SoutheastAsia in the Age of Commerce, 1450–1680: Volume One, The Lands below the Winds. New Haven, CT: Yale University Press.

[135] Hall, K.R. (2011), A History of Early SoutheastAsia: Maritime Trade and Societal Development, 100–1500. Lanham, MD: Rowman & Littlefield Publishers.

of these interactions. This includes the blending of Hindu-Buddhist and Islamic traditions, as well as the incorporation of indigenous beliefs and practices into these foreign religious frameworks. Further investigation into the ways in which local communities adapted and transformed these influences can shed light on the processes of cultural change and continuity in the region. Additionally, research into the material culture of early Indonesian societies, including archaeology and art history, can provide valuable insights into the everyday lives of people during this period and the ways in which they engaged with and contributed to the broader networks of exchange.[136] Finally, future research should also focus on the political history of early Indonesian kingdoms, particularly the processes of state formation and decline. This includes the examination of the factors that contributed to the rise and fall of powerful polities such as Srivijaya and Majapahit, as well as the role of local elites and regional powers in shaping the political landscape of the archipelago. By investigating these dynamics, scholars can develop a more nuanced understanding of the complex and multifaceted history of early Indonesia and its significance within the broader context of Southeast Asian and global history.[137]

References

Acri, A. (2017), Esoteric Buddhism in Mediaeval Maritime Asia: Networks of Masters, Texts, Icons. ISEAS—Yusof Ishak Institute.

Andaya, B.W. (2001), To Live as Brothers: Southeast Sumatra in the Seventeenth and Eighteenth Centuries. University of Hawaii Press.

Azra, A. (2004), The Origins of Islamic Reformism in Southeast Asia: Networks of Malay-Indonesian and Middle Eastern 'Ulamā' in the Seventeenth and Eighteenth Centuries. Allen & Unwin.

Azra, A. (2006), The Origins of Islamic Reformism in Southeast Asia: Networks of Malay-Indonesian and Middle Eastern 'Ulamā' in the Seventeenth and Eighteenth Centuries. Allen & Unwin.

[136] Vickers, A. (2005), A History of Modern Indonesia. Cambridge: Cambridge University Press.

[137] Heidhues, M.S. (2000), SoutheastAsia: A Concise History. London: Thames & Hudson.

Barrett, D.P. & Worden, R.L. (1995), Early Southeast Asia: Selected Readings. Ithaca, NY: Cornell University Southeast Asia Program Publications.
Bellina, B. (2007), Cultural Exchange Between India and Southeast Asia: Production and Distribution of Hard Stone Ornaments (VIc BC—VIc AD). Paris: École Française d'Extrême-Orient.
Bellina, B. and Glover, I. (2004), Southeast Asia: From Prehistory to History. Routledge.
Christie, J.W. (1995), States without Cities: Demographic Trends in Early Java. Indonesia, 60, pp. 23–40.
Cœdès, G. (1968), The Indianized States of Southeast Asia. Australian National University Press.
Davison, J. (2003), Balinese Architecture: Towards an Encyclopedia. Tuttle Publishing.
Guy, J. (1998), Oriental Trade Ceramics in South-East Asia, Ninth to Sixteenth Centuries: With a Catalogue of Chinese, Vietnamese and Thai Wares in Australian Collections. Oxford University Press.
Hall, K.R. (2011), A History of Early Southeast Asia: Maritime Trade and Societal Development, 100–1500. Rowman & Littlefield Publishers.
Heidhues, M.S. (2000), Southeast Asia: A Concise History. London: Thames & Hudson.
Johns, A.H. (1995), Sufism in Southeast Asia: Reflections and Reconsiderations. Journal of Southeast Asian Studies.
Kempers, A.J. (1991), Monumental Bali: Introduction to Balinese Archaeology & Guide to the Monuments. Periplus Editions.
Kieven, L. (2013), Following the Cap-Figure in Majapahit Temple Reliefs: A New Look at the Religious Function of East Javanese Temples. Brill.
Kulke, H. (1990), A History of India. Routledge.
Kumar, A. (2019), Javanese Literature in Surakarta Manuscripts. Cornell University Press.
Lombard, D. (2000), Le carrefour javanais: Essai d'histoire globale. Paris: Éditions de l'EHESS.
Lombard, D. (1990), Le carrefour javanais. Essai d'histoire globale (The Javanese Crossroads: Towards a Global History). Éditions de l'École des hautes études en sciences sociales.
Majumdar, R.C. (1986), History of Southeast Asia. McMillan.
Manguin, P.-Y. (2010), Early trading polities of Southeast Asia: Their markets and the Indian Ocean trade network. Journal of Southeast Asian Studies.
Michaels, A. (2004), Hinduism. Past and present. Princeton University Press.
Miksic, J. (2011), Singapore and the Silk Road of the Sea, 1300–1800. NUS Press.
Munoz, P.M. (2006), Early Kingdoms of the Indonesian Archipelago and the Malay Peninsula. Editions Didier Millet.

Napier, A.D. (1988), The Age of Batik: The Art and Craft of Batik in Asia. Southeast Asia Publications.

Pigeaud, T.G.T. (1960), Java in the 14th Century: A Study in Cultural History. The Hague: Martinus Nijhoff.

Ptak, R. (1998), China's Seaborne Trade with South and Southeast Asia (1200–1750). Ashgate.

Reid, A. (1988), Southeast Asia in the Age of Commerce, 1450–1680: Volume One, The Lands below the Winds. Yale University Press.

Reid, A. (1993), Southeast Asia in the Age of Commerce, 1450–1680: Volume Two, Expansion and Crisis. Yale University Press.

Reid, A. (2015), A History of Southeast Asia: Critical Crossroads. Chichester: Wiley Blackwell.

Ricklefs, M.C. (2008), A History of Modern Indonesia Since c.1200. 4th edn. London: Palgrave Macmillan.

Ricklefs, M.C. (2006), A History of Modern Indonesia Since c.1200. Palgrave Macmillan.

Robson, S.O. (1995), Desawarnana (Nagarakrtagama) by Mpu Prapanca. Leiden: KITLV Press

Rodrigues, H. (2006), Introducing Hinduism. Routledge.

Schoppert, P. (1997), Bali: Cultural Tourism and Touristic Culture. Archipelago Press.

Steinberg, D.J., et al. (1987), In Search of Southeast Asia: A Modern History. University of Hawaii Press.

Vickers, A. (2005), A History of Modern Indonesia. Cambridge: Cambridge University Press.

Wade, G. (2009), The Asian Seas: Trade, Travel, and Visions of the Other (1400–1750). Ashgate.

Wang, G. (1998), China and the Chinese Overseas. Times Academic Press.

Wolters, O.W. (1967), Early Indonesian Commerce: A Study of the Origins of Srīvijaya. Cornell University Press.

Wolters, O.W. (1999), History, Culture, and Region in Southeast Asian Perspectives. Institute of Southeast Asian Studies.

CHAPTER 4

The Influence of Hindu-Buddhist States (200–1500 AD)

Introduction

The spread of Hinduism and Buddhism in Southeast Asia from the early centuries AD played a significant role in shaping the region's cultural, religious, and political landscapes. The influence of these religions is evident in the architecture, literature, and social structures that emerged in various Southeast Asian polities, such as the kingdoms of Srivijaya, Majapahit, and Angkor. Hindu-Buddhist principles were introduced primarily through trade routes and the interactions between Southeast Asian states and Indian civilizations. These religions provided the ideological foundations for the formation of centralized states and the legitimization of royal authority.[1] Hinduism and Buddhism played a pivotal role in shaping the sociopolitical and cultural landscape of early Indonesian kingdoms. The introduction of these religions brought sophisticated frameworks for governance and statecraft, which were instrumental in the formation of centralized states and the legitimization of royal authority. For instance, the adoption of Hindu concepts such as the devaraja (god-king) ideology allowed rulers to position themselves as divine representatives on Earth, consolidating their power and uniting disparate communities under centralized governance. This is evident in the early kingdoms of

[1] Hall, K.R. (2011), A History of Early SoutheastAsia: Maritime Trade and Societal Development, 100–1500. Lanham, MD: Rowman & Littlefield Publishers.

S. Ramesh, *The Political Economy of Indonesia's Economic Development, Volume I*, https://doi.org/10.1007/978-3-031-94350-8_4

Srivijaya and Majapahit, where rulers employed Hindu-Buddhist rituals and iconography to assert their divine status and political legitimacy.[2] Additionally, Buddhist principles of dharma provided ethical guidelines for rulers, reinforcing the idea of kingship as a moral and spiritual duty. In Java, inscriptions such as the Nalanda Copperplate attest to the role of Buddhist monasteries in supporting and legitimizing royal authority through their spiritual influence and administrative capabilities.[3] These monasteries often functioned as centres of learning and diplomacy, further strengthening the state's centralized structure. Furthermore, Hindu and Buddhist cosmology influenced architectural and urban planning, as seen in the construction of monumental structures like Borobudur and Prambanan. These temples not only served as religious centres but also symbolized the ruler's divine mandate and the state's grandeur, promoting social cohesion and political stability.[4] Such structures physically manifested the ideological underpinnings of the state, blending spiritual and temporal authority into a cohesive system of governance. Overall, the infusion of Hinduism and Buddhism into Indonesia provided a robust ideological foundation for centralized state formation, legitimized royal authority through divine association, and left enduring cultural and architectural legacies that shaped the region's history.[5] The diffusion of Hindu-Buddhist culture across Southeast Asia also facilitated the development of complex social hierarchies and the patronage of monumental architecture, as seen in the construction of iconic religious structures like Borobudur and Prambanan in Java, which reflect a synthesis of Indian and local artistic traditions.[6]

Borobudur and Prambanan, two monumental structures in Java, Indonesia, were constructed during distinct periods and reflect the religious and political landscapes of their times. Borobudur, a massive Buddhist stupa and temple complex, was built between the eighth

[2] Geertz, C. (1980). Negara: The Theatre State in Nineteenth-Century Bali. Princeton University Press.

[3] Kulke, H., & Rothermund, D. (2016). A History of India. Routledge.

[4] Miksic, J. (2013). Singapore and the Silk Road of the Sea, 1300–1800. NUS Press.

[5] Ricklefs, M.C. (2001). A History of Modern Indonesia Since c.1200. Stanford University Press.

[6] Lombard, D. (2000), Le carrefour javanais: Essai d'histoire globale. Paris: Éditions de l'EHESS.

and ninth centuries AD during the Sailendra Dynasty. Its construction reflected the dynasty's devotion to Mahayana Buddhism and their desire to legitimize their rule by aligning with a powerful religious tradition.[7] The temple's intricate carvings narrate stories from Buddhist texts and serve as a guide for spiritual enlightenment, suggesting that it was intended not only as a place of worship but also as a tool for spiritual education.

The Sailendra rulers, particularly King Samaratungga, are credited with initiating Borobudur's construction. The choice of location on a volcanic plain near Magelang is significant, as it symbolizes the merging of earthly and cosmic realms, aligning with Buddhist cosmology.[8] The structure is designed as a mandala, reflecting Buddhist concepts of the universe. Its layers represent the journey from the earthly realm to nirvana, with hundreds of Buddha statues and relief panels depicting the life of the Buddha and teachings from the Jataka tales.[9]

Prambanan, a Hindu temple complex, was built in the ninth century under the Mataram Kingdom, likely as a response to the rise of Buddhism and to assert Hinduism's prominence in the region. The complex, dedicated to the Trimurti gods (Brahma, Vishnu, and Shiva), showcases Hindu cosmology and mythological narratives through its detailed reliefs.[10] Rakai Pikatan, a ruler of the Mataram Kingdom, is often credited with the construction of Prambanan. Some sources suggest it was a statement of political and religious rivalry with the Sailendra dynasty, which had supported Buddhism.[11] Prambanan's central temple is dedicated to Shiva, towering at 47 meters, surrounded by smaller temples for other deities. The reliefs on the temple walls depict episodes from the Ramayana, emphasizing themes of dharma and divine intervention, which were central to Hindu statecraft and culture. The construction of Borobudur and Prambanan highlights the interplay between religion and

[7] Miksic, J. N. (2011). Old Javanese Gold: The Hunter Thompson Collection at the Yale University Art Gallery. Yale University Press.

[8] Ricklefs, M. C. (2001). A History of Modern Indonesia Since c.1200. Stanford University Press.

[9] Woodward, M. R. (2003). Java, Indonesia,and Islam. Springer.

[10] Fontein, J. (1990). The Art of SoutheastAsia: Temples and Sculpture. Thames & Hudson.

[11] Miksic, J. N. (2011). Old Javanese Gold: The Hunter Thompson Collection at the Yale University Art Gallery. Yale University Press.

politics in early Javanese history. These monumental projects symbolized the rulers' divine authority, their ability to mobilize vast resources, and their engagement with global religious and cultural exchanges.

The emergence of Hindu-Buddhist states in Southeast Asia between 200 and 1500 AD is closely linked to the region's participation in long-distance trade networks that connected it to South Asia, China, and beyond. The Indianization of Southeast Asia began as early as the first century AD, driven by the movement of traders, priests, and scholars who brought with them religious texts, artistic styles, and political concepts from the Indian subcontinent.[12] This period saw the rise of powerful kingdoms like Funan, Chenla, and later, Srivijaya and Majapahit, which adopted Hindu-Buddhist ideologies to legitimize their rule and consolidate power. The establishment of these states marked a significant shift in the region's political landscape, as local rulers began to adopt the Indian concept of divine kingship and the associated rituals and ceremonies to reinforce their authority.[13] This historical context underscores the importance of religious and cultural exchange in the formation of early Southeast Asian states and their subsequent development.

The primary objective of this chapter is to explore the influence of Hindu-Buddhist states on the development of Southeast Asia from 200 to 1500 AD, focusing on the ways in which these religions shaped the region's political structures, cultural practices, and social hierarchies. The chapter will examine the introduction and spread of Hinduism and Buddhism through trade and diplomatic relations, the establishment of centralized states that drew on Indian models of governance, and the integration of Hindu-Buddhist beliefs into local traditions.[14] Additionally, the chapter will analyze the enduring legacy of these early states on modern Southeast Asian societies, particularly in terms of religious practices, architectural heritage, and cultural identities. By providing a comprehensive overview of the historical and cultural dynamics of the

[12] Kulke, H. & Rothermund, D. (2010), A History of India. 5th edn. London: Routledge.

[13] Coedès, G. (1968), The Indianized States of SoutheastAsia. Honolulu: University of Hawaii Press.

[14] Mabbett, I.W. & Chandler, D.P. (1995), The Khmers. Oxford: Blackwell.

period, this chapter aims to contribute to a deeper understanding of the complexities of Southeast Asia's pre-colonial history.[15]

The Introduction and Spread of Hinduism and Buddhism in Southeast Asia

Origins of Hinduism and Buddhism in the Indian Subcontinent

Hinduism and Buddhism originated in the Indian subcontinent, with Hinduism developing from the Vedic traditions around 1500 BCE and Buddhism emerging in the sixth century BCE as a reformist movement led by Siddhartha Gautama, the Buddha. Hinduism, characterized by its complex pantheon of gods, ritual practices, and the concept of dharma (cosmic law and order), provided a comprehensive framework for social and religious life in ancient India. Buddhism, on the other hand, challenged the established Vedic order by promoting the idea of enlightenment through personal effort and ethical conduct, rejecting the rigid caste system that was integral to Hindu society.[16] Both religions offered a set of philosophical and ethical teachings that would later profoundly influence the cultural and religious landscapes of Southeast Asia. The spread of these religions beyond the Indian subcontinent was facilitated by their adaptability and the appeal of their spiritual and moral teachings, which resonated with the existing beliefs and practices of the Southeast Asian peoples.[17] The dissemination of Hinduism and Buddhism beyond the Indian subcontinent into Southeast Asia was significantly shaped by their inherent adaptability and the universal appeal of their spiritual and moral frameworks. These religions were not imposed but rather integrated into local cultures, finding resonance with pre-existing animistic and ancestral worship practices, which enabled their acceptance and proliferation.[18] The integration of Hinduism and Buddhism into local Southeast Asian cultures was a process of mutual adaptation,

[15] Wolters, O.W. (1999), History, Culture, and Region in Southeast Asian Perspectives. Revised edn. Ithaca, NY: Cornell University SoutheastAsia Program Publications.

[16] Flood, G. (1996), An Introduction to Hinduism. Cambridge: Cambridge University Press.

[17] Gombrich, R. (1988), Theravada Buddhism: A Social History from Ancient Benares to Modern Colombo. London: Routledge.

[18] Kulke, H., & Rothermund, D. (2016). A History of India. Routledge.

where these religions were not imposed but rather assimilated harmoniously into pre-existing animistic and ancestral worship traditions. This blending was facilitated by the religions' flexible doctrines, which allowed them to coexist with indigenous practices rather than replace them.[19] For instance, Hindu deities were often syncretized with local spirits and deities, as seen in Bali, where the Hindu pantheon was adapted into Balinese cosmology alongside indigenous beliefs about the supernatural and nature spirits.[20] Similarly, Buddhism's emphasis on ethical conduct and compassion resonated with ancestral worship practices, which stressed moral behaviour and veneration of forebears. In mainland Southeast Asia, such as in present-day Myanmar and Thailand, Buddhist rituals and monasteries became focal points for community life, integrating with pre-existing practices like spirit worship (nat cults in Myanmar) to provide a unifying moral framework.[21] Moreover, the architectural styles of religious monuments exemplify this synthesis. At Borobudur in Java, for instance, Buddhist teachings are depicted alongside indigenous symbols, reflecting a blending of Mahayana Buddhism with local traditions.[22] Similarly, the Hindu temple complex of Prambanan incorporates elements that resonate with Southeast Asian artistic styles, showing a deliberate effort to align imported religious ideals with local cultural aesthetics.[23]

This integration was also politically advantageous. Local rulers adopted elements of Hindu and Buddhist governance, such as the Hindu devaraja concept, which aligned with the indigenous view of kings as intermediaries between the divine and human realms. This alignment legitimized their rule and facilitated the religions' widespread acceptance.[24]

The adaptability of these religions lay in their capacity to merge with Indigenous traditions without erasing them, creating a syncretic cultural and religious landscape. For instance, in Java, Hinduism's

[19] Kulke, H., & Rothermund, D. (2016). A History of India. Routledge.

[20] Geertz, C. (1980). Negara: The Theatre State in Nineteenth-Century Bali. Princeton University Press.

[21] Woodward, M. R. (2003). Java, Indonesia,and Islam. Springer.

[22] Miksic, J. N. (2011). Old Javanese Gold: The Hunter Thompson Collection at the Yale University Art Gallery. Yale University Press.

[23] Fontein, J. (1990). The Art of SoutheastAsia: Temples and Sculpture. Thames & Hudson.

[24] Ricklefs, M. C. (2001). A History of Modern Indonesia Since c.1200. Stanford University Press.

complex pantheon complemented local beliefs in spirits and deities, while Buddhism's emphasis on compassion and karmic justice reinforced existing moral frameworks.[25] Additionally, Hinduism and Buddhism were promoted by trade networks that connected South Asia with Southeast Asia. Merchants, monks, and scholars facilitated cultural exchanges, spreading texts, rituals, and ideas that appealed to local elites seeking to enhance their legitimacy and governance structures.[26] Hindu notions of kingship, such as the devaraja concept, were particularly influential, as they provided rulers with divine justification for their authority, while Buddhist monasteries became centres of education and political influence.[27] Moreover, the religions' teachings on ethical behaviour, cosmology, and spiritual attainment addressed universal human concerns, making them appealing to a broad audience. For example, the Buddhist emphasis on moral conduct and the pursuit of enlightenment resonated with local rulers' aspirations to present themselves as just and enlightened leaders.[28] This alignment between religious values and local governance priorities further entrenched these religions in Southeast Asian societies. Critically, while Hinduism and Buddhism facilitated cultural and political sophistication in Southeast Asia, their influence was uneven. Coastal polities with stronger trade connections adopted these religions more comprehensively, whereas interior regions retained Indigenous practices more prominently. This selective adoption highlights the nuanced interplay between external influence and local agency.[29]

Mechanisms of Religious and Cultural Transmission to Southeast Asia

The transmission of Hinduism and Buddhism to Southeast Asia was facilitated by a multifaceted combination of trade, migration, and diplomatic exchanges between the Indian subcontinent and Southeast Asian polities.

[25] Ricklefs, M. C. (2001). A History of Modern Indonesia Since c.1200. Stanford University Press.

[26] Miksic, J. N. (2011). Old Javanese Gold: The Hunter Thompson Collection at the Yale University Art Gallery. Yale University Press.

[27] Geertz, C. (1980). Negara: The Theatre State in Nineteenth-Century Bali. Princeton University Press.

[28] Fontein, J. (1990). The Art of SoutheastAsia: Temples and Sculpture. Thames & Hudson.

[29] Woodward, M. R. (2003). Java, Indonesia,and Islam. Springer.

Maritime trade routes, notably those across the Bay of Bengal and the South China Sea, were pivotal in connecting these regions, forming a vibrant network of commercial and cultural exchange. These routes were utilized not only for the exchange of goods such as spices, textiles, and precious metals but also for the dissemination of religious and philosophical ideas. The strategic position of Southeast Asia as a nexus between East and South Asia made it a melting pot of Indian cultural influences, with ports such as Oc Eo in present-day Vietnam and Palembang in Sumatra becoming thriving hubs of interaction. The port of Oc Eo, located in the Mekong Delta near Thoai Son in An Giang Province, Vietnam, was a prominent hub of the Funan Kingdom (first to seventh centuries CE), playing a key role in connecting Southeast Asia to the broader Indian Ocean trading world. The port's strategic location enabled it to thrive as a conduit for goods, people, and cultural exchange, fostering the spread of Hinduism and Buddhism to the region.[30,31] Oc Eo was crucial to the maritime Silk Road, linking Indian traders and Chinese merchants to Southeast Asia's indigenous communities.

Prior to Indianization, the indigenous populations of the Mekong Delta practiced animistic and agricultural spiritual traditions cantered around local deities and nature spirits.[32] The integration of Hinduism and Buddhism did not erase these practices; rather, the new religions were localized to fit existing belief systems. For example, Indian deities like Shiva and Vishnu were sometimes equated with local protective spirits. Archaeological discoveries at Oc Eo, such as Shiva lingams and Buddhist relics, underscore how elites adopted external religious practices while blending them with indigenous traditions.[33] Evidence of Mahayana Buddhist influence at Oc Eo, including Bodhisattva statues and Buddhist

[30] Manguin, P.-Y. (2016). "Early Maritime Trade and Cultural Exchange in the Indian Ocean." In Manguin, P.-Y., Mani, A., & Wade, G. (Eds.), Early Interactions Between South and SoutheastAsia: Reflections on Cross-Cultural Exchange (pp. 1–22). Singapore: ISEAS Publishing.

[31] Higham, C. (2001). The Civilization of Angkor. London: Weidenfeld & Nicolson.

[32] Hall, K. R. (2011). A History of Early SoutheastAsia: Maritime Trade and Societal Development, 100–1500. Lanham, MD: Rowman & Littlefield.

[33] Stark, M. T. (2006). "From Funanto Angkor: Collapse and Regeneration in Ancient Cambodia." In Schwartz, G. M., & Nichols, J. J. (Eds.), After Collapse: The Regeneration of Complex Societies (pp. 144–167). Tucson: University of Arizona Press.

amulets, highlights the role of the port as a centre for the dissemination of Buddhist thought.[34] Mahayana's spread was facilitated by religious intermediaries—Buddhist monks, Hindu priests, and Indian merchants—who translated religious texts and teachings into forms that resonated with local populations. These intermediaries played an essential role in transmitting Sanskrit-based texts, as well as religious iconography and rituals. Such interactions laid the foundation for Buddhist traditions that later flourished in mainland Southeast Asia, particularly in Cambodia and Thailand.[35] Diplomatic exchanges between Funan and other major civilizations were instrumental in the cultural significance of Oc Eo. Chinese records, such as the Records of the Liang Dynasty, describe Funan's rulers sending emissaries to China, often bearing luxury goods such as pearls and ivory, while receiving Chinese support in return.[36] These diplomatic missions extended to India, where links with Gupta-period rulers brought Hindu and Buddhist texts, which were subsequently adapted by the Funanese elites. Kings used these religions to legitimize their rule, blending Indian religious symbols with Indigenous governance traditions.[37,38]

Excavations at Oc Eo by French archaeologist Louis Malleret revealed a treasure trove of artifacts that confirmed its role as a major trade and cultural hub. Finds included Roman coins, Indian jewellery, and Chinese ceramics, demonstrating the port's connections to global trade networks.[39] Gold jewellery and religious statues discovered in the area reflect how the Funan Kingdom synthesized local craftsmanship with

[34] Manguin, P.-Y. (2016). "Early Maritime Trade and Cultural Exchange in the Indian Ocean." In Manguin, P.-Y., Mani, A., & Wade, G. (Eds.), Early Interactions Between South and SoutheastAsia: Reflections on Cross-Cultural Exchange (pp. 1–22). Singapore: ISEAS Publishing.

[35] Coedes, G. (1968). The Indianized States of SoutheastAsia. Honolulu: University of Hawaii Press.

[36] Hall, K. R. (2011). A History of Early SoutheastAsia: Maritime Trade and Societal Development, 100–1500. Lanham, MD: Rowman & Littlefield.

[37] Higham, C. (2001). The Civilization of Angkor. London: Weidenfeld & Nicolson.

[38] Coedes, G. (1968). The Indianized States of SoutheastAsia. Honolulu: University of Hawaii Press.

[39] Malleret, L. (1959). L'Archéologie du Delta du Mékong. Paris: Ecole Française d'Extrême-Orient.

Indian artistic traditions.[40] Such discoveries underscore the role of Oc Eo in facilitating intercultural exchange. The port of Oc Eo and the Funan Kingdom played a foundational role in embedding Hindu-Buddhist traditions in Southeast Asia. These traditions were carried forward by successor states such as Chenla and Angkor, as seen in the widespread use of Indian-derived iconography, temple architecture, and state rituals. The influence of Funan's integration of religion, trade, and diplomacy extended beyond its decline, shaping the religious and cultural landscapes of Southeast Asia for centuries (Higham 2001; Hall 2011). Indian traders were instrumental in this cultural transmission. They often functioned as conduits for introducing Hindu and Buddhist religious traditions to local populations, particularly the ruling elites. For example, inscriptions found in Champa (Vietnam) and Funan (Cambodia) reference the presence of Indian merchants and their role in the local economy and governance.[41] However, this was not a simple process of imposition. Local communities adapted these foreign beliefs to align with their Indigenous traditions and worldviews. For example, animistic practices that emphasized reverence for spirits, ancestors, and sacred natural sites were integrated into the new Hindu and Buddhist frameworks. The practice of syncretism allowed Hindu and Buddhist deities to be incorporated into local pantheons, while rituals such as spirit offerings were merged with Brahmanical ceremonies. This synthesis is evident in the Javanese shadow puppet theatre (wayang kulit), which depicts episodes from the Ramayana and Mahabharata but incorporates local cosmologies and ethical teachings. Furthermore, the role of religious intermediaries, such as Buddhist monks and Hindu priests, was central to this process of cultural exchange. Buddhist missionaries, particularly those following the Mahayana tradition, played a crucial role in establishing religious institutions and spreading teachings across Southeast Asia. Unlike Theravada Buddhism, which was more focused on the individual path to enlightenment, Mahayana Buddhism emphasized the role of bodhisattvas—enlightened beings who delay their own enlightenment to help others achieve liberation. This compassionate

[40] Stark, M. T. (2006). "From Funanto Angkor: Collapse and Regeneration in Ancient Cambodia." In Schwartz, G. M., & Nichols, J. J. (Eds.), After Collapse: The Regeneration of Complex Societies (pp. 144–167). Tucson: University of Arizona Press.

[41] Hall, K. R. (2011). A History of Early SoutheastAsia: Maritime Trade and Societal Development, 100–1500. Lanham, MD: Rowman & Littlefield.

and inclusive approach resonated with local rulers, who often patronized Mahayana monasteries to legitimize their authority and demonstrate moral leadership. Monastic centres such as those in Srivijaya became influential hubs of learning, drawing students and scholars from across the region and even as far as China, as evidenced by the records of the Chinese Buddhist monk I Ching, who studied in Sumatra during the late seventh century.[42] Hindu priests, on the other hand, contributed to the development of political and social structures in Southeast Asia. They introduced Sanskrit as a language of administration and religious ceremony, which became a tool of political legitimacy for Southeast Asian rulers. For example, the inscriptions of King Jayavarman II in Cambodia, often credited with founding the Khmer Empire, describe the establishment of a devaraja (god-king) cult that fused Hindu political theory with indigenous concepts of kingship. Hindu priests also introduced sophisticated rituals, such as the royal consecration ceremony (rajasuya), which symbolized the divine authority of the king and integrated local beliefs about the sacred nature of the land and its rulers.

Diplomatic exchanges further reinforced this cultural transmission, creating networks of mutual influence between Indian and Southeast Asian polities. Southeast Asian rulers actively sought alliances and cultural ties with Indian kingdoms to enhance their prestige and consolidate their power. For instance, the rulers of Funan in Cambodia and the Srivijaya Empire in Sumatra sent emissaries to Indian courts to establish trade agreements and gain access to Indian cultural resources. Such exchanges often involved the gifting of religious texts, icons, and skilled artisans who could create temples, sculptures, and other symbols of divine authority. Inscriptions from the Srivijaya kingdom, for instance, highlight its rulers' patronage of Indian monasteries, particularly Nalanda, one of the most renowned centres of Buddhist learning.[43] These diplomatic exchanges not only facilitated the flow of ideas but also established a shared cultural framework that transcended national and linguistic boundaries. The physical evidence of these cultural interactions is visible in the artistic and architectural achievements of Southeast Asia, which reflect a blend of Indian and local influences. The temple complex of Borobudur in Java, for

[42] Wolters, O.W. (1999). History, Culture, and Region in Southeast Asian Perspectives. Cornell University Southeast Asia Program Publications.

[43] Coedès, G. (1968). The Indianized States of SoutheastAsia. East-West Center Press.

instance, is one of the most iconic examples of Mahayana Buddhist architecture. Its nine stacked platforms, adorned with over 2,500 relief panels, narrate Buddhist teachings while incorporating local artistic motifs. Similarly, the bas-reliefs of Angkor Wat in Cambodia depict scenes from Hindu epics like the Mahabharata and Ramayana but also incorporate indigenous themes, such as the Khmer understanding of cosmology and kingship.

The transmission of Hinduism and Buddhism to Southeast Asia was a complex and dynamic process that involved trade, migration, religious intermediaries, and diplomatic exchanges. These interactions were not unidirectional but rather characterized by adaptation and syncretism, resulting in the creation of unique religious and cultural traditions that continue to shape the region today. These interactions were often formalized through marriage alliances and the establishment of religious institutions, which served as centres for the dissemination of Hindu-Buddhist culture.[44] The process of Indianization was not a one-way transmission but involved significant adaptation and synthesis, as local rulers and communities selectively integrated Indian religious and cultural elements into their own traditions, creating a unique Southeast Asian expression of Hinduism and Buddhism.[45]

Role of Traders, Priests, and Pilgrims in the Spread of Religions

Traders, priests, and pilgrims played a pivotal role in the spread of Hinduism and Buddhism across Southeast Asia, facilitating the transmission of religious and cultural traditions over centuries. Indian traders, who were among the first to establish commercial links with Southeast Asia, brought with them not only goods but also religious ideas and practices. The port cities of Southeast Asia, such as Oc Eo in present-day Vietnam and Palembang in Sumatra, served as key nodes where trade and cultural exchange occurred. These traders, who often settled in these port cities, became influential figures in local societies.[46] By interacting with local elites, they played a significant role in integrating Hindu-Buddhist

[44] Mabbett, I.W. (1977), The Indianization of SoutheastAsia: Reflections on the Historical Sources. Journal of Southeast Asian Studies, 8(1), pp. 1–14.

[45] Wolters, O.W. (1999), History, Culture, and Region in Southeast Asian Perspectives. Revised edn. Ithaca, NY: Cornell University SoutheastAsia Program Publications.

[46] Hall, K.R. (2011), A History of Early SoutheastAsia: Maritime Trade and Societal Development, 100–1500. Lanham, MD: Rowman & Littlefield Publishers.

cultural practices into the political and social frameworks of Southeast Asian polities.[47] For example, the Indianized kingdoms of Funan and Srivijaya became major centres of Buddhist learning, a direct result of these trade-based interactions.[48] Hindu and Buddhist priests also played a critical role in the transmission of religious traditions, often accompanying traders to conduct rituals and provide spiritual guidance. They introduced sacred texts such as the Ramayana and Mahabharata and performed ceremonial practices that aligned with Hindu and Buddhist doctrines. These priests contributed to the formation of Southeast Asia's royal courts, where Hindu-Buddhist concepts like devaraja (god-king) ideology were adopted to legitimize the rule of monarchs.[49] The cultural exchange facilitated by priests is evident in the architectural achievements of the time, such as the temples of Angkor in Cambodia and Borobudur in Indonesia, which incorporate Indian religious symbols and reflect the integration of Hindu-Buddhist thought.[50]

Pilgrims and monks functioned as mobile cultural intermediaries who linked Indian subcontinental traditions with Southeast Asia's indigenous practices. Buddhist monks, particularly those following the Mahayana tradition, travelled extensively, spreading Buddhist philosophy, texts, and rituals. For instance, Chinese records recount the journey of the monk I Ching, who described the flourishing Buddhist culture in the Srivijayan empire.[51] These pilgrimages not only transported sacred relics and scriptures but also facilitated cross-cultural exchanges, blending Indian religious traditions with local animistic and ancestor worship beliefs. This syncretism gave rise to distinct forms of Hindu-Buddhist practices in Southeast Asia, such as the amalgamation of Vishnu worship with indigenous serpent or naga deities.[52] In addition to their individual

[47] Coedès, G. (1968). The Indianized States of SoutheastAsia. University of Hawaii Press.

[48] Hall, K.R. (2011). A History of Early SoutheastAsia: Maritime Trade and Societal Development, 100–1500. Rowman & Littlefield.

[49] Higham, C. (2001). The Civilization of Angkor. Weidenfeld & Nicolson.

[50] Stark, M.T. (2006). 'From Funanto Angkor: Collapse and Regeneration in Ancient Cambodia', in G.M. Schwartz & J.J. Nichols (eds), After Collapse: The Regeneration of Complex Societies, University of Arizona Press, pp. 144–167.

[51] Miksic, J.N. & Goh, G.Y. (2017) Ancient SoutheastAsia. London: Routledge.

[52] Malleret, L. (1959). L'archéologie du Delta du Mékong. Tome premier, L'exploration archéologique et les fouilles d'Oc-Èo. École française d'Extrême-Orient.

contributions, these groups were supported by broader diplomatic and cultural exchanges. For example, rulers from Southeast Asia sent emissaries to Indian kingdoms to establish alliances and learn about Indian religion and culture. Southeast Asian rulers who sent emissaries to Indian kingdoms include the rulers of Funan, Srivijaya, and Champa. These interactions involved prominent Indian polities, such as the Gupta Empire and the Pallava dynasty, and played a significant role in facilitating the cultural and religious exchange between the regions.

The rulers of Funan (located in present-day Cambodia and southern Vietnam) were among the first to establish contact with Indian kingdoms. Historical records, including Chinese sources such as the History of the Liang Dynasty, mention that Funanese kings sent emissaries to Indian courts to establish alliances and gain access to Indian religious texts and advisors.[53] The Funanese court adopted Hinduism, particularly the worship of Vishnu and Shiva, as evidenced by the numerous lingams and yoni artifacts discovered at archaeological sites in the Mekong Delta.

The rulers of the Srivijaya Empire, cantered in Sumatra, maintained close connections with Indian kingdoms, particularly during the Gupta period. Srivijaya is renowned for its role as a hub of Buddhist learning and exchange. Inscriptions, such as the Nalanda copper plate inscription, record that Srivijayan King Balaputra sent emissaries to Indian Buddhist monasteries, including Nalanda, to establish learning centres and secure the support of Indian scholars for religious and educational development in Southeast Asia.[54] This helped Srivijaya become a vital center for Mahayana Buddhism in the region. In Champa (modern-day central and southern Vietnam), rulers fostered diplomatic and religious ties with South Indian kingdoms, particularly the Pallava dynasty. The adoption of Shaivism (worship of Shiva) in Champa, as seen in the temples at My Son, reflects these connections. Pallava architects and artisans accompanied emissaries to assist in the construction of Champa's temples, introducing South Indian architectural styles and techniques.[55]

The Gupta Empire was a significant partner in these interactions due to its prominence as a center of Hindu and Buddhist intellectual and

[53] Coedès, G. (1968). The Indianized States of SoutheastAsia. University of Hawaii Press.

[54] Hall, K.R. (2011). A History of Early SoutheastAsia: Maritime Trade and Societal Development, 100–1500. Rowman & Littlefield.

[55] Miksic, J.N. & Goh, G.Y. (2017). Ancient SoutheastAsia. Routledge.

cultural life. The Pallava dynasty, based in Tamil Nadu, was also deeply involved, particularly with kingdoms like Champa, due to their shared maritime trade routes and cultural exchanges. These emissaries served not only as diplomats but also as conduits for transmitting religious doctrines, artistic traditions, and governance structures. The religious texts and advisors they brought back profoundly influenced the sociopolitical and religious systems of Southeast Asia, leading to the development of Indianized states like Angkor and Srivijaya. These diplomatic missions often returned with priests, scholars, and artisans who further disseminated Hindu-Buddhist ideas.[56] This multi-layered interaction between traders, priests, and pilgrims created a dynamic network of cultural transmission, deeply influencing the sociopolitical and religious landscapes of Southeast Asia. Priests and monks, who travelled alongside traders, were instrumental in establishing religious institutions and disseminating religious teachings. Buddhist monks, in particular, were active in translating and transmitting religious texts, contributing to the spread of Buddhism throughout the region.[57] Pilgrims also played a significant role, as they travelled to and from sacred sites in India, bringing back religious relics, texts, and practices that further reinforced the presence of Hinduism and Buddhism in Southeast Asia.[58]

Early Evidence of Hindu-Buddhist Influence in Southeast Asia

The earliest evidence of Hindu-Buddhist influence in Southeast Asia dates back to the first few centuries AD, as seen in archaeological findings, inscriptions, and architectural remains. The discovery of Hindu-Buddhist temples and shrines, such as those at My Son in Vietnam, Borobudur in Java, and Prambanan in Java, provides tangible evidence of the spread and adaptation of these religions in the region. These sites reflect a blend of Indian and local artistic styles, indicating a complex process

[56] Hall, K.R. (2011). A History of Early SoutheastAsia: Maritime Trade and Societal Development, 100–1500. Rowman & Littlefield.

[57] Ray, H.C. (1994), Buddhist Saints in India: A Study in Buddhist Values and Orientations. Cambridge: Cambridge University Press.

[58] Coedès, G. (1968), The Indianized States of SoutheastAsia. Honolulu: University of Hawaii Press.

of cultural synthesis.[59] Inscriptions found in these sites, often written in Sanskrit or Pali, also attest to the presence of Indian religious concepts and the role of local rulers in promoting Hindu-Buddhist practices.[60] The widespread adoption of Indian iconography and religious motifs in Southeast Asian art and architecture further illustrates the deep influence of Hinduism and Buddhism on the region's cultural landscape.[61] This cultural transmission is evident in various aspects of Southeast Asian artistic expression, including monumental architecture, sculpture, and decorative arts. Temple complexes such as Angkor Wat in Cambodia and Prambanan in Indonesia embody these influences through their design and symbolism. Angkor Wat, initially dedicated to Vishnu, reflects Indian cosmological concepts such as Mount Meru, the mythical axis of the universe. The temple's intricate bas-reliefs depict scenes from the Hindu epics Ramayana and Mahabharata, merging Indian mythology with Khmer artistic traditions.[62,63] Similarly, Prambanan, dedicated to the Trimurti—Brahma, Vishnu, and Shiva—integrates Indian architectural principles with Javanese stylistic elements, emphasizing local adaptations of imported ideas.[64] In sculpture, the influence of Indian art is equally prominent. Statues of Hindu deities such as Vishnu and Shiva found across Southeast Asia closely resemble Indian prototypes, incorporating distinct iconographic elements like mudras (gestures) and asanas (postures). Buddhist sculptures, such as those depicting the Buddha and bodhisattvas, also reflect Indian stylistic conventions, particularly those from the Gupta and post-Gupta periods, while adapting to local cultural and aesthetic sensibilities. For example, the serene expressions and flowing

[59] Dupont, P. (1959), The Archaeology of Thailandand Cambodia. Oxford: Oxford University Press.

[60] Miksic, J.N. (2011), Old Javanese Gold: The Hunter Thompson Collection at the Yale University Art Gallery. New Haven, CT: Yale University Press.

[61] Ricklefs, M.C. (2001), A History of Modern Indonesia Since c.1200. 3rd edn. Stanford, CA: Stanford University Press.

[62] Coedès, G. (1968). The Indianized States of SoutheastAsia. University of Hawaii Press.

[63] Dhar, P.P. (2018). 'Monuments, Motifs, Myths: Architecture and its Transformations in Early Indiaand SoutheastAsia', in S. Saran (ed.), Cultural and Civilisational Links Between Indiaand SoutheastAsia: Historical and Contemporary Dimensions. Palgrave Macmillan, pp. 325–345.

[64] Miksic, J.N. & Goh, G.Y. (2017). Ancient SoutheastAsia. Routledge.

robes of Buddha statues in Borobudur reveal both Indian influence and local innovation.[65] Moreover, the integration of indigenous motifs such as the naga (serpent deity) into Hindu-Buddhist iconography highlights the blending of local traditions with Indian religious frameworks.[66] Indian-inspired motifs extended beyond monumental works to decorative arts, including textiles, pottery, and jewellery. Patterns such as the lotus flower, symbolizing purity and spiritual awakening in Hinduism and Buddhism, became widespread in Southeast Asia. The use of intricate floral and geometric patterns in temple carvings and household artifacts further reflects Indian influence, often reinterpreted to suit local aesthetics and cultural practices. For instance, temple reliefs in central Java not only depict scenes from Indian mythology but also incorporate representations of local flora, fauna, and daily life, creating a unique Southeast Asian artistic identity.[67] This integration of Indian iconography into Southeast Asian art and architecture was not a simple process of replication but one of adaptation and localization. Local artisans and architects synthesized Indian religious and cultural motifs with indigenous materials, techniques, and symbolic traditions, resulting in a distinctive Southeast Asian aesthetic. The blending of Indian concepts such as sacred geometry with local styles produced monumental works that are as much a reflection of regional creativity as they are of Indian influence. These artistic and architectural achievements underscore the depth of cultural exchanges facilitated by trade, migration, and religious missions, leaving an enduring legacy on Southeast Asia's cultural and religious landscapes.

The Establishment of Hindu-Buddhist States (200–500 AD)

The formation of early Hindu-Buddhist kingdoms such as Funan in present-day Cambodia and Vietnam and Tarumanagara in modern Indonesia illustrates the deep influence of Indian cultural, religious, and political systems on early Southeast Asia. Both kingdoms emerged as

[65] Mabbett, I.W. (1977). 'The "Indianization"of SoutheastAsia: Reflections on the Historical Sources', Journal of Southeast Asian Studies, 8(2), pp. 143–161.

[66] Higham, C. (2001). The Civilization of Angkor. Weidenfeld & Nicolson.

[67] Stark, M.T. (2006). 'From Funanto Angkor: Collapse and Regeneration in Ancient Cambodia', in G.M. Schwartz & J.J. Nichols (eds), After Collapse: The Regeneration of Complex Societies, University of Arizona Press, pp. 144–167.

centres of trade, governance, and cultural exchange, laying the foundations for the region's Indianized states. Funan, often regarded as one of the earliest Indianized states in Southeast Asia, thrived from the first to the sixth century CE. Its location in the Mekong Delta made it a key hub for maritime trade, connecting India, China, and the wider Southeast Asian region. Indian traders played a significant role in Funan's political and cultural development, introducing Hindu and Buddhist practices that were adopted by the ruling elite.[68] The Funanese kings integrated Indian concepts of governance, such as the devaraja (god-king) ideology, to legitimize their rule. This adoption is evidenced by inscriptions, such as those in Sanskrit, which record Funan's rulers performing Hindu rituals to assert their divine authority.[69] Additionally, Funan served as an intermediary in the transmission of Buddhism to China, with monks traveling through its territory to study at Indian centres of learning. The Chinese monk I Ching's travelogues highlight Funan's pivotal role in the spread of Mahayana Buddhism across the region.[70]

Tarumanagara, situated in western Java, emerged in the early fifth century CE as a Hindu kingdom that also displayed strong Indian influences. Its rulers adopted Hinduism as a state religion, as evidenced by the Tugu and Ciaruteun inscriptions, which are written in Sanskrit and Old Javanese and refer to King Purnawarman, a devotee of Vishnu. These inscriptions celebrate Purnawarman's construction of canals and irrigation systems, linking his accomplishments to divine authority.[71] The inscriptions' language and script demonstrate the kingdom's integration of Indian cultural and religious elements, while the emphasis on waterworks reflects the adaptation of Hindu ideals to local geographical and agricultural contexts.

Both Funan and Tarumanagara also reflected a fusion of Indian and local traditions in their governance, art, and religious practices. Funan's maritime orientation allowed for the accumulation of wealth through

[68] Coedès, G. (1968). The Indianized States of SoutheastAsia. University of Hawaii Press.

[69] Mabbett, I.W. (1977). 'The "Indianization"of SoutheastAsia: Reflections on the Historical Sources', Journal of Southeast Asian Studies, 8(2), pp. 143–161.

[70] Miksic, J.N. & Goh, G.Y. (2017). Ancient SoutheastAsia. Routledge.

[71] Hall, K.R. (2011). A History of Early SoutheastAsia: Maritime Trade and Societal Development, 100–1500. Rowman & Littlefield.

trade, and this prosperity funded temple-building projects that incorporated Indian architectural styles while using local materials and techniques.[72] Similarly, Tarumanagara's use of Hindu motifs in its inscriptions and art demonstrates how Indian religious traditions were localized to fit indigenous cultural frameworks. The early Hindu-Buddhist kingdoms of Funan and Tarumanagara illustrate the dynamic processes of cultural transmission, adaptation, and integration that characterized Southeast Asia's Indianization. These states not only adopted Indian religious and political systems but also transformed them, creating unique cultural syntheses that shaped the region's history.

Political and Religious Strategies of Early Rulers

The establishment and consolidation of Hindu-Buddhist states in Indonesia between 200 and 500 AD were underpinned by sophisticated political and religious strategies that early rulers employed to legitimize and strengthen their power. By adopting Hinduism and Buddhism, these rulers incorporated Indian political ideologies and religious practices into their governance, blending them with local traditions to create unique and enduring state systems.[73]

Early Indonesian rulers embraced the Indian concept of divine kingship, portraying themselves as earthly manifestations of deities such as Vishnu or Shiva. This devaraja (god-king) ideology was instrumental in legitimizing their authority. For instance, the Yupa inscriptions from the kingdom of Kutai in East Kalimantan commemorate King Mulawarman's performance of Vedic rituals and his patronage of Brahmanical priests. These inscriptions, written in Sanskrit and dated to the fourth century AD, highlight the early adoption of Indian religious concepts to reinforce royal authority.[74] Similarly, inscriptions from Tarumanagara in West Java, attributed to King Purnawarman, emphasize his dedication to Vishnu

[72] Stark, M.T. (2006). 'From Funanto Angkor: Collapse and Regeneration in Ancient Cambodia', in G.M. Schwartz & J.J. Nichols (eds.), After Collapse: The Regeneration of Complex Societies. University of Arizona Press, pp. 144–167.

[73] Kulke, H., & Rothermund, D. (2016). A History of India. Routledge.

[74] Sarkar, H.B. (1985). Trade and Trade Routes in Ancient India. Abhinav Publications.

through the construction of irrigation canals, aligning his rule with divine favour and societal prosperity.[75]

Maritime states like Funan and Srivijaya adapted Indian administrative frameworks to effectively organize their territories and manage extensive trade networks. The use of Sanskrit as a courtly and administrative language enabled rulers to project their power and connect with the broader Indianized world.[76] The control of interregional trade routes allowed these rulers to amass wealth, which they redistributed through monumental temple-building projects. This strategy not only consolidated their power but also linked their rule to divine favour, as seen in the construction of religious structures such as Borobudur and Prambanan.[77]

The integration of Hindu-Buddhist practices into statecraft played a crucial role in strengthening the political authority of these early rulers. Religious rituals, temple construction, and patronage of the priestly class served as tools for consolidating power. The Prambanan temple complex, dedicated to the Hindu Trimurti (Brahma, Vishnu, Shiva), symbolized the ruler's divine connection and reinforced their role as protector and sustainer of cosmic order (dharma).[78] Similarly, the Borobudur monument, constructed in Central Java, highlights Mahayana Buddhist ideals. Its design as a massive mandala symbolizing the path to enlightenment reflects the ruler's alignment with Buddhist principles, presenting the king as both a moral leader and a patron of spiritual advancement.[79] Mahayana Buddhism also played a central role in the political strategies of states like Srivijaya. Mahayana texts emphasized the ruler's duty to be a cakravartin (universal ruler), a concept embraced by Srivijayan kings who positioned themselves as patrons of the Buddhist world. The Nalanda inscription records King Balaputra's endowment of a Buddhist monastery in India, reflecting Srivijaya's dual strategy of religious patronage and diplomatic engagement.[80] Rulers also employed religious syncretism to

[75] Wolters, O.W. (1999). History, Culture, and Region in Southeast Asian Perspectives. Cornell University Southeast Asia Program Publications.

[76] Schmidt, B. (2010). Entangled Histories: Regionalism, Trade, and Identity in Early SoutheastAsia. National University of Singapore Press.

[77] Miksic, J.N., & Goh, G.Y. (2017). Ancient SoutheastAsia. Routledge.

[78] Higham, C. (2001). The Civilization of Angkor. Weidenfeld & Nicolson.

[79] Hall, K.R. (2011). A History of Early SoutheastAsia: Maritime Trade and Societal Development, 100–1500. Rowman & Littlefield.

[80] Sarkar, H.B. (1985). Trade and Trade Routes in Ancient India. Abhinav Publications.

appeal to diverse populations, blending Hindu and Buddhist elements with local animistic and ancestor worship practices. This adaptability is evident in the integration of indigenous motifs, such as the naga (serpent deities), into Hindu-Buddhist iconography. Temples like Candi Sukuh in Java combine Hindu cosmological symbolism with local fertility rituals, exemplifying this fusion.[81] The political and religious strategies employed by early rulers of Hindu-Buddhist states in Indonesia reflect their ingenuity in adapting Indian influences to local contexts. These strategies not only legitimized their rule but also laid the foundation for the enduring influence of Hinduism and Buddhism in Indonesia's cultural and political history.

Integration of Hindu-Buddhist Concepts into Governance and Society

The integration of Hindu-Buddhist concepts into governance and society in Indonesia from 200 to 500 AD marked a transformative period in its political, cultural, and social history. This era saw the establishment of Indianized states that adapted Hindu-Buddhist ideologies to local contexts, blending imported ideas with Indigenous traditions to create unique systems of governance and cultural expression. Hindu-Buddhist ideas significantly influenced the structure of early Indonesian states, particularly through the concept of divine kingship. The adoption of the devaraja (god-king) ideology allowed rulers to position themselves as earthly representatives of divine power. In kingdoms such as Tarumanagara and Kutai, this concept legitimized royal authority by linking it to Hindu deities like Vishnu and Shiva.[82] Inscriptions, such as the Yupa inscriptions of Kutai, demonstrate how rulers used Sanskrit to proclaim their piety and divine mandate. These inscriptions highlight King Mulawarman's performance of Vedic sacrifices, aligning his rule with Brahmanical ideals of governance.[83]

[81] Manguin, P.-Y., Mani, A., & Wade, G. (Eds.). (2011). Early Interactions Between South and SoutheastAsia: Reflections on Cross-Cultural Exchange. ISEAS–Yusof Ishak Institute.

[82] Kulke, H., & Rothermund, D. (2016). A History of India. Routledge.

[83] Coedès, G. (1968). The Indianized States of SoutheastAsia. University of Hawaii Press.

Buddhism also played a vital role in governance, particularly in maritime states like Srivijaya, which embraced Mahayana Buddhist principles. Mahayana texts emphasized the ideal of the cakravartin (universal ruler), a figure responsible for ensuring the welfare of the realm through Buddhist principles of compassion and justice. Srivijayan rulers actively promoted Buddhism through patronage of monasteries and scholars, fostering intellectual and cultural ties with Indian centers of learning such as Nalanda. The Nalanda inscription, which records King Balaputra's endowment of a monastery in India, underscores the integration of Buddhist values into state governance.[84] Hindu-Buddhist concepts were also reflected in societal organization and legal systems. The adoption of Indian dharmaśāstra (law codes) influenced local practices, particularly in the administration of justice and social hierarchies. For example, the concept of varna (social classes) was adapted to fit indigenous systems of stratification. However, these Indian-derived ideas were not imposed wholesale but were selectively incorporated into existing structures, resulting in unique hybrid systems that resonated with local populations.[85]

The integration of Hindu-Buddhist concepts extended to monumental architecture and public works, which served both political and religious purposes. Temples such as Prambanan and Borobudur functioned as centres of worship and symbols of state power. Prambanan, dedicated to the Hindu Trimurti, embodies the integration of Indian cosmological ideas into architectural form, with its towering spires representing Mount Meru, the axis of the universe.[86] Similarly, Borobudur, designed as a massive mandala, illustrates the centrality of Buddhist ideals in society and governance, promoting the ruler as both a spiritual guide and a worldly protector.[87]

The adaptation of Hindu-Buddhist concepts to local beliefs and practices was crucial to their acceptance. Indigenous animistic traditions, such as reverence for naga (serpent deities) and ancestor worship, were

[84] Miksic, J.N., & Goh, G.Y. (2017). Ancient SoutheastAsia. Routledge.

[85] Hall, K.R. (2011). A History of Early SoutheastAsia: Maritime Trade and Societal Development, 100–1500. Rowman & Littlefield.

[86] Higham, C. (2001). The Civilization of Angkor. Weidenfeld & Nicolson.

[87] Stark, M.T. (2006). 'From Funanto Angkor: Collapse and Regeneration in Ancient Cambodia', in G.M. Schwartz & J.J. Nichols (eds.), After Collapse: The Regeneration of Complex Societies. University of Arizona Press, pp. 144–167.

seamlessly integrated into Hindu-Buddhist iconography and rituals. For instance, the naga motif is frequently depicted in temple carvings, symbolizing the connection between the sacred and the earthly.[88] Additionally, localized Hindu rituals often incorporated elements of fertility and agricultural cycles, aligning them with the spiritual and material concerns of agrarian communities. This integration of Hindu-Buddhist concepts into governance and society fostered political stability and cultural flourishing, enabling the emergence of sophisticated state systems. By blending Indian influences with Indigenous traditions, early Indonesian rulers established a legacy that profoundly shaped the region's historical trajectory.

The Rise of Srivijaya and the Spread of Mahayana Buddhism (Seventh–Thirteenth Century)

Srivijaya's Role as a Major Centre of Buddhist Learning

The Srivijaya Empire, cantered in present-day Sumatra, Indonesia, emerged as a dominant maritime and cultural power between the seventh and thirteenth centuries. Its strategic position along the Strait of Malacca allowed it to control key trade routes linking India, China, and Southeast Asia, while also fostering the exchange of goods, ideas, and religious practices. Central to Srivijaya's legacy was its role as a major center of Mahayana Buddhist learning and pilgrimage, a status that significantly shaped the religious and cultural dynamics of the region.

Srivijaya's influence as a Buddhist center is evidenced by its patronage of religious institutions and scholars. Mahayana Buddhism, which emphasizes the ideals of universal compassion and the Bodhisattva path, flourished under Srivijayan rulers. Inscriptions such as those found in Kedukan Bukit and Talang Tuwo (seventh century) highlight the rulers' dedication to Buddhist principles, describing their endowments to monasteries and other religious foundations.[89] Srivijayan kings positioned themselves as patrons of Buddhism, thereby reinforcing their legitimacy as rulers and aligning their authority with divine sanction.

[88] Manguin, P.-Y., Mani, A., & Wade, G. (Eds.). (2011). Early Interactions Between South and SoutheastAsia: Reflections on Cross-Cultural Exchange. ISEAS–Yusof Ishak Institute.

[89] Coedès, G. (1968). The Indianized States of SoutheastAsia. University of Hawaii Press.

The Nalanda inscription (ninth century) provides further evidence of Srivijaya's prominence as a center for Buddhist learning. It records that King Balaputra, a Srivijayan monarch, endowed a monastery at Nalanda in India, one of the most renowned Buddhist educational centres of the time. This act not only underscores the empire's strong ties to Indian Buddhism but also reflects Srivijaya's active engagement in transregional religious and intellectual networks.[90] By supporting institutions such as Nalanda, Srivijaya positioned itself as a key intermediary in the transmission of Buddhist knowledge between India and the broader Southeast Asian world.

Srivijaya's capital city, often identified with the archaeological site of Palembang, housed numerous Buddhist monasteries and served as a major hub for pilgrims traveling to and from India. Chinese records, such as the accounts of the monk Yijing[91] emphasize the role of Srivijaya as a vital stopover for Chinese pilgrims journeying to Indian monasteries. Yijing spent several years in Srivijaya, studying Sanskrit and Buddhist texts, and he praised the city for its rigorous training in Buddhist philosophy and its hospitality to travellers.[92] His writings attest to Srivijaya's reputation as a center of religious learning and its ability to attract scholars and pilgrims from across Asia.

Architectural and artistic remains further highlight Srivijaya's Buddhist heritage. Stupas, statues, and other artifacts discovered at sites such as Muara Jambi in Sumatra demonstrate the blending of Indian Buddhist iconography with local artistic traditions. These artifacts often depict Bodhisattvas and other Mahayana Buddhist figures, reflecting the depth of Buddhist devotion and the integration of imported religious ideas into local contexts.[93] In addition to its religious contributions, Srivijaya's role as a Buddhist center had significant political and economic dimensions. By promoting itself as a protector and patron of Buddhism, the empire enhanced its prestige and influence in regional and international diplomacy. Its ability to provide safe passage and resources for pilgrims and traders bolstered its economic prosperity and strengthened its status as

[90] Miksic, J.N., & Goh, G.Y. (2017). Ancient SoutheastAsia. Routledge.

[91] Yijing (1896). A Record of the Buddhist Religion as Practised in India and the Malay Archipelago (A.D. 671–695), translated by J. Takakusu. Oxford: Clarendon Press.

[92] Hall, K.R. (2011). A History of Early SoutheastAsia: Maritime Trade and Societal Development, 100–1500. Rowman & Littlefield.

[93] Higham, C. (2001). The Civilization of Angkor. Weidenfeld & Nicolson.

a maritime power. The intertwining of religion and commerce not only ensured Srivijaya's wealth but also solidified its place as a cultural and spiritual hub in the Buddhist world.[94] The decline of Srivijaya in the thirteenth century, partly due to the rise of rival powers such as the Chola dynasty in South India and the Majapahit Empire in Java, did not erase its impact on the region's religious and cultural history. The legacy of Srivijaya's Buddhist institutions and its role in the dissemination of Mahayana Buddhism continued to influence Southeast Asia long after its fall.

Cultural and Religious Contributions of Srivijaya

Srivijaya (seventh–thirteenth century) played a pivotal role in shaping Indonesia's cultural and religious landscape, fostering its economic development. As a prominent maritime empire based in Palembang, Srivijaya controlled critical trade routes in the Strait of Malacca, linking India, China, and Southeast Asia. This strategic position not only advanced economic prosperity but also enabled significant cultural and religious contributions.[95] Culturally, Srivijaya was a melting pot of diverse influences due to its active participation in international trade. The empire facilitated the exchange of knowledge, art, and traditions between India and China, contributing to the flourishing of Indonesian society. For example, the construction of monumental Buddhist structures such as Borobudur, although built later during the Shailendra dynasty associated with Srivijaya, showcases the blending of Indian architectural techniques with local artistry. These architectural achievements attracted pilgrims and promoted cultural tourism, which in turn boosted regional economies. Srivijaya's wealth from maritime trade directly financed these projects, demonstrating how cultural advancements were intertwined with economic growth.[96] Srivijaya's dominance over maritime trade directly funded its cultural d religious advancements, revealing the interdependence of economic growth and cultural development during the empire's peak. Srivijaya's strategic location in the Strait of Malacca and Sunda Strait enabled it to control critical trade routes between India and

[94] Kulke, H., & Rothermund, D. (2016). A History of India. Routledge.

[95] Coedès, George. The Indianized States of SoutheastAsia. University of Hawaii Press, 1968.

[96] Hall, Kenneth R. Maritime Trade and State Development in Early SoutheastAsia. University of Hawaii Press, 1985.

China. The empire earned substantial revenue by levying taxes and tolls on passing ships and facilitating the exchange of luxury goods like spices, silk, and ceramics.[97] These revenues formed the foundation of the empire's wealth and enabled large-scale cultural investments. For instance, Srivijaya allocated significant resources to building and maintaining Buddhist monasteries and educational centres, which became influential across Southeast Asia. The Chinese pilgrim Yijing, who stayed in Srivijaya in 671 AD, described Palembang as a vibrant centre of Buddhist learning, hosting over a thousand monks and serving as a hub for the study and translation of religious texts.[98] Such religious and scholarly endeavours required significant funding, which Srivijaya's trade-based economy provided. Moreover, monumental structures such as Borobudur, while directly attributed to the Shailendra dynasty, were influenced by the economic and cultural prosperity fostered under Srivijaya. It has been observed that the close ties between Srivijaya and the Shailendra rulers suggest that Srivijaya's economic power indirectly supported these projects, further intertwining economic and cultural achievements.[99] The funding of these projects also had a ripple effect on the local economy. Artisans, labourers, and traders benefited from the demand for materials, construction expertise, and religious artifacts. This economic activity not only strengthened local industries but also attracted pilgrims and scholars to Srivijaya, increasing commerce and reinforcing its position as a cultural and religious hub.[100] Thus, Srivijaya's wealth from maritime trade was a critical driver of its cultural advancements, creating a virtuous cycle in which economic prosperity fuelled cultural projects, which in turn enhanced its prestige and attracted more trade and pilgrim traffic. This dynamic showcases the interconnected nature of economic and cultural growth in the Srivijaya empire.

Religiously, Srivijaya was a major centre for Mahayana Buddhism. It was documented in 671 AD that Palembang hosted over a thousand

[97] Hall, Kenneth R. Maritime Trade and State Development in Early SoutheastAsia. University of Hawaii Press, 1985.

[98] Yijing. A Record of Buddhist Practices Sent Home from the Southern Sea. Translated by Takakusu J., Clarendon Press, 1896.

[99] Coedès, George. The Indianized States of SoutheastAsia. University of Hawaii Press, 1968.

[100] Miksic, John N. Southeast Asian Ceramics: New Light on Old Pottery. Southeast Asian Ceramic Society, 2009.

Buddhist monks and was a hub for religious scholarship.[101] Monastic education flourished as texts and teachings from India were disseminated through Srivijaya to other parts of Southeast Asia. This role as a centre of Buddhist learning not only elevated Srivijaya's cultural standing but also attracted scholars and pilgrims, increasing economic activity in the form of trade and pilgrimage.[102] The empire's rulers actively supported Buddhist practices, commissioning religious texts and endowing temples that solidified Srivijaya's status as a spiritual and intellectual hub.[103] The economic implications of these cultural and religious contributions were profound. By controlling trade routes, Srivijaya generated immense wealth, which was reinvested in cultural and religious projects. The influx of pilgrims and scholars further stimulated the local economy, creating demand for services, goods, and infrastructure. Srivijaya's integration of cultural, religious, and economic priorities demonstrates how the empire's contributions laid a foundation for Indonesia's historical development.

The Influence of Srivijaya on Neighbouring Regions

Srivijaya (seventh–thirteenth century) significantly influenced neighbouring regions through its cultural and religious contributions, which in turn impacted Indonesia's economic development. As a powerful maritime empire cantered in Palembang, Srivijaya's strategic position allowed it to exert cultural, economic, and religious influence across Southeast Asia. Culturally, Srivijaya promoted Old Malay as the lingua franca across the Malay Archipelago, facilitating trade and communication. The use of Old Malay in administrative, commercial, and religious contexts was instrumental in uniting the diverse ethnic groups within and beyond Srivijaya's realm. This language standardization helped merchants, officials, and religious scholars communicate effectively, promoting cross-cultural exchange and enabling the smooth functioning of trade networks between India, China, and the Middle East. Old Malay inscriptions, such as the Kedukan Bukit inscription (683 AD), reflect Srivijaya's role in

[101] Yijing. A Record of Buddhist Practices Sent Home from the Southern Sea. Translated by Takakusu J., Clarendon Press, 1896.

[102] Yijing. A Record of Buddhist Practices Sent Home from the Southern Sea. Translated by Takakusu J., Clarendon Press, 1896.

[103] Miksic, John N. Southeast Asian Ceramics: New Light on Old Pottery. Southeast Asian Ceramic Society, 2009.

formalizing this linguistic system, further enhancing regional cohesion.[104] By establishing a shared linguistic framework, Srivijaya laid the foundation for a thriving maritime economy and cultural network across the region. Religiously, Srivijaya emerged as a major centre for Mahayana Buddhism. The empire was renowned for hosting scholars and pilgrims, particularly from China and India, who sought spiritual and academic enrichment. Chinese pilgrim Yijing, who visited Srivijaya in the late seventh century, noted the presence of over a thousand monks engaged in Buddhist studies and the meticulous translations of sacred texts.[105] These religious activities, supported by royal patronage, elevated Srivijaya's status as a spiritual hub and a crucial link in the spread of Buddhism across Southeast Asia. The rulers' commissioning of Buddhist texts and temple construction attracted pilgrims and scholars, generating economic benefits through increased trade and cultural tourism.[106] These cultural and religious contributions fostered regional cohesion and economic prosperity. Srivijaya's strategic control of trade routes, combined with its cultural and religious influence, ensured a steady influx of wealth, which was reinvested in infrastructure, religious institutions, and the arts. The integration of commerce, culture, and spirituality created a dynamic economy that left an enduring legacy in Indonesia's historical development.

The Majapahit Kingdom and Its Hindu-Buddhist Legacy (Thirteenth–Fifteenth Century)

Origins and Expansion of Majapahit

The Majapahit Kingdom (thirteenth–fifteenth century) was a significant Hindu-Buddhist empire in Southeast Asia, influencing regional culture, religion, and economic systems. Founded in 1293 by Raden Wijaya after defeating the Mongol forces of Kublai Khan, the kingdom emerged as a dominant power in maritime Southeast Asia. It reached its peak under the reign of Hayam Wuruk (1350–1389) and his prime minister, Gajah

[104] Miksic, J. N., and Yian, C. (2016). Ancient SoutheastAsia. Routledge.

[105] Takakusu, J. (1896). A Record of the Buddhist Religion as Practised in India and the Malay Archipelago (A.D. 671–695) by I-Tsing. Clarendon Press.

[106] Hall, K. R. (2011). A History of Early SoutheastAsia: Maritime Trade and Societal Development, 100–1500. Rowman & Littlefield.

Mada, whose policies and military campaigns expanded the empire's influence across the Indonesian archipelago and beyond.[107] Hayam Wuruk, often referred to as Rajasanagara, presided over a period of cultural and economic prosperity. Under his leadership, Majapahit consolidated its control over key trade routes and extended its influence to areas such as Sumatra, Borneo, Sulawesi, and even as far as the Malay Peninsula and the Philippines.[108] Gajah Mada, Majapahit's renowned prime minister, was pivotal in this expansion. He articulated his famous "Sumpah Palapa" oath, pledging to unify the Nusantara (the Indonesian archipelago) under Majapahit rule. Through both diplomatic means and military campaigns, he successfully subdued rival polities and established a vast network of tributary states, which paid homage and provided resources to the empire.[109] The 1365 Nagarakretagama, a Javanese court poem, details the extensive territorial reach of Majapahit during this era, listing numerous vassal states under its influence, reflecting Gajah Mada's ambition and effectiveness in realizing a unified Nusantara.[110] This era of expansion not only solidified Majapahit's political dominance but also enhanced its economic standing as it controlled critical maritime trade routes. By commanding these strategic passages, Majapahit became a central player in the spice trade and other lucrative exchanges between India, China, and the Middle East. The economic prosperity fuelled cultural and artistic advancements, marking this period as the golden age of Majapahit.[111]

The cultural contributions of Majapahit were profound. The promotion of Javanese culture during its expansion led to the widespread dissemination of its art, literature, and architecture. Traditional performing arts, such as wayang kulit (shadow puppetry), became integral to Javanese and later Balinese cultural identity. The Nagarakretagama, a Javanese epic poem written in 1365, extolled the glory of Majapahit and described its

[107] Hall, K. R. (2011). A History of Early SoutheastAsia: Maritime Trade and Societal Development, 100–1500. Rowman & Littlefield.

[108] Hall, K. R. (2011). A History of Early SoutheastAsia: Maritime Trade and Societal Development, 100–1500. Rowman & Littlefield.

[109] Miksic, J. N., and Yian, C. (2016). Ancient SoutheastAsia. Routledge.

[110] Robson, S. O. (1995). Nagarakretagama (Desawarnana). KITLV Press.

[111] Reid, A. (1988). SoutheastAsia in the Age of Commerce, 1450–1680: The Lands Below the Winds. Yale University Press.

vast tributary network, showcasing its cultural hegemony.[112] Architectural innovations, including the use of red brick in temple construction, were significant during this era. Temples such as Trowulan and Tikus serve as examples of the kingdom's architectural ingenuity, which influenced later Balinese religious structures.[113] Religiously, Majapahit played a central role in sustaining and disseminating Hindu-Buddhist traditions throughout Southeast Asia. The kingdom's rulers were patrons of Hindu and Buddhist institutions, commissioning temples and supporting the production of religious texts. For example, the Candi Sukuh and Candi Cetho temples reflect the syncretism of Hindu-Buddhist beliefs, blending religious symbolism with Javanese mysticism. This legacy influenced Balinese Hinduism, which remains a vibrant tradition today. The fall of Majapahit in the late fifteenth century saw an exodus of its intellectual and spiritual elites to Bali, preserving the kingdom's cultural and religious practices in the region.[114]

The economic impact of Majapahit's cultural and religious contributions was substantial. The promotion of Old Javanese as a lingua franca facilitated trade and administration across the diverse regions under Majapahit's influence. Control over key maritime trade routes allowed Majapahit to dominate the spice trade, generating wealth that was reinvested into religious and cultural projects. This economic prosperity created a legacy, establishing Majapahit as a critical foundation for Indonesia's historical development.[115]

Syncretism of Hinduism and Buddhism in Majapahit

The Majapahit Kingdom, which thrived from the thirteenth to the fifteenth century in East Java, Indonesia, is a testament to the syncretic fusion of Hinduism and Buddhism. This cultural and religious amalgamation left a profound impact on the region's traditions and practices, visible in literature, architecture, and governance. One of the clearest examples

[112] Robson, S. O. (1995). Nagarakretagama (Desawarnana). KITLV Press.

[113] Miksic, J. N., and Yian, C. (2016). Ancient SoutheastAsia. Routledge.

[114] Geertz, C. (1980). Negara: The Theatre State in Nineteenth-Century Bali. Princeton University Press.

[115] Reid, A. (1988). SoutheastAsia in the Age of Commerce, 1450–1680: The Lands Below the Winds. Yale University Press.

of this syncretism is found in the Kakawin Sutasoma, a fourteenth-century epic poem by Mpu Tantular. The work introduced the concept of "Bhinneka Tunggal Ika," translated as "Unity in Diversity," which underscores the harmonious coexistence of Hindu and Buddhist beliefs.[116] This phrase has transcended its historical context to become Indonesia's national motto, symbolizing the legacy of religious tolerance fostered during the Majapahit era. Architectural evidence further illustrates this religious synthesis. Temples such as Candi Jawi and Candi Jago feature an intentional blending of Hindu and Buddhist elements. Candi Jawi, for instance, is a Shivaite sanctuary crowned with a Buddhist ornament, symbolizing the integration of these two religious traditions.[117] Similarly, the reliefs at Candi Jago depict both Hindu and Buddhist iconography, demonstrating a deliberate fusion that reflects the religious and cultural ethos of the time. The rulers of Majapahit embraced a policy of inclusivity through the Shiva-Buddha doctrine, which highlighted the equivalence of the Hindu god Shiva and the Buddha. This approach not only strengthened internal cohesion but also reinforced the rulers' legitimacy over their diverse subjects. King Kertarajasa Jayawardhana, the founder of Majapahit, exemplified this syncretic tradition by being posthumously depicted as Harihara, a deity combining aspects of Shiva and Vishnu.[118] The syncretism of Hinduism and Buddhism during Majapahit contributed significantly to the cultural richness of the era. This blending of religious traditions fostered tolerance and pluralism, elements that have remained integral to Indonesian identity throughout its history.[119] (Al Makin 2016).

[116] Pratiwi, Y., Numan, I., & Idham, N. C. (2024). "The Synchronization of HinduBuddhist Spatial and Architecture in Traditional Javanese Mosques." Journal of Architectural Research and Design Studies, 8(2), 45–60.

[117] Pratiwi, Y., Numan, I., & Idham, N. C. (2024). "The Synchronization of HinduBuddhist Spatial and Architecture in Traditional Javanese Mosques." Journal of Architectural Research and Design Studies, 8(2), 45–60.

[118] Acri, A. (2015). Revisiting the Cult of Śiva-Buddha in Javaand Bali. Journal of Southeast Asian Studies, 46(1), 60–79.

[119] Al Makin. (2016). Unearthing Nusantara's Concept of Religious Pluralism: Harmonization and Syncretism in Hindu-Buddhist and Islamic Classical Texts. Al-Jāmi'ah: Journal of Islamic Studies, 54(1), 1–30.

Majapahit's Role in Southeast Asian Politics and Culture

The Majapahit Kingdom (circa 1293–1500 AD) significantly influenced Southeast Asian politics and culture through its extensive trade networks, diplomatic relations, and cultural dissemination. Majapahit's strategic location enabled it to become a central hub in regional trade, facilitating economic and cultural exchanges across the archipelago and beyond. Its ports attracted merchants from various regions, fostering a cosmopolitan environment that encouraged the blending of diverse cultural and religious traditions.[120]

Diplomatically, Majapahit engaged with contemporary kingdoms across Southeast Asia, including those in present-day Malaysia, Thailand, and the Philippines. These interactions were characterized by both alliances and conflicts, as Majapahit sought to expand its influence and control over vital trade routes. The kingdom's political dynamics were complex, involving negotiations and power struggles with neighbouring states.[121] Culturally, Majapahit played a pivotal role in the dissemination of art, literature, and religious practices throughout the region. The Panji stories, originating from Java during the Majapahit period, became popular across Southeast Asia, influencing local literatures and performing arts in countries like Thailand, Cambodia, and Malaysia. These narratives not only entertained but also conveyed social and moral values, reflecting the cultural milieu of the time.[122] Furthermore, Majapahit's architectural styles and urban planning concepts left a lasting legacy, particularly evident in the traditional architecture of Bali. The synchronization of Hindu-Buddhist spatial and architectural elements in Majapahit structures influenced the design of religious and communal buildings in subsequent

[120] Munandar, A. A. (2020). "Majapahit and the Contemporary Kingdoms: Interactions and Views." Berkala Arkeologi, 40(2), 145–160. (https://ejournal.brin.go.id).

[121] Munandar, A. A. (2020). "Majapahit and the Contemporary Kingdoms: Interactions and Views." Berkala Arkeologi, 40(2), 145–160. (https://ejournal.brin.go.id).

[122] Vickers, A. (2014). "Majapahit and Panji Stories." In C. Kubuontubuh & P. Carey (Eds.), Majapahit: Inspiration for the World (pp. 47–66). Jakarta: Arsari. (https://www.academia.edu).

Southeast Asian societies.[123] In summary, Majapahit's role in Southeast Asian politics and culture was multifaceted, encompassing economic dominance, diplomatic engagements, and cultural contributions that have had a lasting impact on the region's historical trajectory.

Artistic and Architectural Achievements of Majapahit

The Majapahit Kingdom (thirteenth–fifteenth century) is renowned for its significant artistic and architectural achievements, which have left a lasting impact on Indonesian culture. Majapahit architecture is characterized by the extensive use of red brick, a departure from the stone materials favoured in earlier periods. This innovation is evident in structures such as the Bajang Ratu and Wringin Lawang gates in Trowulan, which showcase the kingdom's mastery in brick construction. The Bajang Ratu gate, for instance, is an elegant red brick paduraksa (roofed gate) adorned with intricate bas-reliefs depicting stories from Javanese mythology.[124] The temple architecture of Majapahit follows the East Javanese style, characterized by slender and tall structures with multi-tiered roofs that create an illusion of greater height. Temples such as Candi Jabung and Candi Pari exemplify this style, with their towering structures and intricate carvings. The use of red brick in these temples not only demonstrates the architectural innovation of the Majapahit period but also reflects the kingdom's adaptation to local materials and conditions.[125] The Majapahit era also witnessed a flourishing of the arts, particularly in stone sculpture. Majapahit stone sculptures from the fourteenth to fifteenth centuries are noted for their intricate details and symbolic significance. These sculptures often depict deities from the Hindu-Buddhist pantheon, reflecting the syncretic religious landscape of the period. The artisanry of these

[123] Setiawan, B. (2017). "Ancient Architectural Influence Between Baliand Majapahit: Drawing Upon the Past for the Future." In M. Santoso & I. Budi (Eds.), Proceedings of the International Conference on Southeast Asian Studies (pp. 213–225). Singapore: Springer. (link.springer.com).

[124] Wijaya, A. A., Widiastuti, & Mudra, I. K. (2018). "Application of Majapahit Architectural Elements in the Design of the Prapanca Secondary Market in Mojokerto, Jawa Timur." Journal of A Sustainable Global South, 2(2), 11–20.

[125] Setiawan, B. (2017). "Ancient Architectural Influence Between Baliand Majapahit: Drawing Upon the Past for the Future." In M. Santoso & I. Budi (Eds.), Proceedings of the International Conference on Southeast Asian Studies (pp. 213–225). Singapore: Springer.

sculptures indicates an elevated level of artistic development and a deep understanding of religious iconography.[126]

The artistic and architectural innovations of the Majapahit Kingdom have had a profound influence on subsequent Indonesian art and architecture. The use of red brick and the development of specific architectural forms, such as the paduraksa gate, have been incorporated into later Javanese and Balinese architecture. The aesthetic principles established during the Majapahit era continue to inspire contemporary Indonesian art and architecture, underscoring the enduring legacy of this remarkable period in Indonesia's history.[127,128]

Religious and Cultural Syncretism in Southeast Asia

Blending of Indigenous and Indian Religious Traditions

The period between 200 and 1500 AD in Southeast Asia was marked by significant religious and cultural syncretism, particularly the blending of indigenous traditions with Indian Hindu-Buddhist influences. This fusion is evident in various aspects of Southeast Asian societies, including religious practices, art, and architecture. One prominent example is the worship of the deity Hari-Hara, a syncretic figure combining aspects of the Hindu gods Vishnu (Hari) and Shiva (Hara). This amalgamation symbolized the integration of different religious sects and was prevalent in regions like the Khmer Empire. Temples such as Angkor Wat and the Bayon reflect this syncretism through their architectural designs and

[126] Pullen, L. (2021). "Majapahit: Stone Sculpture from the Fourteenth to the Fifteenth Century." In Patterned Splendour: Textiles Presented on Javanese Metal and Stone Sculptures; Eighth to Fifteenth Century (pp. 223–250). Singapore: ISEAS Publishing.

[127] Setiawan, B. (2017). "Ancient Architectural Influence Between Baliand Majapahit: Drawing Upon the Past for the Future." In M. Santoso & I. Budi (Eds.), Proceedings of the International Conference on Southeast Asian Studies (pp. 213–225). Singapore: Springer.

[128] Wijaya, A. A., Widiastuti, & Mudra, I. K. (2018). "Application of Majapahit Architectural Elements in the Design of the Prapanca Secondary Market in Mojokerto, Jawa Timur." Journal of A Sustainable Global South, 2(2), 11–20.

iconography, serving both religious and political purposes by promoting unity and legitimizing royal authority.[129]

In the Brahmaputra Valley, the assimilation of tribal and Brahmanical practices led to unique localized forms of worship. Indigenous deities were often equated with Hindu gods, creating a syncretic pantheon recognized by local populations. This melding allowed for a flexible spiritual landscape, where elements of both belief systems coexisted.[130] Similarly, the interplay between Hindu and animistic traditions in Southeast Asia gave rise to syncretic religious practices. Ceremonial life often integrated elements from both systems, with rituals incorporating Hindu and animistic symbols, chants, and offerings. Temples and shrines frequently housed altars dedicated to both Hindu gods and indigenous spirits, reflecting a harmonious coexistence of beliefs.[131] This syncretism extended beyond religious practices to art, literature, and governance. The adoption and adaptation of Indian cultural elements were facilitated by trade and the movement of peoples, leading to a unique cultural mosaic in Southeast Asia. Cultural exchanges brought Hindu-Buddhist iconography, temple architecture, and storytelling traditions to the region, where they were localized and interwoven with indigenous customs.[132] The blending of indigenous and Indian religious traditions in Southeast Asia resulted in a rich tapestry of syncretic practices. This fusion not only enriched the cultural and religious landscape of the region but also played a crucial role in the formation of spiritual and social models that have persisted through the centuries.

[129] Patowary, K. N. (2023). "Hari-Hara: Tradition of Syncretism in SoutheastAsia Special Reference." ShodhKosh: Journal of Visual and Performing Arts, 4(1). Available at: https://granthaalayahpublication.org.

[130] Patowary, K. N. (2023). "Hari-Hara: Tradition of Syncretism in SoutheastAsia Special Reference." ShodhKosh: Journal of Visual and Performing Arts, 4(1). Available at: https://granthaalayahpublication.org.

[131] "Syncretism in South and SoutheastAsia: Adoption and Adaptation." (2023). Asia Research News. Available at: https://www.asiaresearchnews.com.

[132] "Syncretism in South and SoutheastAsia: Adoption and Adaptation." (2023). Asia Research News. Available at: https://www.asiaresearchnews.com.

Development of Localized Forms of Hinduism and Buddhism

The spread of Hinduism and Buddhism from the Indian subcontinent to Southeast Asia between 200 and 1500 AD led to the development of localized forms of these religions, deeply influencing the region's cultural and religious landscapes. Hinduism was introduced through trade and cultural exchanges, leading to its integration with Indigenous beliefs. In Bali, for example, Hinduism developed uniquely, blending traditional Balinese customs with Hindu practices, resulting in a vibrant and enduring Hindu culture distinct from its Indian origins.[133] Similarly, in mainland Southeast Asia, Hinduism coexisted with Buddhism, influencing local art, architecture, and social structures. The Khmer Empire initially embraced Hinduism, as evidenced by the construction of temples like Angkor Wat, which was dedicated to the Hindu god Vishnu.[134] Buddhism entered Southeast Asia via maritime trade routes, leading to the establishment of Theravada Buddhism as the dominant form in countries like Thailand, Burma, and Laos. This form of Buddhism was deeply influenced by local traditions, resulting in unique practices and interpretations. For example, the Thai Buddhist tradition incorporates elements of animism, reflecting the region's indigenous beliefs.[135] In contrast, Mahayana Buddhism spread to maritime Southeast Asia, including regions like Vietnam and Indonesia, through interactions with Chinese traders and monks. This form of Buddhism integrated with local customs, leading to distinct practices and artistic expressions.[136] The interaction between Hinduism, Buddhism, and Indigenous beliefs led to syncretic practices, where elements from different traditions were combined. For instance, many Buddhist rituals, such as the sprinkling of holy water and the tying of a white string on a person's wrist, are influenced by Hindu

[133] Ardhana, I. K. (2019) 'Buddhismin SoutheastAsia: A Study of Philosophy, Religion and a Model of a Multicultural Society', Journal of Multidisciplinary Studies, 6(1), pp. 1–10. Available at: https://crimsonpublishers.com/nrs/pdf/NRS.000582.pdf.

[134] Britannica (2024) 'Hinduism- SoutheastAsia, Pacific, Religion', Encyclopedia Britannica. Available at: https://www.britannica.com/topic/Hinduism/The-spread-of-Hinduism-in-Southeast-Asia-and-the-Pacific.

[135] Britannica (2024) 'Buddhismin SoutheastAsia', Encyclopedia Britannica. Available at: https://www.britannica.com/topic/Buddhism/Southeast-Asia.

[136] Heikkilä-Horn, M.-L. (2019) 'Hinduismin SoutheastAsia', in Encyclopedia of Hinduism. Springer, pp. 1–5. Available at: https://link.springer.com/referenceworkentry/10.1007/978-94-024-1188-1_70.

rituals. Temples and shrines frequently housed altars dedicated to both Hindu gods and indigenous spirits, reflecting a harmonious coexistence of beliefs.[137] This syncretism extended beyond religious practices to art, literature, and governance. The adoption and adaptation of Indian cultural elements were facilitated by trade and the movement of peoples, leading to a unique cultural mosaic in Southeast Asia. Cultural exchanges brought Hindu-Buddhist iconography, temple architecture, and storytelling traditions to the region, where they were localized and interwoven with indigenous customs.[138] The development of localized forms of Hinduism and Buddhism in Southeast Asia was a dynamic process, characterized by the adaptation of Indian religious traditions to local contexts and their integration with indigenous beliefs. This syncretism resulted in rich and diverse religious landscapes across the region.

The Role of Temples and Monasteries in Religious Syncretism

Between 200 and 1500 AD, Southeast Asia witnessed significant religious syncretism, particularly between Hinduism and Buddhism. Temples and monasteries played a pivotal role in this process, serving as centres for religious convergence and cultural integration. In the Khmer Empire, the temple complex of Angkor Wat exemplifies this syncretism. Originally constructed in the early twelfth century as a Hindu temple dedicated to Vishnu, it was later converted into a Buddhist temple in the fourteenth century. This transition reflects the fluidity between Hindu and Buddhist practices, with architectural and iconographic elements accommodating both traditions. The coexistence of Hindu and Buddhist iconography within the same sacred space facilitated a blended religious experience for worshippers.[139] Similarly, the Bayon Temple, also located in Angkor, illustrates the integration of Hindu and Buddhist elements.

[137] Heikkilä-Horn, M.-L. (2019) 'Hinduismin SoutheastAsia', in Encyclopedia of Hinduism. Springer, pp. 1–5. Available at: https://link.springer.com/referenceworkentry/10.1007/978-94-024-1188-1_70.

[138] Ardhana, I. K. (2019) 'Buddhismin SoutheastAsia: A Study of Philosophy, Religion and a Model of a Multicultural Society', Journal of Multidisciplinary Studies, 6(1), pp. 1–10. Available https://crimsonpublishers.com/nrs/pdf/NRS.000582.pdf.

[139] Copplestone, L. (2024) 'Temple-Monasteries, Buddhist Monks, and Architectural Exchange Between India, Java, and Tibet in the Late eighth Century', Religions, 15(11), p. 1338. Available at: https://www.mdpi.com/2077-1444/15/11/1338.

Built in the late twelfth century by King Jayavarman VII, the temple features towers adorned with enigmatic smiling faces, believed to represent the Bodhisattva Avalokiteshvara, intertwined with the king's likeness. The temple's galleries depict scenes from Hindu mythology alongside everyday life, indicating a harmonious blend of religious narratives.[140] In Java, Indonesia, the Prambanan Temple complex stands as a testament to religious syncretism. Constructed in the ninth century, it comprises several temples dedicated to Hindu deities such as Shiva, Vishnu, and Brahma. Adjacent to Prambanan is the Sewu Temple complex, a Buddhist sanctuary from the same period. The proximity and contemporaneity of these complexes suggest a society where Hinduism and Buddhism coexisted and influenced each other, fostering a syncretic religious environment.[141] Monasteries also contributed to religious syncretism by serving as educational and cultural hubs. Buddhist monks travelled extensively across regions, facilitating the exchange of religious ideas and practices. The architectural design of temple-monasteries, such as those in Paharpur (Bangladesh), Candi Sewu (Java), and Samye (Tibet), reflects a blend of indigenous and Indian influences, indicating a syncretic approach to religious architecture.[142] These examples demonstrate that temples and monasteries were instrumental in the syncretic development of Southeast Asian religions. By accommodating multiple religious traditions within their structures and practices, they facilitated cultural integration and the emergence of unique, localized expressions of faith.

Examples of Syncretic Art and Architecture

Between 200 and 1500 AD, Southeast Asia experienced a rich blending of artistic and architectural traditions, resulting in syncretic forms that fused Hindu, Buddhist, and indigenous influences. This integration is evident

[140] Copplestone, L. (2024) 'Temple-Monasteries, Buddhist Monks, and Architectural Exchange Between India, Java, and Tibet in the Late 8th Century', Religions, 15(11), p. 1338. Available at: https://www.mdpi.com/2077-1444/15/11/1338.

[141] Angkor Database (n.d.) 'The Syncretism of Religions in SoutheastAsia, Especially in the Khmer Empire'. Available at: https://cdn.angkordatabase.asia/libs/docs/publications/the-syncretism-of-religions-in-southeast-asia-especially-in-the-khmer-empire/syncretism-briggs.pdf.

[142] Copplestone, L. (2024) 'Temple-Monasteries, Buddhist Monks, and Architectural Exchange Between India, Java, and Tibet in the Late eighth Century', Religions, 15(11), p. 1338. Available at: https://www.mdpi.com/2077-1444/15/11/1338.

in major cultural landmarks, demonstrating the region's ability to adapt external religious ideas to local contexts, creating unique expressions of art and architecture.

The Borobudur Temple in Central Java, Indonesia, is a prominent example of this syncretism. Constructed between the eighth and ninth centuries, Borobudur is a Buddhist monument incorporating Indigenous Javanese design principles. The temple's nine stacked platforms, adorned with intricate bas-reliefs depicting scenes from Buddhist cosmology, reflect a harmonious blending of Buddhist narratives and local artistic sensibilities. The design also incorporates the mandala, a symbol central to both Buddhist and Indigenous spiritual traditions, showcasing the region's cultural fusion.[143] Borobudur's physical layout integrates with the surrounding natural environment, emphasizing a holistic spiritual experience influenced by local animistic traditions. In Vietnam, the Champa kingdom provides another compelling example of syncretic art and architecture. The Cham people, deeply influenced by Hinduism, developed a unique artistic style that combined Indian Hindu motifs with local elements. The My Son Sanctuary, a UNESCO World Heritage site, features brick temples dedicated to Hindu deities such as Shiva and Vishnu. These temples are adorned with intricate carvings of divine figures and mythological scenes, integrating indigenous patterns and symbols into their designs.[144] The Champa sculptures, often carved from sandstone, reflect a localized interpretation of Hindu religious iconography, making them distinct from their Indian counterparts. Further evidence of syncretic architecture can be found in the Prambanan Temple complex in Java, Indonesia. Constructed in the ninth century, Prambanan is a Hindu temple dedicated to the Trimurti—Brahma, Vishnu, and Shiva. The towering central spires reflect Indian architectural principles, yet the intricate carvings and layout exhibit adaptations to Javanese aesthetics and beliefs. Adjacent to Prambanan is the Sewu Temple complex, a Buddhist sanctuary from the same era, illustrating the coexistence and mutual

[143] Smarthistory (n.d.) 'Cultural exchange and syncretism in the arts of South Asia since 1200'. Available at: https://smarthistory.org/reframing-art-history/cultural-exchange-syncretism-arts-south-asia-since-1200/.

[144] Smarthistory (n.d.) 'Cultural exchange and syncretism in the arts of South Asia since 1200'. Available at: https://smarthistory.org/reframing-art-history/cultural-exchange-syncretism-arts-south-asia-since-1200/.

influence of Hinduism and Buddhism in the region.[145] Beyond individual monuments, temple-monasteries served as centers for the exchange of ideas, blending artistic and religious traditions across Southeast Asia. Monasteries like those at Candi Sewu in Java and Paharpur in Bangladesh reflect a synthesis of Indian, Buddhist, and local architectural influences. These structures often incorporated indigenous materials and construction techniques, adapting Indian design principles to local needs and environments.[146] The art and architecture of Southeast Asia during this period illustrate a remarkable syncretic tradition. By integrating Hindu, Buddhist, and indigenous elements, Southeast Asian artisans created unique cultural expressions that reflected the diversity and dynamism of the region's religious and artistic landscapes.

The Decline of Hindu-Buddhist States and the Rise of Islam (Fourteenth–Fifteenth Century)

Factors Contributing to the Decline of Hindu-Buddhist Kingdoms.

Between the fourteenth and fifteenth centuries, the decline of Hindu-Buddhist kingdoms in Southeast Asia was driven by a combination of internal, economic, cultural, and environmental factors, which collectively facilitated the rise of Islamic states. One key factor was political fragmentation within major Hindu-Buddhist kingdoms such as the Majapahit Empire in Java. Internal conflicts and succession disputes weakened central authority, leading to the disintegration of these states into smaller, more vulnerable polities.[147] This fragmentation undermined their ability to respond to external pressures and compete effectively with emerging Islamic powers.

[145] Ardhana, I. K. (2019) 'Buddhismin SoutheastAsia: A Study of Philosophy, Religion and a Model of a Multicultural Society', Journal of Multidisciplinary Studies, 6(1), pp. 1–10. Available at: https://crimsonpublishers.com/nrs/pdf/NRS.000582.pdf.

[146] Heikkilä-Horn, M.-L. (2019) 'Hinduismin SoutheastAsia', in Encyclopedia of Hinduism. Springer, pp. 1–5. Available at: https://link.springer.com/referenceworkentry/10.1007/978-94-024-1188-1_70.

[147] Preceden (2024) 'Kingdoms of SoutheastAsia Timeline'. Available at: https://www.preceden.com/timeline/kingdoms-of-southeast-asia.

Economic shifts also played a significant role in the decline of these kingdoms. During this period, maritime trade routes were increasingly dominated by Muslim traders from the Middle East, India, and Persia. These traders established strong commercial ties with local rulers and merchants, who were incentivized to adopt Islam to gain access to lucrative trade networks. The integration of Islamic principles into commerce and governance diminished the influence of Hindu-Buddhist traditions.[148] The spread of Islam in Southeast Asia was further accelerated by its adaptability and the efforts of Sufi missionaries. These missionaries employed a syncretic approach, integrating Islamic teachings with local customs and spiritual practices. This cultural inclusivity made Islam appealing to diverse populations, contributing to its widespread adoption across the region.[149] As Islam gained prominence, the cultural and religious institutions of Hindu-Buddhist kingdoms gradually lost their relevance and support.

Environmental factors also contributed to the decline of certain Hindu-Buddhist kingdoms. For instance, the Khmer Empire, a Hindu-Buddhist state, faced severe environmental challenges, including prolonged droughts followed by intense monsoons. These events disrupted agricultural production and weakened the empire's economic stability, hastening its decline.[150] Such environmental stressors exacerbated existing vulnerabilities and made these kingdoms less resilient to external influences. The decline of Hindu-Buddhist kingdoms in Southeast Asia was a multifaceted process influenced by internal instability, economic realignments, cultural transformations, and environmental challenges. These factors not only facilitated the rise of Islamic states but also reshaped the cultural and religious landscape of the region.

The Spread of Islam in Southeast Asia and Indonesia

Between the fourteenth and fifteenth centuries, Islam spread throughout Southeast Asia and Indonesia through a combination of trade, missionary

[148] Asia Society (2024) 'TheArrival of Islamin SoutheastAsia'. Available at: https://sites.asiasociety.org/education/islam_in_seasia/curriculum-arrival.htm.

[149] Islamweb (2024) 'The Spread of Islamin SoutheastAsia'. Available at: https://islamweb.net/en/article/136127/the-spread-of-islam-in-southeast-asia.

[150] Islamweb (2024) 'The Spread of Islamin SoutheastAsia'. Available at: https://islamweb.net/en/article/136127/the-spread-of-islam-in-southeast-asia.

activities, and political changes. This period marked a significant transformation in the region's religious landscape, with Islam gradually supplanting Hindu-Buddhist traditions. Trade played a pivotal role in the dissemination of Islam. Muslim merchants from the Middle East, India, and China established extensive trade networks across Southeast Asia, facilitating not only the exchange of goods but also the transmission of religious and cultural ideas. The strategic location of port cities like Malacca and Pasai made them central hubs for these interactions, leading to the establishment of Muslim communities and the eventual Islamization of local populations.[151] Missionary efforts, particularly by Sufi mystics, were instrumental in spreading Islam. Sufis adapted Islamic teachings to align with local customs and traditions, making the religion more accessible and acceptable to Indigenous communities. Their emphasis on personal spirituality and incorporation of local cultural practices facilitated a syncretic form of Islam that resonated with the diverse populations of Southeast Asia.[152] Political dynamics also influenced the spread of Islam. As local rulers and elites converted to Islam, they often adopted the religion as a means to strengthen trade relations with Muslim merchants and to consolidate their own political power. The conversion of ruling classes led to the establishment of Islamic sultanates, such as the Sultanate of Malacca, which became influential centres of Islamic culture and learning.[153] The decline of Hindu-Buddhist kingdoms, due to internal strife and external pressures, created a power vacuum that facilitated the rise of Islamic states. The adaptability of Islam, combined with its appeal to both the elite and common people, enabled it to become the dominant religion in the region by the end of the fifteenth century.[154] The spread of Islam in Southeast Asia and Indonesia during

[151] Aljunied, K. (2019) 'Islamin SoutheastAsia', Oxford Research Encyclopedia of Religion. Available at: https://oxfordre.com/religion/view/10.1093/acrefore/9780199340378.001.0001/acrefore-9780199340378-e-658.

[152] Ali, M. (2019) 'Islamin SoutheastAsia', Oxford Research Encyclopedia of Asian History. Available at: https://oxfordre.com/asianhistory/view/10.1093/acrefore/9780190277727.001.0001/acrefore-9780190277727-e-40.

[153] Aljunied, K. (2019) 'Islamin SoutheastAsia', Oxford Research Encyclopedia of Religion. Available at: https://oxfordre.com/religion/view/10.1093/acrefore/9780199340378.001.0001/acrefore-9780199340378-e-658.

[154] Ali, M. (2019) 'Islamin SoutheastAsia', Oxford Research Encyclopedia of Asian History. Available at: https://oxfordre.com/asianhistory/view/10.1093/acrefore/9780190277727.001.0001/acrefore-9780190277727-e-40.

the fourteenth and fifteenth centuries was a multifaceted process driven by trade, missionary activities, and political transformations. This period of Islamization significantly shaped the cultural and religious landscape of the region, laying the foundation for the diverse expressions of Islam observed in Southeast Asia today.

Transition from Hindu-Buddhist to Islamic States

Between the fourteenth and fifteenth centuries, Southeast Asia underwent a significant transition from Hindu-Buddhist states to Islamic polities. This transformation was driven by a combination of trade networks, the activities of Sufi missionaries, and political dynamics. One key factor in this transition was the influence of maritime trade. The region's strategic location along major maritime routes facilitated interactions with Muslim traders from the Middle East, India, and China. These traders not only engaged in commerce but also introduced Islamic practices and beliefs to local rulers and communities. The port city of Malacca emerged as a pivotal centre for Islamization during this period, with its rulers converting to Islam to secure advantageous trade relations and alliances with Muslim merchants.[155] This conversion set the stage for the establishment of the Malacca Sultanate, which became a prominent Islamic power in the region. Another significant contributor was the role of Sufi missionaries. Sufis employed a syncretic approach, blending Islamic teachings with local customs and traditions, which made the religion more accessible to diverse populations. For example, in Java, the Wali Songo, or "Nine Saints," were instrumental in spreading Islam through a combination of religious teachings, integration with indigenous culture, and the establishment of mosques.[156] The adaptability of Sufi practices allowed Islam to coexist with pre-existing Hindu-Buddhist traditions, easing the transition for local communities. Political factors also played a crucial role. The decline of Hindu-Buddhist kingdoms, such as Majapahit, due to internal conflicts and external pressures, created a power vacuum that Islamic states filled. The conversion of local rulers, who often sought to

[155] Ricklefs, M. C. (2008) A History of Modern Indonesia since c. 1200. 4th edn. London: Palgrave Macmillan.

[156] Ali, M. (2019) 'Islamin SoutheastAsia to c. 1800', Oxford Research Encyclopedia of Asian History. Available at: https://oxfordre.com/asianhistory/display/10.1093/acrefore/9780190277727.001.0001/acrefore-9780190277727-e-40.

legitimize their authority through association with a broader Islamic identity, further accelerated the transition. The rulers of Pasai in Sumatra, for instance, adopted Islam to strengthen their political and economic ties with the Islamic world.[157] The adaptability and inclusivity of Islam contributed to its success in replacing Hindu-Buddhist traditions. For instance, many elements of Hindu-Buddhist culture were incorporated into Islamic practices, such as the use of traditional art forms and architecture. Mosques in Java, such as the Demak Great Mosque, reflect this synthesis, incorporating traditional Javanese architectural styles alongside Islamic religious functions.[158] The transition from Hindu-Buddhist to Islamic states in Southeast Asia was a complex and multifaceted process. Driven by trade, missionary activities, and political changes, this transformation reshaped the religious and cultural landscape of the region, laying the foundations for the Islamic societies that dominate Southeast Asia today.

Legacy of Hindu-Buddhist Practices in Post-Islamic Indonesia

The transition from Hindu-Buddhist kingdoms to Islamic states in Indonesia during the fourteenth and fifteenth centuries did not erase pre-existing cultural and religious practices. Instead, many Hindu-Buddhist traditions were assimilated into the evolving Islamic society, leaving a lasting legacy evident in various aspects of Indonesian culture. For example, the Borobudur temple, constructed in the eighth century as a Buddhist monument, remains a significant cultural and religious landmark in Indonesia. Its preservation and the rituals associated with it reflect the enduring influence of Indonesia's Buddhist heritage.[159] In Bali, Hinduism persisted despite the widespread adoption of Islam throughout the rest of the archipelago. Balinese Hinduism, known

[157] Reid, A. (1988) SoutheastAsia in the Age of Commerce 1450–1680: Volume 1, The Lands below the Winds. New Haven: Yale University Press.

[158] Aljunied, S. M. (2019) 'SoutheastAsia and the Spread of Islam', Oxford Research Encyclopedia of Religion. Available at: https://oxfordre.com/religion/view/10.1093/acrefore/9780199340378.001.0001/acrefore-9780199340378-e-658.

[159] Bloembergen, M. and Eickhoff, M. (2015) 'Save Borobudur! The Moral Dynamics of Heritage Formation in Indonesia across Orders and Borders, 1930s–1980s', in Cultural Heritage as Civilizing Mission. Springer, pp. 119–146. Available at: https://link.springer.com/chapter/10.1007/978-3-319-13638-7_5.

as Agama Hindu Dharma, incorporates elements of Buddhism and indigenous animistic beliefs, demonstrating a syncretic tradition that has endured over centuries. This blend highlights the resilience and adaptability of Hindu-Buddhist traditions in Indonesia.[160] Additionally, the artistic and architectural styles of Hindu-Buddhist traditions are evident in various Islamic structures. For instance, mosques in Java, such as the Demak Great Mosque, display architectural features that draw heavily on Hindu-Buddhist aesthetics, showcasing the syncretic nature of Indonesian religious practices.[161] These examples illustrate how Hindu-Buddhist practices have been preserved and integrated into Indonesia's cultural and religious landscape, even after the rise of Islam. The syncretic nature of Indonesian spirituality underscores the complex interplay between different religious traditions and the enduring legacy of the archipelago's Hindu-Buddhist past.

Art and Architecture of the Hindu-Buddhist States

Key Architectural Monuments: Borobudur, Prambanan, and Angkor Wat

Borobudur, Prambanan, and Angkor Wat are monumental testaments to the architectural and cultural zenith of Hindu-Buddhist states in Southeast Asia between 200 and 1500 AD. These structures demonstrate advanced engineering, religious devotion, and the syncretic cultural evolution of their respective societies. Borobudur, located in Central Java, Indonesia, is the world's largest Buddhist temple, constructed in the ninth century during the Sailendra Dynasty. Its design reflects a mandala, symbolizing Buddhist cosmology, with a pyramidal base, five concentric square terraces, and three circular platforms topped by a central stupa. The temple's intricate bas-reliefs narrate the life of Siddhartha Gautama and illustrate Javanese society of the time. This architectural complexity

[160] Picard, M. (2011) 'BalineseHinduism and the Indonesian State: Recent Developments', Archipel, 81(1), pp. 127–154. Available at: https://www.jstor.org/stable/27864809.

[161] Noseworthy, W. (2022) 'Seeking Dharma Below the Winds: Hindu Particularism in Island SoutheastAsia', International Journal of Hindu Studies, 26, pp. 393–423. Available at: https://link.springer.com/article/10.1007/s11407-022-09321-2.

and symbolic depth highlight the advanced state of Javanese art and religious thought during this period.[162] Prambanan, also in Central Java, is a ninth-century Hindu temple complex dedicated to the Trimurti: Brahma, Vishnu, and Shiva. The largest temple, Candi Shiva Mahadeva, rises to 47 meters, showcasing the verticality typical of Hindu temple architecture. The complex's layout and the intricate carvings depicting scenes from the Ramayana reflect the profound influence of Indian culture on Javanese civilization. Prambanan exemplifies the zenith of classical Javanese art and the syncretic nature of Indonesian spirituality, where Hinduism and indigenous beliefs coalesced.[163] Angkor Wat, situated in present-day Cambodia, is the largest religious monument globally, originally constructed in the early twelfth century as a Hindu temple dedicated to Vishnu under King Suryavarman II. Its architectural plan represents Mount Meru, the mythical center of the universe in Hindu and Buddhist cosmology. The temple's extensive bas-reliefs and devatas (deity carvings) exhibit the zenith of Khmer art. Angkor Wat's transformation into a Buddhist temple by the end of the twelfth century illustrates the fluidity and syncretism of religious practices in the region.[164] These architectural masterpieces not only represent religious devotion but also reflect the political power and cultural sophistication of their respective societies. The similarities in architectural styles and motifs among Borobudur, Prambanan, and Angkor Wat suggest a shared cultural and religious milieu across Southeast Asia, facilitated by trade routes and the movement of artisans and ideas. The study of these monuments provides insight into

[162] Situngkir, H. (2015) 'Borobudur was Built Algorithmically'. Available at: https://arxiv.org/abs/1508.03649 (Accessed: 19 December 2024).

[163] Martinus, A. and Herwindo, R. P. (2019) 'Comparative Study of Type-Morphology Architecture Borobudur-Prambanan Temple of AngkorWat: Case Study on Mass Processes, Looks, Socks, and Ornaments'. Available at: https://www.academia.edu/39859579/COMPARATIVE_STUDY_OF_TYPE_MORPHOLOGY_ARCHITECTURE_BOROBUDUR_PRAMBANAN_TEMPLE_OF_ANGKOR_WAT_CASE_STUDY_ON_MASS_PROCESSES_LOOKS_SOCKS_AND_ORNAMENTS.

[164] Martinus, A. and Herwindo, R. P. (2019) 'Comparative Study of Type-Morphology Architecture Borobudur-PrambananTempleof AngkorWat: Case Study on Mass Processes, Looks, Socks, and Ornaments'. Available at: https://www.academia.edu/39859579/COMPARATIVE_STUDY_OF_TYPE_MORPHOLOGY_ARCHITECTURE_BOROBUDUR_PRAMBANAN_TEMPLE_OF_ANGKOR_WAT_CASE_STUDY_ON_MASS_PROCESSES_LOOKS_SOCKS_AND_ORNAMENTS.

the interconnectedness of the region's historical development and the syncretic evolution of its religious and cultural landscapes.[165]

Development of Religious Iconography

The development of religious iconography in Southeast Asia between 200 and 1500 AD reflects a dynamic interplay between indigenous traditions and external influences, particularly from India. Early sculptures and reliefs in the region closely mirrored Indian prototypes, highlighting the initial influence of Indian artistic and religious traditions. Over time, artisans began to reinterpret these forms, integrating indigenous aesthetics and spiritual concepts. This syncretic approach led to the creation of distinctive regional styles that, while acknowledging their Indian origins, stood apart in their originality.[166] One example of this adaptation is the depiction of Buddhist deities, such as the Bodhisattva Avalokiteshvara. In Southeast Asia, Avalokiteshvara's iconography evolved to incorporate local symbols and motifs, reflecting indigenous concepts of kingship and spirituality. Similarly, Hindu deities like Vishnu and Shiva were reimagined in ways that resonated with local audiences, often incorporating elements from native traditions. These adaptations not only enriched the visual culture of the region but also facilitated the acceptance and spread of Hinduism and Buddhism by making these religions more accessible to local populations.[167]

New iconographic forms unique to Southeast Asia also emerged during this period. For instance, religious sculptures and temple carvings in regions like Java and Cambodia combined Indian influences with local artistic preferences, resulting in a visual language that reflected the

[165] Situngkir, H. (2015) 'Borobudur was Built Algorithmically'. Available at: https://arxiv.org/abs/1508.03649.

[166] Singh, A. S. (2018) 'A Historical and Cultural Study of Buddhist Art in Early South-EastAsia'. International Journal of Social Science and Humanity, 6(8), pp. 591–595. Available at: https://www.ijssh.org/vol6/711-H10004.pdf.

[167] Guy, J. (2014) 'Lost Kingdoms: Hindu-Buddhist Sculpture of Early SoutheastAsia'. The Metropolitan Museum of Art. Available at: https://www.metmuseum.org/met-publications/lost-kingdoms-hindu-buddhist-sculpture-of-early-southeast-asia.

complex cultural and religious landscape of the region.[168] These innovations demonstrated the creativity and adaptability of Southeast Asian artisans, who successfully blended external religious ideals with indigenous practices. The development of religious iconography in Southeast Asia during this era exemplifies a process of adaptation and innovation. By blending Indian influences with Indigenous artistic traditions, Southeast Asian artisans created a rich and diverse visual language that continues to reflect the syncretic and dynamic nature of the region's history.

Influence of Indian Art Styles and Local Adaptations

The art and architecture of Southeast Asia between 200 and 1500 AD were profoundly influenced by Indian styles, which were subsequently adapted to local cultures, resulting in unique syncretic expressions. This cultural transmission, often referred to as "Indianization," encompassed religious, artistic, and political elements that were selectively integrated by Southeast Asian societies.[169,170]

Indian influence is evident in the adoption of Hindu-Buddhist iconography, temple architecture, and Sanskrit inscriptions across Southeast Asia. For example, the temple complexes of Angkor Wat in Cambodia and Prambanan in Indonesia exhibit architectural styles reminiscent of Indian prototypes, such as the use of corbelled arches and intricate bas-reliefs depicting scenes from the Ramayana and Mahabharata. However, these structures also display local adaptations, including indigenous motifs and construction techniques, reflecting a blend of imported and native artistic

[168] Revire, N. (2022) 'The Creative South: Buddhistand Hindu Art in Mediaeval Maritime Asia'. https://www.Academia.edu. Available at: https://www.academia.edu/77136262/2022_The_Creative_South_Buddhist_and_Hindu_Art_in_Mediaeval_Maritime_Asia_Vol_1_TOC_Intro_.

[169] Guy, J. (2014) Lost Kingdoms: Hindu-Buddhist Sculpture of Early SoutheastAsia. New York: The Metropolitan Museum of Art. Available at: https://www.metmuseum.org/met-publications/lost-kingdoms-hindu-buddhist-sculpture-of-early-southeast-asia.

[170] Singh, A. S. (2018) 'A Historical and Cultural Study of Buddhist Art in Early South-EastAsia', International Journal of Social Science and Humanity, 6(8), pp. 591–595. Available at: https://www.ijssh.org/vol6/711-H10004.pdf.

traditions.[171,172] The process of Indianization was not a passive reception of Indian culture but involved active selection and modification by Southeast Asian societies. Local artisans and patrons adapted Indian artistic conventions to fit indigenous aesthetic preferences and sociopolitical contexts. This is evident in the regional variations of temple architecture and sculpture, where Indian motifs were reinterpreted to align with local beliefs and practices.[173,174] The transmission of Indian culture to Southeast Asia was facilitated by trade networks and the movement of artisans, merchants, and religious figures. These interactions led to the exchange of artistic techniques and religious ideas, which were then localized to create distinctive cultural expressions. For example, the spread of Buddhism from India to Southeast Asia resulted in the development of unique Buddhist art forms that, while drawing on Indian prototypes, incorporated local elements and symbolism.[175,176,177] The influence of Indian art styles on Southeast Asian art and architecture during this period was significant, but it was characterized by a dynamic process of adaptation and localization. Southeast Asian societies did not simply replicate Indian models; instead, they integrated and transformed these influences

[171] Pandya Dhar, P. (2018) 'Monuments, Motifs, Myths: Architecture and its Transformations in Indiaand SoutheastAsia'. In S. Saran (ed.), Cultural and Civilizational Links Between Indiaand SoutheastAsia: Historical and Contemporary Dimensions. Palgrave Macmillan, pp. 325–345. Available at: https://www.academia.edu/37364963.

[172] Singh, A. S. (2018) 'A Historical and Cultural Study of Buddhist Art in Early South-EastAsia', International Journal of Social Science and Humanity, 6(8), pp. 591–595. Available at: https://www.ijssh.org/vol6/711-H10004.pdf.

[173] Guy, J. (2014) Lost Kingdoms: Hindu-Buddhist Sculpture of Early SoutheastAsia. New York: The Metropolitan Museum of Art. Available at: https://www.metmuseum.org/met-publications/lost-kingdoms-hindu-buddhist-sculpture-of-early-southeast-asia.

[174] Revire, N. (2022) 'The Creative South: Buddhistand Hindu Art in Mediaeval Maritime Asia', International Journal of Hindu Studies, 26, pp. 393–423. Available at: https://www.academia.edu/77136262.

[175] Guy, J. (2014) Lost Kingdoms: Hindu-Buddhist Sculpture of Early SoutheastAsia. New York: The Metropolitan Museum of Art. Available at: https://www.metmuseum.org/met-publications/lost-kingdoms-hindu-buddhist-sculpture-of-early-southeast-asia.

[176] Singh, A. S. (2018) 'A Historical and Cultural Study of Buddhist Art in Early South-EastAsia', International Journal of Social Science and Humanity, 6(8), pp. 591–595. Available at: https://www.ijssh.org/vol6/711-H10004.pdf.

[177] Libretexts (n.d.) Art of SoutheastAsia. Available at: https://human.libretexts.org/Bookshelves/Art/Art_History/11%3A_Art_of_South_and_Southeast_Asia_Before_1200_CE/11.04%3A_Art_of_Southeast_Asia.

to create unique artistic and architectural forms that reflected their own cultural identities.

Conservation and Study of Hindu-Buddhist Art in Southeast Asia

The conservation and study of Hindu-Buddhist art in Southeast Asia have been pivotal in preserving the region's rich cultural heritage and advancing scholarly understanding of its historical contexts. Significant efforts have been undertaken by both local governments and international organizations to safeguard and research these artistic traditions. For example, the restoration of the Ta Prohm temple in Cambodia was led by the Archaeological Survey of India (ASI). Constructed during the reign of Khmer King Jayavarman VII, Ta Prohm is renowned for its intertwining of architecture and nature. India and Cambodia signed an agreement in 2002 to restore this temple, with significant portions of the temple complex, including the Hall of Dancers, completed by 2012.[178] Scholarly research has also been instrumental in deepening the understanding of Hindu-Buddhist art in the region. Publications have introduced the sculptural traditions of Southeast Asia to broader audiences.[179] Scholarly work, associated with an exhibition at The Metropolitan Museum of Art, explores the religious art of early Southeast Asian kingdoms, contextualizing these artifacts within their historical settings.[180] Academic journals further contribute to the study of Southeast Asian art.[181] Additionally, scientific analyses of sculptures by institutions such as the National Museum of Asian Art have provided technical insights. Studies on casting technologies and stone materials used in ancient Cambodia, Thailand, and Vietnam have advanced knowledge about the craftsmanship

[178] VIF (2024) 'India's Role in the Conservation of Cultural Heritage in SoutheastAsia'. Available at: https://www.vifindia.org/article/2024/july/31/India-s-Role-in-the-Conservation-of-Cultural-Heritage-in-Southeast-Asia.

[179] Guy, J. (2014) Lost Kingdoms: Hindu-Buddhist Sculpture of Early SoutheastAsia. New York: The Metropolitan Museum of Art. Available at: https://www.metmuseum.org/met-publications/lost-kingdoms-hindu-buddhist-sculpture-of-early-southeast-asia.

[180] Guy, J. (2014) Lost Kingdoms: Hindu-Buddhist Sculpture of Early SoutheastAsia. New York: The Metropolitan Museum of Art. Available at: https://www.metmuseum.org/met-publications/lost-kingdoms-hindu-buddhist-sculpture-of-early-southeast-asia.

[181] Pratu: Journal of Buddhistand Hindu Art, Architecture and Archaeology of Ancient to Premodern SoutheastAsia (n.d.) Available at: https://pratujournal.org/.

of the time and informed conservation strategies.[182] The conservation and study of Hindu-Buddhist art in Southeast Asia involve a collaborative effort between practical restoration projects and academic research. Restoration efforts like those at Ta Prohm highlight the importance of preserving physical heritage, while scholarly publications and technical studies contribute to a nuanced understanding of the artistic and historical landscapes of the region.

Legacy of Hindu-Buddhist States in Modern Indonesia and Southeast Asia

Cultural and Religious Continuities

The enduring legacy of Hindu-Buddhist states in modern Indonesia and Southeast Asia is evident through various cultural and religious continuities that have persisted despite the region's Islamification and Western colonization. These continuities manifest in religious practices, artistic expressions, and societal structures, reflecting a deep-seated historical influence. In Indonesia, particularly on the island of Bali, Hinduism remains the predominant religion. Balinese Hinduism, while rooted in Indian traditions, has evolved uniquely by integrating Indigenous animistic beliefs and local customs. This syncretic form of Hinduism is characterized by rituals, ceremonies, and art forms that are distinct to Balinese culture, demonstrating the adaptation and resilience of Hindu traditions in a predominantly Muslim nation.[183] Similarly, in Thailand, Buddhism has incorporated elements of Hinduism, evident in the veneration of Hindu deities such as Brahma and Ganesha within Buddhist temples. This syncretism highlights the intertwined nature of Hindu and Buddhist traditions in the region, a legacy of historical interactions and cultural exchanges.[184] The influence of Hindu-Buddhist art and architecture is also prominent. Monuments like the Prambanan temple complex

[182] National Museum of Asian Art (NMAA) (n.d.) Conservation and Scientific Research. Available at: https://asia.si.edu/research/conservation-scientific-research/.

[183] Rao, R. (2023) 'Hindu Culture in Indonesia', Academia.edu. Available at: https://www.academia.edu/95892347/Hindu_Culture_in_Indonesia.

[184] Vadassery, S. (2017) 'The Dance of Life: Leisure, Culture and Religious Experience', in Cultural Traditions and Contemporary Challenges in SoutheastAsia. Available at: https://crvp.org/publications/Series-IIID/IIID-3.pdf.

in Java, Indonesia, and the Angkor Wat in Cambodia stand as testaments to the region's Hindu-Buddhist heritage. These structures not only serve as cultural landmarks but also continue to play roles in contemporary religious and cultural practices, attracting both worshippers and tourists, thereby contributing to national identities and economies.[185] Furthermore, traditional performing arts in Southeast Asia often draw upon Hindu epics such as the Ramayana and Mahabharata. In Indonesia, the Wayang Kulit shadow puppet theatre narrates stories from these epics, preserving and propagating Hindu-Buddhist narratives through generations. This continuity underscores the enduring impact of Hindu-Buddhist literature and mythology on the region's cultural fabric.[186] The cultural and religious continuities from the Hindu-Buddhist era in modern Indonesia and Southeast Asia are profound. They are manifested in religious syncretism, monumental architecture, and traditional arts, reflecting a rich historical legacy that continues to shape the region's cultural and religious landscapes.

Influence on Modern Indonesian and Southeast Asian Identity

The legacy of Hindu-Buddhist states has left an indelible mark on the cultural and national identities of modern Indonesia and Southeast Asia. This influence is evident in religious practices, artistic traditions, political ideologies, and societal structures across the region. In Indonesia, Hindu-Buddhist legacies are particularly prominent in Bali, where Hinduism remains the dominant religion. Balinese Hinduism integrates local animistic beliefs and cultural practices, creating a distinct form of Hindu tradition unique to the island. Religious ceremonies such as Nyepi (Balinese Day of Silence) and artistic traditions like Legong dance and Wayang Kulit shadow puppetry illustrate the integration of Hindu-Buddhist narratives into local culture.[187] These practices underscore how Hindu-Buddhist ideas continue to shape Balinese identity and contribute

[185] Guy, J. (2014) Lost Kingdoms: Hindu-Buddhist Sculpture of Early SoutheastAsia. New York: The Metropolitan Museum of Art. Available at: https://www.metmuseum.org/met-publications/lost-kingdoms-hindu-buddhist-sculpture-of-early-southeast-asia.

[186] Agarwal, R. (2013) 'Hinduismin SoutheastAsia', http://www.Academia.edu. Available at: https://www.academia.edu/4185602/Hinduism_in_Southeast_Asia.

[187] Geertz, C. (1973) The Interpretation of Cultures: Selected Essays. New York: Basic Books.

to the preservation of cultural heritage. Similarly, in Java, the Majapahit Kingdom's historical narratives influence modern Indonesian nationalism. The Majapahit symbol, often invoked in political discourse, represents the golden age of Indonesia's history, promoting unity amidst diversity. Indonesia's national motto, "Bhinneka Tunggal Ika" (Unity in Diversity), originates from a Majapahit text, highlighting the enduring cultural and political significance of Hindu-Buddhist traditions in shaping the modern Indonesian state.[188] The architectural heritage of Hindu-Buddhist states also plays a pivotal role in regional identity. Iconic structures such as Borobudur and Prambanan in Indonesia and Angkor Wat in Cambodia serve as cultural touchstones for their respective nations. These monuments, originally religious sites, have been repurposed as symbols of national pride and tourism. Their preservation and use in cultural diplomacy emphasize the role of Hindu-Buddhist architecture in shaping modern identity.[189] In Southeast Asia more broadly, Hindu-Buddhist elements remain integrated into Buddhism, which dominates the religious landscape. Thai Buddhism, for instance, incorporates the veneration of Hindu deities such as Brahma and Ganesha alongside traditional Buddhist practices. The syncretism of these traditions reflects historical interactions and underscores their enduring relevance in cultural identity.[190] Moreover, the narratives from Hindu epics like the Ramayana and Mahabharata continue to influence performing arts and literature in Southeast Asia. In countries like Indonesia, Thailand, and Cambodia, these stories are retold through traditional theatre, dances, and festivals. These cultural expressions not only preserve historical narratives but also reinforce shared cultural heritage across the region.[191] The influence of Hindu-Buddhist states on modern Southeast Asian identity is profound and multifaceted. From shaping religious practices and artistic traditions to influencing political ideologies and national symbols, the legacy of these ancient states continues to resonate in the region's cultural and national consciousness.

[188] Ricklefs, M. C. (2008) A History of Modern Indonesia since c. 1200. 4th edn. London: Palgrave Macmillan.

[189] Winter, T. (2010) 'Heritage Tourism and National Identity in SoutheastAsia', Annals of Tourism Research, 37(3), pp. 715–731.

[190] Reynolds, F. E. (2005) 'Buddhist Continuities in Thai Religion and Culture', in Smith, B. K. (ed.) Hinduism and Modernity. Oxford: Blackwell, pp. 167–185.

[191] Acri, A. (2015) 'Revisiting the Cult of Śiva-Buddha in Javaand Bali', Journal of Southeast Asian Studies, 46(1), pp. 60–79.

Preservation and Revival of Hindu-Buddhist Traditions

The preservation and revival of Hindu-Buddhist traditions in modern Indonesia and Southeast Asia represent efforts to maintain and celebrate the region's rich cultural heritage. These efforts are evident in the restoration of ancient monuments, the continuation of traditional practices, and the promotion of historical narratives that align with national identities. In Indonesia, the restoration of Hindu-Buddhist monuments such as Borobudur and Prambanan highlights the commitment to preserving these cultural landmarks. Borobudur, a UNESCO World Heritage Site, has undergone extensive restoration under both Indonesian and international initiatives. The restoration project, led by UNESCO in the 1970s, not only saved the structure from further degradation but also positioned it as a center for religious ceremonies and international tourism. Similarly, the Prambanan temple complex, dedicated to the Trimurti (Brahma, Vishnu, and Shiva), continues to serve as a pilgrimage site and a venue for cultural performances, such as the Ramayana Ballet, which attracts both locals and tourists.[192] The revival of Hindu-Buddhist festivals and ceremonies further illustrates the ongoing cultural significance of these traditions. In Bali, Hindu rituals such as Galungan and Nyepi (Day of Silence) underscore the integration of ancient practices into daily life. These festivals, steeped in historical symbolism, have evolved to reflect both traditional values and modern contexts. Similarly, in Cambodia, Buddhist rituals and ceremonies, often linked to Angkor Wat, underscore the temple's enduring spiritual and cultural relevance.[193] Education and research also play critical roles in the preservation and revival of Hindu-Buddhist traditions. Institutions like the Nalanda-Sriwijaya Centre in Singapore promote scholarly exchanges and research focused on the cultural and historical connections between India and Southeast Asia. These initiatives emphasize the shared heritage of Hindu-Buddhist civilizations and their influence on the region's development.[194] In Thailand,

[192] Winter, T. (2010) 'Heritage Tourism and National Identity in SoutheastAsia', Annals of Tourism Research, 37(3), pp. 715–731.

[193] Geertz, C. (1973) The Interpretation of Cultures: Selected Essays. New York: Basic Books.

[194] Ricklefs, M. C. (2008) A History of Modern Indonesia since c. 1200. 4th edn. London: Palgrave Macmillan.

the preservation of Hindu-Buddhist traditions is evident in the integration of these elements into Buddhist practices. The veneration of Hindu deities such as Brahma and Ganesha within Thai Buddhist temples reflects the syncretic nature of religious traditions in the region. This blending of traditions is also apparent in the country's performing arts, where stories from the Ramayana are reenacted in classical dances like Khon.[195] Efforts to preserve and revive Hindu-Buddhist traditions also contribute to cultural diplomacy. Programs promoting shared heritage, such as India's Act East Policy, emphasize the historical and cultural connections between India and Southeast Asia. These initiatives foster mutual understanding and cooperation, demonstrating the relevance of Hindu-Buddhist traditions in contemporary international relations.[196] The preservation and revival of Hindu-Buddhist traditions in modern Indonesia and Southeast Asia serve as a testament to the region's dedication to maintaining its historical and cultural identity. Through restoration projects, continued religious practices, education, and cultural diplomacy, these traditions remain integral to the social and cultural fabric of the region.

Conclusion

This chapter builds upon the foundational narratives established in Chapters 1–3 by examining the pivotal role of Hindu-Buddhist states in shaping Southeast Asia's sociopolitical and cultural dynamics. Chapter 1 lays the groundwork by introducing the overarching themes of Indonesia's political economy, including the interplay between local innovation and external influences. This framing is critical for understanding how Hindu-Buddhist ideas were selectively adopted and adapted by local rulers, a process explored in depth in this chapter.

Chapter 2 traces the early migration and settlement patterns in Indonesia, emphasizing the region's diverse ecological and cultural foundations. This context is essential for appreciating the emergence of Hindu-Buddhist states, as their integration of Indian ideas into local contexts reflects the adaptability seen in earlier societal formations. For instance, the spread of Indian cosmology and religious practices, detailed

[195] Reynolds, F. E. (2005) 'Buddhist Continuities in Thai Religion and Culture', in Smith, B. K. (ed.) Hinduism and Modernity. Oxford: Blackwell, pp. 167–185.

[196] Acri, A. (2015) 'Revisiting the Cult of Śiva-Buddha in Javaand Bali', Journal of Southeast Asian Studies, 46(1), pp. 60–79.

in this chapter, echoes the earlier adaptability and innovation described in Chapter 2's account of prehistoric migrations and the Austronesian expansion. Chapter 3 provides a detailed account of the growth of trade networks and early kingdoms, setting the stage for the Indianization of Southeast Asia. It highlights how the region's strategic position as a nexus of maritime trade facilitated the inflow of Indian cultural, religious, and political ideas. This chapter elaborates on these dynamics, showing how rulers such as those of Srivijaya and Majapahit leveraged their control over trade routes to legitimize their authority through the adoption of Hindu-Buddhist traditions.

The discussion in this chapter critically evaluates the transformative impact of these states, demonstrating their role in fostering syncretic cultural forms and laying the groundwork for enduring architectural and artistic legacies. This analysis also underscores a key continuity from Chapter 3: the region's ability to synthesize diverse influences into uniquely Southeast Asian forms of governance and culture. Moreover, this chapter transitions effectively into the broader historical trajectory by addressing the decline of Hindu-Buddhist states and the rise of Islam, themes that will be expanded in subsequent chapters. It frames this transition not as a rupture but as part of the ongoing negotiation of identity and power that has characterized Indonesian history, linking back to the long-term processes introduced in Chapters 1 and 2. In conclusion, this chapter not only enriches the narrative by detailing the Hindu-Buddhist era but also connects seamlessly with the earlier chapters. It highlights how early migrations, trade networks, and local ingenuity set the stage for the profound cultural and political transformations that would define the region's premodern history.

References

Acri, A. (2015). Revisiting the Cult of Śiva-Buddha in Java and Bali. Journal of Southeast Asian Studies, 46(1), 60–79.

Agarwal, R. (2013) 'Hinduism in Southeast Asia', Academia.edu. Available at: https://www.academia.edu/4185602/Hinduism_in_Southeast_Asia.

Aljunied, K. (2019) 'Islam in Southeast Asia', Oxford Research Encyclopedia of Religion. Available at: https://doi.org/10.1093/acrefore/9780199340378.001.0001/acrefore-9780199340378-e-658

Al Makin. (2016). Unearthing Nusantara's Concept of Religious Pluralism: Harmonization and Syncretism in Hindu-Buddhist and Islamic Classical Texts. Al-Jāmi'ah: Journal of Islamic Studies, 54(1), 1–30.

Ali, M. (2019) 'Islam in Southeast Asia', Oxford Research Encyclopedia of Asian History. Available at: https://doi.org/10.1093/acrefore/9780190277727.001.0001/acrefore-9780190277727-e-40

AncientScholar (2023) 'Hindu and Animistic Deities in Southeast Asia.' Available at: https://ancientscholar.org/hindu-and-animistic-deities-in-southeast-asia

Angkor Database (n.d.) 'The Syncretism of Religions in Southeast Asia, Especially in the Khmer Empire'. Available at: https://cdn.angkordatabase.asia/libs/docs/publications/the-syncretism-of-religions-in-southeast-asia-especially-in-the-khmer-empire/syncretism-briggs.pdf.

Ardhana, I. K. (2019) 'Buddhism in Southeast Asia: A Study of Philosophy, Religion and a Model of a Multicultural Society', Journal of Multidisciplinary Studies, 6(1), pp. 1–10. Available at: https://crimsonpublishers.com/nrs/pdf/NRS.000582.pdf.

Asia Research News (2023) 'Syncretism in South and Southeast Asia: Adoption and Adaptation.' Available at: https://www.asiaresearchnews.com/html/calendar.php/eid/1345/cid/2/research/culture/administrator_account/syncretism_in_south_and_southeast_asia.

Asia Society (2024) 'The Arrival of Islam in Southeast Asia'. Available at: https://sites.asiasociety.org/education/islam_in_seasia/curriculum-arrival.htm.

Bloembergen, M. and Eickhoff, M. (2015) 'Save Borobudur! The Moral Dynamics of Heritage Formation in Indonesia across Orders and Borders, 1930s–1980s', in Cultural Heritage as Civilizing Mission. Springer, pp. 119–146. Available at: https://doi.org/10.1007/978-3-319-13638-7_5

Britannica (2024) 'Buddhism in Southeast Asia', Encyclopedia Britannica. Available at: https://www.britannica.com/topic/Buddhism/Southeast-Asia.

Britannica (2024) 'Hinduism - Southeast Asia, Pacific, Religion', Encyclopedia Britannica. Available at: https://www.britannica.com/topic/Hinduism/The-spread-of-Hinduism-in-Southeast-Asia-and-the-Pacific.

Coedès, G. (1968), The Indianized States of Southeast Asia. Honolulu: University of Hawaii Press.

Copplestone, L. (2024) 'Temple-Monasteries, Buddhist Monks, and Architectural Exchange Between India, Java, and Tibet in the Late 8th Century', Religions, 15(11), p. 1338. Available at: https://www.mdpi.com/2077-1444/15/11/1338.

Dhar, P.P. (2018). 'Monuments, Motifs, Myths: Architecture and its Transformations in Early India and Southeast Asia', in S. Saran (ed.), Cultural and Civilisational Links Between India and Southeast Asia: Historical and Contemporary Dimensions, Palgrave Macmillan, pp. 325–345.

Flood, G. (1996), An Introduction to Hinduism. Cambridge: Cambridge University Press.
Fontein, J. (1990). The Art of Southeast Asia: Temples and Sculpture. Thames & Hudson.
Geertz, C. (1973) The Interpretation of Cultures: Selected Essays. New York: Basic Books.
Geertz, C. (1980). Negara: The Theatre State in Nineteenth-Century Bali. Princeton University Press.
Gombrich, R. (1988), Theravada Buddhism: A Social History from Ancient Benares to Modern Colombo. London: Routledge.
Guy, J. (2014) 'Lost Kingdoms: Hindu-Buddhist Sculpture of Early Southeast Asia'. The Metropolitan Museum of Art. Available at: https://www.metmuseum.org/met-publications/lost-kingdoms-hindu-buddhist-sculpture-of-early-southeast-asia.
Hall, K.R. (1985). Maritime Trade and State Development in Early Southeast Asia. University of Hawaii Press.
Hall, K.R. (2011) A History of Early Southeast Asia: Maritime Trade and Societal Development, 100-1500. Lanham, MD: Rowman & Littlefield Publishers.
Heikkilä-Horn, M.-L. (2019) 'Hinduism in Southeast Asia', in Encyclopedia of Hinduism. Springer, pp. 1–5. Available at: https://doi.org/10.1007/978-94-024-1188-1_70.
Higham, C. (2001). The Civilization of Angkor. London: Weidenfeld & Nicolson.
I-Ching (2009). A Record of the Buddhist Religion as Practised in India and the Malay Archipelago. Munshiram Manoharlal Publishers.
Islamweb (2024) 'The Spread of Islam in Southeast Asia'. Available at: https://islamweb.net/en/article/136127/the-spread-of-islam-in-southeast-asia
Kulke, H. & Rothermund, D. (2010) A History of India. 5th edn. London: Routledge.
Kulke, H., & Rothermund, D. (2016). A History of India. Routledge.
Libretexts (n.d.) Art of Southeast Asia. Available at: https://human.libretexts.org/Bookshelves/Art/Art_History/11%3A_Art_of_South_and_Southeast_Asia_Before_1200_CE/11.04%3A_Art_of_Southeast_Asia.
Lombard, D. (2000) Le carrefour javanais: Essai d'histoire globale. Paris: Éditions de l'EHESS.
Mabbett, I.W. (1977), The Indianization of Southeast Asia: Reflections on the Historical Sources. Journal of Southeast Asian Studies, 8(1), pp. 1–14.
Mabbett, I.W. & Chandler, D.P. (1995), The Khmers. Oxford: Blackwell.
Malleret, L. (1959). L'Archéologie du Delta du Mékong. Paris: Ecole Française d'Extrême-Orient.

Manguin, P.-Y., Mani, A., & Wade, G. (Eds.). (2011). Early Interactions Between South and Southeast Asia: Reflections on Cross-Cultural Exchange. ISEAS–Yusof Ishak Institute.

Manguin, P.-Y. (2016). "Early Maritime Trade and Cultural Exchange in the Indian Ocean." In Manguin, P.-Y., Mani, A., & Wade, G. (Eds.), Early Interactions Between South and Southeast Asia: Reflections on Cross-Cultural Exchange (pp. 1–22). Singapore: ISEAS Publishing.

Martinus, A. and Herwindo, R. P. (2019) 'Comparative Study of Type-Morphology Architecture Borobudur-Prambanan Temple of Angkor Wat: Case Study on Mass Processes, Looks, Socks, and Ornaments'. Available at: https://www.academia.edu/39859579/COMPARATIVE_STUDY_OF_TYPE_MORPHOLOGY_ARCHITECTURE_BOROBUDUR_PRAMBANAN_TEMPLE_OF_ANGKOR_WAT_CASE_STUDY_ON_MASS_PROCESSES_LOOKS_SOCKS_AND_ORNAMENTS.

Miksic, J.N. (2009), Southeast Asian Ceramics: New Light on Old Pottery. Southeast Asian Ceramic Society, 2009.

Miksic, J. N. (2011). Old Javanese Gold: The Hunter Thompson Collection at the Yale University Art Gallery. Yale University Press.

Miksic, J. (2013). Singapore and the Silk Road of the Sea, 1300–1800. NUS Press.

Miksic, J. N., and Yian, C. (2016). Ancient Southeast Asia. Routledge.

Miksic, J.N. & Goh, G.Y. (2017). Ancient Southeast Asia. Routledge.

Munandar, A. A. (2020). "Majapahit and the Contemporary Kingdoms: Interactions and Views." Berkala Arkeologi, 40(2), 145–160. (ejournal.brin.go.id).

National Museum of Asian Art (NMAA) (n.d.) Conservation and Scientific Research. Available at: https://asia.si.edu/research/conservation-scientific-research/.

Noseworthy, W. (2022) 'Seeking Dharma Below the Winds: Hindu Particularism in Island Southeast Asia', International Journal of Hindu Studies, 26, pp. 393–423. Available at: https://doi.org/10.1007/s11407-022-09321-2.

Pandya Dhar, P. (2018) 'Monuments, Motifs, Myths: Architecture and its Transformations in India and Southeast Asia'. In S. Saran (ed.), Cultural and Civilizational Links Between India and Southeast Asia: Historical and Contemporary Dimensions. Palgrave Macmillan, pp. 325–345. Available at: https://www.academia.edu/37364963.

Patowary, K. N. (2023). "Hari-Hara: Tradition of Syncretism in South East Asia Special Reference." ShodhKosh: Journal of Visual and Performing Arts, 4(1). Available at: www.granthaalayahpublication.org.

Picard, M. (2011) 'Balinese Hinduism and the Indonesian State: Recent Developments', Archipel, 81(1), pp. 127–154. Available at: https://www.jstor.org/stable/27864809.

Pratiwi, Y., Numan, I., & Idham, N. C. (2024). "The Synchronization of Hindu Buddhist Spatial and Architecture in Traditional Javanese Mosques." Journal of Architectural Research and Design Studies, 8(2), 45–60.

Pratu: Journal of Buddhist and Hindu Art, Architecture and Archaeology of Ancient to Premodern Southeast Asia (n.d.) Available at: https://pratujournal.org/.

Preceden (2024) 'Kingdoms of Southeast Asia Timeline'. Available at: https://www.preceden.com/timeline/kingdoms-of-southeast-asia.

Pullen, L. (2021). "Majapahit: Stone Sculpture from the Fourteenth to the Fifteenth Century." In Patterned Splendour: Textiles Presented on Javanese Metal and Stone Sculptures; Eighth to Fifteenth Century (pp. 223–250). Singapore: ISEAS Publishing.

Rao, R. (2023) 'Hindu Culture in Indonesia', Academia.edu. Available at: https://www.academia.edu/95892347/Hindu_Culture_in_Indonesia.

Ray, H.C. (1994), Buddhist Saints in India: A Study in Buddhist Values and Orientations. Cambridge: Cambridge University Press.

Reid, A. (1988). Southeast Asia in the Age of Commerce, 1450–1680: The Lands Below the Winds. Yale University Press.

Revire, N. (2022) 'The Creative South: Buddhist and Hindu Art in Mediaeval Maritime Asia'. Academia.edu. Available at: https://www.academia.edu/77136262/2022_The_Creative_South_Buddhist_and_Hindu_Art_in_Mediaeval_Maritime_Asia_Vol_1_TOC_Intro_.

Reynolds, F. E. (2005) 'Buddhist Continuities in Thai Religion and Culture', in Smith, B. K. (ed.) Hinduism and Modernity. Oxford: Blackwell, pp. 167–185.

Ricklefs, M.C. (2001), A History of Modern Indonesia Since c.1200. 3rd edn. Stanford, CA: Stanford University Press.

Ricklefs, M. C. (2008) A History of Modern Indonesia since c. 1200. 4th edn. London: Palgrave Macmillan.

Robson, S. O. (1995). Nagarakretagama (Desawarnana). KITLV Press.

Sarkar, H.B. (1985). Trade and Trade Routes in Ancient India. Abhinav Publications.

Schmidt, B. (2010). Entangled Histories: Regionalism, Trade, and Identity in Early Southeast Asia. National University of Singapore Press.

Setiawan, B. (2017). "Ancient Architectural Influence Between Bali and Majapahit: Drawing Upon the Past for the Future." In M. Santoso & I. Budi (Eds.), Proceedings of the International Conference on Southeast Asian Studies (pp. 213–225). Singapore: Springer. (link.springer.com).

Singh, A. S. (2018) 'A Historical and Cultural Study of Buddhist Art in Early South-East Asia'. International Journal of Social Science and Humanity, 6(8), pp. 591–595. Available at: https://www.ijssh.org/vol6/711-H10004.pdf (Accessed: 19 December 2024).

Situngkir, H. (2015) 'Borobudur was Built Algorithmically'. Available at: https://arxiv.org/abs/1508.03649.

Smarthistory (n.d.) 'Cultural exchange and syncretism in the arts of South Asia since 1200'. Available at: https://smarthistory.org/reframing-art-history/cultural-exchange-syncretism-arts-south-asia-since-1200/.

Stark, M. T. (2006). "From Funan to Angkor: Collapse and Regeneration in Ancient Cambodia." In Schwartz, G. M., & Nichols, J. J. (Eds.), After Collapse: The Regeneration of Complex Societies (pp. 144–167). Tucson: University of Arizona Press.

Takakusu, J. (1896). A Record of the Buddhist Religion as Practised in India and the Malay Archipelago (A.D. 671–695) by I-Tsing. Clarendon Press.

Vadassery, S. (2017) 'The Dance of Life: Leisure, Culture and Religious Experience', in Cultural Traditions and Contemporary Challenges in Southeast Asia. Available at: https://crvp.org/publications/Series-IIID/IIID-3.pdf.

Vickers, A. (2014). "Majapahit and Panji Stories." In C. Kubuontubuh & P. Carey (Eds.), Majapahit: Inspiration for the World (pp. 47–66). Jakarta: Arsari. (www.academia.edu).

VIF (2024) 'India's Role in the Conservation of Cultural Heritage in Southeast Asia'. Available at: https://www.vifindia.org/article/2024/july/31/India-s-Role-in-the-Conservation-of-Cultural-Heritage-in-Southeast-Asia.

Wijaya, A. A., Widiastuti, & Mudra, I. K. (2018). "Application of Majapahit Architectural Elements in the Design of the Prapanca Secondary Market in Mojokerto, Jawa Timur." Journal of A Sustainable Global South, 2(2), 11–20.

Winter, T. (2010) 'Heritage Tourism and National Identity in Southeast Asia', Annals of Tourism Research, 37(3), pp. 715–731.

Wolters, O.W. (1999) History, Culture, and Region in Southeast Asian Perspectives. Revised edn. Ithaca, NY: Cornell University Southeast Asia Program Publications.

Woodward, M. R. (2003). Java, Indonesia, and Islam. Springer.

Yijing. A Record of Buddhist Practices Sent Home from the Southern Sea. Translated by Takakusu J., Clarendon Press, 1896.

PART II

The Colonial Impact

CHAPTER 5

The Arrival of European Powers (1500–1800)

Introduction

The period between 1500 and 1800 marked a profound transformation in the history of Indonesia, characterized by the arrival and establishment of European colonial powers that dramatically altered the archipelago's political, economic, and social landscapes. This era witnessed the gradual displacement of indigenous kingdoms and trading networks by European entities, most notably the Portuguese and the Dutch, who sought to control the lucrative spice trade and exert their influence over Southeast Asia.[1] The incursion of these foreign powers set in motion a series of events that would not only reshape Indonesia's internal dynamics but also integrate it into the emerging global economic system of the early modern period.

The Portuguese were the first Europeans to arrive in the Indonesian archipelago in the early sixteenth century, motivated by the desire to dominate the spice trade and spread Christianity.[2] Establishing footholds in strategic locations such as Malacca and the Moluccas, they introduced new military technologies and mercantile practices that disrupted

[1] Ricklefs, M.C. (2001), A History of Modern Indonesia Since c.1200. 3rd edn. Stanford, CA: Stanford University Press.

[2] Boxer, C.R. (1965) The Portuguese Seaborne Empire, 1415–1825. London: Hutchinson.

S. Ramesh, *The Political Economy of Indonesia's Economic Development, Volume I*, https://doi.org/10.1007/978-3-031-94350-8_5

existing trade patterns and political alliances.[3] However, their influence remained relatively limited due to strong resistance from local powers and competition from other European rivals. The Dutch emergence in the region during the late sixteenth and early seventeenth centuries marked a turning point in Indonesian history. The establishment of the Dutch East India Company (Vereenigde Oostindische Compagnie or VOC) in 1602 signalled the beginning of a systematic and sustained effort to control trade and territory across the archipelago.[4] Leveraging superior naval power and strategic diplomacy, the VOC succeeded in establishing a monopoly over the spice trade by subjugating local kingdoms and controlling key ports, most notably founding Batavia (modern-day Jakarta) as their administrative and commercial hub.[5] The Dutch colonial administration implemented exploitative economic policies, such as the forced cultivation system, which had profound and often devastating effects on the indigenous populations and economies.[6]

The arrival and entrenchment of European powers also led to significant social and cultural transformations within Indonesian society. The introduction of Christianity, European legal systems, and new social hierarchies disrupted traditional structures and practices, leading to both assimilation and resistance among local communities.[7] Moreover, the colonial period intensified patterns of migration and urbanization, as people were drawn to colonial centres for labour opportunities or displaced from their lands due to colonial policies.[8] These changes laid the foundations for modern Indonesian society, embedding complex legacies of colonialism that continue to influence the nation's development trajectory.

[3] Reid, A. (1993), SoutheastAsia in the Age of Commerce, 1450–1680: Volume Two, Expansion and Crisis. New Haven, CT: Yale University Press.

[4] Gaastra, F.S. (2003), The DutchEastIndiaCompany: Expansion and Decline. Zutphen: Walburg Pers.

[5] Taylor, J.G. (2003), Indonesia: Peoples and Histories. New Haven, CT: Yale University Press.

[6] Elson, R.E. (1994), Village Java under the Cultivation System, 1830–1870. Sydney: Allen & Unwin.

[7] Knaap, G. & Teitler, G. (2004), Between Discipline and Disgust: Deserters of the VOC Army in Eighteenth Century Asia. Itinerario, 28(2), pp. 55–76.

[8] Boomgaard, P. (1990), Children of the Colonial State: Population Growth and Economic Development in Java, 1795–1880. Amsterdam: Free University Press.

This chapter seeks to explore the multifaceted impacts of European colonialism on Indonesia between 1500 and 1800, examining how the interventions of the Portuguese and Dutch reshaped the archipelago's political economy and social fabric. Through an analysis of colonial strategies, indigenous responses, and the resulting economic and cultural transformations, the chapter aims to provide a comprehensive understanding of this critical period in Indonesian history. Drawing upon a range of academic sources, it will delve into the mechanisms of colonial control, the restructuring of trade networks, and the long-term consequences of colonial rule, highlighting the resilience and adaptability of Indonesian societies in the face of foreign domination.[9,10]

The Impact of European Colonialism on Indigenous Polities

European colonialism between 1500 and 1800 profoundly transformed the indigenous polities of Indonesia, reshaping the region's political, economic, and cultural fabric. The arrival of European powers, particularly the Dutch through the Vereenigde Oost-Indische Compagnie (VOC), marked a turning point in the history of the archipelago. The Dutch employed a system of indirect rule, which preserved traditional governance while subjugating local rulers to colonial authority. By maintaining Indigenous regents under Dutch oversight, the VOC undermined the autonomy of indigenous political structures. This hierarchical governance model replaced collaborative and localized power systems, eroded local governance practices, and introduced political instability. These changes created dependency on Dutch authority, with indigenous elites often reduced to instruments of colonial control rather than independent rulers.[11,12] The destabilizing impact of this indirect rule extended to the fabric of governance itself. Local leaders, or bupati, were co-opted into

[9] Cribb, R. (2000), Historical Dictionary of Indonesia. 2nd edn. Lanham, MD: Scarecrow Press.

[10] Vickers, A. (2005), A History of Modern Indonesia. Cambridge: Cambridge University Press.

[11] Ricklefs, M. C. (2008). A History of Modern Indonesia since c. 1200. 4th edn. London: Palgrave Macmillan.

[12] Taylor, J. G. (2003). Indonesia: Peoples and Histories. New Haven: Yale University Press.

the colonial system through promises of personal enrichment, leading to the erosion of traditional legitimacy and an increasing reliance on coercive measures to maintain control. The dual governance system also bred corruption, as indigenous rulers were caught between local expectations and colonial demands, resulting in widespread dissatisfaction and a gradual fragmentation of political authority.[13] Economically, the VOC's monopolistic practices were particularly detrimental. By controlling lucrative trade commodities like spices, the VOC marginalized indigenous traders and undermined traditional trade networks that had connected the archipelago with broader Indian Ocean trading systems for centuries. The Cultivation System (Cultuurstelsel), formalized in the nineteenth century but rooted in earlier VOC policies, forced local farmers to dedicate a portion of their agricultural output to cash crops like sugar, coffee, and indigo, destined for European markets. This extraction-based economic model enriched Dutch coffers while plunging Indigenous communities into poverty. Many farmers were forced to reduce subsistence agriculture, leading to widespread food insecurity and famine. These economic disruptions also contributed to the entrenchment of regional inequalities, with some areas, such as Java, bearing a disproportionate burden of colonial exploitation.[14,15] The cultural impact of European colonialism was equally profound. The imposition of centralized European legal systems marginalized adat—customary laws that governed land use, dispute resolution, and social relations in Indigenous communities. By replacing adat with rigid statute-based legal frameworks, the Dutch fundamentally altered the social fabric of the region. In the context of Indonesia, "adat" refers to the traditional customary laws, norms, and practices that govern social, cultural, and legal interactions within local communities. It encompasses a wide range of practices, including the regulation of interpersonal relationships, community responsibilities, and conflict resolution

[13] Henley, D. (2004). Conflict, Justice, and the Stranger-King: Indigenous Roots of Colonial Rule in Indonesia and Elsewhere. Modern Asian Studies, 38(1), pp. 85–144.

[14] Booth, A. (1998). The Indonesian Economy in the Nineteenth and Twentieth Centuries: A History of Missed Opportunities. London: Palgrave Macmillan.

[15] Henley, D. (2004). Conflict, Justice, and the Stranger-King: Indigenous Roots of Colonial Rule in Indonesia and Elsewhere. Modern Asian Studies, 38(1), pp. 85–144.

within a local or tribal context.[16,17] Adat also governs communal land ownership and resource management, emphasizing collective rights and responsibilities over individual property rights.[18] It prescribes religious and cultural rituals, including marriage, funerals, and harvest celebrations, reflecting the spiritual and cultural values of the community.[19] As a form of customary law, adat operates alongside formal state law, providing local frameworks for resolving disputes and maintaining order.[20] Adat varies widely across Indonesia's diverse ethnic and regional communities, reflecting their unique historical and cultural contexts. During colonial rule, adat often conflicted with imposed legal systems, as colonial powers sought to replace or marginalize it with Western-style, centralized laws.[21] However, adat remains an important aspect of Indonesian identity and continues to influence local governance and societal norms in many parts of the country.[22] Changes to adat disenfranchised many indigenous people, as land previously held under communal or customary arrangements was increasingly privatized and appropriated by the colonial state or European settlers.[23] Social stratification was also reinforced by the creation of a Eurasian community, born out of unions between Europeans and locals. While Eurasians served as intermediaries in the colonial

[16] Davidson, J. S., and Henley, D. (2007). The Revival of Tradition in Indonesian Politics: The Deployment of Adat from Colonialism to Indigenism. London: Routledge.

[17] Henley, D. (2004). Conflict, Justice, and the Stranger-King: Indigenous Roots of Colonial Rule in Indonesia and Elsewhere. Modern Asian Studies, 38(1), pp. 85–144.

[18] Fitzpatrick, D. (2008). "Beyond Dualism: Land Acquisition and Law in Indonesia." In Indonesian Law and Society, edited by T. Lindsey, pp. 74–94. Sydney: Federation Press.

[19] Bowen, J. R. (2003). Muslims through Discourse: Religion and Ritual in Gayo Society. Princeton: Princeton University Press.

[20] Burns, P. (2004). The Leiden Legacy: Concepts of Law in Indonesia. Leiden: KITLV Press.

[21] Hooker, M. B. (1978). Adat Law in Modern Indonesia. Kuala Lumpur: Oxford University Press.

[22] Davidson, J. S., and Henley, D. (2007). The Revival of Tradition in Indonesian Politics: The Deployment of Adat from Colonialism to Indigenism. London: Routledge.

[23] Waites, B. (1999). Europe and the Third World: From Colonisation to Decolonisation c. 1500–1998. London: Macmillan Press.

system, they often faced systemic discrimination and ambiguous legal status, embodying the contradictions and inequities of colonial rule.[24]

The architectural legacy of the colonial period highlights the cultural dominance exercised by European powers. Cities like Batavia (modern-day Jakarta) were transformed into hubs of Dutch colonial authority, with imposing administrative buildings and fortifications that symbolized European power. These structures were often built using local labour and materials, demonstrating the exploitation inherent in colonial governance. Simultaneously, the redirection of resources towards colonial architectural projects stifled the development of indigenous architecture, reflecting the broader suppression of local cultural expression.[25] The hybrid architectural styles that emerged, blending European designs with local influences, also illustrate how indigenous communities adapted and resisted cultural domination, subtly asserting their identities within the confines of colonial rule.[26] Despite the pervasive disruptions caused by colonialism, indigenous resistance persisted, often manifesting in strategic adaptations rather than outright rebellion. The Sultanate of Banten in western Java provides a compelling example of this resistance. By leveraging its control over critical trade routes, Banten managed to maintain a degree of autonomy, negotiating with Dutch authorities while safeguarding its internal governance structures. Such instances highlight the agency of indigenous rulers in navigating the colonial landscape, balancing accommodation with defiance to preserve their political and cultural identities.[27,28] The broader implications of this period reveal a dual narrative of exploitation and resilience. While colonial powers dismantled traditional political systems and imposed new economic and cultural hierarchies, Indigenous communities demonstrated remarkable

[24] Andaya, B.W. (1993). To Live as Brothers: SoutheastSumatra in the Seventeenth and Eighteenth Centuries. Honolulu: University of Hawaii Press.

[25] Vink, M. (2019). 'From the Cape to Canton: The DutchIndian Ocean World, 1600–1800—A Littoral Census', Journal of Indian Ocean World Studies, 3, pp. 13–37.

[26] Taylor, J. G. (2003). Indonesia: Peoples and Histories. New Haven: Yale University Press.

[27] Reid, A. (1993). SoutheastAsia in the Age of Commerce, 1450–1680: Expansion and Crisis. New Haven: Yale University Press.

[28] Henley, D. (2004). Conflict, Justice, and the Stranger-King: Indigenous Roots of Colonial Rule in Indonesia and Elsewhere. Modern Asian Studies, 38(1), pp. 85–144.

adaptability. They resisted complete subjugation by reinterpreting colonial policies and preserving key aspects of their heritage. The legacy of this era is evident in the modern political and cultural landscape of Indonesia, where the historical memory of colonialism continues to inform debates about national identity, governance, and development.

European colonialism profoundly and multifacetedly impacted indigenous polities in Indonesia between 1500 and 1800. Through political subjugation, economic exploitation, and cultural imposition, colonial powers reshaped the sociopolitical and economic fabric of the archipelago. However, the resilience and adaptability of Indigenous communities underscore the complexity of this transformative period, revealing a nuanced narrative of domination and resistance that continues to inform Indonesia's historical and contemporary identity.

The Role of the Dutch East India Company (VOC) in Reshaping the Indonesian Economy

The Dutch East India Company (Vereenigde Oostindische Compagnie, or VOC) fundamentally transformed the Indonesian economy between 1602 and its dissolution in 1799. Initially established as a commercial enterprise, the VOC quickly evolved into a quasi-sovereign entity, wielding unprecedented economic and political power in the archipelago. Its control over trade, agriculture, and governance profoundly altered indigenous economic systems, trade networks, and labour practices.

The Dutch East India Company (Vereenigde Oostindische Compagnie, or VOC) fundamentally transformed Indonesia's economic landscape through its monopolistic control over trade, its restructuring of agricultural systems, and its imposition of exploitative labour practices. By monopolizing the lucrative spice trade, the VOC disrupted traditional trade networks that had linked the archipelago to broader Indian Ocean commerce for centuries. These networks, which had fostered relatively equitable exchanges between local producers and regional traders, were supplanted by VOC-dominated systems that marginalized indigenous merchants and consolidated wealth within Dutch hands.[29] Through exclusive contracts, price manipulation, and the use of military force,

[29] Ricklefs, M. C. (2008). A History of Modern Indonesia since c. 1200. 4th edn. London: Palgrave Macmillan.

the VOC coerced local producers into selling their goods at artificially low prices, undermining the economic independence of indigenous communities.[30] Agricultural practices were also profoundly altered by the VOC. In areas like Java, the company introduced systems such as the Preanger System, which required farmers to cultivate cash crops like coffee for export markets under coercive conditions. This shift disrupted subsistence farming, leaving local populations dependent on imported food and vulnerable to famine.[31] Moreover, the focus on monoculture led to environmental degradation and reduced agricultural diversity, compounding the socio-economic challenges faced by local communities.[32] The focus on monoculture during the VOC period, particularly under exploitative systems like the Preanger System in Java, had profound environmental and socio-economic consequences. Monoculture refers to the large-scale cultivation of a single crop, such as coffee or sugar, driven by European demand and enforced by colonial policies. While it maximized short-term profits for the Dutch East India Company, it disrupted traditional agricultural practices and eroded the ecological balance of the regions under its control. By replacing diversified farming systems, monoculture led to soil depletion, as the repeated planting of a single crop stripped essential nutrients from the land. This degradation made the soil less fertile over time, reducing agricultural productivity and increasing the vulnerability of local populations to food insecurity.[33] The replacement of subsistence crops with export-oriented cash crops, such as coffee, left communities dependent on volatile global markets and imported food supplies, heightening their exposure to famine during economic or climatic disruptions.[34] In addition to soil degradation, monoculture also disrupted local water systems. Large-scale coffee and

[30] Reid, A. (1993). SoutheastAsia in the Age of Commerce, 1450–1680: Expansion and Crisis. New Haven: Yale University Press.

[31] Booth, A. (1998). The Indonesian Economy in the Nineteenth and Twentieth Centuries: A History of Missed Opportunities. London: Palgrave Macmillan.

[32] Henley, D. (2004). Fertility, Food, and Fever: Population, Economy, and Environment in North and Central Sulawesi, 1600–1930. Leiden: KITLV Press.

[33] Henley, D. (2004). Fertility, Food, and Fever: Population, Economy, and Environment in North and Central Sulawesi, 1600–1930. Leiden: KITLV Press.

[34] Booth, A. (1998). The Indonesian Economy in the Nineteenth and Twentieth Centuries: A History of Missed Opportunities. London: Macmillan Press.

sugar plantations often required significant irrigation, leading to overextraction of water resources and altering natural hydrological patterns. This, in turn, contributed to the erosion of arable land and the loss of biodiversity, as native plant species were displaced to accommodate colonial crops.[35] These ecological changes had cascading effects on local ecosystems, reducing the resilience of both the environment and the communities that depended on it. The socio-economic challenges caused by monoculture extended beyond environmental degradation. Forced labour systems imposed by the VOC compelled farmers to cultivate cash crops under exploitative conditions, leaving them with little time or resources to maintain their subsistence farming practices. Forced labour under Dutch colonial rule, particularly during the era of the Dutch East India Company (VOC), had profound effects on Indonesian farmers, leaving them with insufficient time and resources to sustain their subsistence farming practices. The VOC imposed systems like the Preanger System in Java, which coerced farmers into cultivating cash crops such as coffee under exploitative conditions.[36] These systems prioritized export production for European markets, leaving farmers with limited opportunities to grow food crops essential for their survival. The quotas enforced by the VOC demanded substantial labour input, forcing farmers to divert time away from their own subsistence needs, which weakened their ability to produce sufficient food for their families.[37] Additionally, the VOC's policies reallocated fertile lands, traditionally used for diverse subsistence farming, to cash crops required for export. This shift to monoculture reduced agricultural diversity, undermining food security and leaving communities vulnerable to famine during economic or climatic disruptions.[38] The lack of compensation for forced labour further compounded the farmers' plight. Many received minimal or no payment for their work, which restricted their ability to invest in essential farming tools, seeds, or other resources needed for their

[35] Henley, D. (2004). Fertility, Food, and Fever: Population, Economy, and Environment in North and Central Sulawesi, 1600–1930. Leiden: KITLV Press.

[36] Booth, A. (1998). The Indonesian Economy in the Nineteenth and Twentieth Centuries: A History of Missed Opportunities. London: Macmillan Press.

[37] Henley, D. (2004). Fertility, Food, and Fever: Population, Economy, and Environment in North and Central Sulawesi, 1600–1930. Leiden: KITLV Press.

[38] Henley, D. (2004). Fertility, Food, and Fever: Population, Economy, and Environment in North and Central Sulawesi, 1600–1930. Leiden: KITLV Press.

subsistence activities.[39] Instead, they were often driven into debt as they struggled to meet colonial demands while still providing for their families. The focus on monoculture under VOC rule not only disrupted traditional farming practices but also degraded the land. Soil depletion caused by the repetitive cultivation of single crops like coffee or sugar rendered the land less productive over time, further constraining farmers' ability to maintain subsistence agriculture.[40] This ecological degradation exacerbated food insecurity and increased farmers' reliance on expensive or scarce imported food supplies controlled by colonial markets, leaving them exposed to famine during periods of market volatility.[41] Furthermore, labour systems imposed by the VOC also physically exhausted farmers, leaving them unable to devote energy to their own agricultural needs. The rigorous demands of forced labour, combined with the time taken away from tending their own fields, disrupted traditional agricultural cycles and community-based farming systems. These practices eroded the self-sufficiency of rural communities and undermined social structures that had traditionally supported collective farming and food production.[42] Consequently, the socio-economic inequality embedded in forced labour systems persisted long after the VOC's rule, leaving a legacy of poverty and dependency among Indonesia's farming communities. The reliance on forced labour to sustain VOC profits illustrates the extractive nature of colonial systems that prioritized short-term economic gain over sustainable development. By reshaping traditional agricultural practices and exploiting local labour, the VOC created conditions that entrenched cycles of poverty and vulnerability, significantly affecting the long-term resilience of Indonesian farmers and their communities.[43,44]

[39] Taylor, J. G. (2003). Indonesia: Peoples and Histories. New Haven: Yale University Press.

[40] Booth, A. (1998). The Indonesian Economy in the Nineteenth and Twentieth Centuries: A History of Missed Opportunities. London: Macmillan Press.

[41] Ricklefs, M. C. (2008). A History of Modern Indonesia since c.1200. 4th ed. Basingstoke: Palgrave Macmillan.

[42] Reid, A. (1993). SoutheastAsia in the Age of Commerce, 1450–1680: Volume Two, Expansion and Crisis. New Haven: Yale University Press.

[43] Taylor, J. G. (2003). Indonesia: Peoples and Histories. New Haven: Yale University Press.

[44] Henley, D. (2004). Fertility, Food, and Fever: Population, Economy, and Environment in North and Central Sulawesi, 1600–1930. Leiden: KITLV Press.

The spillover effects of colonial administration practices thus led to cycles of debt and poverty, as farmers were unable to meet both their subsistence needs and the demands of colonial administrators.[45] Additionally, the focus on monoculture reduced the agricultural diversity that had traditionally provided communities with nutritional security and economic stability, further compounding their vulnerability to external shocks.[46] The emphasis on monoculture under VOC rule created a series of interconnected challenges, including environmental degradation, reduced biodiversity, and increased socio-economic inequality. These practices undermined the long-term sustainability of local agricultural systems, leaving a legacy of vulnerability that persisted well beyond the colonial period.

Labor practices under the VOC further exacerbated economic inequalities. The company relied heavily on systems of forced labour, including corvée labour, in which local populations were compelled to work on VOC-controlled plantations and infrastructure projects. These practices disrupted traditional livelihoods and imposed significant physical and economic burdens on indigenous workers.[47] The Hongi expeditions in the Moluccas exemplify the VOC's coercive strategies, as naval patrols enforced the destruction of unauthorized spice cultivation to maintain the company's monopoly, often displacing entire communities and intensifying social instability.[48]

The VOC's extractive policies created a dualistic economy in Indonesia. While the colonial export economy flourished, indigenous systems were systematically undermined, fostering economic dependency

[45] Taylor, J. G. (2003). Indonesia: Peoples and Histories. New Haven: Yale University Press.

[46] Ricklefs, M. C. (2008). A History of Modern Indonesia since c.1200. 4th ed. Basingstoke: Palgrave Macmillan.

[47] Taylor, J. G. (2003). Indonesia: Peoples and Histories. New Haven: Yale University Press.

[48] Henley, D. (2004). Fertility, Food, and Fever: Population, Economy, and Environment in North and Central Sulawesi, 1600–1930. Leiden: KITLV Press.

and deepening socio-economic stratification. Local elites who collaborated with the VOC were rewarded with privileges, but these arrangements often alienated broader populations and entrenched hierarchies that persisted into the post-colonial era.[49,50]

While the VOC brought immense wealth to the Netherlands and became a model for corporate enterprise globally, its legacy in Indonesia was marked by systemic exploitation, deepening inequality, and entrenched economic dependency. The VOC's economic strategy cantered on monopolizing the lucrative spice trade, exploiting Indonesia's dominance as the world's leading producer of nutmeg, cloves, and mace. By imposing exclusive contracts and using military force to suppress unauthorized trade, the VOC disrupted pre-existing trade networks that had sustained equitable exchanges between local producers and Indian Ocean markets for centuries.[51] These traditional trade systems were integral to local economies, fostering regional interdependence and shared prosperity. In contrast, the VOC's monopolistic policies marginalized indigenous traders, compelling them to sell at artificially low prices while the company monopolized profits in European markets.[52] This reallocation of wealth created stark economic disparities, shifting resources from local communities to the Dutch colonial rulers. The VOC's reliance on coercion to enforce its monopoly is epitomized by the Hongi system in the Moluccas. This naval patrol destroyed unauthorized spice cultivation and trade, ensuring strict compliance with VOC policies. While the Hongi system secured the company's dominance, it caused widespread hardship for local communities. Entire populations were uprooted, traditional agricultural practices were abandoned, and local economies were

[49] Ricklefs, M. C. (2008). A History of Modern Indonesia since c.1200. 4th ed. Basingstoke: Palgrave Macmillan.

[50] Reid, A. (1993). SoutheastAsia in the Age of Commerce, 1450–1680: Volume Two, Expansion and Crisis. New Haven: Yale University Press.

[51] Ricklefs, M. C. (2008). A History of Modern Indonesia since c.1200. 4th ed. Basingstoke: Palgrave Macmillan.

[52] Reid, A. (1993). SoutheastAsia in the Age of Commerce, 1450–1680: Volume Two, Expansion and Crisis. New Haven: Yale University Press.

left destabilized.[53] The resulting population displacement and food insecurity illustrate the human cost of the VOC's extractive economic policies, which prioritized profit over social stability.

Trade hubs such as Batavia (modern Jakarta) further consolidated the VOC's economic dominance and reflected its exploitative colonial model. Established as the administrative and commercial centre of VOC operations, Batavia epitomized the extractive nature of Dutch colonial urbanization. The city's development prioritized European commercial interests at the expense of indigenous welfare, often relying on forced labour and displacing local populations to support its infrastructure. Batavia also became a site of concentrated economic and political power, where local elites were co-opted into the colonial system, further entrenching inequalities.[54] This pattern of urban exploitation highlighted the VOC's role in restructuring Indonesia's economy to serve European needs, often at the expense of local populations. Beyond trade, the VOC's influence extended to agricultural practices, fundamentally reshaping local economies. The Preanger System in West Java serves as a striking example of this transformation. Under this system, local farmers were forced to cultivate coffee for export markets, dedicating significant portions of their labour and land to crops that benefited European markets rather than their own needs. These arrangements often left farmers in a state of perpetual debt and vulnerability, as they received little to no compensation for their labour.[55] The focus on monoculture not only disrupted subsistence farming but also exposed communities to environmental degradation and economic volatility, further compounding their hardships. The dualistic economy introduced by the VOC deepened socio-economic stratification in Indonesia. While the export-driven colonial economy thrived, local economies were systematically undermined, leaving Indigenous communities reliant on subsistence agriculture and informal trade networks. Indigenous elites who collaborated with the VOC were rewarded with wealth and privileges, creating a class of intermediaries who perpetuated the system of exploitation.

[53] Henley, D. (2004). Fertility, Food, and Fever: Population, Economy, and Environment in North and Central Sulawesi, 1600–1930. Leiden: KITLV Press.

[54] Taylor, J. G. (2003). Indonesia: Peoples and Histories. New Haven: Yale University Press.

[55] Booth, A. (1998). The Indonesian Economy in the Nineteenth and Twentieth Centuries: A History of Missed Opportunities. London: Macmillan Press.

During Dutch colonial rule in India, particularly in regions where the Dutch East India Company (VOC) held sway, the collaboration of indigenous elites was a cornerstone of the VOC's governance strategy. These elites—local rulers, zamindars (landlords), or community leaders—were co-opted into the colonial system by being granted wealth, privileges, and authority. In exchange, they functioned as intermediaries, facilitating the VOC's exploitative economic policies, such as forced labour, cash crop cultivation, and monopolistic trade practices. This collaboration entrenched a dualistic economic structure where the colonial export economy thrived at the expense of Indigenous communities.[56] The rewards given to these elites often included control over land and labour, tax exemptions, and shares in the profits of the colonial economy. By creating incentives for their loyalty, the VOC ensured that the local population was managed with minimal direct intervention. These elites, seeking to preserve their newfound status, often enforced the VOC's exploitative policies with greater zeal than the Dutch officials themselves. This led to a system where the burden of colonial extraction fell disproportionately on the lower strata of society, particularly the peasantry.[57] The intermediaries' vested interests in maintaining the colonial order perpetuated systems of exploitation. They collected taxes, ensured compliance with forced cultivation policies, and suppressed dissent, often profiting from the very systems that impoverished the broader population. This dual role as both enforcers of colonial authority and beneficiaries of its policies alienated the elites from most of their communities, deepening social and economic divisions.[58] The long-term effects of this arrangement were profound. The intermediary class became integral to the functioning of colonial rule and the broader economy, ensuring that the VOC could maximize profits while avoiding the costs of direct administration. Over time, this class of elites embedded themselves into the colonial hierarchy, contributing to the stratification of society and perpetuating inequality. Even after the decline of Dutch influence in India, these patterns of inequality and the legacy of exploitation persisted, influencing

[56] Chaudhuri, K. N. (1985). Trade and Civilisation in the Indian Ocean: An Economic History from the Rise of Islam to 1750. Cambridge: Cambridge University Press.

[57] Prakash, O. (1998). European Commercial Enterprise in Pre-Colonial India. Cambridge: Cambridge University Press.

[58] Arasaratnam, S. (1986). Merchants, Companies, and Commerce on the Coromandel Coast, 1650–1740. Delhi: Oxford University Press.

post-colonial governance structures and socio-economic dynamics.[59] This collaboration between the Dutch colonial rulers and the indigenous elite further alienated the broader population and reinforced existing hierarchies, embedding patterns of inequality that would persist long after the VOC's dissolution.[60] These dynamics highlight the broader implications of the VOC's policies, which prioritized economic extraction over sustainable development. In colonial Indonesia, the Dutch East India Company (VOC) strategically co-opted indigenous elites to maintain control over the vast and diverse archipelago. These elites, often local rulers, village heads, or influential figures, were rewarded with wealth, privileges, and positions of authority in exchange for their collaboration with the colonial administration. This collaboration created a class of intermediaries who played a key role in perpetuating the system of exploitation imposed by the VOC. These elites were instrumental in enforcing policies like forced labour and cash crop cultivation, as they acted as mediators between the colonial authorities and the local population, often benefiting from the oppressive systems they helped administer.[61] By granting these elites significant economic and social advantages, the VOC entrenched a dualistic economic structure that separated colonial and indigenous systems. The elites were often given access to land, monopolies on local trade, or tax exemptions, which set them apart from the broader population and incentivized their loyalty to the colonial regime.[62] This collaboration not only alienated the elites from the general populace but also ensured the continuation of exploitative practices, as the elites had vested interests in maintaining the status quo.[63] Furthermore, the privileges extended to these elites created hierarchies that deepened socio-economic stratification. The intermediary class, benefiting from colonial policies, often used

[59] Bayly, C. A. (1988). Indian Society and the Making of the British Empire. Cambridge: Cambridge University Press.

[60] Reid, A. (1993). SoutheastAsia in the Age of Commerce, 1450–1680: Volume Two, Expansion and Crisis. New Haven: Yale University Press.

[61] Ricklefs, M. C. (2008). A History of Modern Indonesia since c.1200. 4th ed. Basingstoke: Palgrave Macmillan.

[62] Taylor, J. G. (2003). Indonesia: Peoples and Histories. New Haven: Yale University Press.

[63] Henley, D. (2004). Fertility, Food, and Fever: Population, Economy, and Environment in North and Central Sulawesi, 1600–1930. Leiden: KITLV Press.

their power to extract additional labour or taxes from the local population, compounding the burdens already imposed by the VOC. This perpetuated cycles of exploitation and poverty for the majority of the population while consolidating the power and wealth of the elites.[64] The reliance on this intermediary class was not just a mechanism of control but also a cost-effective strategy for the VOC, as it allowed the colonial administration to maintain dominance with minimal direct oversight. The long-term consequences of this arrangement were significant. The collaboration entrenched patterns of inequality and dependency that persisted into the post-colonial period, as many elites transitioned seamlessly into roles of authority within the modern state. These dynamics highlight the VOC's broader strategy of governance, which prioritized short-term stability and profit over equitable development or sustainable governance structures.[65] The resulting social fragmentation and economic disparities became a lasting legacy of colonial exploitation in Indonesia.

Despite its initial success, the VOC faced significant internal challenges that undermined its dominance. By the eighteenth century, inefficiencies and corruption had eroded the company's financial standing. Corruption among VOC officials, combined with growing resistance from local populations and increased competition from other European powers, exposed the limits of the company's extractive economic model.[66] The company's inability to adapt to changing political and economic conditions, coupled with mismanagement, led to its eventual dissolution in 1799. However, the Dutch colonial state absorbed many of the VOC's assets and practices, perpetuating the exploitative systems it had established. The VOC's two-century presence in Indonesia profoundly reshaped the region's economy, leaving a complex and often damaging legacy. While its monopolistic control over trade and forced agricultural practices generated immense wealth for the Netherlands, these policies entrenched economic dependency, disrupted traditional systems, and exacerbated inequalities across the archipelago. The company's reliance on coercion and its prioritization of profit over sustainability created long-lasting structural imbalances

[64] Reid, A. (1993). SoutheastAsia in the Age of Commerce, 1450–1680: Volume Two, Expansion and Crisis. New Haven: Yale University Press.

[65] Booth, A. (1998). The Indonesian Economy in the Nineteenth and Twentieth Centuries: A History of Missed Opportunities. London: Macmillan Press.

[66] Taylor, J. G. (2003). Indonesia: Peoples and Histories. New Haven: Yale University Press.

that continue to influence Indonesia's development. At the same time, the VOC's role as a pioneer of corporate enterprise and global trade underscores the duality of its legacy: a testament to the power of commerce and capitalism, but also a stark reminder of the human costs of colonial exploitation.

The Transformation of Trade Networks Under European Dominance

The arrival of European powers in Indonesia during the early modern period (1500–1800) fundamentally altered the archipelago's trade networks, reshaping them to prioritize European economic interests. For centuries prior to European influence, Indonesian trade operated through decentralized and interconnected maritime exchange systems. These networks linked local producers with major trading hubs such as Malacca, Aceh, and Makassar, which acted as critical nodes connecting Southeast Asia to the broader Indian Ocean economy. Through these systems, Indonesia's rich natural resources, including spices, textiles, and timber, flowed freely to markets in India, China, the Middle East, and beyond, fostering regional prosperity and autonomy.[67] Autonomy refers to the regional economies and local trade systems in Indonesia and the surrounding areas. Before European intervention, these systems operated independently, with local producers, merchants, and port cities having significant control over trade routes, production, and economic exchanges. European dominance undermined this independence by imposing monopolies and centralized control, effectively stripping local and regional stakeholders of their economic self-determination.

The Portuguese were the first European power to disrupt these indigenous networks, capturing Malacca in 1511. Malacca had been a key port for traders from Java, Sumatra, and the Spice Islands, facilitating the flow of goods like nutmeg, cloves, and mace to international markets. Portuguese control introduced militarized trade routes and high tariffs, which marginalized traditional merchants and dismantled local economic systems. While the Portuguese influence in the region waned by the late sixteenth century, their monopolistic approach to trade left a legacy,

[67] Chaudhuri, K. N. (1985). Trade and Civilisation in the Indian Ocean: An Economic History from the Rise of Islam to 1750. Cambridge: Cambridge University Press.

paving the way for other European powers, particularly the Dutch, to impose even more rigid systems of control.[68]

The establishment of the Dutch East India Company (VOC) in 1602 marked a turning point in the transformation of trade networks. The VOC institutionalized European dominance by combining military might with corporate monopolies. Through a combination of force and diplomacy, the company secured exclusive contracts with local rulers, compelling them to supply spices like nutmeg and cloves at fixed, often unfair prices. This monopoly was further enforced through the Hongi system, a naval campaign in the Moluccas aimed at destroying unauthorized spice cultivation. The Hongi expeditions devastated local economies and communities, displacing populations and ensuring VOC control over production and trade routes.[69] Centralization of trade operations was another significant aspect of the VOC's transformation of Indonesian trade. The Dutch established Batavia (modern Jakarta) as the administrative and commercial centre of their Southeast Asian empire. This centralization marked a departure from the decentralized trading systems that had characterized the region for centuries. While Batavia flourished as a hub for the export of spices, coffee, and textiles, it marginalized secondary ports like Banten and Makassar, which had previously been vibrant centres of regional trade. The shift to centralized control also meant that local economies were increasingly restructured to serve European markets, with little regard for the needs of Indigenous populations.[70]

The VOC's monopolistic practices created a dualistic economic structure in Indonesia. On one side, the colonial export economy thrived, driven by the exploitation of labour and resources to meet European demand. On the other, local subsistence economies were systematically undermined. Indigenous merchants and producers were often forced into subordinate roles or excluded entirely from lucrative trade activities. The suppression of inter-island trade networks, which had traditionally integrated regional economies, further weakened local economic resilience. The focus on single commodities, such as spices, coffee,

[68] Reid, A. (1993). SoutheastAsia in the Age of Commerce, 1450–1680: Volume Two, Expansion and Crisis. New Haven: Yale University Press.

[69] Ricklefs, M. C. (2008). A History of Modern Indonesia since c.1200. 4th ed. Basingstoke: Palgrave Macmillan.

[70] Henley, D. (2004). Fertility, Food, and Fever: Population, Economy, and Environment in North and Central Sulawesi, 1600–1930. Leiden: KITLV Press.

and sugar, exposed the Indonesian economy to the volatility of global markets, leaving local populations vulnerable to price fluctuations and environmental shocks.[71]

The British interregnum in Java (1811–1816) under Sir Stamford Raffles momentarily disrupted Dutch control but did not significantly alter the trajectory of European dominance. Raffles sought to liberalize trade and dismantle some of the VOC's monopolistic structures. He introduced reforms such as land taxation to replace forced cultivation systems, aiming to restore some degree of economic autonomy to local populations. However, these efforts were short-lived, and the Dutch quickly re-established control in 1816. Upon their return, the Dutch expanded forced cultivation systems like the Preanger System, which required farmers in West Java to dedicate land and labour to coffee production for export. This system further entrenched Indonesia's integration into global markets at the expense of local subsistence farming and economic self-reliance.[72] The transformation of trade networks under European dominance had profound long-term consequences for Indonesian society and economy. The militarization and monopolization of commerce disrupted indigenous economic systems that had previously fostered regional interdependence and prosperity. Centralized trade operations redirected resources to European markets, leaving local populations impoverished and dependent. The colonial focus on export-driven economies exacerbated social inequalities, creating a dualistic structure where colonial elites and their local collaborators thrived at the expense of the majority. These dependencies and inequalities persisted well beyond the colonial period, shaping Indonesia's economic and political trajectories into the modern era.[73] The colonial policies and structures established by European powers, particularly the Dutch East India Company (VOC) and later the Dutch colonial state, created systemic dependencies and inequalities that left a lasting imprint on Indonesia's economic and political development. These dependencies stemmed from the transformation of Indonesia's economy into one that prioritized the extraction and

[71] Booth, A. (1998). The Indonesian Economy in the Nineteenth and Twentieth Centuries: A History of Missed Opportunities. London: Macmillan Press.

[72] Taylor, J. G. (2003). Indonesia: Peoples and Histories. New Haven: Yale University Press.

[73] Ricklefs, M. C. (2008). A History of Modern Indonesia since c.1200. 4th ed. Basingstoke: Palgrave Macmillan.

export of resources for European markets, rather than fostering local economic resilience or diversification. This focus on monoculture and export-oriented production left Indonesia vulnerable to global market fluctuations, as well as reliant on colonial infrastructure and systems of governance to sustain economic activity.[74] The inequalities introduced during the colonial period were deeply embedded in social and economic hierarchies. Indigenous elites who collaborated with colonial powers were rewarded with privileges, land, and positions of authority, creating a class of intermediaries who perpetuated the system of exploitation. Meanwhile, much of the population was subjected to forced labour and the cultivation of cash crops, such as coffee and sugar, which disrupted subsistence farming and exacerbated poverty. These social divisions created a dualistic economy in which the colonial export sector thrived, while local communities faced economic stagnation and limited opportunities for upward mobility.[75]

These colonial legacies persisted well into the post-colonial era. For example, the economic dependency on exporting raw materials and cash crops continued after Indonesia's independence, as the new nation struggled to industrialize and diversify its economy. The infrastructure and administrative systems inherited from the colonial period were often ill-suited to addressing the needs of a modern, independent state. Furthermore, the social hierarchies entrenched during the colonial era, including the concentration of land ownership among a small elite, continued to exacerbate economic inequality and hinder social mobility.[76] These hierarchies were sustained through mechanisms such as the forced cultivation system (cultuurstelsel) and land ownership structures that prioritized the interests of the Dutch colonial administration and their local collaborators. Under the cultuurstelsel introduced in the nineteenth century, peasants were required to allocate a portion of their land and labour to grow cash crops like coffee and sugar for export. While the profits from these exports flowed primarily to the colonial government and

[74] Ricklefs, M. C. (2008). A History of Modern Indonesia since c.1200. 4th ed. Basingstoke: Palgrave Macmillan.

[75] Booth, A. (1998). The Indonesian Economy in the Nineteenth and Twentieth Centuries: A History of Missed Opportunities. London: Macmillan Press.

[76] Taylor, J. G. (2003). Indonesia: Peoples and Histories. New Haven: Yale University Press.

European markets, local village elites (priyayi), who acted as intermediaries, were rewarded with privileges such as control over large tracts of land and administrative authority. This arrangement solidified their socio-economic dominance while impoverishing most rural farmers who were left with insufficient resources to sustain their subsistence farming needs.[77] Another example can be seen in the redistribution of land during colonial reforms in the late nineteenth and early twentieth centuries, which often formalized land ownership in favour of colonial plantations and wealthy local elites. In regions like Java, large estates were owned either by Dutch planters or by Indigenous aristocrats who collaborated with the colonial administration. Meanwhile, the rural population was often relegated to tenant farming or sharecropping, which left them vulnerable to exploitative practices and perpetuated cycles of poverty.[78] These patterns of land concentration and economic disparity did not disappear with the end of colonial rule. After independence, many of the landownership structures remained intact, as large landowners were often politically influential and resisted land redistribution efforts. For instance, in post-independence Indonesia, the land reform laws of the 1960s faced significant resistance from both traditional elites and the military, resulting in limited redistribution of land to smallholders. This perpetuated rural poverty and constrained opportunities for social mobility for most of the population.[79] In essence, the colonial concentration of land ownership created a rigid social hierarchy where a small elite controlled vast economic resources while the majority of the population remained marginalized. This hierarchy hindered social mobility by limiting access to land, capital, and opportunities for education or entrepreneurship, effectively locking many Indonesians into cycles of poverty that persisted well into the modern era.

Politically, the colonial period also left a legacy of centralized governance and authoritarian practices. The Dutch colonial administration had relied on hierarchical and centralized structures to maintain control, which were subsequently adopted by Indonesia's post-independence

[77] Booth, A. (1998). The Indonesian Economy in the Nineteenth and Twentieth Centuries: A History of Missed Opportunities. London: Macmillan Press.

[78] Henley, D. (2004). Fertility, Food, and Fever: Population, Economy, and Environment in North and Central Sulawesi, 1600–1930. Leiden: KITLV Press.

[79] Ricklefs, M. C. (2008). A History of Modern Indonesia since c.1200. 4th ed. Basingstoke: Palgrave Macmillan.

governments. This contributed to the concentration of power in Jakarta and a top-down approach to governance, which often marginalized rural and regional populations. The political inequalities and tensions rooted in the colonial era were further compounded by the economic disparities, shaping the trajectory of Indonesia's development and contributing to periods of instability and conflict.[80] One notable example was the Java War (1825–1830), led by Prince Diponegoro, which arose from widespread discontent with Dutch colonial policies, including the cultuurstelsel (forced cultivation system) and disruptive land reforms. These policies alienated the Javanese aristocracy and rural population, sparking a massive rebellion against the colonial regime.[81] Similarly, throughout the mid-nineteenth century, localized revolts emerged as rural communities resisted the cultuurstelsel, which had imposed significant labour and land burdens on farmers to prioritize Dutch economic interests. These uprisings underscored the growing frustrations among Indonesians over the exploitation and political marginalization they faced.[82] After Indonesia declared independence in 1945, the inequalities and tensions inherited from colonial rule fuelled the Indonesian National Revolution (1945–1949). This four-year conflict between Indonesian nationalists and Dutch forces reflected long-standing grievances over political exclusion and economic exploitation under colonial rule. The revolution became a defining moment in dismantling colonial structures, although many of these inequalities persisted in post-independence governance.[83] In the 1950s, regional rebellions such as the Darul Islam insurgency in West Java and the Permesta rebellion in Sulawesi arose from dissatisfaction with centralized governance, another colonial legacy. These conflicts highlighted the lingering regional imbalances in political power and resource

[80] Henley, D. (2004). Fertility, Food, and Fever: Population, Economy, and Environment in North and Central Sulawesi, 1600–1930. Leiden: KITLV Press.

[81] Ricklefs, M. C. (2008). A History of Modern Indonesia since c.1200. 4th ed. Basingstoke: Palgrave Macmillan.

[82] Booth, A. (1998). The Indonesian Economy in the Nineteenth and Twentieth Centuries: A History of Missed Opportunities. London: Macmillan Press.

[83] Taylor, J. G. (2003). Indonesia: Peoples and Histories. New Haven: Yale University Press.

distribution that had been reinforced during the Dutch era.[84] The anti-communist purge of 1965–1966 further illustrated the enduring impact of colonial inequalities. Rural poverty and marginalization, legacies of the Dutch system, made the communist movement (PKI) appealing to many Indonesians. The eventual suppression of the PKI, following an alleged coup attempt, resulted in mass killings and marked one of the most destabilizing periods in Indonesia's history. This event not only reflected Cold War geopolitics but also underscored how colonial-era divisions left Indonesia vulnerable to internal conflict.[85] Additionally, the East Timor independence struggle (1975–1999) demonstrated the lingering challenges of centralized governance, which Indonesia inherited from the Dutch colonial state. The suppression of regional autonomy in East Timor, rooted in unequal development policies, prolonged instability and violence in the region.[86] These examples illustrate how the colonial era's embedded inequalities—political marginalization, economic disparities, and centralized governance—persisted well into Indonesia's modern history. They contributed to recurring cycles of instability and conflict, shaping the country's post-colonial development and political identity in profound ways. The dependencies and inequalities established during Indonesia's colonial period did not simply vanish with independence. Instead, they became structural features of the post-colonial state, influencing the nation's economic policies, social hierarchies, and political dynamics well into the modern era. These legacies highlight the enduring impact of colonial exploitation on Indonesia's development.

The arrival of European powers transformed Indonesian trade networks from decentralized systems of regional exchange into centralized, monopolistic structures serving European economic interests. Through militarized trade, centralized operations, and the suppression of local commerce, the Portuguese, Dutch, and British fundamentally reshaped Indonesia's role in the global economy. These changes, driven by short-term profit motives, left a legacy of dependency and inequality

[84] Henley, D. (2004). Fertility, Food, and Fever: Population, Economy, and Environment in North and Central Sulawesi, 1600–1930. Leiden: KITLV Press.

[85] Ricklefs, M. C. (2008). A History of Modern Indonesia since c.1200. 4th ed. Basingstoke: Palgrave Macmillan.

[86] Taylor, J. G. (2003). Indonesia: Peoples and Histories. New Haven: Yale University Press.

that continued to influence Indonesia long after the colonial period ended.

Socioeconomic Consequences of Colonial Rule

The arrival of European powers in Indonesia between 1500 and 1800 brought transformative changes to the archipelago's socio-economic structures, fundamentally altering the livelihoods, social hierarchies, and economic trajectories of Indonesian communities. These changes were driven by monopolistic policies, exploitative labour systems, and land-use transformations imposed by colonial powers like the Portuguese, Dutch, and British. The restructuring of trade networks, land ownership patterns, and labour relations was carried out primarily to serve European economic interests, often at the expense of local autonomy and well-being. One of the most profound consequences of colonial rule was the monopolization of Indonesia's trade networks. The Dutch East India Company (VOC) institutionalized these changes by centralizing operations in Batavia (modern Jakarta) and securing exclusive control over high-demand commodities like nutmeg, cloves, and mace. VOC policies, such as the Hongi system, involved the systematic destruction of unauthorized spice cultivation in the Moluccas to enforce their monopoly, displacing communities and undermining local economies.[87] The Dutch East India Company's (VOC) use of the Hongi system to enforce its monopoly on spices like nutmeg and cloves in the Moluccas had devastating effects on local economies. This policy involved deploying naval expeditions to destroy unauthorized spice cultivation and punish those who violated the VOC's trade restrictions. The aim was to eliminate competition and ensure the VOC's control over the highly lucrative spice trade. However, these actions had far-reaching consequences for the local populations and their economies. By destroying unauthorized spice gardens, the VOC disrupted the livelihoods of local farmers who depended on cultivating and trading spices as their primary source of income. Many communities in the Moluccas had long relied on a decentralized trade system, exchanging their spices for goods like rice, textiles,

[87] Ricklefs, M. C. (2008). A History of Modern Indonesia since c.1200. 4th ed. Basingstoke: Palgrave Macmillan.

and other essentials from nearby regions.[88] The systematic destruction of these gardens not only eradicated their immediate economic activity but also severed the trade networks that sustained their broader economies. The VOC's monopoly forced local populations to sell their spices at fixed, often artificially low prices dictated by the company. This significantly reduced the income of local producers, preventing them from reinvesting in their own communities or maintaining sustainable livelihoods. The displacement of communities further compounded this economic disruption. Entire villages were uprooted, either because their land was deemed unsuitable for VOC-approved cultivation or because they were targeted for punitive measures after violating VOC regulations.[89] In addition, the focus on enforcing a spice monopoly meant that other aspects of local economies, such as subsistence farming and artisanal production, were neglected or suppressed. Communities that had traditionally relied on a mixed economy were pushed into dependency on the VOC for food and goods. This created a cycle of economic vulnerability, as these communities became increasingly reliant on the VOC for survival while losing their capacity for self-sustenance and autonomous economic activity.[90].The long-term effects of these policies further entrenched economic inequalities. The VOC's prioritization of short-term profit over the well-being of local populations led to widespread poverty and dependency. By undermining the ability of local economies to function independently, the VOC's policies left a legacy of economic fragility in the Moluccas that persisted long after the end of colonial rule.[91] This deliberate destruction of local economic structures exemplifies the extractive nature of colonial exploitation, where the interests of the colonial power were prioritized at the expense of the communities it controlled. Furthermore, smaller ports like Banten and Makassar, once vibrant hubs of regional trade, were marginalized as the Dutch redirected resources to support

[88] Henley, D. (2004). Fertility, Food, and Fever: Population, Economy, and Environment in North and Central Sulawesi, 1600–1930. Leiden: KITLV Press.

[89] Ricklefs, M. C. (2008). A History of Modern Indonesia since c.1200. 4th ed. Basingstoke: Palgrave Macmillan.

[90] Reid, A. (1993). SoutheastAsia in the Age of Commerce, 1450–1680: Volume Two, Expansion and Crisis. New Haven: Yale University Press.

[91] Booth, A. (1998). The Indonesian Economy in the Nineteenth and Twentieth Centuries: A History of Missed Opportunities. London: Macmillan Press.

their centralized operations in Batavia.[92] This restructuring created a dualistic economy in which the export-oriented sectors thrived, while indigenous trade and subsistence systems stagnated.[93] The introduction of the cultuurstelsel (forced cultivation system) in the nineteenth century further entrenched economic inequalities. Under this system, farmers were coerced into dedicating significant portions of their land and labour to cash crops such as coffee and sugar for export markets. The colonial government profited immensely, using revenues to finance Dutch industrialization, while rural populations faced impoverishment and food insecurity. Subsistence farming was neglected, leaving communities vulnerable to famine during poor harvests or economic downturns.[94] The Preanger System in West Java, for instance, required farmers to grow coffee for the VOC with minimal compensation, exacerbating poverty and hindering subsistence farming.[95] This imbalance not only drained local economies but also perpetuated a reliance on exploitative labour arrangements. The colonial administration also reshaped Indonesia's social hierarchies by concentrating wealth and power in the hands of European settlers and indigenous elites who collaborated with the colonial regime. Local aristocrats, or priyayi, were co-opted into the system by being granted administrative authority and control over land. These privileges created a class of intermediaries who enforced colonial policies and benefited disproportionately from the colonial economy. For example, the Dutch rewarded cooperative elites with tax exemptions and land rights, further entrenching social stratification and widening the gap between the elite and the rural poor.[96] This stratification limited opportunities for social mobility, locking many Indonesians into cycles of poverty and reinforcing the exploitation of labour.

[92] Henley, D. (2004). Fertility, Food, and Fever: Population, Economy, and Environment in North and Central Sulawesi, 1600–1930. Leiden: KITLV Press.

[93] Reid, A. (1993). SoutheastAsia in the Age of Commerce, 1450–1680: Volume Two, Expansion and Crisis. New Haven: Yale University Press.

[94] Booth, A. (1998). The Indonesian Economy in the Nineteenth and Twentieth Centuries: A History of Missed Opportunities. London: Macmillan Press.

[95] Bosma, U. (2013). The Sugar Plantation in Indiaand Indonesia: Industrial Production, 1770–2010. Cambridge: Cambridge University Press.

[96] Taylor, J. G. (2003). Indonesia: Peoples and Histories. New Haven: Yale University Press.

Environmental degradation was another long-term consequence of colonial rule, particularly due to the emphasis on monoculture and resource extraction. The forced cultivation of single crops, such as coffee, sugar, and tobacco, led to soil exhaustion and a decline in agricultural biodiversity. Over time, the repetitive cultivation of these crops depleted nutrients in the soil, reducing agricultural productivity and the resilience of local farming systems.[97] Deforestation and overextraction of water resources to support plantations further disrupted ecosystems, compounding the environmental vulnerabilities faced by rural communities.[98] These ecological damages persisted well beyond the colonial period, leaving Indonesia with degraded land and limited agricultural potential.

Labor systems during the colonial period became increasingly coercive. In addition to the cultuurstelsel, systems of corvée labour and other forced arrangements placed significant burdens on rural populations. Farmers and labourers were compelled to meet production quotas for cash crops, often at the expense of their own subsistence farming. These labour systems created cycles of debt and dependency, as workers struggled to repay taxes or loans while meeting the demands of colonial administrators.[99] Communal support systems that had traditionally sustained rural communities were eroded under the pressures of forced labour and land dispossession, leaving many Indonesians economically and socially vulnerable. The socio-economic consequences of colonial rule in Indonesia were far-reaching and deeply entrenched. By prioritizing European economic interests, colonial powers disrupted traditional trade networks, imposed exploitative labor systems, and entrenched social inequalities that marginalized the majority of the population. The legacies of these policies persisted well into the post-colonial period, shaping Indonesia's development trajectory. Poverty, environmental degradation, and social stratification, rooted in the colonial era, continued to influence the nation's economic and political landscape for centuries to come.

[97] Henley, D. (2004). Fertility, Food, and Fever: Population, Economy, and Environment in North and Central Sulawesi, 1600–1930. Leiden: KITLV Press.

[98] Peluso, N. L. (1992). Rich Forests, Poor People: Resource Control and Resistance in Java. Berkeley: University of California Press.

[99] Bosma, U. (2013). The Sugar Plantation in Indiaand Indonesia: Industrial Production, 1770–2010. Cambridge: Cambridge University Press.

The Long-Term Legacy of Early Colonialism in Indonesia's Political Economy

The arrival of European colonial powers between 1500 and 1800 fundamentally transformed Indonesia's political economy, creating legacies that have shaped the nation's development for centuries. Early colonialism, particularly under the Dutch East India Company (VOC), disrupted indigenous economic systems, centralized trade, entrenched social hierarchies, and introduced extractive policies that prioritized European profits over the welfare of local populations. These transformations have left an enduring impact on Indonesia's economic structures, governance, and social dynamics, which continue to influence the nation's trajectory.

One of the most significant long-term impacts of colonialism was the centralization of trade networks under European control. Prior to the VOC, Indonesian trade networks were decentralized and interconnected, enabling local producers to benefit from a dynamic regional economy. Ports like Malacca, Aceh, and Makassar thrived as trading hubs, facilitating the flow of spices, textiles, and other goods across Southeast Asia and beyond.[100] Malacca, in particular, was renowned as one of the most important trading ports of the era. Its strategic location on the Strait of Malacca allowed it to function as a meeting point for traders from the East and West. The port's cosmopolitan character and inclusive trade policies enabled it to attract merchants from a wide range of cultural and economic backgrounds, fostering a dynamic and diverse economic ecosystem. Similarly, Aceh on the northern tip of Sumatra became a key player in the pepper trade, leveraging its fertile lands and favourable geographic position to dominate the global spice market. The wealth generated through trade not only sustained local economies but also allowed port cities like Aceh to emerge as powerful political entities capable of influencing regional affairs.[101]

Makassar, on the island of Sulawesi, played a crucial role as a major entrepôt in the eastern Indonesian archipelago. It connected the spice-producing regions of the Moluccas with markets in Java and beyond. Unlike the monopolistic tendencies later imposed by European powers,

[100] Chaudhuri, K. N. (1985). Trade and Civilisation in the Indian Ocean: An Economic History from the Rise of Islam to 1750. Cambridge: Cambridge University Press.

[101] Reid, A. (1993). SoutheastAsia in the Age of Commerce, 1450–1680: Volume Two, Expansion and Crisis. New Haven: Yale University Press.

Makassar's trade policies were characterized by openness and flexibility, allowing merchants of various nationalities to operate freely. This inclusivity fostered competition and innovation, enabling local producers to secure favourable prices for their goods while importing a variety of commodities to sustain their communities. The city's vibrant trade networks and autonomous governance structure exemplified the decentralized economic systems that prevailed prior to European intervention.[102] These pre-VOC trade networks not only enabled the equitable distribution of wealth across the region but also stimulated cultural and technological exchange. The flow of goods through these ports was often accompanied by the spread of ideas, religions, and innovations, which enriched the social and intellectual fabric of Southeast Asia. The dynamism and resilience of these networks provided a robust foundation for the local economy, ensuring that wealth was not concentrated in a single centre but rather distributed across multiple regions. This decentralized system allowed for economic diversification, making the region less vulnerable to external shocks or monopolistic practices. However, this equilibrium was disrupted with the arrival of the VOC, which sought to centralize trade and enforce monopolistic control, undermining the interconnected and inclusive nature of these pre-colonial systems (Ricklefs, 2008). The VOC's entry into this dynamic environment marked a drastic shift towards centralization and monopolistic control, as the company sought to dominate the lucrative spice trade and eliminate competition. The VOC's strategy cantered on centralizing trade operations in Batavia (modern Jakarta), which became the administrative and commercial hub of its Southeast Asian empire. This centralization involved redirecting trade flows away from traditional ports like Makassar and Banten, which had previously thrived as regional trading hubs. By forcing goods to pass through Batavia under VOC supervision, the company not only marginalized these ports but also disrupted the decentralized nature of trade networks that had allowed wealth and resources to be distributed more evenly across the archipelago.[103] Smaller ports and regional economies suffered as their traditional trading partners were co-opted into VOC-controlled routes, leading to economic stagnation and dependency. To

[102] Henley, D. (2004). Fertility, Food, and Fever: Population, Economy, and Environment in North and Central Sulawesi, 1600–1930. Leiden: KITLV Press.

[103] Ricklefs, M. C. (2008). A History of Modern Indonesia since c.1200. 4th ed. Basingstoke: Palgrave Macmillan.

enforce its monopoly, the VOC employed coercive measures such as exclusive contracts with local rulers, heavy tariffs, and military interventions. One of the most infamous examples of this was the Hongi system, a naval campaign that targeted unauthorized spice cultivation in the Moluccas. Under this system, VOC forces destroyed spice trees that were not under their control, punishing communities that violated VOC trade restrictions. This eradicated competition but also displaced communities and dismantled local economies that had relied on the spice trade for centuries.[104] The focus on centralized control and monopoly undermined the inclusive trade practices of pre-colonial systems, which had allowed merchants of different nationalities and ethnicities to participate freely in regional commerce. The VOC's monopolistic practices also replaced the collaborative and reciprocal relationships that had characterized earlier trade systems with exploitative ones. Under pre-colonial systems, local producers were active participants in the trade network, negotiating prices and exchanging goods on equal terms with foreign merchants. In contrast, the VOC imposed fixed prices for spices and other commodities, often paying local producers far below market value. This exploitative system redirected the economic benefits of trade away from local communities and towards European markets, creating a stark imbalance in wealth and resources.[105] Furthermore, the VOC's centralization of trade disrupted the cultural and social exchanges that had been integral to the interconnected pre-colonial systems. The flow of goods through decentralized networks was often accompanied by the spread of ideas, technologies, and cultural practices. These networks, which connected Indonesian ports like Aceh, Malacca, and Makassar to the wider Indian Ocean economy, served as conduits for intellectual and cultural interactions that enriched local societies. One notable example of this cultural exchange was the spread of Islam to Indonesia, which was facilitated by trade networks connecting Southeast Asia to the Middle East and South Asia. Muslim merchants and scholars traveling through ports like Aceh introduced Islamic teachings, which were gradually adopted by local communities. Aceh, known as the "Verandah of Mecca," became a center of Islamic learning, attracting scholars and fostering the development of

[104] Ricklefs, M. C. (2008). A History of Modern Indonesia since c.1200. 4th ed. Basingstoke: Palgrave Macmillan.

[105] Henley, D. (2004). Fertility, Food, and Fever: Population, Economy, and Environment in North and Central Sulawesi, 1600–1930. Leiden: KITLV Press.

a vibrant Islamic intellectual tradition in the region.[106] Another example is the influence of Indian culture, including Hinduism and Buddhism, which entered Indonesia through maritime trade routes long before the arrival of Europeans. These religions profoundly shaped Indonesia's cultural and political landscapes, as seen in the establishment of Hindu-Buddhist kingdoms like Majapahit and Srivijaya. Along with religious ideas, Indian trade networks brought advancements in architecture, governance, and art, exemplified by the construction of Borobudur and Prambanan temples, which remain iconic symbols of Indonesia's cultural heritage.[107] The influence of Indian trade networks on Indonesia brought significant advancements in architecture, governance, and art, which have left a lasting legacy in the region. These exchanges enriched Indonesian society and are exemplified by monumental structures, administrative innovations, and artistic traditions that demonstrate the integration of Indian ideas with local culture.

In architecture, the construction of monumental Hindu-Buddhist temples such as Borobudur and Prambanan exemplifies the profound impact of Indian architectural principles. Borobudur, built in the eighth–ninth centuries by the Sailendra dynasty, reflects the influence of Indian Buddhist stupas. The massive structure is designed as a mandala, symbolizing the Buddhist cosmology, and is adorned with intricate bas-reliefs depicting scenes from the life of the Buddha. Similarly, the Prambanan temple complex, dedicated to the Hindu deity Shiva and constructed by the Mataram Kingdom in the ninth century, showcases Indian temple architecture through its towering spires and detailed carvings of Hindu epics like the Ramayana. These temples not only highlight the adoption of Indian architectural styles but also show how local craftsmen integrated these influences with Indigenous traditions, creating a uniquely Indonesian aesthetic.[108]

In governance, Indian models of statecraft and administration were adopted and adapted by Indonesian kingdoms. The concept of the divine kingship (devaraja), which portrayed rulers as semi-divine figures with

[106] Reid, A. (1993). SoutheastAsia in the Age of Commerce, 1450–1680: Volume Two, Expansion and Crisis. New Haven: Yale University Press.

[107] Chaudhuri, K. N. (1985). Trade and Civilisation in the Indian Ocean: An Economic History from the Rise of Islam to 1750. Cambridge: Cambridge University Press.

[108] Chaudhuri, K. N. (1985). Trade and Civilisation in the Indian Ocean: An Economic History from the Rise of Islam to 1750. Cambridge: Cambridge University Press.

a sacred duty to govern, was derived from Indian Hindu and Buddhist traditions. This ideology legitimized the authority of rulers and became a central feature of political organization in kingdoms like Majapahit and Srivijaya. Additionally, Indian influence introduced administrative systems, including the use of Sanskrit as a language of governance and religious texts. The inscriptions found at various sites, such as the Kedukan Bukit inscription from Srivijaya, illustrate how Indian political and religious concepts were localized to suit the needs of Indonesian rulers.[109]

In art, the Indian influence is evident in the adoption of iconography, sculpture, and decorative motifs. Hindu and Buddhist deities, such as Vishnu, Shiva, and the Buddha, were depicted in statues and carvings that adorned temples and palaces. These artistic representations often followed Indian iconographic conventions, including specific postures (mudras) and symbolic attributes, while incorporating local elements such as indigenous flora and fauna. The bas-reliefs of Borobudur, for instance, combine Indian narrative techniques with scenes of Javanese life, illustrating a synthesis of foreign and local artistic traditions. Beyond sculpture, Indian influence extended to textiles and crafts, with patterns and techniques introduced through trade, enriching Indonesian artistic production.[110] The enduring legacy of these advancements can be seen not only in physical monuments but also in the cultural and administrative systems that persisted long after the decline of Hindu-Buddhist kingdoms. The integration of Indian ideas with local traditions created a uniquely Indonesian identity that remains an essential part of the country's cultural heritage. The trade networks also facilitated technological exchanges. For instance, Chinese merchants introduced new techniques in ceramic production and metalworking to Indonesian artisans. Chinese influence is evident in the production of high-quality ceramics and the adoption of sophisticated metallurgical practices in regions like Java and Sumatra. These technologies not only enhanced local industries but also allowed Indonesian goods to compete effectively in international markets.[111] (Henley,

[109] Ricklefs, M. C. (2008). A History of Modern Indonesia since c.1200. 4th ed. Basingstoke: Palgrave Macmillan.

[110] Henley, D. (2004). Fertility, Food, and Fever: Population, Economy, and Environment in North and Central Sulawesi, 1600–1930. Leiden: KITLV Press.

[111] Henley, D. (2004). Fertility, Food, and Fever: Population, Economy, and Environment in North and Central Sulawesi, 1600–1930. Leiden: KITLV Press.

2004). The introduction of advanced techniques in ceramic production enabled Indonesian artisans to produce high-quality goods that were highly valued both domestically and internationally. Chinese potters brought with them the knowledge of glazing, firing, and decoration techniques that allowed for the production of durable and aesthetically refined ceramics. These innovations were adopted and localized in regions such as Java and Sumatra, where local artisans began producing ceramics with unique designs that reflected a blend of Chinese and indigenous styles.[112] For example, Chinese celadon and porcelain influenced the development of Indonesian ceramics, leading to the production of vessels and tableware that were not only functional but also served as status symbols among local elites. These ceramics became important trade commodities, enhancing Indonesia's role in the broader Indian Ocean trade network. Artifacts discovered at archaeological sites, such as those in Trowulan (the capital of the Majapahit Kingdom), show the extent to which Chinese techniques were integrated into local craftsmanship. The presence of Chinese-style ceramics in these sites also indicates the high demand for such goods among Southeast Asian consumers and beyond.[113] In addition to ceramics, Chinese metallurgical practices influenced local industries. Chinese traders and settlers introduced advanced methods of working with metals such as bronze and iron, which were essential for the production of tools, weapons, and ornamental objects. These techniques allowed for the creation of more efficient agricultural tools, enhancing productivity in farming communities, as well as superior weaponry that strengthened the military capacities of kingdoms like Majapahit and Srivijaya. The use of iron plows, for instance, revolutionized farming practices in Java, contributing to the economic prosperity of the region.[114] Furthermore, Chinese metallurgical expertise enabled the production of intricate bronze and gold artifacts, such as jewellery and religious objects, which were highly prized in both local and international markets. These items not only became important symbols of

[112] Henley, D. (2004). Fertility, Food, and Fever: Population, Economy, and Environment in North and Central Sulawesi, 1600–1930. Leiden: KITLV Press.

[113] Chaudhuri, K. N. (1985). Trade and Civilisation in the Indian Ocean: An Economic History from the Rise of Islam to 1750. Cambridge: Cambridge University Press.

[114] Reid, A. (1993). SoutheastAsia in the Age of Commerce, 1450–1680: Volume Two, Expansion and Crisis. New Haven: Yale University Press.

wealth and status but also served as trade goods that bolstered Indonesia's participation in global commerce. The fusion of Chinese techniques with indigenous designs resulted in unique artistic expressions, exemplified by the ornate gold and bronze items unearthed in sites across Sumatra and Java, which demonstrate both technical skill and cultural hybridity.[115] The adoption of Chinese technologies and practices allowed Indonesian goods to compete effectively in international markets, strengthening the region's position in the global trade networks of the Indian Ocean. By integrating Chinese innovations into local industries, Indonesia developed a reputation for producing high-quality goods that were in demand across Asia and beyond. This integration of Chinese influence contributed to the economic and cultural dynamism of pre-colonial Indonesia, laying the groundwork for its continued prominence in regional and global trade. Cultural practices were another significant aspect of this exchange. The arrival of Indian and Arab merchants introduced diverse culinary traditions, textiles, and musical instruments to Indonesia, enriching local cultures. The batik tradition in Java, for example, shows influences from Indian textile patterns, adapted to local tastes and aesthetics. Similarly, the gamelan musical ensemble reflects a synthesis of indigenous, Indian, and Southeast Asian influences, demonstrating how cultural practices evolved through cross-cultural interactions facilitated by trade.[116] In addition to material and intellectual exchanges, these trade networks contributed to the development of cosmopolitan port cities like Malacca, which became melting pots of cultures, languages, and religions. The diversity of these cities created opportunities for collaboration and innovation, enabling the region to thrive as a dynamic centre of commerce and culture before the disruption caused by Dutch colonization.[117]

By monopolizing trade routes and restricting access to certain regions, the VOC curtailed these exchanges, reducing the opportunities for cross-cultural interaction and innovation that had previously enriched Southeast

[115] Wolters, O. W. (1999). History, Culture, and Region in Southeast Asian Perspectives. 2nd ed. Ithaca: Cornell University Press.

[116] Ricklefs, M. C. (2008). A History of Modern Indonesia since c.1200. 4th ed. Basingstoke: Palgrave Macmillan.

[117] Reid, A. (1993). SoutheastAsia in the Age of Commerce, 1450–1680: Volume Two, Expansion and Crisis. New Haven: Yale University Press.

Asia's diverse societies.[118] The long-term impact of the VOC's monopolistic policies was profound. By undermining the decentralized and inclusive nature of pre-colonial trade systems, the VOC not only disrupted regional economies but also entrenched patterns of inequality and dependency that would persist into the colonial and post-colonial periods. The destruction of traditional trade networks, coupled with the centralization of power in Batavia, left Indonesia with a fragmented economic landscape that was heavily oriented towards serving external markets rather than fostering internal development.[119] The VOC's monopolistic policies, such as exclusive contracts with local rulers and the militarized enforcement of trade restrictions, centralized economic power in Batavia (modern Jakarta). This centralization marginalized smaller ports, like Banten and Makassar, and redirected wealth towards European-controlled centres. The Hongi system, which involved the destruction of unauthorized spice cultivation, further disrupted local economies and displaced communities, exacerbating regional inequalities.[120] The Hongi system implemented by the Dutch East India Company (VOC) exacerbated regional inequalities in Indonesia by selectively benefiting certain areas while marginalizing others. This system involved the use of naval expeditions to destroy unauthorized spice cultivation in the Moluccas, ensuring that the VOC maintained a monopoly over high-value commodities like nutmeg, cloves, and mace. While the VOC concentrated its efforts and investments in regions under its control, such as Ambon and certain areas of the Banda Islands, other regions were systematically excluded from the economic benefits of the spice trade. The destruction of unauthorized spice gardens displaced communities that had relied on the cultivation and trade of these commodities for their livelihoods. This forced displacement often targeted smaller villages and independent producers, undermining their local economies and leaving them dependent on the VOC for economic survival. At the same time, the VOC redirected resources and wealth generated from the spice trade to central hubs like Batavia (modern Jakarta), deepening the divide between economically

[118] Reid, A. (1993). SoutheastAsia in the Age of Commerce, 1450–1680: Volume Two, Expansion and Crisis. New Haven: Yale University Press.

[119] Booth, A. (1998). The Indonesian Economy in the Nineteenth and Twentieth Centuries: A History of Missed Opportunities. London: Macmillan Press.

[120] Ricklefs, M. C. (2008). A History of Modern Indonesia since c.1200. 4th ed. Basingstoke: Palgrave Macmillan.

integrated regions and those left on the periphery.[121] Regions that were able to align themselves with the VOC, often through collaboration by local elites, gained some economic advantages, albeit within the restrictive framework of the VOC's monopolistic policies. These areas benefited from infrastructure development, administrative attention, and access to European markets. However, these benefits were limited to a select few, often exacerbating disparities within these regions between the collaborating elite and the broader population.[122] The VOC's operations in Indonesia created a stark divide between regions that were economically integrated into its trade network and those left on the periphery. Economically integrated regions, such as Batavia (modern Jakarta), Ambon, and the Banda Islands, were central to the VOC's commercial activities. Batavia, established as the administrative and commercial hub, benefited from significant investments in infrastructure, including ports, warehouses, and fortifications, which facilitated the processing and export of spices and other goods. This concentration of resources made Batavia a dominant economic centre, with wealth flowing disproportionately to its urban elite and the VOC itself.[123] Similarly, Ambon and the Banda Islands, located in the Moluccas, became focal points for the VOC's spice trade. The VOC enforced a strict monopoly over the production of nutmeg, mace, and cloves in these areas, often through coercive measures like the Hongi system and forced labour. While local elites who collaborated with the VOC received privileges, the broader population faced displacement and exploitation, as exemplified by the massacre in the Banda Islands in 1621, which depopulated the region and introduced enslaved labour for plantation agriculture.[124] The Banda Island massacre of 1621 was one of the most infamous and brutal episodes of VOC colonial rule in Indonesia, highlighting the lengths to which the company would go to secure its monopoly over the lucrative spice trade. The Banda Islands, located in the Moluccas, were among the world's

[121] Ricklefs, M. C. (2008). A History of Modern Indonesia since c.1200. 4th ed. Basingstoke: Palgrave Macmillan.

[122] Henley, D. (2004). Fertility, Food, and Fever: Population, Economy, and Environment in North and Central Sulawesi, 1600–1930. Leiden: KITLV Press.

[123] Ricklefs, M. C. (2008). A History of Modern Indonesia since c.1200. 4th ed. Basingstoke: Palgrave Macmillan.

[124] Henley, D. (2004). Fertility, Food, and Fever: Population, Economy, and Environment in North and Central Sulawesi, 1600–1930. Leiden: KITLV Press.

primary sources of nutmeg and mace, spices that were highly valued in European markets. The local Bandanese population had traditionally operated within decentralized trade networks, selling their spices to various merchants, including Javanese, Malay, and Arab traders. This open trade system, however, conflicted with the VOC's ambition to monopolize the spice trade.[125] Under the leadership of Governor-General Jan Pieterszoon Coen, the VOC launched a campaign in 1621 to suppress resistance and enforce its monopoly. The Bandanese had resisted VOC efforts to control their trade, refusing to enter into exclusive agreements that would have forced them to sell their spices solely to the Dutch at artificially low prices. In retaliation, Coen ordered a military assault on the islands. The campaign resulted in the systematic slaughter of thousands of Bandanese men, women, and children, effectively depopulating the islands. It is estimated that of the approximately 15,000 inhabitants of the Banda Islands, only a few hundred survived, either fleeing to other regions or being enslaved.[126] Following the massacre, the VOC took control of the depopulated islands and transformed them into plantation economies to produce nutmeg and mace exclusively for Dutch export. To sustain these plantations, the VOC imported enslaved labourers from other parts of the Indonesian archipelago and beyond, including Java, Sulawesi, and even as far as India and Africa. These enslaved workers faced harsh conditions, forced to cultivate spices under the supervision of VOC administrators and plantation managers. The introduction of this plantation system marked a significant shift in the region's economic structure, replacing the indigenous trade-based economy with a coercive export-oriented model.[127]

The Banda Island massacre had long-term implications for both the local population and the broader region. The destruction of the Bandanese society erased a vibrant culture that had thrived on trade and autonomy. The VOC's actions set a precedent for the use of extreme violence to enforce economic policies, establishing a pattern of exploitation and domination that would characterize Dutch colonial

[125] Ricklefs, M. C. (2008). A History of Modern Indonesia since c.1200. 4th ed. Basingstoke: Palgrave Macmillan.

[126] Henley, D. (2004). Fertility, Food, and Fever: Population, Economy, and Environment in North and Central Sulawesi, 1600–1930. Leiden: KITLV Press.

[127] Taylor, J. G. (2003). Indonesia: Peoples and Histories. New Haven: Yale University Press.

rule in Indonesia. Furthermore, the reliance on enslaved labour and the establishment of monoculture plantations foreshadowed the extractive economic practices that would persist throughout the colonial period, leaving a legacy of inequality and underdevelopment.[128] The Banda Island massacre of 1621 was a turning point in the VOC's colonization of Indonesia. It demonstrated the company's willingness to use extreme violence to secure its economic interests, depopulating entire regions and replacing local systems of trade and governance with exploitative plantation economies. The massacre not only devastated the Bandanese population but also entrenched patterns of forced labour and economic extraction that would define the Dutch colonial project in the archipelago.

In contrast, regions left on the periphery, such as Makassar in Sulawesi and Aceh in northern Sumatra, experienced economic marginalization due to the VOC's monopolistic practices. Makassar, once a vibrant and cosmopolitan trading hub, saw its economic significance diminish after the VOC redirected trade routes to Batavia and launched military campaigns to suppress its independence, including its capture in 1667. This undermined Makassar's role in the spice trade and left the region reliant on subsistence agriculture and small-scale commerce.[129] Similarly, Aceh, which had previously thrived as a regional power in the pepper trade, was sidelined as the VOC focused its efforts on controlling spice-producing regions. The redirection of trade and exclusionary policies diminished Aceh's economic prominence, leaving it increasingly isolated from the broader trading network.[130]

Many of Indonesia's outer islands, such as Kalimantan, Nusa Tenggara, and Papua, were excluded from the VOC's economic network altogether because they lacked significant spice production or other high-value commodities. These areas were left to subsistence economies with minimal investment in infrastructure or trade development. This neglect reinforced regional disparities, creating a legacy of underdevelopment in these peripheral regions that persisted well into the modern

[128] Chaudhuri, K. N. (1985). Trade and Civilisation in the Indian Ocean: An Economic History from the Rise of Islam to 1750. Cambridge: Cambridge University Press.

[129] Reid, A. (1993). SoutheastAsia in the Age of Commerce, 1450–1680: Volume Two, Expansion and Crisis. New Haven: Yale University Press.

[130] Henley, D. (2004). Fertility, Food, and Fever: Population, Economy, and Environment in North and Central Sulawesi, 1600–1930. Leiden: KITLV Press.

era.[131] By prioritizing economic integration in select areas like Batavia and the Banda Islands while marginalizing others, the VOC entrenched regional inequalities, disrupting traditional trade networks and leaving many regions economically stagnant or impoverished.

The Hongi system also intensified inequality by prioritizing the production of spices for export over local needs. Communities that were displaced or forced to cultivate spices under VOC control often struggled to maintain subsistence farming, leading to food shortages and economic vulnerabilities. Meanwhile, regions that were less involved in the spice trade or resisted VOC control saw their economies stagnate as trade routes were rerouted and their access to external markets curtailed.[132] The Hongi system disrupted traditional trade and agricultural systems, benefiting regions and individuals aligned with the VOC while marginalizing others. This selective economic integration exacerbated existing regional inequalities, creating a legacy of uneven development that persisted long after the VOC's decline. The focus on exporting high-value commodities like nutmeg, cloves, and mace to European markets created a dualistic economy in which the outward-looking colonial sector thrived at the expense of subsistence economies. This economic dualism reinforced regional imbalances, as resource-rich areas were integrated into global markets while others were excluded, leading to uneven development. Such patterns persisted into the post-colonial period, as Indonesia continued to grapple with economic dependency and underdevelopment in many regions.[133] The introduction of the cultuurstelsel (forced cultivation system) in the nineteenth century further entrenched economic dependency and inequality. Farmers were coerced into dedicating significant portions of their land and labour to cash crops like coffee and sugar, which were exported to finance Dutch industrialization. While these policies generated immense profits for the Dutch state, they are left rural populations impoverished, as subsistence farming was neglected and food security deteriorated. For example, the prevalence of famines in Java during this period can be directly linked to the prioritization

[131] Booth, A. (1998). The Indonesian Economy in the Nineteenth and Twentieth Centuries: A History of Missed Opportunities. London: Macmillan Press.

[132] Reid, A. (1993). SoutheastAsia in the Age of Commerce, 1450–1680: Volume Two, Expansion and Crisis. New Haven: Yale University Press.

[133] Henley, D. (2004). Fertility, Food, and Fever: Population, Economy, and Environment in North and Central Sulawesi, 1600–1930. Leiden: KITLV Press.

of export crops over staple foods.[134] The economic patterns established by the cultuurstelsel persisted into the modern era, as Indonesia's post-independence economy remained reliant on the export of raw materials and cash crops, limiting opportunities for diversification and industrialization.[135] Colonial policies also reshaped social hierarchies by concentrating wealth and power among a small elite, consisting of European settlers and indigenous collaborators. The VOC co-opted local rulers and aristocrats, granting them privileges such as land ownership and administrative authority in exchange for their support. These collaborators, often Javanese aristocrats (priyayi), played a key role in enforcing exploitative policies like the cultuurstelsel, further alienating rural communities and deepening social stratification.[136] The inequalities entrenched during the colonial period persisted into the post-independence era, as land reforms and redistributive policies were often ineffective or resisted by powerful elites.

The environmental consequences of early colonialism also left a legacy. The emphasis on monoculture for cash crops led to soil depletion, reduced biodiversity, and long-term ecological damage. Plantation agriculture, particularly for coffee and sugar, disrupted traditional farming practices and eroded the natural resilience of Indonesia's agricultural systems. For example, deforestation and the overextraction of water resources for plantation irrigation not only degraded the environment but also made rural communities more vulnerable to climatic shocks.[137] These environmental vulnerabilities persisted into the modern era, as Indonesia faced challenges related to deforestation, land degradation, and agricultural sustainability.

Politically, the governance structures established by the VOC laid the foundation for centralized and authoritarian rule in Indonesia. The VOC

[134] Booth, A. (1998). The Indonesian Economy in the Nineteenth and Twentieth Centuries: A History of Missed Opportunities. London: Macmillan Press.

[135] Elson, R. E. (1997). 'The Cultivation System and "Agricultural Involution": A View from the Water's Edge', in Boomgaard, P. and Brown, I. (eds.) Weathering the Storm: The Economies of SoutheastAsia in the 1930s Depression. Singapore: Institute of Southeast Asian Studies, pp. 231–258.

[136] Taylor, J. G. (2003). Indonesia: Peoples and Histories. New Haven: Yale University Press.

[137] Peluso, N. L. (1992). Rich Forests, Poor People: Resource Control and Resistance in Java. Berkeley: University of California Press.

relied on a hierarchical and militarized system to maintain its monopoly, marginalizing local governance structures and concentrating power in Batavia. These patterns were inherited by the Dutch colonial state and later by post-independence governments. For instance, the centralization of power in Jakarta during the New Order era under Suharto can be directly linked to the governance models introduced during the colonial period (Reid, 1993). This centralization has contributed to regional tensions and uneven development, as peripheral areas often feel excluded from decision-making processes and resource allocation.

The long-term legacy of early colonialism in Indonesia's political economy is evident in the centralized trade networks, economic dependency on cash crops, entrenched social hierarchies, environmental degradation, and authoritarian governance structures that continue to shape the nation's development. By prioritizing European economic interests over the well-being of local populations, colonial powers created structural imbalances that have persisted into the modern era. These legacies underscore the profound and enduring impact of colonialism on Indonesia's political and economic trajectory.

Conclusion

The arrival of European powers between 1500 and 1800 initiated profound transformations in Indonesia's political economy, marking a critical juncture in the region's development. Before European intervention, the Indonesian archipelago was part of a dynamic and decentralized network of maritime trade. Ports such as Malacca, Aceh, and Makassar served as thriving hubs for the exchange of goods, ideas, and cultural practices, linking Indonesia to a broader Indian Ocean economy that had historically balanced commercial interdependence with regional autonomy.[138] The trade routes facilitated not only economic prosperity but also the integration of technological and cultural innovations, as evidenced by the influence of Indian and Chinese civilizations on governance, agriculture, and religious practices.[139]

[138] Chaudhuri, K. N. (1985). Trade and Civilisation in the Indian Ocean: An Economic History from the Rise of Islam to 1750. Cambridge: Cambridge University Press.

[139] Wolters, O. W. (1999). History, Culture, and Region in Southeast Asian Perspectives. 2nd ed. Ithaca: Cornell University Press.

The Portuguese, and later the Dutch East India Company (VOC), disrupted this equilibrium, imposing monopolistic trade practices that centralized wealth and power in European hands. Through the Hongi system, unauthorized spice cultivation was systematically eradicated, forcing communities into dependency while marginalizing traditional trade centres like Banten and Makassar. The consolidation of trade in Batavia (modern Jakarta) under VOC dominance exemplified the shift from decentralized regional networks to a rigid, extractive colonial economy.[140] This centralization not only displaced indigenous traders but also redirected the economic benefits of Indonesia's resources to European markets, deepening regional inequalities.[141]

The integration of Indonesia's economy into global markets through forced cultivation systems, such as the cultuurstelsel, entrenched patterns of exploitation. Farmers were coerced into growing cash crops like coffee and sugar for export at the expense of subsistence agriculture, leading to widespread poverty and vulnerability to famine.[142] Such systems echoed pre-colonial patterns of agrarian dependency but were amplified under colonial rule, cementing economic imbalances that persisted into the post-colonial period. In the context of Indonesia, colonial systems of economic exploitation, such as the cultuurstelsel (Cultivation System), were built upon pre-existing patterns of agrarian dependency but amplified their effects, resulting in structural imbalances that persisted into the post-colonial era. Prior to European intervention, Indonesia's agrarian economy operated within a hierarchical framework where peasants provided labor and a share of their agricultural output to local rulers or aristocratic elites (priyayi). These elites, in turn, had reciprocal obligations to their communities, including the provision of protection and infrastructure. This decentralized system allowed for some degree of local autonomy and sustainability, as communities retained a significant degree

[140] Ricklefs, M. C. (2008). A History of Modern Indonesia Since c.1200. 4th ed. Stanford, CA: Stanford University Press.

[141] Henley, D. (2004). Fertility, Food, and Fever: Population, Economy, and Environment in North and Central Sulawesi, 1600–1930. Leiden: KITLV Press.

[142] Booth, A. (1998). The Indonesian Economy in the Nineteenth and Twentieth Centuries: A History of Missed Opportunities. London: Macmillan Press.

of control over their agricultural resources.[143,144] Under Dutch colonial rule, these pre-existing systems were co-opted and expanded to serve the interests of the colonial administration. The cultuurstelsel, introduced in Java in the nineteenth century, required farmers to allocate a significant portion of their land and labour to produce export-oriented cash crops like coffee, sugar, and indigo. Unlike the reciprocal obligations of pre-colonial systems, the colonial framework prioritized the extraction of surplus for the benefit of the Dutch state, leaving rural communities impoverished and vulnerable. Food shortages and famines became a recurring issue as subsistence farming was neglected in favour of cash crop production.[145,146] The system relied heavily on the existing social hierarchy, with local elites enlisted as intermediaries to enforce colonial policies. These elites, rewarded with privileges and exemptions, deepened social stratification, further alienating the broader population.[147]

The intensification of agrarian dependency during the colonial period had enduring consequences. The focus on monoculture and cash crops entrenched an economic structure heavily reliant on volatile global markets, limiting Indonesia's opportunities for industrialization and economic diversification. Even after independence, Indonesia's economy remained tied to the export of raw materials, as the colonial system had underinvested in industrial and human capital development. This dependency created significant barriers to self-sufficiency and sustainable economic growth.[148] Additionally, the collaboration of local elites with colonial authorities ensured that the wealth and power disparities of the colonial period persisted into the post-colonial era, as land reforms

[143] Geertz, C. (1963). Agricultural Involution: The Processes of Ecological Change in Indonesia. Berkeley: University of California Press.

[144] Reid, A. (1993). SoutheastAsia in the Age of Commerce, 1450–1680: Volume Two, Expansion and Crisis. New Haven: Yale University Press.

[145] Booth, A. (1998). The Indonesian Economy in the Nineteenth and Twentieth Centuries: A History of Missed Opportunities. London: Macmillan Press.

[146] Elson, R. E. (1997). 'The Cultivation System and "Agricultural Involution": A View from the Water's Edge,' in Boomgaard, P. and Brown, I. (eds.) Weathering the Storm: The Economies of SoutheastAsia in the 1930s Depression. Singapore: Institute of Southeast Asian Studies.

[147] Ricklefs, M. C. (2008). A History of Modern Indonesia since c.1200. 4th ed. Basingstoke: Palgrave Macmillan.

[148] Peluso, N. L. (1992). Rich Forests, Poor People: Resource Control and Resistance in Java. Berkeley: University of California Press.

and redistributive policies in the twentieth century were only partially successful in addressing these inequalities.[149,150] The cultuurstelsel and other colonial economic policies not only intensified pre-existing agrarian dependencies but also institutionalized them within a centralized and exploitative framework. This transformation disrupted local economies and entrenched structural inequalities that continue to shape Indonesia's political and economic landscape. The colonial amplification of dependency and extraction exemplifies the long-lasting impact of these policies on Indonesia's development trajectory.

Colonial rule also reconfigured social hierarchies, empowering local elites who collaborated with European authorities while exacerbating inequalities among the broader population. For instance, the Javanese Preyasi class played a key role in enforcing colonial policies, perpetuating cycles of economic and social stratification. These dynamics were rooted in pre-colonial governance structures, where rulers sought legitimacy through religious and political patronage, but under colonialism, these mechanisms became tools of European dominance.[151] The environmental consequences of European interventions further compounded Indonesia's challenges. Monoculture plantations disrupted ecological systems, leading to soil depletion and biodiversity loss. Such transformations, as explored in Chapter 3, undermined the resilience of Indonesia's agrarian economy, which had historically been characterized by diversified agricultural practices.[152]

The arrival of European powers profoundly altered Indonesia's political economy, shifting it from a decentralized, culturally rich maritime hub to a centralized, extractive colonial system. These changes laid the groundwork for economic dependency, social stratification, and environmental degradation that persisted into the modern era. By juxtaposing these developments with the achievements of pre-colonial trade and governance systems, this chapter underscores the long-term implications of

[149] Geertz, C. (1963). Agricultural Involution: The Processes of Ecological Change in Indonesia. Berkeley: University of California Press.

[150] Henley, D. (2004). Fertility, Food, and Fever: Population, Economy, and Environment in North and Central Sulawesi, 1600–1930. Leiden: KITLV Press.

[151] Taylor, J. G. (2003). Indonesia: Peoples and Histories. New Haven: Yale University Press.

[152] Peluso, N. L. (1992). Rich Forests, Poor People: Resource Control and Resistance in Java. Berkeley: University of California Press.

colonialism on Indonesia's economic and political trajectory, as explored in subsequent sections of this volume.

References

Andaya, B.W. (1993). To Live as Brothers: Southeast Sumatra in the Seventeenth and Eighteenth Centuries. Honolulu: University of Hawaii Press

Arasaratnam, S. (1986). Merchants, Companies, and Commerce on the Coromandel Coast, 1650–1740. Delhi: Oxford University Press.

Bayly, C. A. (1988). Indian Society and the Making of the British Empire. Cambridge: Cambridge University Press.

Boomgaard, P. (1990), Children of the Colonial State: Population Growth and Economic Development in Java, 1795–1880. Amsterdam: Free University Press.

Booth, A. (1998). The Indonesian Economy in the Nineteenth and Twentieth Centuries: A History of Missed Opportunities. London: Palgrave Macmillan.

Bosma, U. (2013). The Sugar Plantation in India and Indonesia: Industrial Production, 1770–2010. Cambridge: Cambridge University Press.

Bowen, J. R. (2003). Muslims through Discourse: Religion and Ritual in Gayo Society. Princeton: Princeton University Press.

Boxer, C.R. (1965) The Portuguese Seaborne Empire, 1415–1825. London: Hutchinson

Burns, P. (2004). The Leiden Legacy: Concepts of Law in Indonesia. Leiden: KITLV Press.

Chaudhuri, K. N. (1985). Trade and Civilisation in the Indian Ocean: An Economic History from the Rise of Islam to 1750. Cambridge: Cambridge University Press.

Cribb, R. (2000), Historical Dictionary of Indonesia. 2nd edn. Lanham, MD: Scarecrow Press.

Davidson, J. S., and Henley, D. (2007). The Revival of Tradition in Indonesian Politics: The Deployment of Adat from Colonialism to Indigenism. London: Routledge.

Elson, R.E. (1994), Village Java under the Cultivation System, 1830–1870. Sydney: Allen & Unwin.

Elson, R.E. (1997). 'The Cultivation System and "Agricultural Involution": A View from the Water's Edge', in Boomgaard, P. and Brown, I. (eds.) Weathering the Storm: The Economies of Southeast Asia in the 1930s Depression. Singapore: Institute of Southeast Asian Studies, pp. 231–258.

Fitzpatrick, D. (2008). "Beyond Dualism: Land Acquisition and Law in Indonesia." In Indonesian Law and Society, edited by T. Lindsey, pp. 74–94. Sydney: Federation Press.

Gaastra, F.S. (2003), The Dutch East India Company: Expansion and Decline. Zutphen: Walburg Pers.
Geertz, C. (1963). Agricultural Involution: The Processes of Ecological Change in Indonesia. Berkeley: University of California Press.
Henley, D. (2004). Conflict, Justice, and the Stranger-King: Indigenous Roots of Colonial Rule in Indonesia and Elsewhere. Modern Asian Studies, 38(1), pp. 85–144.
Hooker, M. B. (1978). Adat Law in Modern Indonesia. Kuala Lumpur: Oxford University Press.
Knaap, G. & Teitler, G. (2004), Between Discipline and Disgust: Deserters of the VOC Army in Eighteenth Century Asia. Itinerario, 28(2), pp. 55–76.
Peluso, N. L. (1992). Rich Forests, Poor People: Resource Control and Resistance in Java. Berkeley: University of California Press.
Prakash, O. (1998). European Commercial Enterprise in Pre-Colonial India. Cambridge: Cambridge University Press.
Reid, A. (1993), Southeast Asia in the Age of Commerce, 1450–1680: Volume Two, Expansion and Crisis. New Haven, CT: Yale University Press.
Ricklefs, M.C. (2001), A History of Modern Indonesia Since c.1200. 3rd edn. Stanford, CA: Stanford University Press.
Ricklefs, M. C. (2008). A History of Modern Indonesia since c. 1200. 4th edn. London: Palgrave Macmillan.
Taylor, J.G. (2003), Indonesia: Peoples and Histories. New Haven, CT: Yale University Press.
Vickers, A. (2005), A History of Modern Indonesia. Cambridge: Cambridge University Press.
Waites, B. (1999). Europe and the Third World: From Colonisation to Decolonisation c. 1500–1998. London: Macmillan Press.

CHAPTER 6

Dutch Colonial Economy (1800–1942)

Introduction

The Dutch colonial period in Indonesia, spanning from 1800 to 1942, was a formative era that significantly influenced the country's political economy and set the stage for its future development trajectory. This chapter examines the economic structures, policies, and impacts of Dutch colonial rule, focusing on how these elements shaped Indonesia's path toward economic development.

During the nineteenth century, the Dutch East Indies, as Indonesia was then known, became a crucial part of the global economy, primarily due to its rich natural resources. The Dutch colonial administration implemented the Cultivation System (Cultuurstelsel), which forced indigenous farmers to grow export crops such as coffee, sugar, and indigo, leading to significant changes in land use and rural livelihoods,[1,2] This system was not only economically exploitative but also politically repressive,

[1] Elson, R. E. (1984), Village Java under the Cultivation System 1830–1870. Sydney: Allen & Unwin.

[2] Fernando, M. R. (2006), 'The Cultivation Systemin Java: The Social and Economic Effects of Dutch Colonial Policy in the Mid-Nineteenth Century', Journal of Southeast Asian Studies, 37(3), pp. 435–456.

S. Ramesh, *The Political Economy of Indonesia's Economic Development, Volume I*, https://doi.org/10.1007/978-3-031-94350-8_6

consolidating Dutch control over the archipelago while creating a dualistic economy that separated the indigenous population from European settlers.[3] As the century progressed, the Dutch shifted from the Cultivation System to a more liberal economic approach, allowing private enterprises to invest in the colony. The Dutch colonial administration in Indonesia transitioned from the Cultivation System (Cultuurstelsel) to a more liberal economic approach, a shift that significantly reshaped the colony's economy and social structure. The Cultivation System, implemented in 1830, required Indonesian farmers to allocate a portion of their land and labour to grow export crops, such as coffee, sugar, and indigo, which were sold at fixed prices to the colonial government. While this system generated substantial revenue for the Dutch, it caused widespread suffering among local populations, leading to famine, poverty, and resistance.[4] The system prioritized colonial revenue over the welfare of local communities, disrupting traditional agricultural practices and food security. Farmers were forced to divert significant portions of their land from subsistence farming to export-oriented production, reducing the availability of staple crops like rice. This reallocation of resources led to chronic food shortages and widespread famine, particularly during periods of poor harvests or natural disasters. For example, during the 1840s, famines devastated parts of Central Java, resulting in tens of thousands of deaths as local populations struggled to survive.[5] Poverty deepened under the Cultivation System, as farmers were burdened with high quotas and strict penalties for failing to meet production targets. Many were compelled to borrow money at exorbitant interest rates to meet their obligations, plunging them into cycles of debt and dependency. The exploitation extended beyond economic terms, as labour requirements often demanded gruelling physical work under harsh conditions. The system resembled a form of forced labour, with local leaders acting

[3] Booth, A. (1998), The Indonesian Economy in the Nineteenth and Twentieth Centuries: A History of Missed Opportunities. London: Macmillan.

[4] Fasseur, C. (1992). The Politics of Colonial Exploitation: Java, the Dutch, and the Cultivation System. Ithaca, NY: Cornell University Press.

[5] Booth, A. (1998). The Indonesian Economy in the Nineteenth and Twentieth Centuries: A History of Missed Opportunities. London: Palgrave Macmillan.

as intermediaries to enforce compliance, further entrenching inequalities within rural communities.[6] Resistance to the Cultivation System emerged in various forms. Farmers engaged in subtle acts of defiance, such as sabotaging crops, reducing yields, or fleeing their villages. More overt rebellions occurred in certain regions, as communities protested the oppressive conditions. Additionally, criticism of the system grew within the Netherlands itself, where liberal politicians and humanitarians condemned the exploitative nature of colonial rule. This backlash eventually led to reforms in the 1860s, culminating in the adoption of the Liberal Policy, which sought to replace the Cultivation System with a framework encouraging private enterprise and foreign investment.[7] The Cultivation System highlights the dual legacy of colonial economic policies. This included the generation of wealth for the Dutch at the expense of severe social and economic dislocation for the colonized. While it enabled the Dutch to fund public works at home, pay off national debt, and strengthen their colonial administration, it left a legacy of inequality, poverty, and resentment among Indonesia's rural populations. By the 1860s, growing criticism of the Cultivation System from liberal politicians and humanitarians in the Netherlands, combined with declining profitability and administrative inefficiencies and prompted reforms. The Liberal Policy (Vrije Politiek), introduced in the 1870s, aimed to open the colonial economy to private enterprise. This policy allowed private investors, particularly Dutch and European companies, to lease land and establish plantations, mining operations, and trade businesses in the archipelago.[8] The shift to a liberal economic approach was facilitated by legal and institutional changes, such as the 1870 Agrarian Law, which prevented the outright sale of native land to foreign companies but allowed long-term leases. This framework aimed to balance the interests of local communities with the demands of foreign investors. In practice, however, the law often marginalized Indigenous farmers, as large tracts

[6] Elson, R.E. (1997). The End of the Peasantry in SoutheastAsia: A Social and Economic History of Peasant Livelihood, 1800–1990s. Basingstoke: Macmillan.

[7] Furnivall, J.S. (1948). Colonial Policy and Practice: A Comparative Study of Burma and NetherlandsIndia. Cambridge: Cambridge University Press.

[8] Elson, R.E. (1997). The End of the Peasantry in SoutheastAsia: A Social and Economic History of Peasant Livelihood, 1800–1990s. Basingstoke: Macmillan.

of fertile land were leased to private companies, displacing local populations and reducing their access to resources and the ability to maintain a sustainable livelihood.[9]

The liberalization of the economy encouraged the expansion of export-oriented agriculture, particularly in crops like rubber, tea, and tobacco. It also fostered the growth of infrastructure, such as railways, ports, and irrigation systems, built to support the export economy. These developments integrated the Indonesian economy more closely into global trade networks and generated significant profits for European investors. However, the benefits of this economic transformation were unevenly distributed. While the Dutch economy flourished, most Indonesians continued to face exploitation, low wages, and limited access to land.[10] Additionally, the influx of private capital and the expansion of plantations contributed to significant environmental and social changes. Deforestation and soil degradation became pressing issues, as large-scale monoculture replaced traditional farming practices. Socially, the reliance on indentured labour led to harsh working conditions and frequent labour unrest, with indigenous workers often subjected to exploitative contracts and poor living standards.[11] The Dutch shift from the Cultivation System to a more liberal economic approach marked a significant turning point in Indonesia's economic development. While it introduced elements of modernization and integration into global markets, it also entrenched and increased economic inequalities among the Indigenous Indonesians and social tensions that would shape the country's colonial and post-colonial trajectory. The transition from the Cultivation System to a Liberal System marked the rise of the plantation economy, particularly in Java and Sumatra, where European and Chinese entrepreneurs dominated the cultivation of rubber, tea, and tobacco.[12,13] However,

[9] Booth, A. (1998). The Indonesian Economy in the Nineteenth and Twentieth Centuries: A History of Missed Opportunities. London: Palgrave Macmillan.

[10] Furnivall, J.S. (1948). Colonial Policy and Practice: A Comparative Study of Burma and NetherlandsIndia. Cambridge: Cambridge University Press.

[11] Stoler, A.L. (1985). Capitalism and Confrontation in Sumatra's Plantation Belt, 1870–1979. New Haven, CT: Yale University Press.

[12] Breman, J. (2015), Mobilizing Labour for the Global Coffee Market: Profits from an Unfree Work Regime in Colonial Java. Amsterdam: Amsterdam University Press.

[13] Mackie, J. A. C. (1976), 'Economic Problems of the Dutchin Indonesia during the 1930s', Bulletin of Indonesian Economic Studies, 12(1), pp. 19–30.

this liberalization also exacerbated social and economic inequalities, as the benefits of economic expansion were unevenly distributed, with indigenous populations often marginalized and confined to low-wage labour.[14]

The chapter will also explore the vulnerabilities inherent in the colonial economy, particularly its dependence on global markets. The Great Depression of the 1930s highlighted these vulnerabilities, leading to economic decline, social unrest, and the rise of nationalist movements that questioned Dutch authority and sought economic as well as political independence.[15,16]

Dutch Colonial Power in Indonesia

The Dutch established themselves as a colonial power in Indonesia through a multifaceted strategy of military conquest, alliances with local rulers, and administrative innovations, culminating in the implementation of the Cultivation System in 1830. These methods enabled the Dutch to consolidate their authority and exploit Java's agricultural wealth, making it a vital economic resource for the Netherlands while imposing significant hardships on the Indigenous population. The Dutch settlement of Indonesia began in the early seventeenth century, spearheaded by the Dutch East India Company (VOC), which sought to establish a monopoly over the lucrative spice trade in the region. The Dutch succeeded in consolidating their presence and ultimately becoming a colonial power through a combination of military force, strategic alliances with indigenous rulers, and the exploitation of regional political and economic dynamics. The VOC established its first permanent foothold in Indonesia in 1603 with the construction of a trading post in Banten, a key port on Java's northwest coast. However, the turning point came in 1619 when the Dutch captured and established Batavia (modern-day Jakarta) as their administrative and commercial centre. This strategic move was facilitated by the disintegration of larger kingdoms like Majapahit and the rivalry among smaller polities, which the Dutch exploited to their

[14] Geertz, C. (1963), Agricultural Involution: The Processes of Ecological Change in Indonesia. Berkeley: University of California Press.

[15] Cribb, R. (1994), Historical Dictionary of Indonesia. Lanham, MD: Scarecrow Press.

[16] Kahin, G. M. (1952), Nationalism and Revolution in Indonesia. Ithaca, NY: Cornell University Press.

advantage.[17] Moreover, the Dutch employed military force to overpower indigenous rulers who resisted their influence. One such example was Sultan Agung of Mataram, a powerful Javanese ruler who attempted to expel the Dutch from Batavia during the 1620s and 1630s. Despite his efforts, the superior naval and military capabilities of the Dutch allowed them to repel his forces and solidify their control over the area. By defeating local resistance, the Dutch secured key territories that would become the foundation of their colonial empire.[18] In addition to military conquest, the Dutch were adept at forging alliances with local rulers to expand their influence. These alliances often involved mutual benefits, such as military support from the Dutch in exchange for trade privileges and political stability for the indigenous rulers. For instance, the Sultanate of Ternate in the Maluku Islands allied with the Dutch to counter its rival, the Sultanate of Tidore. By aligning themselves with Ternate, the Dutch gained access to the spice trade and began consolidating control over the region's valuable clove and nutmeg production.[19] Another critical factor in Dutch success was their ability to exploit internal divisions within indigenous polities. The Javanese kingdom of Mataram, for example, was weakened by succession disputes following the death of Sultan Agung. The Dutch capitalized on this instability by supporting rival claimants to the throne, thereby gaining influence over the kingdom and securing economic concessions.[20] The Dutch also introduced administrative and financial innovations that supported their expansion. They established a bureaucratic system to manage their growing territories and ensure efficient resource extraction. The Dutch East India Company (VOC) established a bureaucratic system in Indonesia to manage its expanding territories and ensure the efficient extraction of resources. This system transformed the VOC from a trading company into a quasi-state, enabling it to consolidate power and maximize profits. At the centre of this bureaucracy was the Governor-General, based in Batavia (modern-day Jakarta),

[17] Ricklefs, M.C. (2008). A History of Modern Indonesia Since c. 1200. Stanford, CA: Stanford University Press.

[18] Andaya, B.W., & Andaya, L.Y. (2016). A History of Early Modern SoutheastAsia, 1400–1830. Cambridge: Cambridge University Press.

[19] Kumar, A. (1997). Java and Modern Europe: Ambiguous Encounters. Richmond: Curzon Press.

[20] Ricklefs, M.C. (2008). A History of Modern Indonesia Since c. 1200. Stanford, CA: Stanford University Press.

who held supreme authority over VOC operations. Batavia became the administrative and commercial hub, from which policies were formulated and directives issued to regional offices. Below the Governor-General, a hierarchy of officials managed the various regions and aspects of the VOC's operations, supported by an extensive network of records and correspondences that ensured the centralized flow of information and effective decision-making.[21,22]

The VOC's bureaucratic system played a critical role in resource extraction, particularly in enforcing monopolies on lucrative commodities such as spices from the Maluku Islands. By imposing exclusive trading rights and controlling production and distribution, the VOC secured dominance over global spice markets. This involved setting quotas for indigenous communities, who were required to cultivate specific amounts of export crops, which were then transported to Batavia for redistribution to European markets. The meticulous record-keeping and strict oversight inherent in the VOC's bureaucracy ensured the efficient functioning of these monopolistic practices, although they often came at a severe cost to local populations.[23] The severe costs to local populations under the VOC's monopolistic practices were both economic and social, reflecting the exploitative nature of Dutch colonial administration. These costs stemmed from forced labour, land dispossession, loss of economic autonomy, and significant disruptions to traditional ways of life. Indigenous communities were compelled to participate in the production of export crops, such as cloves, nutmeg, and mace, often at the expense of cultivating food crops needed for subsistence. The VOC imposed strict quotas on these communities, requiring them to allocate their labour and land to fulfil the company's demands. This practice frequently led to food shortages and famines, as local populations could not produce enough rice or other staples to sustain themselves. For example, during the seventeenth century, entire villages in the Maluku Islands were depopulated due to starvation and forced relocations aimed at ensuring compliance

[21] Ricklefs, M.C. (2008). A History of Modern Indonesia Since c. 1200. Stanford, CA: Stanford University Press.

[22] Bosma, U., & Raben, R. (2008). Being "Dutch" in the Indies: A History of Creolisation and Empire, 1500–1920. Athens: Ohio University Press.

[23] Andaya, B.W., & Andaya, L.Y. (2016). A History of Early Modern SoutheastAsia, 1400–1830. Cambridge: Cambridge University Press.

with VOC policies.[24] The Maluku Islands, also known as the Moluccas or the Spice Islands, are located in eastern Indonesia, between Sulawesi to the west and New Guinea to the east, with the Banda Sea to the south. These islands form part of the larger region of eastern Indonesia and fall within the province of Maluku, with Ambon as its provincial capital.[25] Historically, the Maluku Islands were the primary source of highly prized spices such as nutmeg, mace, and cloves. These commodities were in high demand in Europe during the Age of Exploration, making the islands central to early global trade networks. European powers, including the Portuguese, Dutch, and British, vied for control over the region. The Dutch East India Company (VOC) ultimately succeeded in the seventeenth century, establishing a monopoly on the spice trade by employing both military force and strategic alliances with local rulers. This dominance was cemented through the brutal suppression of local resistance, such as the massacre and depopulation of the Banda Islands in the early 1600s to gain direct control over nutmeg production.[26] The key islands within the Maluku group include:

Ambon:	A major administrative and trading hub during Dutch colonial rule.
Banda Islands:	Historically, the only global source of nutmeg and mace until the eighteenth century.
Ternate and Tidore:	These sultanates played pivotal roles in the spice trade, acting as intermediaries and centres of political power in the region.[27] Today, while the spice trade no longer defines their economic significance, the Maluku Islands remain culturally and historically rich. Their lush forests, volcanic landscapes, and pristine beaches contribute to their reputation as one of

[24] Ricklefs, M.C. (2008). A History of Modern Indonesia Since c. 1200. Stanford, CA: Stanford University Press.

[25] Andaya, B.W., & Andaya, L.Y. (2016). A History of Early Modern SoutheastAsia, 1400–1830. Cambridge: Cambridge University Press.

[26] Ricklefs, M.C. (2008). A History of Modern Indonesia Since c. 1200. Stanford, CA: Stanford University Press.

[27] Kumar, A. (1997). Java and Modern Europe: Ambiguous Encounters. Richmond: Curzon Press.

> Indonesia's most beautiful regions. The islands continue to attract historians, researchers, and travellers interested in their unique blend of natural and historical heritage.

The enforcement of monopolistic practices involved significant physical and psychological coercion. Indigenous workers were often subjected to harsh working conditions and brutal punishments if they failed to meet production quotas or attempted to resist VOC policies. Forced relocations were common, with communities uprooted and resettled to areas where their labour could be more easily controlled. In the Banda Islands, for example, VOC forces massacred thousands of residents in the early seventeenth century to establish direct control over nutmeg production, replacing the local population with enslaved labourers imported from other regions.[28] Economic exploitation was another key burden. The prices paid by the VOC for export crops were often far below-market value, ensuring significant profits for the company while leaving local producers in poverty. The inability to negotiate fair prices or diversify economic activities meant that many communities became entirely dependent on the VOC for their livelihoods, perpetuating cycles of poverty and indebtedness. Additionally, the company's monopolistic policies stifled local trade networks, as indigenous merchants and producers were unable to compete with the VOC's control over production and distribution (Bosma & Raben, 2008). One notable example was the VOC's impact on the Banda Islands, historically the world's only source of nutmeg and mace. Local Banda merchants had traditionally traded these spices with a variety of buyers, including Malay, Javanese, Arab, and Chinese traders. However, when the VOC established its monopoly in the early seventeenth century, it systematically dismantled this vibrant trade network. The VOC forcibly took control of nutmeg production and distribution, massacring, or forcibly displacing much of the local population in the Banda Massacre of 1621. The survivors were either enslaved or forced into labour on VOC-controlled plantations. The VOC then imported enslaved workers to replace the indigenous population and directly managed all nutmeg exports, ensuring that no rival traders

[28] Andaya, B.W., & Andaya, L.Y. (2016). A History of Early Modern SoutheastAsia, 1400–1830. Cambridge: Cambridge University Press.

could access the lucrative spice market.[29] In Java, local trade networks suffered a similar fate under VOC policies. The company-imposed quotas and forced farmers to grow specific export crops, such as sugar and coffee, at the expense of food crops. This restricted the ability of local merchants to participate in traditional trade markets, as much of the agricultural output was diverted to VOC-controlled channels. For example, Javanese peasants and traders who had previously supplied local markets were now forced to sell their produce at fixed, artificially low prices to the VOC. This left little surplus for local trade and severely undercut indigenous merchants, who could not compete with the VOC's monopoly on pricing and export rights.[30] Another significant disruption occurred in the Maluku Islands, where the VOC imposed strict controls over clove production. The company implemented a policy of "extirpation," which involved destroying clove trees in areas not under VOC control to prevent unauthorized production. This not only suppressed local trade but also disrupted traditional agricultural systems and livelihoods, as many communities relied on clove cultivation for subsistence and regional commerce. Indigenous traders and producers who resisted these policies faced harsh punishments, including confiscation of property and forced labour.[31] These examples illustrate how the VOC's monopolistic policies decimated local trade networks and marginalized indigenous merchants, ensuring that economic activity in Indonesia served the interests of the company and its European shareholders. The long-term consequences included economic dependency, social disruption, and the erosion of traditional systems of commerce, which further entrenched Dutch colonial control. Social structures and traditional practices were also severely disrupted. The VOC's reliance on local elites, such as village heads, to enforce its policies created tensions within communities. These elites, incentivized with financial rewards and political favours, often prioritized their loyalty to the VOC over their responsibilities to their own people. This dynamic eroded trust within communities, undermining traditional

[29] Andaya, B.W., & Andaya, L.Y. (2016). A History of Early Modern SoutheastAsia, 1400–1830. Cambridge: Cambridge University Press.

[30] Furnivall, J.S. (1948). Colonial Policy and Practice: A Comparative Study of Burma and NetherlandsIndia. Cambridge: Cambridge University Press.

[31] Ricklefs, M.C. (2008). A History of Modern Indonesia Since c. 1200. Stanford, CA: Stanford University Press.

governance structures and social cohesion.[32] The environmental impact of the VOC's policies further exacerbated the suffering of local populations. Large-scale monoculture agriculture, driven by the company's focus on export crops, led to soil depletion and deforestation, reducing the availability of resources for indigenous use. This ecological degradation compounded the economic and social challenges faced by local communities, leaving them increasingly vulnerable to natural disasters and economic downturns.[33] The severe costs to local populations under the VOC's monopolistic practices included widespread poverty, food insecurity, forced labour, social disintegration, and environmental degradation. These consequences highlight the deeply exploitative nature of Dutch colonial policies, which prioritized profit over the welfare of the Indigenous people in Indonesia.

The system imposed by the VOC also managed labour and land to support resource extraction. Forced labour systems, such as corvée labour, were frequently employed, with local populations compelled to work under harsh conditions without fair compensation. The VOC relied heavily on co-opting local elites, such as village heads and regional rulers, to enforce compliance with its policies. In return, these elites received privileges, creating a system of indirect rule that minimized administrative costs while consolidating VOC authority. However, this approach exacerbated the exploitation of Indigenous communities, deepening poverty and fostering resentment.[34] Despite its efficiency in resource extraction, the VOC's bureaucratic system was plagued by corruption and inefficiency. Many officials exploited their positions for personal gain, engaging in illicit trade and misappropriating resources, which undermined the company's monopoly. Corruption within the bureaucracy, coupled with inefficiencies in governance, gradually weakened the VOC's economic and administrative structures. Additionally, the exploitative nature of the system alienated local populations, leading to resistance and uprisings that further strained VOC resources and authority. These factors contributed to the eventual decline of the VOC, which dissolved in 1799, paving

[32] Elson, R.E. (1997). The End of the Peasantry in SoutheastAsia: A Social and Economic History of Peasant Livelihood, 1800–1990s. Basingstoke: Macmillan.

[33] Furnivall, J.S. (1948). Colonial Policy and Practice: A Comparative Study of Burma and NetherlandsIndia. Cambridge: Cambridge University Press.

[34] Elson, R.E. (1997). The End of the Peasantry in SoutheastAsia: A Social and Economic History of Peasant Livelihood, 1800–1990s. Basingstoke: Macmillan.

the way for direct colonial administration by the Dutch state.[35,36] The bureaucratic system established by the VOC reflected the Dutch commitment to centralizing authority and maximizing economic gains. While it enabled the VOC to dominate the region's economy for nearly two centuries, its reliance on exploitative practices and systemic corruption ultimately undermined its stability and effectiveness, leaving a mixed legacy of control and conflict in Indonesia. Moreover, the VOC operated as a quasi-state, complete with its own military and legal system, allowing it to function autonomously in its dealings with indigenous rulers. This organizational sophistication gave the Dutch a significant advantage over rival European powers and local rulers alike.[37]

By the nineteenth century, the Dutch had transitioned from a trading power to a colonial authority, a shift marked by the dissolution of the VOC in 1799 and the direct administration of Indonesia by the Dutch state. The Napoleonic Wars and subsequent British occupation of Java (1811–1816) briefly interrupted Dutch control, but the return of Java to the Dutch after the war allowed them to consolidate their governance. This culminated in the implementation of the Cultivation System in 1830, a mechanism that institutionalized their economic dominance over Java while exploiting the labour and resources of the Indigenous population.[38]

The Dutch East India Company (VOC), founded in 1602, served as the foundation of Dutch colonial dominance in Indonesia. With a monopoly on trade in the East Indies, the VOC established fortified trading posts and strategic alliances with local rulers. Batavia (modern-day Jakarta) became the centre of VOC operations, serving as a base for trade and military campaigns. The VOC exploited rivalries between indigenous polities in the Indonesian archipelago to weaken opposition, such as in the wars against the Mataram Kingdom, allowing the Dutch

[35] Furnivall, J.S. (1948). Colonial Policy and Practice: A Comparative Study of Burma and NetherlandsIndia. Cambridge: Cambridge University Press.

[36] Fasseur, C. (1992). The Politics of Colonial Exploitation: Java, the Dutch, and the Cultivation System. Ithaca, NY: Cornell University Press.

[37] Bosma, U., & Raben, R. (2008). Being "Dutch" in the Indies: A History of Creolisation and Empire, 1500–1920. Athens: Ohio University Press.

[38] Furnivall, J.S. (1948). Colonial Policy and Practice: A Comparative Study of Burma and NetherlandsIndia. Cambridge: Cambridge University Press.

to extract resources and assert control over key territories.[39,40] However, the VOC's operations were plagued by corruption, mismanagement, and financial difficulties, ultimately leading to its dissolution in 1799. Control of VOC territories transitioned to the Dutch government, marking a shift toward centralized governance. This transition coincided with global political upheavals, including the Napoleonic Wars and the British occupation of Java (1811–1816). During this period, the Dutch realized the need for a more robust administrative system to stabilize their rule and address financial pressures in the Netherlands.[41] The Napoleonic Wars had drained Dutch resources, and Java's agricultural potential was seen as a critical asset for economic recovery. The implementation of the Cultivation System in 1830 reflected the Dutch government's intent to formalize colonial economic extraction. The system required Javanese farmers to dedicate a portion of their land and labour to producing export crops such as coffee, sugar, and indigo, which were sold to the Dutch government at fixed prices. These goods were then resold on international markets for significant profit for the Dutch government. The system relied heavily on the feudal hierarchy of Javanese society, co-opting village heads and the priyayi (Javanese aristocracy) into the colonial administration. These intermediaries enforced the system's requirements, ensuring compliance from local populations while receiving financial and political rewards that bolstered Dutch control.[42,43]

Military conquest and suppression were equally integral to Dutch dominance. The Diponegoro War (1825–1830) was a pivotal conflict, as it mobilized widespread resistance against colonial rule, driven by grievances over taxation, land confiscations, and cultural tensions. Despite significant losses, the Dutch ultimately prevailed, demonstrating their military superiority and decisively subduing one of the most formidable

[39] Ricklefs, M.C. (2008). A History of Modern Indonesia Since c. 1200. Stanford, CA: Stanford University Press.

[40] Andaya, B.W., & Andaya, L.Y. (2016). A History of Early Modern SoutheastAsia, 1400–1830. Cambridge: Cambridge University Press.

[41] Furnivall, J.S. (1948). Colonial Policy and Practice: A Comparative Study of Burma and NetherlandsIndia. Cambridge: Cambridge University Press.

[42] Elson, R.E. (1997). The End of the Peasantry in SoutheastAsia: A Social and Economic History of Peasant Livelihood, 1800–1990s. Basingstoke: Macmillan.

[43] Cribb, R. (1994). The Late Colonial State in Indonesia: Political and Economic Foundations of the Netherlands Indies, 1880–1942. Leiden: KITLV Press.

challenges to their authority.[44,45] The war's conclusion coincided with the implementation of the Cultivation System, which benefited from the pacification of rural Java and the expansion of Dutch administrative and military presence.

Administrative innovations played a critical role in sustaining Dutch colonial rule. Detailed record-keeping and centralized oversight allowed the Dutch to maximize the efficiency of the Cultivation System. For instance, revenue from Java's agricultural exports funded public works and reduced the Dutch national debt, while also financing military campaigns to expand control over the outer islands.[46,47] However, the system's success came at a significant cost to the local population, who suffered from land displacement, labour exploitation, and declining food security. Famines and rural poverty became widespread, particularly during periods of poor harvests.[48] The Dutch also established a monopoly over key resources and trade routes, ensuring their economic dominance. By controlling the production and distribution of cash crops, they marginalized local producers and traders, consolidating wealth within colonial enterprises. This economic centralization reinforced the structural inequalities between the colonial administration and the indigenous population, perpetuating resentment and resistance.[49] By combining military force, strategic alliances with local elites, and innovative administrative practices, the Dutch institutionalized their economic and political authority in Indonesia. The Cultivation System exemplified their capacity to integrate economic extraction with political control, transforming Java into the linchpin of Dutch colonial wealth. However, the social and economic costs borne by the Javanese population left

[44] Ricklefs, M.C. (2008). A History of Modern Indonesia Since c. 1200. Stanford, CA: Stanford University Press.

[45] Carey, P. (2007). The Power of Prophecy: Prince Dipanagara and the End of an Old Order in Java, 1785–1855. Leiden: KITLV Press.

[46] Booth, A. (1998). The Indonesian Economy in the Nineteenth and Twentieth Centuries: A History of Missed Opportunities. London: Palgrave Macmillan.

[47] Bosma, U., & Raben, R. (2008). Being "Dutch" in the Indies: A History of Creolisation and Empire, 1500–1920. Athens: Ohio University Press.

[48] Fasseur, C. (1992). The Politics of Colonial Exploitation: Java, the Dutch, and the Cultivation System. Ithaca, NY: Cornell University Press.

[49] Kumar, A. (1997). Java and Modern Europe: Ambiguous Encounters. Richmond: Curzon Press.

a legacy of inequality and exploitation that persisted throughout the colonial era.

The Cultivation System and Its Impacts

The Cultivation System (cultuurstelsel), implemented in Java by the Dutch colonial administration in 1830, marked a pivotal era in Indonesia's economic history. Designed to address the financial troubles of the Netherlands following the Napoleonic Wars, the system forced Javanese farmers to dedicate a significant portion of their land and labour to the production of export-oriented cash crops such as coffee, sugar, and indigo. The surplus generated was transported to Europe, where it contributed significantly to the Dutch state's revenue, financing infrastructure projects and national development.[50] While the Cultivation System was financially advantageous for the Dutch, its impacts on Indonesian society and economy were profoundly detrimental, exacerbating inequalities, poverty, and environmental degradation. Under the system, farmers were required to cultivate cash crops on 20% of their arable land or provide equivalent labour to colonial plantations. In practice, these demands often exceeded the stipulated percentage, leaving inadequate land and resources for subsistence farming. As a result, rural communities faced chronic food shortages, malnutrition, and periodic famines, with devastating human consequences. One of the most severe famines occurred in the 1840s, leading to significant loss of life in parts of Java, a direct consequence of the system's prioritization of exports over local food security.[51] This famine was a direct consequence of the cultuurstelsel (Cultivation System), which prioritized the production of cash crops such as coffee, sugar, and indigo for export over the cultivation of staple food crops like rice that were essential for local food security. Under the system, farmers were required to dedicate a sizeable portion of their land and labour to the cultivation of export crops, leaving insufficient

[50] Booth, A. (1998). The Indonesian Economy in the Nineteenth and Twentieth Centuries: A History of Missed Opportunities. London: Macmillan Press.

[51] Elson, R. E. (1997). 'The Cultivation System and "Agricultural Involution": A View from the Water's Edge,' in Boomgaard, P. and Brown, I. (eds.) Weathering the Storm: The Economies of SoutheastAsia in the 1930s Depression. Singapore: Institute of Southeast Asian Studies.

resources for subsistence farming. Moreover, the system's rigid enforcement meant that even during periods of poor harvests, farmers were obligated to meet quotas for cash crops, exacerbating food shortages.[52] The famine was particularly devastating in regions such as Cirebon and Priangan in West Java, where local populations were already struggling with the demands of the cultuurstelsel. The overextraction of agricultural resources, combined with poor weather conditions, led to catastrophic food shortages. Entire villages were left without adequate sustenance, forcing families to sell their possessions, migrate in search of food, or succumb to starvation. Reports from the time indicate that thousands of people perished, with many more enduring extreme malnutrition and disease caused by the famine.[53]

The colonial administration's indifference to the plight of rural communities further exacerbated the crisis. Resources that could have been directed toward famine relief were instead diverted to sustain the export economy, ensuring continued profits for the Dutch state and VOC shareholders. The prioritization of export-oriented agriculture over local food production highlighted the exploitative nature of the cultuurstelsel, which treated the rural population to extract wealth rather than as a community to be supported and sustained.[54] This famine exemplifies the structural vulnerabilities introduced by the cultuurstelsel. By dismantling traditional agricultural practices and imposing monoculture systems, the colonial regime created an economic framework that left rural communities highly susceptible to food shortages and environmental shocks. The events of the 1840s underscore the human cost of colonial economic policies and their long-term impact on Indonesia's agrarian society, as they entrenched patterns of inequality and dependency that persisted long after the abolition of the cultuurstelsel. This exploitative arrangement entrenched patterns of agrarian dependency, with farmers becoming trapped in cycles of debt and poverty due to their inability

[52] Elson, R. E. (1997). 'The Cultivation System and "Agricultural Involution": A View from the Water's Edge,' in Boomgaard, P. and Brown, I. (eds.) Weathering the Storm: The Economies of SoutheastAsia in the 1930s Depression. Singapore: Institute of Southeast Asian Studies.

[53] Booth, A. (1998). The Indonesian Economy in the Nineteenth and Twentieth Centuries: A History of Missed Opportunities. London: Macmillan Press.

[54] Ricklefs, M. C. (2008). A History of Modern Indonesia Since c.1200. 4th ed. Basingstoke: Palgrave Macmillan.

to sustain their subsistence needs while meeting colonial demands. The Cultivation System also reinforced and expanded existing social hierarchies. Indigenous elites, particularly the Javanese priyayi, played a crucial role as intermediaries in enforcing the system. These elites benefited from their collaboration with the colonial administration, receiving privileges such as land grants and financial incentives. However, their collaboration deepened divisions within Indonesian society, as the broader rural population endured the most of the system's exploitative practices.[55] This dynamic contributed to the entrenchment of social stratification, leaving lasting inequalities that would persist beyond the colonial period.

Economically, the Cultivation System's reliance on monoculture and cash crop production created vulnerabilities for both local communities and the colonial economy. By focusing on export crops, the system neglected the diversification of agriculture and industrial development, making Indonesia dependent on volatile global markets for revenue. The environmental consequences of this focus were also significant. Monoculture farming practices degraded soil fertility and reduced agricultural biodiversity, undermining the sustainability of local ecosystems and leaving rural communities more susceptible to environmental shocks.[56] The depletion of resources and ecological imbalance caused by the Cultivation System created long-term challenges for Indonesia's agrarian economy. Despite its exploitative nature, the Cultivation System had broader geopolitical implications for the Dutch colonial state. The revenue generated by the system made the Netherlands one of Europe's wealthiest countries during the nineteenth century, funding the industrialization of the Dutch economy and the expansion of its colonial empire. However, by the mid-nineteenth century, increasing criticism of the system from liberal politicians and humanitarian groups in the Netherlands, combined with mounting resistance from local populations, led to its gradual dismantlement. The abolition of the Cultivation System in the late nineteenth century, however, did not signify the end of exploitation,

[55] Ricklefs, M. C. (2008). A History of Modern Indonesia Since c.1200. 4th ed. Basingstoke: Palgrave Macmillan.

[56] Peluso, N. L. (1992). Rich Forests, Poor People: Resource Control and Resistance in Java. Berkeley: University of California Press.

as new colonial economic structures continued to prioritize the extraction of resources and labour over the welfare of Indonesians.[57]

The Cultivation System had profound and far-reaching impacts on Indonesia. It reoriented the economy toward the needs of the colonial state, at significant social, economic, and environmental costs to local populations. The system entrenched inequalities, undermined food security, and degraded the environment, while ensuring the financial success of the Dutch colonial regime. These legacies of exploitation and dependency would shape Indonesia's economic and social landscape for decades, becoming key elements in the nation's post-independence struggles for equitable development and sustainability.

The Rise of the Plantation Economy

The rise of the plantation economy in Indonesia during the nineteenth and early twentieth centuries was a defining feature of the Dutch colonial economic system. This shift was closely tied to the decline of the cultuurstelsel (Cultivation System) and the emergence of private enterprise as the dominant force in agricultural production. The transition to a plantation-based economy was driven by global demand for cash crops such as sugar, coffee, tea, rubber, and tobacco, which were cultivated on a large scale for export. The plantation economy restructured Indonesia's agrarian landscape, consolidating land under large estates controlled by European companies while transforming local populations into a labour force bound by exploitative systems of control.[58] The plantation economy required significant changes to land ownership and labour systems. Under colonial policies, particularly the Agrarian Law of 1870, vast tracts of land were made available for European private investors, effectively dispossessing local communities. This law allowed the colonial state to lease "unused" land to plantation companies, disregarding indigenous systems of communal land ownership. As a result, many Indonesian farmers were displaced from their land or forced to work on plantations as wage labourers or under coercive arrangements, such as coolie labour

[57] Booth, A. (1998). The Indonesian Economy in the Nineteenth and Twentieth Centuries: A History of Missed Opportunities. London: Macmillan Press.

[58] Boomgaard, P. (1991). Changing Economy in Indonesia: A Selection of Statistical Source Material from the Early 19th Century up to 1940. Amsterdam: Royal Tropical Institute.

contracts, which bound workers to plantations under harsh and often abusive conditions.[59] These contracts were reinforced by a paternalistic and racially hierarchical colonial system that relegated indigenous workers to the lowest rungs of the economic order.[60]

The economic benefits of the plantation economy flowed primarily to European investors and the Dutch colonial state, with limited reinvestment in local infrastructure or welfare. Plantations became the backbone of the colonial export economy, generating significant revenues for the Netherlands while exacerbating inequalities within Indonesia. Regions like East Sumatra became centres of plantation activity, producing rubber and tobacco for global markets. These areas saw a concentration of wealth and development tied to European interests, while other parts of Indonesia, particularly outer islands, remained underdeveloped and excluded from the plantation economy.[61]

The environmental consequences of the plantation economy were equally significant. The focus on monoculture depleted soil fertility and disrupted local ecosystems. Forests were cleared to make way for plantations, leading to deforestation and the loss of biodiversity. The environmental degradation caused by these practices undermined the sustainability of local agricultural systems and contributed to the vulnerability of rural communities to ecological shocks, such as floods and droughts.[62] These ecological transformations also created lasting challenges for post-colonial Indonesia, as degraded lands required significant investment and restoration efforts.

The social impacts of the plantation economy were profound, entrenching patterns of exploitation and inequality. The reliance on forced labour systems, including the use of indentured workers imported from Java and other parts of Indonesia, created a workforce subject to low wages, poor working conditions, and limited mobility. Resistance to these conditions, such as labour strikes and peasant uprisings, was often

[59] Peluso, N. L. (1992). Rich Forests, Poor People: Resource Control and Resistance in Java. Berkeley: University of California Press.

[60] Stoler, A. L. (1985). Capitalism and Confrontation in Sumatra's Plantation Belt, 1870–1979. New Haven: Yale University Press.

[61] Ricklefs, M. C. (2008). A History of Modern Indonesia Since c.1200. 4th ed. Basingstoke: Palgrave Macmillan.

[62] Henley, D. (2004). Fertility, Food, and Fever: Population, Economy, and Environment in North and Central Sulawesi,1600–1930. Leiden: KITLV Press.

met with harsh repression by the colonial authorities. These tensions highlighted the exploitative nature of the plantation economy and its role in perpetuating colonial dominance over Indonesia's resources and people.[63]

The rise of the plantation economy in colonial Indonesia marked a fundamental shift in the country's economic structure. It consolidated land and labour under European control, prioritized export-oriented production, and deepened social and environmental inequalities. While plantations generated substantial wealth for the Dutch and European investors, their legacy in Indonesia was one of dispossession, exploitation, and ecological degradation. The impacts of this system persisted well into the post-colonial period, shaping Indonesia's struggles for economic independence and sustainability.

Economic Liberalization and the Dual Economy

The economic liberalization policies implemented in the late nineteenth and early twentieth centuries under Dutch colonial rule marked a significant shift in Indonesia's economic landscape. These policies, intended to modernize and diversify the colonial economy, led to the emergence of a dual economy, characterized by a stark divide between the modern, export-oriented sector dominated by European interests and the traditional, subsistence-based sector inhabited by the indigenous population. The liberalization process began with the Agrarian Law of 1870, which allowed private European entrepreneurs to lease large tracts of land for plantation agriculture. This policy aimed to attract foreign investment and reduce the Dutch state's direct involvement in economic management, as the state moved away from the exploitative cultuurstelsel toward a market-driven approach.[64] The expansion of the modern sector under liberalization policies was evident in the growth of large-scale plantations producing export commodities such as rubber, tea, tobacco, and sugar. These plantations were financed and managed predominantly by European investors, who benefited from access to infrastructure improvements such as railways, ports, and irrigation systems built by the colonial administration to support export activities. While these developments

[63] Stoler, A. L. (1985). Capitalism and Confrontation in Sumatra's Plantation Belt, 1870–1979. New Haven: Yale University Press.

[64] Booth, A. (1998). The Indonesian Economy in the Nineteenth and Twentieth Centuries: A History of Missed Opportunities. London: Macmillan Press.

contributed to significant economic growth in the export sector, the benefits were concentrated among European companies and their collaborators, including local elites who facilitated the exploitation of labour and resources.[65] This concentration of wealth and resources created stark inequalities, as the indigenous population was largely excluded from the benefits of economic modernization.

The traditional sector, composed of smallholder agriculture and subsistence farming, continued to dominate the livelihoods of most Indonesians. This sector was characterized by low productivity and limited access to the infrastructure and financial capital available to the modern sector. Indigenous farmers faced significant challenges, including limited access to land due to colonial land tenure policies that prioritized European enterprises. The disparities between the modern and traditional sectors became increasingly pronounced, with the traditional sector providing cheap labour for the plantation economy while remaining economically marginalized.[66] The economic marginalization of the traditional sector under colonial rule in Indonesia was the result of deliberate policies and structural imbalances designed to prioritize the modern, export-oriented economy over local agricultural and subsistence systems. The traditional sector, composed primarily of Indigenous smallholder farmers engaged in subsistence agriculture, was systematically excluded from the benefits of economic modernization, leaving it underdeveloped and dependent on the colonial economy. A key reason for this marginalization was the colonial land tenure policies established under the Agrarian Law of 1870, which allowed European investors to lease vast tracts of land for plantation agriculture. While this law aimed to prevent outright land ownership by Europeans, it designated large areas of land as "wastelands" that could be leased to private enterprises. These lands often included communal lands traditionally used by Indigenous farmers, displacing local communities and reducing the amount of arable land available for

[65] Stoler, A. L. (1985). Capitalism and Confrontation in Sumatra's Plantation Belt, 1870–1979. New Haven: Yale University Press.

[66] Elson, R. E. (1997). 'The Cultivation System and "Agricultural Involution": A View from the Water's Edge,' in Boomgaard, P. and Brown, I. (eds.) Weathering the Storm: The Economies of SoutheastAsia in the 1930s Depression. Singapore: Institute of Southeast Asian Studies.

subsistence farming.[67] This policy entrenched landlessness among rural populations and forced many to work as wage labourers on plantations under exploitative conditions.

The focus on export crops such as rubber, sugar, and tobacco further sidelined the traditional sector. Resources and infrastructure development, such as railways and irrigation systems, were concentrated in regions that supported plantation agriculture. The traditional sector, lacking access to these developments, remained reliant on outdated agricultural techniques, limiting its productivity and competitiveness.[68] The colonial administration's neglect of smallholder agriculture not only reduced the capacity of indigenous farmers to generate surplus income but also left them vulnerable to environmental shocks and food insecurity. The labour policies of the colonial regime exacerbated the traditional sector's marginalization. Indigenous workers, often displaced from their land, were coerced into becoming low-wage labour for plantations. Systems such as the coolie labour contracts tied workers to exploitative conditions, leaving little opportunity for economic mobility. These labour arrangements drained the traditional sector of its workforce, as able-bodied individuals were drawn into plantation labour, further weakening smallholder farming systems.[69] Moreover, the dual economy institutionalized a rigid hierarchy that relegated the traditional sector to a subordinate position. The colonial state and European enterprises viewed the traditional sector as a source of cheap labour and low-cost food to sustain the plantation economy. Indigenous farmers were seen as economic tools rather than as stakeholders in development. This perspective was reinforced by colonial taxation systems, which placed disproportionate burdens on rural communities while directing the benefits of economic growth to the colonial administration and European investors.[70]

[67] Peluso, N. L. (1992). Rich Forests, Poor People: Resource Control and Resistance in Java. Berkeley: University of California Press.

[68] Booth, A. (1998). The Indonesian Economy in the Nineteenth and Twentieth Centuries: A History of Missed Opportunities. London: Macmillan Press.

[69] Stoler, A. L. (1985). Capitalism and Confrontation in Sumatra's Plantation Belt, 1870–1979. New Haven: Yale University Press.

[70] Elson, R. E. (1997). 'The Cultivation System and "Agricultural Involution": A View from the Water's Edge,' in Boomgaard, P. and Brown, I. (eds.) Weathering the Storm: The Economies of SoutheastAsia in the 1930s Depression. Singapore: Institute of Southeast Asian Studies.

The marginalization of the traditional sector was also ideological. The colonial administration promoted the notion that the indigenous economy was backward and incapable of modernizing without European intervention. This ideology justified the lack of investment in smallholder agriculture and the extraction of labour and resources for the modern sector. Indigenous farmers were thus trapped in a cycle of underdevelopment, as they were denied access to the education, capital, and infrastructure needed to improve their livelihoods.[71] Therefore, the traditional sector remained economically marginalized under colonial rule due to land tenure policies, the prioritization of export-oriented plantation agriculture, exploitative labour systems, and entrenched social and economic hierarchies. This marginalization not only deepened inequalities between the modern and traditional sectors but also laid the groundwork for structural imbalances that persisted into Indonesia's post-colonial era.

The dual economy also reinforced social hierarchies and racial divisions. European planters and businesspeople occupied the upper echelons of the economic structure, while indigenous workers were relegated to low-wage and physically demanding jobs on plantations. This division was institutionalized through colonial laws and administrative practices, which limited the mobility and opportunities of the Indigenous population. The dual economy thus entrenched patterns of dependency and inequality, as the indigenous sector remained underdeveloped and reliant on the modern sector for employment and income.[72] Despite these inequities, the liberalization policies also had unintended consequences that contributed to resistance and social unrest. The increasing exploitation of labour and resources, combined with the exclusion of Indigenous communities from the benefits of economic growth, led to widespread dissatisfaction. Strikes, peasant revolts, and the rise of nationalist movements in the early twentieth century were fuelled by the grievances generated by the dual economy. This system created stark inequalities, as the Indigenous population bore the burden of labour exploitation, land dispossession, and economic marginalization, while European companies and the colonial state reaped the benefits of economic growth. One key driver of resistance was the exploitative labour practices associated with

[71] Ricklefs, M. C. (2008). A History of Modern Indonesia Since c.1200. 4th ed. Basingstoke: Palgrave Macmillan.

[72] Ricklefs, M. C. (2008). A History of Modern Indonesia Since c.1200. 4th ed. Basingstoke: Palgrave Macmillan.

the plantation economy. Indigenous workers, often displaced from their land due to colonial policies such as the Agrarian Law of 1870, were coerced into low-wage labour on plantations. Systems like coolie contracts bound workers to plantations under harsh and often abusive conditions. These workers faced long hours, poor living conditions, and minimal compensation, leaving them trapped in cycles of poverty and debt. Strikes and labour protests became increasingly common in regions like Sumatra and Java, where plantation economies were most concentrated. These strikes were often organized by emerging labour unions, such as the Sarekat Islam, which mobilized workers around shared grievances and laid the foundation for collective resistance.[73,74]

Peasant revolts were another significant form of resistance. Many rural communities were dispossessed of their land or forced to cultivate cash crops for export under systems like the cultuurstelsel and later plantation-based arrangements. This shift disrupted subsistence farming, leading to food shortages and economic insecurity. In response, peasants organized local uprisings to resist taxation, forced cultivation, and land confiscation. For instance, the 1926–1927 Communist uprisings in Java and Sumatra were driven by peasant frustrations over economic exploitation and the colonial government's repressive policies. Although these revolts were brutally suppressed, they underscored the deep dissatisfaction among rural populations and highlighted the links between economic inequality and political resistance.[75] The dual economy also played a critical role in the rise of nationalist movements. By creating a stark divide between the wealth of the modern sector and the poverty of the traditional sector, the colonial economic system became a focal point for nationalist critique. Organizations like the Indonesian National Party (PNI), founded in 1927 by Sukarno, used these grievances to rally support for independence. Nationalists emphasized the need to reclaim control over Indonesia's economy, redistribute land, and end the exploitation

[73] Stoler, A. L. (1985). Capitalism and Confrontation in Sumatra's Plantation Belt, 1870–1979. New Haven: Yale University Press.

[74] Ricklefs, M. C. (2008). A History of Modern Indonesia Since c.1200. 4th ed. Basingstoke: Palgrave Macmillan.

[75] Elson, R. E. (1997). 'The Cultivation System and "Agricultural Involution": A View from the Water's Edge,' in Boomgaard, P. and Brown, I. (eds.) Weathering the Storm: The Economies of SoutheastAsia in the 1930s Depression. Singapore: Institute of Southeast Asian Studies.

of indigenous labour. These movements were further bolstered by the global rise of anti-colonial sentiment and the spread of socialist and Marxist ideas, which framed the dual economy as a symbol of colonial oppression.[76] Furthermore, the disparities of the dual economy created a sense of shared struggle among workers, peasants, and the emerging nationalist elite. Intellectuals and activists used newspapers, speeches, and political organizations to highlight the inequities of the colonial system and build solidarity across different sectors of society. The establishment of educational institutions like Taman Siswa in 1922 aimed to empower Indonesians through education, fostering a generation of leaders who would articulate the economic and social injustices of colonial rule and mobilize the population toward independence.[77] The grievances generated by Indonesia's dual economy—ranging from labour exploitation and land dispossession to systemic inequalities—became powerful catalysts for resistance in the early twentieth century. Strikes, peasant revolts, and nationalist movements were interlinked responses to the inequities of the colonial economic system. These forms of resistance not only challenged the legitimacy of Dutch colonial rule but also laid the groundwork for Indonesia's eventual independence and its efforts to build a more equitable economy in the post-colonial period. Furthermore, the economic liberalization policies under Dutch colonial rule expanded the modern export-oriented economy but did so at the expense of deepening inequalities and reinforcing the dual economy. This divide between the modern and traditional sectors not only marginalized the Indigenous population but also created structural imbalances that persisted into the post-colonial era, shaping Indonesia's economic and social challenges in its quest for equitable development and modernization.

The Vulnerabilities of a Colonial Economy

The vulnerabilities of Indonesia's colonial economy under Dutch rule stemmed from its structural reliance on a narrow range of export commodities, its dependence on external markets, and the systemic exploitation of its labour force. The economy was heavily geared toward

[76] Ricklefs, M. C. (2008). A History of Modern Indonesia Since c.1200. 4th ed. Basingstoke: Palgrave Macmillan.

[77] Taylor, J. G. (2003). Indonesia: Peoples and Histories. New Haven: Yale University Press.

the production of cash crops such as sugar, rubber, coffee, and tobacco, which were cultivated on plantations for export to global markets. While this model generated substantial revenues for the colonial state and European investors, it left the economy vulnerable to global market fluctuations. For instance, the Great Depression of the 1930s led to a collapse in commodity prices, significantly reducing export revenues and exposing the fragility of an economic system overly reliant on external demand.[78] This vulnerability was exacerbated by the absence of industrial diversification, as colonial policies deliberately restricted investment in local industries to ensure that Indonesia remained an exporter of raw materials rather than a competitor in global manufacturing.[79] The prioritization of export-oriented agriculture also undermined food security and exacerbated poverty among the indigenous population. Monoculture farming practices, which replaced traditional diversified agricultural systems, reduced the availability of staple crops such as rice, leaving rural communities dependent on volatile markets for imported food. Periodic famines, such as those experienced in Java in the 1840s, were direct consequences of this imbalance, as the colonial economy prioritized exports over the subsistence needs of the local population.[80] Furthermore, the environmental degradation caused by extensive plantation agriculture, including deforestation and soil depletion, weakened the sustainability of rural livelihoods and contributed to long-term ecological vulnerabilities.[81]

The exploitative labour systems underpinning the colonial economy added another layer of vulnerability. The reliance on forced labour and exploitative contracts, such as the coolie system, created widespread discontent among workers. These conditions not only perpetuated poverty and inequality but also fuelled labour strikes, peasant revolts, and broader resistance movements that challenged the colonial regime. The

[78] Booth, A. (1998). The Indonesian Economy in the Nineteenth and Twentieth Centuries: A History of Missed Opportunities. London: Macmillan Press.

[79] Ricklefs, M. C. (2008). A History of Modern Indonesia Since c.1200. 4th ed. Basingstoke: Palgrave Macmillan.

[80] Elson, R. E. (1997). 'The Cultivation System and "Agricultural Involution": A View from the Water's Edge,' in Boomgaard, P. and Brown, I. (eds.) Weathering the Storm: The Economies of SoutheastAsia in the 1930s Depression. Singapore: Institute of Southeast Asian Studies.

[81] Peluso, N. L. (1992). Rich Forests, Poor People: Resource Control and Resistance in Java. Berkeley: University of California Press.

dual economy, which divided the modern, export-oriented sector from the traditional, subsistence-based sector, institutionalized these inequalities and marginalized the majority of Indonesians from the benefits of economic growth. This lack of inclusive development entrenched social and economic disparities that persisted into the post-colonial period.[82]

Colonial policies also failed to build resilience against external shocks. Infrastructure development, such as railways and ports, was concentrated in areas that supported export production, neglecting broader investments in health, education, and rural development. This uneven distribution of resources compounded the vulnerabilities of rural communities, which were left ill-equipped to cope with economic crises or natural disasters. The collapse of global trade during the Great Depression starkly revealed these weaknesses, as the colonial government was forced to impose austerity measures that disproportionately affected the already impoverished indigenous population.[83] The vulnerabilities of Indonesia's colonial economy were rooted in its dependence on export commodities, its exclusion of the majority population from meaningful economic participation, and its neglect of social and environmental sustainability. These structural weaknesses not only undermined the stability of the colonial economy but also left a legacy of inequality and underdevelopment that shaped Indonesia's post-independence challenges. The colonial emphasis on short-term profit and resource extraction created a fragile economic foundation that would take decades to address in the context of nation-building and economic reform.

Nationalism and Economic Discontent

The vulnerabilities of Indonesia's colonial economy under Dutch rule stemmed from its structural reliance on a narrow range of export commodities, its dependence on external markets, and the systemic exploitation of its labour force. The economy was heavily geared toward the production of cash crops such as sugar, rubber, coffee, and tobacco, which were cultivated on plantations for export to global markets. While this model generated substantial revenues for the colonial state and

[82] Stoler, A. L. (1985). Capitalism and Confrontation in Sumatra's Plantation Belt, 1870–1979. New Haven: Yale University Press.

[83] Ricklefs, M. C. (2008). A History of Modern Indonesia Since c.1200. 4th ed. Basingstoke: Palgrave Macmillan.

European investors, it left the economy vulnerable to global market fluctuations. For instance, the Great Depression of the 1930s led to a collapse in commodity prices, significantly reducing export revenues and exposing the fragility of an economic system overly reliant on external demand.[84] This vulnerability was exacerbated by the absence of industrial diversification, as colonial policies deliberately restricted investment in local industries to ensure that Indonesia remained an exporter of raw materials rather than a competitor in global manufacturing.[85] The prioritization of export-oriented agriculture also undermined food security and exacerbated poverty among the indigenous population. Monoculture farming practices, which replaced traditional diversified agricultural systems, reduced the availability of staple crops such as rice, leaving rural communities dependent on volatile markets for imported food. Periodic famines, such as those experienced in Java in the 1840s, were direct consequences of this imbalance, as the colonial economy prioritized exports over the subsistence needs of the local population.[86] Furthermore, the environmental degradation caused by extensive plantation agriculture, including deforestation and soil depletion, weakened the sustainability of rural livelihoods and contributed to long-term ecological vulnerabilities.[87] The exploitative labour systems underpinning the colonial economy added another layer of vulnerability. The reliance on forced labour and exploitative contracts, such as the coolie system, created widespread discontent among workers. These conditions not only perpetuated poverty and inequality but also fuelled labour strikes, peasant revolts, and broader resistance movements that challenged the colonial regime. The dual economy, which divided the modern, export-oriented sector from the traditional, subsistence-based sector, institutionalized these inequalities and marginalized the majority of Indonesians from

[84] Booth, A. (1998). The Indonesian Economy in the Nineteenth and Twentieth Centuries: A History of Missed Opportunities. London: Macmillan Press.

[85] Ricklefs, M. C. (2008). A History of Modern Indonesia Since c.1200. 4th ed. Basingstoke: Palgrave Macmillan.

[86] Elson, R. E. (1997). 'The Cultivation System and "Agricultural Involution": A View from the Water's Edge,' in Boomgaard, P. and Brown, I. (eds.) Weathering the Storm: The Economies of SoutheastAsia in the 1930s Depression. Singapore: Institute of Southeast Asian Studies.

[87] Peluso, N. L. (1992). Rich Forests, Poor People: Resource Control and Resistance in Java. Berkeley: University of California Press.

the benefits of economic growth. This lack of inclusive development entrenched social and economic disparities that persisted into the post-colonial period.[88] Colonial policies also failed to build resilience against external shocks. Infrastructure development, such as railways and ports, was concentrated in areas that supported export production, neglecting broader investments in health, education, and rural development. This uneven distribution of resources compounded the vulnerabilities of rural communities, which were left ill-equipped to cope with economic crises or natural disasters. The collapse of global trade during the Great Depression starkly revealed these weaknesses, as the colonial government was forced to impose austerity measures that disproportionately affected the already impoverished indigenous population.[89] The vulnerabilities of Indonesia's colonial economy were rooted in its dependence on export commodities, its exclusion of the majority population from meaningful economic participation, and its neglect of social and environmental sustainability. These structural weaknesses not only undermined the stability of the colonial economy but also left a legacy of inequality and underdevelopment that shaped Indonesia's post-independence challenges. The colonial emphasis on short-term profit and resource extraction created a fragile economic foundation that would take decades to address in the context of nation-building and economic reform.

Conclusion

The Dutch colonial economy from 1800 to 1942 fundamentally restructured Indonesia's economic landscape, leaving a dual legacy of modernization and exploitation that continues to influence the nation's development. While the introduction of export-oriented plantations, infrastructure investments, and administrative reforms contributed to the integration of Indonesia into the global economy, these developments were marked by stark inequalities, resource extraction, and socio-economic marginalization of the Indigenous population. This chapter has explored

[88] Stoler, A. L. (1985). Capitalism and Confrontation in Sumatra's Plantation Belt, 1870–1979. New Haven: Yale University Press.

[89] Ricklefs, M. C. (2008). A History of Modern Indonesia Since c.1200. 4th ed. Basingstoke: Palgrave Macmillan.

how these policies entrenched structural dependencies, exacerbated socio-economic hierarchies, and shaped the vulnerabilities of Indonesia's colonial economy. Central to the colonial economic framework was the Cultivation System (cultuurstelsel), which compelled Indigenous farmers to prioritize cash crop production for Dutch profit. This system generated substantial revenues for the Netherlands but came at the expense of food security and local welfare, as evidenced by famines such as the devastating crisis in the 1840s.[90] The dualistic economic structure, with its sharp divide between the modern, export-oriented sector and the traditional, subsistence-based sector, marginalized indigenous livelihoods and entrenched economic disparities that persisted beyond the colonial period.[91] These inequalities were further institutionalized through the Agrarian Law of 1870, which enabled the rise of the plantation economy by dispossessing indigenous communities and prioritizing European investors.[92]

The vulnerabilities of the colonial economy became starkly evident during the global economic crises of the 1930s, when Indonesia's dependence on volatile international markets resulted in widespread hardship. The prioritization of export crops over subsistence agriculture left rural populations particularly exposed, while the lack of investment in local industries or infrastructure ensured that economic benefits remained concentrated in the hands of colonial elites and their local collaborators.[93] This structural fragility contributed to social unrest, labour strikes, and peasant revolts, highlighting the growing discontent with colonial policies and fuelling the rise of nationalist movements seeking economic and political emancipation.[94] In broader historical context, the colonial economy reinforced patterns of resource extraction and underdevelopment that have their roots in earlier European interventions, as discussed

[90] Henley, D. (2004). Fertility, Food, and Fever: Population, Economy, and Environment in North and Central Sulawesi,1600–1930. Leiden: KITLV Press.

[91] Booth, A. (1998). The Indonesian Economy in the Nineteenth and Twentieth Centuries: A History of Missed Opportunities. London: Macmillan Press.

[92] Peluso, N. L. (1992). Rich Forests, Poor People: Resource Control and Resistance in Java. Berkeley: University of California Press.

[93] Bosma, U. (2013). The Sugar Plantation in Indiaand Indonesia: Industrial Production, 1770–2010. Cambridge: Cambridge University Press.

[94] Elson, R. E. (1997). The End of the Peasantry in SoutheastAsia: A Social and Economic History of Peasant Livelihoods, 1800–1990s. Basingstoke: Palgrave Macmillan.

in Chapter 5. The monopolization of trade networks and the centralization of economic power under the VOC disrupted traditional systems of local exchange, consolidating economic benefits within colonial centres like Batavia while peripheral regions were systematically neglected.[95] This centralization laid the groundwork for regional inequalities that persist in contemporary Indonesia, where disparities between urban and rural areas mirror colonial-era imbalances. Critically, the plantation economy's environmental consequences underscore the shortsightedness of colonial economic policies. The widespread deforestation, soil degradation, and reliance on monoculture diminished agricultural resilience and contributed to long-term ecological challenges, as highlighted in previous chapters' discussions of Indonesia's agrarian development.[96] These ecological costs compounded the socio-economic challenges faced by indigenous communities, deepening their dependency on colonial systems and limiting opportunities for self-sufficiency.

The rise of nationalist movements in the early twentieth century, discussed extensively in this chapter, reflects the culmination of grievances rooted in colonial economic exploitation. Organizations like the Sarekat Islam and the Indonesian National Party mobilized broad coalitions of workers, peasants, and intellectuals, drawing attention to the inequalities of the dual economy and laying the ideological groundwork for independence.[97] These movements not only challenged the legitimacy of Dutch rule but also articulated visions of economic sovereignty that would shape Indonesia's post-independence trajectory.

The economy from 1800 to 1942 exemplifies the complexities of modernization under colonial rule. While the era brought infrastructural development and greater integration into global markets, it did so through exploitative systems that entrenched inequalities, undermined local resilience, and prioritized colonial interests over indigenous welfare. The legacies of this period—economic dualism, environmental degradation, and sociopolitical fragmentation—continue to influence Indonesia's path toward equitable and sustainable development. As the subsequent

[95] Ricklefs, M. C. (2008). A History of Modern Indonesia since c.1200. 4th ed. Basingstoke: Palgrave Macmillan.

[96] Peluso, N. L. (1992). Rich Forests, Poor People: Resource Control and Resistance in Java. Berkeley: University of California Press.

[97] Taylor, J. G. (2003). Indonesia: Peoples and Histories. New Haven: Yale University Press.

chapters will explore, addressing these structural imbalances has been a central challenge in Indonesia's post-colonial history, shaping the nation's efforts to achieve inclusive growth and national integration.

References

Andaya, B.W., & Andaya, L.Y. (2016). A History of Early Modern Southeast Asia, 1400–1830. Cambridge: Cambridge University Press.

Boomgaard, P. (1991). Changing Economy in Indonesia: A Selection of Statistical Source Material from the Early 19th Century up to 1940. Amsterdam: Royal Tropical Institute.

Booth, A. (1998), The Indonesian Economy in the Nineteenth and Twentieth Centuries: A History of Missed Opportunities. London: Macmillan.

Bosma, U., & Raben, R. (2008). Being "Dutch" in the Indies: A History of Creolisation and Empire, 1500–1920. Athens: Ohio University Press.

Breman, J. (2015), Mobilizing Labour for the Global Coffee Market: Profits from an Unfree Work Regime in Colonial Java. Amsterdam: Amsterdam University Press.

Carey, P. (2007). The Power of Prophecy: Prince Dipanagara and the End of an Old Order in Java, 1785–1855. Leiden: KITLV Press.

Cribb, R. (1994), Historical Dictionary of Indonesia. Lanham, MD: Scarecrow Press.

Elson, R. E. (1984), Village Java under the Cultivation System 1830–1870. Sydney: Allen & Unwin.

Elson, R. E. (1997). 'The Cultivation System and "Agricultural Involution": A View from the Water's Edge,' in Boomgaard, P. and Brown, I. (eds.) Weathering the Storm: The Economies of Southeast Asia in the 1930s Depression. Singapore: Institute of Southeast Asian Studies.

Elson, R.E. (1997). The End of the Peasantry in Southeast Asia: A Social and Economic History of Peasant Livelihood, 1800–1990s. Basingstoke: Macmillan.

Fasseur, C. (1992). The Politics of Colonial Exploitation: Java, the Dutch, and the Cultivation System. Ithaca, NY: Cornell University Press.

Fernando, M. R. (2006), 'The Cultivation System in Java: The Social and Economic Effects of Dutch Colonial Policy in the Mid-Nineteenth Century', Journal of Southeast Asian Studies, 37(3), pp. 435–456.

Furnivall, J.S. (1948). Colonial Policy and Practice: A Comparative Study of Burma and Netherlands India. Cambridge: Cambridge University Press.

Geertz, C. (1963), Agricultural Involution: The Processes of Ecological Change in Indonesia. Berkeley: University of California Press.

Henley, D. (2004). Fertility, Food, and Fever: Population, Economy, and Environment in North and Central Sulawesi, 1600–1930. Leiden: KITLV Press.

Kahin, G. M. (1952), Nationalism and Revolution in Indonesia. Ithaca, NY: Cornell University Press.

Kumar, A. (1997). Java and Modern Europe: Ambiguous Encounters. Richmond: Curzon Press.

Mackie, J. A. C. (1976), 'Economic Problems of the Dutch in Indonesia during the 1930s', Bulletin of Indonesian Economic Studies, 12(1), pp. 19–30.

Peluso, N. L. (1992). Rich Forests, Poor People: Resource Control and Resistance in Java. Berkeley: University of California Press.

Ricklefs, M. C. (2008). A History of Modern Indonesia Since c.1200. 4th ed. Basingstoke: Palgrave Macmillan.

Stoler, A. L. (1985). Capitalism and Confrontation in Sumatra's Plantation Belt, 1870–1979. New Haven: Yale University Press.

CHAPTER 7

World War II and Japanese Occupation (1942–1945)

Introduction

The period of World War II and the Japanese occupation of Indonesia (1942–1945) was a pivotal era that profoundly reshaped the political, economic, and social landscape of the region. As the Dutch colonial regime was abruptly dismantled, the Japanese administration imposed a military-driven economic agenda that mobilized Indonesia's resources to serve Japan's wartime needs. This reorganization prioritized resource extraction and labour exploitation, resulting in widespread famine, economic dislocation, and social upheaval.[1] The occupation disrupted existing economic institutions and infrastructure, leaving a legacy of devastation that persisted well into the post-war period. Nevertheless, it also inadvertently fostered Indonesian nationalist movements, unifying diverse populations under a shared vision of independence.

Economically, the Japanese implemented policies aimed at maximizing agricultural and industrial output for their military campaigns. Key commodities such as rice, rubber, and oil were requisitioned in vast quantities, leading to acute shortages and famine, particularly in

[1] Sato, S. (1994). 'War, Nationalism and Peasants: Java under the Japanese Occupation, 1942–45.' Journal of Southeast Asian Studies, 25(2), 268–294.

S. Ramesh, *The Political Economy of Indonesia's Economic Development, Volume I*, https://doi.org/10.1007/978-3-031-94350-8_7

Java, where the dense population exacerbated the crisis.[2] Forced labour systems, including the notorious romusha program, further destabilized rural economies by removing able-bodied workers from agricultural production, intensifying poverty and malnutrition.[3] These extractive policies reflected a continuity with colonial practices under the Dutch, yet their severity highlighted the exploitative nature of foreign-controlled economies, reinforcing nationalist critiques of colonial governance.[4] Simultaneously, the Japanese occupation dismantled Dutch colonial structures and reconfigured governance systems to incorporate local leaders. Prominent nationalists like Sukarno and Hatta were co-opted into the administration, enabling them to consolidate political influence and mobilize support for independence. The Japanese slogan "Asia for Asians" and their promotion of Bahasa Indonesia as an administrative language fostered a sense of unity and national identity that transcended regional and cultural divides.[5] While these initiatives were intended to serve Japanese wartime objectives, they inadvertently empowered Indonesian leaders and galvanized anti-colonial sentiments.

The occupation also exposed the fragility of colonial economic systems, which had prioritized resource extraction for metropolitan benefit over the welfare of local populations. The collapse of the plantation economy and the destruction of infrastructure underscored the need for economic diversification and self-sufficiency in the post-war period.[6] However, the devastation wrought by the Japanese left Indonesia ill-equipped to address these challenges, with limited institutional capacity and significant regional disparities.[7] Despite the suffering inflicted during the occupation, it catalysed significant political and social transformations. The shared

[2] Furnivall, J.S. (1948). Colonial Policy and Practice: A Comparative Study of Burma and NetherlandsIndia. Cambridge: Cambridge University Press.

[3] Cribb, R. (1994). Gangsters and Revolutionaries: The Jakarta People's Militia and the Indonesian Revolution, 1945–1949. Honolulu: University of Hawai'i Press.

[4] Ricklefs, M. C. (2008). A History of Modern Indonesia Since c.1200. 4th ed. Stanford, CA: Stanford University Press.

[5] Elson, R. E. (2009). The Idea of Indonesia: A History. Cambridge: Cambridge University Press.

[6] Booth, A. (1998). The Indonesian Economy in the Nineteenth and Twentieth Centuries: A History of Missed Opportunities. London: Macmillan.

[7] Kurasawa, A. (1988). 'Mobilization and Control: A Study of Social Change in Rural Java,1942–1945.' Indonesia, 46(1), 1–32.

hardships of famine, forced labour, and economic dislocation fostered a collective sense of resilience and purpose among Indonesians. These experiences became a rallying point for independence movements, linking economic liberation with political sovereignty. The Japanese occupation thus marked both a period of immense suffering and a transformative moment in Indonesia's history, laying the groundwork for the nation's eventual emergence as an independent state.[8]

The Japanese Occupation, Economic Policies, and the Impact on Indonesia

The Japanese occupation marked the end of Dutch colonial control, albeit temporarily, and introduced a new set of economic policies that aimed to mobilize Indonesia's resources for Japan's war efforts. These policies included the forced requisition of food and raw materials, the reorganization of agricultural production, and the exploitation of labour for military and industrial purposes.[9,10] The Japanese administration also attempted to cultivate Indonesian nationalism by promoting the concept of "Asia for Asians," which played a crucial role in fostering nationalist sentiments that later fuelled the independence movement.[11] However, the economic impact of the occupation was devastating. The forced extraction of resources led to widespread famine, a collapse of the agricultural sector, and severe inflation.[12,13] The Japanese also dismantled many of the existing economic institutions and infrastructure, leaving the economy in disarray by the end of the occupation. This period of intense hardship significantly altered the economic structure of Indonesia, leading

[8] Reid, A. (1980). The Indonesian National Revolution, 1945–1950. Hawthorn, VIC: Longman Australia.

[9] Kurasawa, A. (1988) 'Mobilization and Control: A Study of Social Change in Rural Java,1942–1945', Indonesia, 46(1), pp. 1–32.

[10] Shiraishi, T. (1990) An Age in Motion: Popular Radicalism in Java, 1912–1926. Ithaca, NY: Cornell University Press.

[11] Reid, A. (1980) The Indonesian National Revolution, 1945–1950. Hawthorn, VIC: Longman Australia.

[12] Vickers, A. (2005) A History of Modern Indonesia. Cambridge: Cambridge University Press.

[13] Cribb, R. (1981) The Indonesian Killings 1965–1966: Studies from Javaand Bali. Clayton, VIC: Centre of Southeast Asian Studies, Monash University.

to a more fractured and localized economy.[14] The forced extraction of resources during the Japanese occupation of Indonesia (1942–1945) had catastrophic effects on the economy and society, resulting in widespread famine, a collapse of the agricultural sector, and severe inflation. The occupation, marked by Japan's focus on exploiting Indonesia's resources for its wartime needs, devastated the local economy and significantly altered the nation's economic structure, with long-lasting consequences. The Japanese administration prioritized the extraction of foodstuffs, raw materials, and labour to support their war effort. Key agricultural products, such as rice, were requisitioned in copious quantities for export to Japan and other occupied territories, often leaving insufficient supplies for local consumption. This policy caused severe food shortages and famine, particularly in Java, where the population density was highest. The famine of 1944–1945 resulted in the deaths of hundreds of thousands, with some estimates suggesting that over 2.4 million Javanese perished due to starvation and related diseases.[15] The agricultural sector, which formed the backbone of Indonesia's economy, collapsed under these conditions. The Japanese requisitioning system disrupted traditional farming practices by compelling farmers to grow export crops instead of staple foods. Additionally, the lack of investment in irrigation systems, tools, and fertilizers further reduced agricultural productivity. The occupation saw a steep decline in food production, exacerbating rural poverty and leading to mass dislocation as villagers fled to urban areas or other regions in search of sustenance.[16] Furthermore, severe inflation compounded the economic hardship. The Japanese-issued copious amounts of fiat currency to finance their war operations, flooding the economy with money while limiting the availability of goods and services. This hyperinflation rendered savings worthless and disrupted trade, further eroding economic stability. For example, the price of rice increased exponentially, making necessities unaffordable for much of the population.[17] The

[14] Ricklefs, M. C. (2008) A History of Modern Indonesia Since c.1200. 4th edn. Stanford, CA: Stanford University Press.

[15] Ricklefs, M.C. (2008). A History of Modern Indonesia Since c. 1200. 4th ed. Basingstoke: Palgrave Macmillan.

[16] Elson, R.E. (1997). The End of the Peasantry in SoutheastAsia: A Social and Economic History of Peasant Livelihood, 1800–1990s. Basingstoke: Macmillan.

[17] Booth, A. (1998). The Indonesian Economy in the Nineteenth and Twentieth Centuries: A History of Missed Opportunities. London: Macmillan.

Japanese occupation also dismantled much of the existing economic institutions and infrastructure inherited from the Dutch colonial regime. Factories, ports, and transportation networks were repurposed or left to decay, as the Japanese focused solely on immediate military needs rather than long-term economic sustainability. Key institutions, such as banks and trading companies, were either closed or reorganized under Japanese control, which disrupted financial systems and trade networks. The destruction of infrastructure and institutional frameworks left the Indonesian economy in disarray by the end of the occupation, making post-war recovery even more challenging.[18] This period of intense hardship significantly altered the economic structure of Indonesia, leading to a more fractured and localized economy. With the collapse of centralized economic management, local elites and military leaders assumed greater control over resources and economic activities, setting the stage for the regionalism and economic fragmentation that would characterize the early years of independence. Local elites included traditional aristocrats, regional rulers, and prominent landowners who leveraged their pre-existing social status to dominate local economies. For instance, the priyayi class in Java—comprising Javanese aristocracy and bureaucratic elites—retained influence over rural agricultural production. They were often co-opted by colonial powers or the Japanese occupation authorities to enforce resource extraction policies, giving them entrenched authority over local labour and land. This class continued to exert economic control in the early independence period, often resisting centralized reforms from Jakarta.[19] Military leaders, many of whom emerged during the Japanese occupation, also played a critical role. Under Japanese rule, Indonesians were recruited into military and paramilitary organizations such as the PETA (Pembela Tanah Air, or Defenders of the Homeland). These groups trained local leaders in military tactics and provided them with organizational experience. Figures like Sudirman, who later became a prominent general in the Indonesian National Revolution, initially gained prominence through such organizations. Similarly, regional commanders like Tan Malaka, though primarily a political leader, operated in the vacuum left by centralized administration to exert influence over

[18] Furnivall, J.S. (1948). Colonial Policy and Practice: A Comparative Study of Burma and NetherlandsIndia. Cambridge: Cambridge University Press.

[19] Elson, R.E. (1997). The End of the Peasantry in SoutheastAsia: A Social and Economic History of Peasant Livelihood, 1800–1990s. Basingstoke: Macmillan.

local resources and political structures.[20] Other examples of local leaders include warlords and militia leaders who emerged during the chaotic transition period. These individuals often controlled critical resources such as food supplies, transportation, and even local markets. In regions such as Sumatra and Sulawesi, local commanders and guerrilla leaders, often with ties to former Japanese-trained units, became de facto authorities, resisting attempts by the nascent Republic of Indonesia to centralize economic and political power.[21] The lack of robust centralized institutions meant that these local elites and military leaders were rarely integrated into a cohesive national framework. Instead, they maintained significant autonomy, which contributed to regionalism and economic fragmentation during the early years of independence. The dominance of such figures hindered efforts to establish equitable national policies and exacerbated disparities between Java and the outer islands.[22] The absence of robust economic institutions also left the country ill-prepared to address the demands of a newly independent state, contributing to the challenges of nation-building in the post-occupation period.[23] More specifically, the absence of robust economic institutions in Indonesia during the post-occupation and early independence period significantly hindered the country's ability to address the demands of nation-building. In this case, robust economic institutions are those that ensure effective governance, equitable resource allocation, financial stability, and the facilitation of trade and development. In Indonesia's case, these institutions were either non-existent, weakened, or misaligned with the needs of a newly independent state.

One critical missing institution was a centralized and functional banking system capable of managing monetary policy and providing credit to spur development. Under Dutch colonial rule, banking was dominated by European institutions such as De Javasche Bank, which primarily

[20] Kahin, G.M. (1952). Nationalism and Revolution in Indonesia. Ithaca, NY: Cornell University Press.

[21] Ricklefs, M.C. (2008). A History of Modern Indonesia Since c. 1200. 4th ed. Basingstoke: Palgrave Macmillan.

[22] Booth, A. (1998). The Indonesian Economy in the Nineteenth and Twentieth Centuries: A History of Missed Opportunities. London: Macmillan.

[23] Kahin, G.M. (1952). Nationalism and Revolution in Indonesia. Ithaca, NY: Cornell University Press.

served the interests of the colonial administration and European businesses. During the Japanese occupation, these institutions were either dismantled or repurposed for military use, and by independence, they were ill-equipped to address Indonesia's domestic economic needs. The lack of access to credit hindered agricultural investment and industrial development, while inflation spiralled out of control due to a lack of monetary oversight.[24,25] Another missing institution was a comprehensive land management system. Under the Dutch, land tenure systems were designed to facilitate plantation agriculture and resource extraction, leaving smallholder farmers with insecure land rights. The Japanese occupation exacerbated this by redistributing land to meet wartime needs, often without formal systems to regulate ownership or resolve disputes. The Japanese forcibly requisitioned agricultural land to increase the production of rice, rubber, and other critical commodities needed for their military campaigns. Farmers were often coerced into growing specific crops, regardless of their traditional farming practices or the suitability of their land for these purposes. This shift disrupted subsistence agriculture, reducing food production and contributing to severe famines, particularly in Java, where food insecurity reached catastrophic levels by 1944–1945.[26] Additionally, the Japanese reallocated land without formalizing ownership structures, creating confusion and disputes among farmers. For example, in their efforts to win support from the rural population, the Japanese redistributed land previously controlled by Dutch plantation owners. However, this redistribution was done arbitrarily and without legal frameworks, leaving many farmers without secure titles or the means to resolve conflicts over land boundaries. This lack of institutional oversight resulted in widespread uncertainty and conflict, which persisted after the occupation ended.[27] The uncertainty and conflict stemming from the arbitrary and legally unregulated land redistribution during the Japanese occupation had profound and lasting impacts on Indonesia's

[24] Furnivall, J.S. (1948). Colonial Policy and Practice: A Comparative Study of Burma and NetherlandsIndia. Cambridge: Cambridge University Press.

[25] Booth, A. (1998). The Indonesian Economy in the Nineteenth and Twentieth Centuries: A History of Missed Opportunities. London: Macmillan.

[26] Ricklefs, M.C. (2008). A History of Modern Indonesia Since c. 1200. 4th ed. Basingstoke: Palgrave Macmillan.

[27] Furnivall, J. S. (1948). Colonial Policy and Practice: A Comparative Study of Burma and NetherlandsIndia. Cambridge: Cambridge University Press.

economic development. These effects were felt both in the immediate post-occupation period and in the long term, as Indonesia struggled to rebuild its economy and address issues of land inequality and rural poverty. The lack of secure land titles meant that many smallholder farmers were unable to establish legal claims over their land, leading to widespread disputes. These disputes disrupted agricultural productivity, as contested lands often lay fallow during protracted conflicts. The uncertainty discouraged investment in agricultural improvements, such as irrigation systems, tools, or soil enhancement, as farmers were reluctant to invest in land they might lose. This lack of investment contributed to stagnation in the agricultural sector, which was critical to Indonesia's economy during the early independence period.[28] The lack of a productivity agricultural sector, and lack of political stability ensured that post-Japanese occupation, Indonesia could not industrialise. Moreover, the unresolved land conflicts also exacerbated rural inequality. Wealthier farmers and local elites, often with better access to informal networks or traditional authority structures, were more likely to consolidate landholdings during the chaotic redistribution process. Meanwhile, poorer farmers and landless labourers were further marginalized. This growing disparity fuelled resentment and social tensions in rural areas, undermining efforts to build a cohesive national economy, fostering regional inequalities that persisted for decades.[29]

Institutionally, the inability to resolve land conflicts weakened the government's authority in rural areas. The absence of a clear legal framework for land ownership during and after the Japanese occupation left the newly independent Indonesian state with a fragmented and ineffective system for managing land disputes. This lack of state capacity hindered efforts to implement land reforms, which were critical for addressing rural poverty and ensuring equitable access to agricultural resources. The failure to address these issues undermined the legitimacy of the central government and contributed to the rise of regionalism and localized power structures.[30] The conflicts over land boundaries

[28] Booth, A. (1998). The Indonesian Economy in the Nineteenth and Twentieth Centuries: A History of Missed Opportunities. London: Macmillan.

[29] Elson, R.E. (1997). The End of the Peasantry in SoutheastAsia: A Social and Economic History of Peasant Livelihood, 1800–1990s. Basingstoke: Macmillan.

[30] Furnivall, J.S. (1948). Colonial Policy and Practice: A Comparative Study of Burma and NetherlandsIndia. Cambridge: Cambridge University Press.

also had broader economic consequences. The agricultural sector, already weakened by the extraction policies of the Japanese occupation, was further destabilized by these disputes. Declining productivity and food shortages in the post-occupation period led to increased reliance on imports and disrupted efforts to achieve self-sufficiency. The inability to stabilize the rural economy delayed Indonesia's transition to a more diversified and industrialized economy, as resources and policy attention remained focused on resolving agrarian challenges.[31] Finally, the uncertainty and conflict contributed to political instability. The unresolved land issues became a rallying point for both communist and nationalist movements, which sought to mobilize rural populations by advocating for land reform. These tensions culminated in periodic social unrest, as competing factions clashed over the redistribution of land and resources. The lack of effective resolution mechanisms made land reform one of the most contentious and enduring challenges in Indonesia's post-independence development.[32] The uncertainty and conflict over land boundaries following the Japanese occupation disrupted agricultural productivity, deepened rural inequality, and weakened the state's capacity to govern effectively. These issues had far-reaching consequences, shaping Indonesia's economic and political trajectory and creating challenges that persisted well into the post-colonial era. Forced labour policies under the Japanese further exacerbated the situation. Many farmers were conscripted as romusha (forced labourers) to work on infrastructure projects, plantations, and other wartime initiatives. This conscription removed significant portions of the rural workforce from agricultural activities, leading to abandoned fields and declining productivity. The absence of able-bodied labourers intensified the challenges faced by smallholder farmers, who were already struggling to meet the demands of forced crop production.[33]

The Japanese occupation also disrupted rural governance structures that had previously mediated land disputes and managed local agricultural systems. Traditional village leadership, which had been co-opted by

[31] Ricklefs, M.C. (2008). A History of Modern Indonesia Since c. 1200. 4th ed. Basingstoke: Palgrave Macmillan.

[32] Kahin, G.M. (1952). Nationalism and Revolution in Indonesia. Ithaca, NY: Cornell University Press.

[33] Booth, A. (1998). The Indonesian Economy in the Nineteenth and Twentieth Centuries: A History of Missed Opportunities. London: Macmillan.

both Dutch and Japanese administrations, was weakened as the Japanese imposed their own administrative frameworks. These changes eroded the capacity of rural communities to address land-related conflicts, further destabilizing the agricultural economy.[34] By the end of the Japanese occupation, Indonesia's land tenure systems were in disarray. The combination of arbitrary land redistribution forced crop production, and the conscription of labour had significantly undermined agricultural stability. These disruptions created a legacy of land inequality and insecurity that persisted into the post-independence period, complicating efforts to implement effective land reforms and rebuild the agricultural sector. After independence, the absence of a national land reform policy meant that large disparities in land ownership persisted, particularly between Java and the outer islands. This inequality fuelled regional tensions and undermined efforts to increase agricultural productivity.[35] Indonesia also lacked effective trade and logistics networks, essential for a cohesive national economy. The colonial infrastructure, such as ports and railways, was built to facilitate the export of resources to Europe rather than to support domestic trade. During the Japanese occupation, much of this infrastructure was damaged or fell into disrepair. The absence of a coordinated strategy for rebuilding and modernizing trade networks after independence hindered the integration of regional economies and the distribution of essential goods.[36] The lack of a coordinated strategy for rebuilding and modernizing trade networks in Indonesia after independence can be attributed to a combination of historical, political, and structural factors that emerged during and after the colonial and occupation periods. These factors collectively hampered the newly independent state's ability to formulate and implement cohesive economic policies, particularly concerning infrastructure and trade. One major reason was the legacy of colonial infrastructure and its limited focus on domestic integration. Under Dutch rule, infrastructure development in Indonesia was primarily designed to serve the export-oriented colonial economy. Railways, ports, and roads were constructed to transport raw materials

[34] Elson, R.E. (1997). The End of the Peasantry in SoutheastAsia: A Social and Economic History of Peasant Livelihood, #1800–1990s. Basingstoke: Macmillan.

[35] Elson, R.E. (1997). The End of the Peasantry in SoutheastAsia: A Social and Economic History of Peasant Livelihood, 1800–1990s. Basingstoke: Macmillan.

[36] Ricklefs, M.C. (2008). A History of Modern Indonesia Since c. 1200. 4th ed. Basingstoke: Palgrave Macmillan.

like sugar, coffee, and rubber from plantations to ports for export to Europe, rather than to connect regions within Indonesia. This export-centric model left the country with a fragmented transportation network that was ill-suited to fostering internal trade and regional integration.[37] After independence, the Indonesian government inherited this uneven and inefficient system, which required significant investment and reconfiguration to serve domestic needs—a task that proved difficult given the country's limited resources and competing priorities. The disruption caused by the Japanese occupation further complicated efforts to develop a coordinated strategy. During the occupation (1942–1945), much of Indonesia's infrastructure was neglected, repurposed for military use, or outright destroyed. The Japanese dismantled parts of the existing network, particularly railways and ports, to prevent Allied forces from utilizing them. By the end of the war, Indonesia's trade networks were in disarray, with limited capacity to transport goods efficiently. This destruction created an additional burden for the nascent Indonesian state, which lacked the technical expertise and capital required for large-scale infrastructure reconstruction.[38] Another critical factor was the political instability and fragmented governance that characterized the early years of independence. The struggle for independence (1945–1949) against Dutch attempts to reassert control consumed much of the new government's focus and resources, leaving little capacity to address economic infrastructure systematically. The revolution also fostered regional power bases, as local leaders and militias played crucial roles in the fight against the Dutch. These regional actors often prioritized their own economic interests, leading to fragmented decision-making and resistance to centralized planning efforts. The resulting decentralization of authority hindered the formulation of a unified national strategy for trade and infrastructure development.[39]

The economic fragmentation and regional disparities that emerged during this period further exacerbated the problem. Different regions

[37] Booth, A. (1998). The Indonesian Economy in the Nineteenth and Twentieth Centuries: A History of Missed Opportunities. London: Macmillan.

[38] Furnivall, J.S. (1948). Colonial Policy and Practice: A Comparative Study of Burma and NetherlandsIndia. Cambridge: Cambridge University Press.

[39] Kahin, G.M. (1952). Nationalism and Revolution in Indonesia. Ithaca, NY: Cornell University Press.

in Indonesia had varying economic priorities and levels of development. Java, the political and administrative centre, was relatively well-connected due to its colonial infrastructure, while the outer islands, such as Sumatra and Kalimantan, were underdeveloped and poorly integrated into the national economy. The government's limited capacity to balance these regional differences and allocate resources equitably prevented the establishment of a cohesive strategy to rebuild and modernize trade networks.[40] Finally, the lack of institutional capacity in the post-independence government played a significant role. The administrative structures inherited from the Dutch were oriented toward maintaining colonial control rather than fostering economic development. Following independence, Indonesia faced a severe shortage of skilled personnel capable of planning and managing large-scale infrastructure projects. Additionally, the early government struggled with limited financial resources, widespread corruption, and competing demands from sectors such as education, health, and defence, all of which further undermined its ability to develop and implement coordinated trade policies.[41] The absence of a coordinated strategy for rebuilding and modernizing trade networks after independence was a result of the export-oriented colonial legacy, the devastation wrought by the Japanese occupation, political instability, regional fragmentation, and the limited institutional and financial capacity of the early Indonesian state. These factors collectively delayed the integration of regional economies and the distribution of essential goods, hindering Indonesia's economic recovery and development in the early years of independence.

Indonesia also suffered from a lack of industrial policy frameworks and institutions to support manufacturing and economic diversification. Under colonial rule, industrial development was minimal and geared toward resource extraction. The Japanese occupation further disrupted nascent industries by prioritizing short-term military needs. By independence, Indonesia lacked institutions capable of fostering industrial growth, such as development banks, regulatory agencies, and technical

[40] Elson, R.E. (1997). The End of the Peasantry in SoutheastAsia: A Social and Economic History of Peasant Livelihood, 1800–1990s. Basingstoke: Macmillan.

[41] Ricklefs, M.C. (2008). A History of Modern Indonesia Since c. 1200. 4th ed. Basingstoke: Palgrave Macmillan.

training institutions, leaving the economy heavily dependent on agriculture and resource exports.[42] Finally, the absence of a well-functioning taxation system and fiscal institutions hampered Indonesia's ability to generate revenue for state-building. The colonial taxation system, focused on extractive industries, failed to create a sustainable framework for equitable revenue collection. After independence, weak administrative capacity and widespread corruption further undermined fiscal stability, limiting the government's ability to invest in infrastructure, education, and health services necessary for economic development.[43,44] These institutional weaknesses left Indonesia ill-prepared to address the challenges of independence. The lack of robust economic institutions made it difficult to implement cohesive policies, manage economic crises, or address regional disparities, contributing to the economic fragmentation and political instability that characterized much of the early post-independence period. The absence of robust economic institutions capable of coordinating national development strategies undermined the government's ability to implement cohesive policies. For instance, the lack of a centralized banking system and effective fiscal policies made it difficult to stabilize the currency, manage inflation, or mobilize domestic resources for infrastructure development.[45] This institutional void was particularly problematic in addressing regional disparities, as Java remained the economic and administrative centre, leaving outlying regions marginalized and underdeveloped.[46]

The political instability that characterized much of the early post-independence period further compounded these economic challenges. Weak governance structures, inherited from both Dutch and Japanese colonial administrations, led to a fragmented bureaucracy that struggled

[42] Booth, A. (1998). The Indonesian Economy in the Nineteenth and Twentieth Centuries: A History of Missed Opportunities. London: Macmillan.

[43] Furnivall, J.S. (1948). Colonial Policy and Practice: A Comparative Study of Burma and NetherlandsIndia. Cambridge: Cambridge University Press.

[44] Kahin, G.M. (1952). Nationalism and Revolution in Indonesia. Ithaca, NY: Cornell University Press.

[45] Booth, A. (1998). The Indonesian Economy in the Nineteenth and Twentieth Centuries: A History of Missed Opportunities. London: Macmillan.

[46] Ricklefs, M. C. (2008). A History of Modern Indonesia Since c.1200. 4th ed. Stanford, CA: Stanford University Press.

to enforce policies effectively. The absence of a unified land management system, for example, resulted in conflicts over land ownership and usage, particularly in rural areas, where economic inequality and tensions between local elites and smallholders persisted.[47] These conflicts often escalated into broader social unrest, highlighting the inability of the nascent Indonesian state to mediate or resolve disputes systematically.[48] Moreover, the economic fragmentation fostered by the Japanese occupation's focus on resource extraction rather than institutional development left Indonesia heavily reliant on commodity exports. This dependence on volatile global markets made the economy highly susceptible to external shocks, further exacerbating the difficulties of economic management during the early independence period.[49] Without the institutional capacity to diversify the economy or invest in industrialization, Indonesia faced persistent cycles of economic stagnation and social discontent.

These structural and institutional deficiencies underscored the significant challenges that Indonesia faced in transitioning from a colonial economy to a self-reliant nation-state. They also highlighted the critical need for institutional reform and capacity-building, which would remain central to the country's developmental struggles throughout the twentieth century.[50]

The Japanese occupation not only inflicted immediate suffering but also reshaped Indonesia's economic landscape in ways that influenced its trajectory for decades. The forced extraction of resources, the collapse of the agricultural sector, and the destruction of economic infrastructure left a legacy of poverty, inequality, and structural challenges that Indonesia grappled with well into the post-colonial era. However, despite the economic turmoil, the Japanese occupation inadvertently laid the groundwork for Indonesia's post-war economic policies. The promotion of Indonesian leadership within the administration, coupled with the harsh realities of occupation, accelerated the push for independence and

[47] Elson, R. E. (2009). The Idea of Indonesia: A History. Cambridge: Cambridge University Press.

[48] Kurasawa, A. (1988). 'Mobilization and Control: A Study of Social Change in Rural Java,1942–1945.' Indonesia, 46(1), 1–32.

[49] Furnivall, J. S. (1948). Colonial Policy and Practice: A Comparative Study of Burma and NetherlandsIndia. Cambridge: Cambridge University Press.

[50] Reid, A. (1980). The Indonesian National Revolution, 1945–1950. Hawthorn, VIC: Longman Australia.

the establishment of a national economy.[51] The chapter will also examine how the occupation influenced Indonesia's economic strategies during the early years of independence, as the new nation sought to rebuild and redefine its economy free from colonial influences.[52]

The Japanese occupation of Indonesia from 1942 to 1945 brought significant changes to the archipelago's economic policies, leaving a profound impact on its political and economic landscape. The Japanese sought to restructure Indonesia's economy to serve their war effort, focusing on the extraction of resources, the reorganization of labour, and the promotion of self-sufficiency under the guise of anti-colonial liberation. While some policies resonated with burgeoning nationalist aspirations, the overall impact was one of severe economic hardship and dislocation for the Indonesian population. Japanese economic policies were cantered on the goal of mobilizing Indonesia's resources to support the Japanese military. Rice and other agricultural commodities were requisitioned in large quantities, leading to acute food shortages and widespread famine, particularly in Java. Farmers were forced to meet production quotas under stringent supervision, and much of their output was diverted to the Japanese war effort. The prioritization of resource extraction over local welfare disrupted traditional agricultural systems, leaving rural populations unable to meet their subsistence needs.[53] In many areas, the Japanese also dismantled the plantation economy that had been developed under Dutch rule, repurposing estates for food production or other strategic uses, which further disrupted the economic balance.[54]

Labour policies under Japanese rule were similarly extractive and coercive. The romusha system, which conscripted millions of Indonesians for forced labour, epitomized the exploitative nature of Japanese economic policies. Workers were subjected to harsh conditions, minimal provisions, and high mortality rates while being deployed to construct infrastructure

[51] Elson, R. E. (2009) The Idea of Indonesia: A History. Cambridge: Cambridge University Press.

[52] Sato, S. (1994) 'War, Nationalism and Peasants: Java under the Japanese Occupation, 1942–45', Journal of Southeast Asian Studies, 25(2), pp. 268–294.

[53] Ricklefs, M. C. (2008). A History of Modern Indonesia Since c.1200. 4th ed. Basingstoke: Palgrave Macmillan.

[54] Elson, R. E. (2009). The Idea of Indonesia: A History. Cambridge: Cambridge University Press.

projects such as railways, airstrips, and military fortifications. The romusha system not only decimated local labour forces but also weakened traditional social structures, as many families were left without able-bodied members to support agricultural production.[55] Despite these hardships, some aspects of Japanese economic policies inadvertently contributed to the rise of Indonesian nationalism. The Japanese promoted anti-Western rhetoric and implemented policies that nominally supported self-sufficiency and local enterprise, presenting themselves as liberators from European colonialism. For example, the Japanese encouraged the establishment of small-scale industries and cooperatives to produce goods for local consumption. These initiatives were framed as part of a broader effort to build a self-reliant Indonesian economy, aligning with nationalist aspirations for economic independence.[56] However, these efforts were often undermined by the overarching priority of resource extraction for Japan's military needs. The Japanese also sought to integrate Indonesia into their Greater East Asia Co-Prosperity Sphere, which emphasized economic integration under Japanese dominance. This policy further entrenched Indonesia's role as a supplier of raw materials and cheap labour, perpetuating patterns of dependency that had been established under Dutch colonial rule. However, the Japanese occupation differed from the Dutch era in its mobilization of Indigenous leaders and institutions. The Japanese co-opted nationalist leaders such as Sukarno and Hatta, giving them platforms to promote nationalist ideas under Japanese supervision. This collaboration, though controversial, allowed Indonesian leaders to organize politically and build the foundations for post-war independence movements.[57]

The Japanese occupation brought significant changes to Indonesia's economic policies, intensifying resource extraction and labour exploitation while disrupting traditional systems of production. The economic hardships and dislocations caused by Japanese policies inflicted severe suffering on the Indonesian population. However, the occupation also provided opportunities for the growth of nationalist sentiments and the

[55] Cribb, R. (1994). Gangsters and Revolutionaries: The Jakarta People's Militia and the Indonesian Revolution, 1945–1949. Honolulu: University of Hawai'i Press.

[56] Bosma, U. (2013). The Sugar Plantation in Indiaand Indonesia: Industrial Production, 1770–2010. Cambridge: Cambridge University Press.

[57] Ricklefs, M. C. (2008). A History of Modern Indonesia Since c.1200. 4th ed. Basingstoke: Palgrave Macmillan.

mobilization of political leadership, setting the stage for Indonesia's struggle for independence. The complex legacy of Japanese economic policies illustrates both the continuity of colonial exploitation and the ways in which these policies inadvertently strengthened Indonesia's nationalist movement.

The Collapse of the Colonial Economy

The collapse of Indonesia's colonial economy during the Japanese occupation (1942–1945) marked a profound rupture in the economic structures that had defined Dutch rule for over three centuries. The Japanese military administration dismantled the existing colonial apparatus, repurposing Indonesia's economy to serve their war effort. Dutch-controlled plantations, trade networks, and financial institutions were confiscated or abandoned, leading to the disintegration of the export-oriented plantation economy. The Japanese policies prioritized strategic needs over economic stability, further unravelling the colonial framework. The abrupt transition from Dutch to Japanese control disrupted established production systems and trade flows, leaving much of the colonial economic infrastructure in disarray. While the collapse of the colonial economy undermined Dutch economic dominance, it exposed the fragility of a system designed primarily for resource extraction and created severe hardships for the Indonesian population.[58]

The Japanese implemented an economic policy of resource mobilization aimed at supporting their war effort. This policy redirected Indonesia's agricultural and industrial outputs to supply Japan's military campaigns. Key commodities like rice, rubber, oil, and other strategic materials were requisitioned in copious quantities. The emphasis on fulfilling Japanese demands diverted labour, capital, and inputs away from local food production, leading to severe shortages of essential goods. Rice production, which was already strained under Dutch rule, declined precipitously due to the mismanagement of agricultural resources and the forced imposition of quotas. These shortages culminated in widespread famine and malnutrition, particularly in Java, where millions suffered

[58] Ricklefs, M. C. (2008). A History of Modern Indonesia Since c.1200. 4th ed. Basingstoke: Palgrave Macmillan.

from hunger-related illnesses and deaths.[59] This disruption exacerbated the vulnerabilities of rural areas, where subsistence farming became the primary means of survival in the absence of functioning market systems. Furthermore, the labour system underwent a drastic transformation that further strained both the economy and society. The Japanese introduced the romusha system, conscripting millions of Indonesians for forced labour on infrastructure projects across Southeast Asia, such as railways, airstrips, and fortifications. This labour mobilization was a cornerstone of Japanese military strategy but came at a devastating human cost. Many romusha labourers were subjected to inhumane working conditions, with insufficient food, rampant disease, and extremely high mortality rates. Communities were often left without able-bodied workers, which weakened local economies and disrupted agricultural productivity. The forced removal of labour from rural areas deepened the economic crisis, exacerbating food shortages and increasing social dislocation.[60]

Despite the severe economic hardships and human suffering inflicted during this period, the collapse of the colonial economy catalysed significant political and social transformations that shaped Indonesia's path to independence. By dismantling Dutch economic control, the Japanese occupation created a power vacuum that allowed Indonesian nationalists to assert greater influence. The occupation also fostered the emergence of nationalist organizations and leadership structures. Prominent figures like Sukarno and Hatta were co-opted into the Japanese administration, ostensibly to mobilize the population for Japan's war effort. However, these leaders used their positions to build networks and mobilize support for independence, linking economic grievances with political liberation. They effectively transformed economic exploitation into a rallying cry for freedom, using the shared suffering under Japanese and Dutch rule as a unifying narrative.[61] The occupation also highlighted the unsustainability of a colonial economic model that prioritized metropolitan interests over local development. The abrupt collapse of Dutch economic control and the inefficiency of Japanese policies underscored the systemic

[59] Elson, R. E. (2009). The Idea of Indonesia: A History. Cambridge: Cambridge University Press.

[60] Cribb, R. (1994). Gangsters and Revolutionaries: The Jakarta People's Militia and the Indonesian Revolution, 1945–1949. Honolulu: University of Hawai'i Press.

[61] Bosma, U. (2013). The Sugar Plantation in Indiaand Indonesia: Industrial Production, 1770–2010. Cambridge: Cambridge University Press.

weaknesses of extractive economies that lacked diversification and equitable resource distribution. This realization strengthened the resolve of Indonesian nationalists to advocate for economic sovereignty as a cornerstone of independence. The period also fostered grassroots resistance and self-reliance, as communities sought to adapt to the economic upheaval through informal trade networks, cooperative farming, and clandestine political activity.[62]

The collapse of Indonesia's colonial economy during the Japanese occupation was both a profound crisis and a transformative turning point. The dismantling of Dutch economic dominance, coupled with the disruptive policies of the Japanese, exposed the fragility of a system built on extraction and exploitation. While the collapse caused immense suffering, it also galvanized nationalist movements and laid the groundwork for Indonesia's eventual independence. The period serves as a stark reminder of the vulnerabilities inherent in colonial economies and the resilience of societies striving for self-determination amidst systemic upheaval.

The Role of Nationalism and Economic Mobilization

Economic mobilization under Japanese rule focused exclusively on supporting Japan's wartime objectives, prioritizing the extraction of critical resources and conscripting labour to meet military demands. Commodities such as rice, rubber, oil, and metals were requisitioned in vast quantities to fuel the Japanese war machine, often with catastrophic consequences for the Indonesian population. The disruption of agricultural systems and the diversion of food supplies to Japan resulted in widespread shortages and malnutrition, particularly in heavily populated regions like Java, where famine and disease claimed the lives of hundreds of thousands. The economic dislocation exposed the inherent weaknesses of the colonial systems, both Dutch and Japanese, as they prioritized external interests over the welfare of the local populace.[63] This heightened awareness among Indonesians of their subjugation under foreign powers, further fuelling calls for systemic change.

[62] Ricklefs, M. C. (2008). A History of Modern Indonesia Since c.1200. 4th ed. Basingstoke: Palgrave Macmillan.

[63] Elson, R. E. (2009). The Idea of Indonesia: A History. Cambridge: Cambridge University Press.

The romusha labour system epitomized the brutal exploitation of human resources during this period. Millions of Indonesians were forcibly conscripted to build military infrastructure, such as railways, roads, and fortifications, across Southeast Asia. These labourers endured inhumane conditions, malnutrition, and rampant disease, with many dying far from their homes. While the Japanese claimed to promote hakko ichiu (universal brotherhood), their policies often mirrored or even exceeded the exploitative practices of European colonial powers. The loss of able-bodied workers further exacerbated economic vulnerabilities in rural communities, reducing agricultural productivity and deepening the cycle of deprivation.[64] The romusha experience became a powerful symbol of foreign exploitation, searing a collective memory that strengthened anti-colonial resolve.

The Japanese administration's decision to involve Indonesian elites in governance, though primarily intended to co-opt them for Japanese objectives, had unintended consequences. By granting limited administrative authority to figures like Sukarno and Hatta, the Japanese inadvertently created platforms for nationalist leaders to consolidate their influence and promote anti-colonial ideals. The use of the Indonesian language in official contexts marked a departure from Dutch colonial policies and fostered a growing sense of national identity. The establishment of organizations such as PETA (Defenders of the Homeland) provided military training and organizational skills to Indonesians, many of whom would later play pivotal roles in the armed struggle for independence. These initiatives, though rooted in Japanese wartime strategy, unintentionally empowered Indonesians and aligned with their aspirations for sovereignty.[65]

Economic discontent under Japanese rule also illuminated broader contradictions in colonial governance. The severe hardships experienced during the occupation—food shortages, labour exploitation, and economic dislocation—deepened popular resentment of foreign domination, whether European or Japanese. Nationalist organizations such as the Indonesian National Party (PNI) and Sarekat Islam used these

[64] Cribb, R. (1994). Gangsters and Revolutionaries: The Jakarta People's Militia and the Indonesian Revolution, 1945–1949. Honolulu: University of Hawai'i Press.

[65] Bosma, U. (2013). The Sugar Plantation in Indiaand Indonesia: Industrial Production, 1770–2010. Cambridge: Cambridge University Press.

grievances to mobilize support for independence, framing economic liberation as inseparable from political freedom. The shared suffering under Japanese occupation forged a stronger collective identity among Indonesians, breaking down regional and class divisions that had previously hindered nationalist unity. Economic grievances became a rallying cry that unified workers, peasants, and intellectuals in their demand for a new, equitable economic order.[66] Critically, the Japanese occupation exposed the fragility of colonial economies built on resource extraction and systemic exploitation. While the occupation created immense suffering, it also demonstrated the power of grassroots mobilization and highlighted the inefficiencies of foreign-controlled economic systems. By dismantling Dutch economic dominance and co-opting local leadership, the Japanese inadvertently accelerated the emergence of a nationalist consciousness and set the stage for Indonesia's independence. This period underscored the enduring link between economic hardship and political activism, as Indonesians leveraged their experiences of exploitation to advocate for a more just and autonomous future.

The intersection of economic mobilization and nationalist sentiment during the Japanese occupation revealed both the vulnerabilities of colonial systems and the resilience of the Indonesian people. While the occupation exacerbated inequalities and inflicted severe hardship, it also fostered a shared vision of independence and self-determination. The lessons of this period became central to Indonesia's post-colonial identity, reinforcing the importance of economic sovereignty as a foundation for nation-building.

Social and Economic Consequences of the Occupation

The Japanese occupation of Indonesia from 1942 to 1945 brought transformative social and economic consequences that profoundly reshaped the archipelago and catalysed the independence movement. Economically, the occupation dismantled the colonial structures that had underpinned Dutch rule for over three centuries, replacing them with a militarized system focused on resource extraction for Japan's war effort. Key

[66] Ricklefs, M. C. (2008). A History of Modern Indonesia Since c.1200. 4th ed. Basingstoke: Palgrave Macmillan.

commodities such as rice, rubber, and oil were requisitioned, disrupting local economies and severely undermining agricultural systems. The diversion of food supplies to Japanese military campaigns caused widespread shortages, particularly in Java, where famine and malnutrition claimed millions of lives. These shortages were exacerbated by Japanese-imposed quotas and forced requisitions, which prioritized military needs over the welfare of local populations.[67] This crisis exposed the vulnerabilities of a colonial economic model designed primarily for export and external exploitation, leaving rural communities impoverished and increasingly reliant on subsistence farming for survival. The plantation economy, a cornerstone of Dutch colonial economic structures, was similarly destabilized. Under Japanese rule, many plantations were repurposed for food production or abandoned entirely as labour and resources were redirected toward military objectives. The production of cash crops such as rubber and sugar plummeted, resulting in economic dislocation and the collapse of export revenues. This not only disrupted rural livelihoods but also underscored the fragility of a mono-crop agricultural system reliant on external markets.[68] As local economies unravelled, the capacity of communities to sustain themselves diminished, further highlighting the long-term consequences of colonial dependency and resource extraction.

Socially, the occupation inflicted deep scars, particularly through the forced labour system known as romusha. This system conscripted millions of Indonesians to work on infrastructure projects across Southeast Asia under brutal conditions, with labourers facing extreme malnutrition, disease, and exhaustion. Mortality rates were alarmingly high, with many labourers dying far from home and leaving families and villages devastated. Entire communities were depopulated of able-bodied men, disrupting traditional social structures and exacerbating the economic hardships of rural areas (Cribb, 1994). The trauma inflicted by the romusha system starkly contrasted with Japanese propaganda, which framed their occupation as a liberation from Western imperialism. This hypocrisy deepened resentment toward foreign rule and intensified anti-colonial sentiments, reinforcing a shared desire for self-determination across diverse Indonesian communities. Despite the severe hardships

[67] Elson, R. E. (2009). The Idea of Indonesia: A History. Cambridge: Cambridge University Press.

[68] Bosma, U. (2013). The Sugar Plantation in Indiaand Indonesia: Industrial Production, 1770–2010. Cambridge: Cambridge University Press.

imposed by Japanese policies, the occupation also had unintended consequences that contributed to the growth of Indonesian nationalism. The Japanese administration co-opted nationalist leaders such as Sukarno and Hatta, integrating them into organizations like Putera (Centre of the People's Power) to mobilize support for the war effort. While this collaboration remains controversial, it allowed these leaders to build political networks and strengthen their influence. Sukarno and Hatta used their positions to articulate a vision of independence and prepare the population for self-governance. The promotion of the Indonesian language in administration and education further unified the population, fostering a national identity that transcended regional, cultural, and linguistic divides.[69] Additionally, the establishment of PETA (Defenders of the Homeland) provided military training to Indonesians, equipping them with organizational and combat skills that would later prove crucial in the independence struggle. Culturally, the occupation disrupted traditional hierarchies and norms, creating opportunities for new leaders to emerge from outside the established aristocracy. The collapse of Dutch control left a power vacuum, and the Japanese emphasis on anti-Western rhetoric and self-sufficiency resonated with many Indonesians, even as the occupation's exploitative policies contradicted these ideals. The shared suffering under Japanese rule—marked by famine, forced labour, and political repression—fostered a collective sense of identity and purpose. This period highlighted the systemic inequalities of colonial economic systems, reinforcing the urgency of establishing a new order that prioritized Indonesian welfare over foreign interests.[70]

The economic dislocation and social fragmentation caused by the occupation were profound, but they also galvanized resistance and set the stage for Indonesia's independence. The shared experiences of hardship united workers, peasants, and intellectuals, breaking down barriers and fostering solidarity. This unity was further strengthened by the realization that the colonial economy's focus on extraction and dependency was unsustainable. The occupation exposed the fragility of these systems, underscoring the necessity of economic sovereignty as a foundation for nation-building. As the Japanese surrendered in 1945, the legacies

[69] Ricklefs, M. C. (2008). A History of Modern Indonesia Since c.1200. 4th ed. Basingstoke: Palgrave Macmillan.

[70] Bosma, U. (2013). The Sugar Plantation in Indiaand Indonesia: Industrial Production, 1770–2010. Cambridge: Cambridge University Press.

of their occupation—both the suffering it caused and the nationalist consciousness it fostered—became pivotal drivers of the independence movement. Indonesians were inspired to rebuild their nation on principles of equality, self-determination, and economic justice, drawing lessons from the exploitative practices of both Dutch and Japanese rule.

The Legacy of the Japanese Occupation on Post-War Economic Development

The Japanese occupation of Indonesia from 1942 to 1945 left a profound and multifaceted legacy on post-war economic development, shaping the nation's trajectory in ways that were both challenging and transformative. Economically, the dismantling of Dutch colonial systems by the Japanese exposed the inherent fragility of an extractive economy that had prioritized exports over local welfare. Under Dutch rule, Indonesia's economy was heavily reliant on the plantation system, producing commodities such as rubber, sugar, and coffee for global markets. During the Japanese occupation, this system was disrupted as plantations were dismantled or repurposed for food production to meet the needs of the Japanese war effort. At the same time, resource extraction intensified, with rice, oil, and rubber being requisitioned to support military campaigns. This abrupt shift revealed the vulnerabilities of an economy designed primarily to serve foreign interests, highlighting the pressing need for a more self-reliant economic framework in the post-war period.[71]

The collapse of the plantation economy had far-reaching consequences, leaving many rural areas in a state of severe disrepair. Food shortages and widespread famine, particularly in Java, underscored the failure of the colonial economic system to meet local needs. Millions of Indonesians suffered from malnutrition and starvation, and the agricultural sector, already strained under Dutch rule, was further weakened by labour shortages and declining productivity. These conditions underscored the dangers of mono-crop agriculture and export dependency, sparking debates among nationalist leaders about the need to diversify the economy and prioritize food security. However, the legacy of this economic dislocation posed significant challenges for the post-war

[71] Elson, R. E. (2009). The Idea of Indonesia: A History. Cambridge: Cambridge University Press.

government, which faced the daunting task of rebuilding infrastructure, revitalizing agriculture, and addressing widespread rural poverty.[72]

Socially, the Japanese occupation played a pivotal role in fostering a sense of collective identity and purpose that carried over into the post-war era. By involving prominent nationalist leaders such as Sukarno and Hatta in their administration, the Japanese inadvertently provided a platform for the growth of nationalist ideologies. These leaders effectively used their positions to articulate visions of independence, linking economic grievances with broader political aspirations. Organizations such as PETA (Defenders of the Homeland) not only provided military training to Indonesians but also cultivated a generation of leaders who were equipped to lead the armed struggle for independence. This military preparedness proved crucial in resisting Dutch attempts to reassert control after the war and helped lay the groundwork for the formation of the Indonesian National Army.[73]

The Japanese emphasis on anti-Western rhetoric and the promotion of the Indonesian language in administration and education further reinforced nationalist sentiments. By encouraging the use of Bahasa Indonesia, the Japanese fostered a sense of unity across diverse ethnic and regional groups, breaking down barriers that had previously hindered the nationalist movement. This linguistic unification played a crucial role in shaping Indonesia's post-war identity as a cohesive nation-state. However, the occupation also left behind deep scars, particularly through the romusha forced labour system, which conscripted millions of Indonesians to work on infrastructure projects under inhumane conditions. The high mortality rates and the displacement of labourers disrupted traditional social structures, leaving communities fragmented and struggling to recover in the immediate aftermath of the war.[74] The occupation also underscored the systemic inequalities of colonial economic systems, highlighting the need for a new economic order. The food shortages and economic dislocation experienced during the Japanese era demonstrated the dangers of prioritizing external markets over domestic

[72] Bosma, U. (2013). The Sugar Plantation in Indiaand Indonesia: Industrial Production, 1770–2010. Cambridge: Cambridge University Press.

[73] Ricklefs, M. C. (2008). A History of Modern Indonesia Since c.1200. 4th ed. Basingstoke: Palgrave Macmillan.

[74] Cribb, R. (1994). Gangsters and Revolutionaries: The Jakarta People's Militia and the Indonesian Revolution, 1945–1949. Honolulu: University of Hawai'i Press.

needs. This realization influenced post-war policy debates, with nationalist leaders emphasizing the importance of economic diversification and self-sufficiency. However, the institutional weaknesses and fragmented infrastructure left by the Japanese posed significant challenges to achieving these goals and refers to the profound challenges Indonesia inherited from the Japanese occupation, which significantly hindered post-war recovery and economic development. During the occupation, the Japanese dismantled much of the Dutch colonial administrative and economic systems to prioritize their war effort. This included the dissolution of the Dutch bureaucratic framework, which, while exploitative, had been essential for coordinating governance and economic activities across the vast archipelago. The Japanese replaced it with a decentralized and militarized administration that lacked cohesion, leaving post-war Indonesia without the institutional capacity to implement unified policies effectively.[75] The infrastructure was also severely fragmented and degraded under Japanese rule. Railways, ports, and communication networks, which had been critical for managing the export-oriented colonial economy, were repurposed for military use and suffered from neglect and overuse. For example, key rail lines in Java were used intensively to transport resources to ports for export to Japan, leading to significant wear and damage. Moreover, forced labour projects under the romusha system, such as the construction of military airstrips and roads, diverted resources and workforce from maintaining existing infrastructure. As a result, by the end of the war, much of Indonesia's transport and communication systems were in disrepair, complicating efforts to rebuild the economy and integrate the nation.[76] The loss of human resources also exacerbated institutional weaknesses. Millions of Indonesians were conscripted into forced labour under harsh conditions, with many dying or suffering long-term health consequences. This depletion of the labour force left many regions without the skilled or able-bodied workers needed to rebuild. Additionally, the Japanese occupation disrupted traditional governance systems at the local level, further weakening the links between the central government and rural areas. This

[75] Elson, R. E. (2009). The Idea of Indonesia: A History. Cambridge: Cambridge University Press.

[76] Cribb, R. (1994). Gangsters and Revolutionaries: The Jakarta People's Militia and the Indonesian Revolution, 1945–1949. Honolulu: University of Hawai'i Press.

fragmentation made it difficult to implement coordinated economic policies, as the government faced resistance and inefficiencies when trying to manage diverse and often disconnected regions.[77]

Another critical aspect of the institutional weaknesses was the absence of robust financial systems. The Japanese had eliminated much of the Dutch banking infrastructure, and their wartime economy operated on coercion and requisition rather than monetary transactions. This left post-war Indonesia with an unstable currency and a lack of financial institutions capable of mobilizing capital for reconstruction. Without access to adequate financial resources, the government struggled to fund large-scale development projects, compounding the challenges of addressing poverty, famine, and long-term economic planning.[78] In sum, the institutional weaknesses and fragmented infrastructure inherited from the Japanese occupation were severe and multifaceted, affecting governance, transportation, human resources, and financial stability. These issues created significant obstacles for nationalist leaders in their efforts to transition from a war-torn colonial economy to an independent and self-sufficient nation. Addressing these structural challenges required not only immediate relief measures but also a long-term vision for economic diversification and institution-building, which proved to be a monumental task in the years following independence. The Indonesian government faced the dual task of addressing the immediate crises of poverty and famine while laying the foundations for long-term economic development. These challenges were compounded by the legacy of war-related destruction, which included damaged transport networks, depleted natural resources, and a lack of skilled labour.[79]

The Japanese occupation had a complex legacy for post-war economic development in Indonesia. On one hand, it exacerbated economic and social dislocation, leaving a weakened infrastructure and deeply fragmented society. On the other, it catalysed the nationalist movement and fostered a collective sense of purpose, laying the groundwork for economic and political transformation. The occupation revealed the

[77] Bosma, U. (2013). The Sugar Plantation in Indiaand Indonesia: Industrial Production, 1770–2010. Cambridge: Cambridge University Press.

[78] Ricklefs, M. C. (2008). A History of Modern Indonesia Since c.1200. 4th ed. Basingstoke: Palgrave Macmillan.

[79] Bosma, U. (2013). The Sugar Plantation in Indiaand Indonesia: Industrial Production, 1770–2010. Cambridge: Cambridge University Press.

fragility of colonial systems while highlighting the resilience of the Indonesian population, who leveraged their shared experiences of hardship to rebuild their nation on principles of economic sovereignty and self-determination. This period serves as a crucial reminder of the interconnectedness of economic policies, social cohesion, and national identity in shaping Indonesia's journey toward independence.

Conclusion

The Japanese occupation of Indonesia from 1942 to 1945 was a period of profound economic and social upheaval, marking a critical juncture in the nation's trajectory toward independence. By dismantling Dutch colonial structures, the Japanese exposed the systemic fragility of an economy deeply entrenched in extractive practices that prioritized external markets over local development. The redirection of Indonesia's resources to meet Japan's wartime needs caused significant disruptions to agricultural and industrial systems. The forced requisitioning of rice, rubber, and oil led to severe shortages of essential goods, while the exploitation of local labour through the romusha system intensified suffering across the archipelago. The famine and malnutrition that ravaged Java during this period, claiming the lives of hundreds of thousands, starkly underscored the failures of colonial economic policies to prioritize the welfare of the local population. These crises laid bare the unsustainability of a model that subordinated domestic needs to foreign economic agendas, reinforcing nationalist critiques of colonial governance.[80,81]

The romusha system, which conscripted millions of Indonesians to work on infrastructure projects under brutal conditions, exemplified the exploitative nature of Japanese policies. These labourers faced starvation, disease, and abuse, with mortality rates reaching catastrophic levels. Entire communities were decimated, leaving families and villages bereft of able-bodied men, further exacerbating rural economic decline. While the Japanese occupation was marked by severe hardship, it also exposed the limitations of colonial governance and the inherent contradictions of imperialism. By presenting themselves as liberators from Western

[80] Elson, R. E. (2009). The Idea of Indonesia: A History. Cambridge: Cambridge University Press.

[81] Cribb, R. (1994). Gangsters and Revolutionaries: The Jakarta People's Militia and the Indonesian Revolution, 1945–1949. Honolulu: University of Hawai'i Press.

imperialism while simultaneously implementing policies of exploitation, the Japanese reinforced nationalist sentiments among Indonesians, who began to view independence as the only viable path to self-determination and economic justice.

Despite the suffering inflicted during the occupation, this period also catalysed significant political and social transformations. The Japanese co-optation of nationalist leaders, including Sukarno and Hatta, provided these figures with platforms to promote independence and mobilize public support. Through organizations like Putera and PETA (Defenders of the Homeland), Indonesians gained political and military experience, building the networks and organizational capacity that would later underpin the independence struggle. The use of the Indonesian language in administration and education further solidified a shared national identity, fostering unity across diverse ethnic and cultural groups. This linguistic and cultural cohesion contrasted sharply with the fragmented governance under Dutch rule, empowering Indonesians to imagine themselves as a single nation.[82] The occupation also revealed the economic vulnerabilities created by reliance on monoculture and export dependency. The collapse of plantation systems and the devastation of infrastructure highlighted the need for economic diversification and self-reliance in the post-war period. The wartime economy's failure to sustain basic subsistence further underscored the necessity of policies that prioritized food security and domestic development over global markets. However, the damage inflicted on infrastructure, such as railways, ports, and irrigation systems, posed significant challenges for recovery. The depletion of human capital through forced labour compounded these difficulties, leaving post-war Indonesia with limited resources to address both immediate crises and long-term development needs.[83] Critically, the Japanese occupation underscored the contradictions of colonial systems. While it dismantled Dutch structures, it failed to establish sustainable alternatives, leaving a power vacuum that nationalist leaders were able to exploit. The occupation's emphasis on anti-Western rhetoric and the promotion of self-sufficiency resonated with Indonesians but clashed with the exploitative realities of Japanese governance. This dissonance

[82] Ricklefs, M. C. (2008). A History of Modern Indonesia Since c.1200. 4th ed. Basingstoke: Palgrave Macmillan.

[83] Bosma, U. (2013). The Sugar Plantation in Indiaand Indonesia: Industrial Production, 1770–2010. Cambridge: Cambridge University Press.

fuelled discontent, strengthening the nationalist movement and fostering a collective desire for sovereignty. At the same time, the occupation exposed deep structural inequalities in Indonesia's political economy, reinforcing the importance of addressing issues such as land ownership, labour exploitation, and regional disparities in the post-colonial period.

In conclusion, the Japanese occupation represents both a period of immense suffering and a transformative moment in Indonesia's political and economic development. It illuminated the systemic failings of colonial rule while catalysing a nationalist movement that linked economic sovereignty with political liberation. The legacy of the occupation underscores the resilience of the Indonesian people, who emerged from this period with a renewed commitment to rebuilding their nation on principles of equality and self-determination. The lessons of this turbulent era—particularly the dangers of economic dependency and the importance of inclusive governance—became foundational to Indonesia's efforts to forge an autonomous identity on the global stage.

References

Booth, A. (1998). The Indonesian Economy in the Nineteenth and Twentieth Centuries: A History of Missed Opportunities. London: Macmillan.

Bosma, U. (2013). The Sugar Plantation in India and Indonesia: Industrial Production, 1770–2010. Cambridge: Cambridge University Press.

Cribb, R. (1981) The Indonesian Killings 1965–1966: Studies from Java and Bali. Clayton, VIC: Centre of Southeast Asian Studies, Monash University.

Cribb, R. (1994). Gangsters and Revolutionaries: The Jakarta People's Militia and the Indonesian Revolution, 1945–1949. Honolulu: University of Hawai'i Press.

Elson, R.E. (1997). The End of the Peasantry in Southeast Asia: A Social and Economic History of Peasant Livelihood, 1800–1990s. Basingstoke: Macmillan.

Elson, R. E. (2009) The Idea of Indonesia: A History. Cambridge: Cambridge University Press.

Furnivall, J.S. (1948). Colonial Policy and Practice: A Comparative Study of Burma and Netherlands India. Cambridge: Cambridge University Press.

Kahin, G.M. (1952). Nationalism and Revolution in Indonesia. Ithaca, NY: Cornell University Press.

Kurasawa, A. (1988) 'Mobilization and Control: A Study of Social Change in Rural Java, 1942–1945', Indonesia, 46(1), pp. 1–32.

Reid, A. (1980) The Indonesian National Revolution, 1945–1950. Hawthorn, VIC: Longman Australia.

Ricklefs, M. C. (2008) A History of Modern Indonesia Since c.1200. 4th edn. Stanford, CA: Stanford University Press.

Sato, S. (1994) 'War, Nationalism and Peasants: Java under the Japanese Occupation, 1942–45', Journal of Southeast Asian Studies, 25(2), pp. 268–294.

Shiraishi, T. (1990) An Age in Motion: Popular Radicalism in Java, 1912–1926. Ithaca, NY: Cornell University Press.

Vickers, A. (2005) A History of Modern Indonesia. Cambridge: Cambridge University Press.

PART III

Post-Independence Struggles and Growth

CHAPTER 8

The Road to Independence (1945–1950)

Introduction

The period between 1945 and 1950 was one of the most critical in Indonesia's history, as the country transitioned from Japanese occupation to the brink of full sovereignty. This era, marked by the struggle for independence, was not only a time of intense political upheaval but also one of significant economic challenges and transformations. Chapter 8: The Road to Independence (1945–1950) explored the complex interplay between political events and economic developments during these formative years, highlighting how the foundations for Indonesia's post-colonial economy were laid.

The Proclamation of Indonesian Independence on August 17, 1945, by Sukarno and Hatta, marked the beginning of a tumultuous struggle against Dutch efforts to reassert control over the archipelago. This period, often referred to as the Indonesian National Revolution, saw widespread military conflict, social upheaval, and economic dislocation.[1,2] The immediate aftermath of the proclamation was characterized by the establishment of a revolutionary government that faced the enormous

[1] Ricklefs, M. C. (2008). A History of Modern Indonesia Since c.1200. 4th ed. Basingstoke: Palgrave Macmillan.

[2] Kahin, G. M. (1952). Nationalism and Revolution in Indonesia. Ithaca: Cornell University Press.

S. Ramesh, *The Political Economy of Indonesia's Economic Development, Volume I*, https://doi.org/10.1007/978-3-031-94350-8_8

task of managing an economy devastated by war and occupation. The challenge of state-building was compounded by the need to secure international recognition and to stabilize an economy suffering from hyperinflation, food shortages, and the collapse of trade.[3,4] One of the central themes of this period was the economic dimension of the independence struggle. The fledgling Indonesian government had to develop strategies for economic survival, including the creation of a national currency, the management of scarce resources, and the negotiation of foreign aid and support.[5] These economic strategies were not just about survival but also about asserting economic sovereignty, as Indonesia sought to break free from the colonial economic structures imposed by the Dutch.[6] This chapter will discuss the various efforts to nationalize Dutch-owned enterprises and the broader implications of these policies for Indonesia's economic development in the post-colonial period.[7] Furthermore, this period witnessed significant social changes, as the population was mobilized for both military and economic purposes. The revolutionary government encouraged a spirit of self-sufficiency and nationalism, which played a crucial role in uniting the diverse population against the common enemy of colonialism.[8] However, these efforts were also met with considerable challenges, including internal divisions, the burden of war, and the complexities of forging a unified national identity in a highly diverse archipelago.[9]

[3] Reid, A. (1974). The Indonesian National Revolution, 1945–1950. Hawthorn: Longman Australia.

[4] Cribb, R. and Brown, C. (1995). Modern Indonesia: A History Since 1945. London: Longman.

[5] Kahin, G. M. (1952). Nationalism and Revolution in Indonesia. Ithaca: Cornell University Press.

[6] Elson, R. E. (2009). The Idea of Indonesia: A History. Cambridge: Cambridge University Press.

[7] Feith, H. (1962). The Decline of Constitutional Democracy in Indonesia. Ithaca: Cornell University Press.

[8] Anderson, B. R. O. G. (1972). Java in a Time of Revolution: Occupation and Resistance, 1944–1946. Ithaca: Cornell University Press.

[9] Vickers, A. (2005). A History of Modern Indonesia. Cambridge: Cambridge University Press.

The Proclamation of Independence and Its Immediate Aftermath

The proclamation of Indonesia's independence on August 17, 1945, marked a watershed moment in the nation's history, signalling the culmination of decades of nationalist resistance against colonial exploitation. Delivered by Sukarno and Hatta, the declaration symbolized Indonesia's break from its colonial past but also initiated a fraught period of uncertainty, as the fledgling republic grappled with the challenges of asserting sovereignty and building a functioning state. Decades of systemic exploitation under Dutch colonial rule, compounded by the devastation of the Japanese occupation, had left Indonesia economically and politically fragile. Infrastructure lay in ruins, industries were incapacitated, and rural areas were mired in poverty and famine. These challenges underscored the monumental task of transitioning from a colony to a unified, independent nation-state.[10]

The economic discontent that fuelled Indonesia's nationalist struggle persisted in the post-independence period. The collapse of the plantation economy during the Japanese occupation had disrupted the agricultural and industrial sectors that had formed the backbone of Dutch colonial revenues. Vast tracts of formerly productive land lay fallow, and rural populations were impoverished by decades of extractive policies and war. Key industries, such as rubber, sugar, and oil, were either severely damaged or abandoned, leaving Indonesia ill-equipped to generate the revenues necessary for reconstruction. Transport networks, integral to economic integration, were also fragmented and barely functional, compounding the difficulty of revitalizing the economy. The war for independence (1945–1949) against the Dutch further strained resources, as much-needed funds, labour, and materials were diverted to support the armed struggle.

The financial burden of funding military operations, combined with the disruption of trade and production, severely constrained the newly declared Republic of Indonesia's ability to establish economic stability in the immediate post-colonial period. Following the Proclamation of Independence in 1945, the republic was engaged in a four-year armed struggle against the Dutch military, which sought to reassert colonial control. The

[10] Ricklefs, M. C. (2008). A History of Modern Indonesia Since c.1200. 4th ed. Basingstoke: Palgrave Macmillan.

war effort drained scarce financial resources, as the newly formed government had to mobilize and supply guerrilla forces, procure weapons, and maintain logistical networks under extreme conditions. Unlike the Dutch, who received substantial financial and military support from the United States and the Marshall Plan, the Indonesian republic relied primarily on internal revenue extraction, war taxes, and the confiscation of Japanese military assets to sustain its resistance.[11] Trade and production were severely disrupted due to the physical destruction of economic infrastructure and the collapse of colonial-era trade networks. During the war, Dutch naval blockades cut off Indonesia's access to global markets, preventing the export of key commodities such as rubber, tin, and oil, which had historically generated foreign exchange for the Dutch East Indies. The blockade also created severe shortages of essential imports, including industrial machinery, medicine, and food supplies, worsening inflation and economic hardship. The impact was particularly pronounced in Java, where urban centres such as Jakarta and Surabaya experienced rising food prices and declining industrial output, leading to economic instability.[12]

The war also disrupted agricultural production, particularly in Java and Sumatra, where many rice-producing regions became battlegrounds. Thousands of farmers were displaced, irrigation systems were destroyed, and rural supply chains collapsed, leading to widespread food shortages and malnutrition. For example, in Java rural supply chains collapsed due to a number of reasons.[13] Firstly, the destruction of irrigation networks led to a reduction in rice yields. Secondly, the military conflict with the Dutch and their naval blockades prevented the transportation of farm produce to areas where there was a need. Finally, farmers fled the conflict zones leading to abandoned agricultural land. The republic attempted to address these crises through forced requisitioning of rice and other staple goods, but this often led to hoarding and underground

[11] Kahin, G.M. (1952). Nationalism and Revolution in Indonesia. Ithaca, NY: Cornell University Press.

[12] Lindblad, J.T. (2008). Bridges to New Business: The Economic Decolonization of Indonesia. Leiden: KITLV Press.

[13] Van der Eng, P. (2008). "Food Supply in Java during War and Decolonisation, 1940–1950." Australian Economic History Review, 48(1), 62–95.

activity, further exacerbating price volatility.[14] The Indonesian government also faced a monetary crisis. With limited tax revenues and no established financial institutions, the republic issued its own emergency currency (Oeang Republik Indonesia, or ORI) in 1946. However, the Dutch and other foreign actors refused to recognize the ORI, leading to hyperinflation and a lack of confidence in the new currency. The monetary instability forced many transactions to be conducted through barter trade or the use of the remaining Japanese occupation currency, further complicating economic recovery.[15] Additionally, industrial production suffered due to damage inflicted during both the Japanese occupation (1942–1945) and the subsequent war of independence. Factories and oil refineries, which had been key sources of employment and economic output under the Dutch, were either destroyed or nationalized under uncertain legal conditions. For example, the Royal Dutch Shell installations in Sumatra and Kalimantan were targeted by both retreating Dutch forces and nationalist fighters, resulting in years of lost production and a lack of investment in the oil sector post-independence.[16] By the time the Netherlands formally recognized Indonesian independence in December 1949, the republic's economy was in a state of near collapse. The prolonged war effort had left the government with crippling debt, a dysfunctional financial system, severe inflation, and a shattered industrial base. The new republic struggled to finance its war effort, relying on extraordinary taxes, forced levies, and the confiscation of Japanese military assets.[17] Unlike the Dutch, who received international financial support through the Marshall Plan, Indonesia had no access to foreign credit markets, forcing the government to print money to sustain military operations. By 1949, international negotiations at the Round Table Conference compelled Indonesia to assume a significant portion of the

[14] Booth, A. (1998). The Indonesian Economy in the Nineteenth and Twentieth Centuries: A History of Missed Opportunities. London: Macmillan.

[15] Lindblad, J.T. (2008). Bridges to New Business: The Economic Decolonization of Indonesia. Leiden: KITLV Press.

[16] Dick, H., Houben, V., Lindblad, J.T., & Wie, T.K. (2002). The Emergence of a National Economy: An Economic History of Indonesia, 1800–2000. Honolulu: University of Hawaii Press.

[17] Booth, A. (1998). The Indonesian Economy in the Nineteenth and Twentieth Centuries: A History of Missed Opportunities. London: Macmillan.

Dutch East Indies' colonial debt, estimated at over 4.3 billion guilders.[18] This placed the young republic in a precarious fiscal position, severely limiting its capacity to invest in economic reconstruction. With much of its revenue directed toward repaying inherited debts, Indonesia entered independence facing immediate financial instability that constrained its ability to rebuild infrastructure and industrial capacity. The war also shattered Indonesia's financial system. The pre-war economy had been dominated by Dutch-controlled financial institutions, with De Javasche Bank acting as the central bank. However, the Japanese occupation had dismantled much of this system, replacing Dutch banking structures with military-controlled financial operations.[19] Therefore, the Japanese occupation of Indonesia (1942–1945) marked a radical transformation of the financial system, as the pre-war Dutch-controlled banking infrastructure was dismantled and replaced with a militarized economic administration designed to serve Japan's war effort. Before the occupation, Indonesia's financial system was dominated by Dutch and European banks, with De Javasche Bank acting as the central bank, regulating currency issuance and controlling major financial transactions.[20] However, once Japan invaded Indonesia and expelled the Dutch colonial administration, the occupation authorities seized control of financial institutions, liquidated Dutch assets, and replaced private banking structures with a military-run economic system that prioritized Japan's wartime economic policies.[21] One of the first measures undertaken by the Japanese military authorities was the closure and seizure of Dutch banks. Dutch-owned institutions such as De Javasche Bank, Nederlandsch-Indische Handelsbank, and Escomptobank were immediately shut down, and their assets were frozen or transferred

[18] Lindblad, J.T. (2008). Bridges to New Business: The Economic Decolonization of Indonesia. Leiden: KITLV Press.

[19] Lindblad, J.T. (2015). Economic Globalization and Indonesian Economy since the Late Nineteenth Century. Singapore: ISEAS-Yusof Ishak Institute.

[20] Lindblad, J.T. (2008). Bridges to New Business: The Economic Decolonization of Indonesia. Leiden: KITLV Press.

[21] Dick, H., Houben, V., Lindblad, J.T., & Wie, T.K. (2002). The Emergence of a National Economy: An Economic History of Indonesia, 1800–2000. Honolulu: University of Hawaii Press.

to Japanese-controlled entities.[22] The Japanese military government liquidated European financial capital, nationalized major banks, and expelled Dutch bankers and financial administrators, effectively eliminating private banking services that had previously underpinned Indonesia's trade and commerce.[23] In their place, the Japanese set up a militarized economic administration, directly controlled by the Southern Development Bank (Nanpo Kaihatsu Ginko), a Tokyo-based financial institution responsible for overseeing the economic policies of Japan's occupied territories.[24]

The Southern Development Bank played a critical role in integrating Indonesia's financial system into Japan's Greater East Asia Co-Prosperity Sphere, effectively subordinating the Indonesian economy to the needs of the Japanese war machine. The bank took control of monetary policy, financial transactions, and credit allocation, ensuring that all economic activities served Japanese military interests. Instead of financing industrial or commercial enterprises, Japanese-controlled financial institutions focused on funding war production, procuring resources, and sustaining military logistics.[25] Local businesses and farmers were forced into Japan's war economy, with financial resources directed toward military supply chains rather than civilian economic development.[26]

A key feature of the military-controlled financial system was the introduction of military scrip currency to replace Dutch banknotes. The Japanese authorities banned the circulation of Dutch guilders and introduced the Japanese-issued rupiah, also known as "invasion money," which became the only legal tender in occupied Indonesia.[27] However, this new

[22] Lindblad, J.T. (2015). Economic Globalization and Indonesian Economy since the Late Nineteenth Century. Singapore: ISEAS-Yusof Ishak Institute.

[23] Booth, A. (1998). The Indonesian Economy in the Nineteenth and Twentieth Centuries: A History of Missed Opportunities. London: Macmillan.

[24] Kahin, G.M. (1952). Nationalism and Revolution in Indonesia. Ithaca, NY: Cornell University Press.

[25] Ricklefs, M.C. (2008). A History of Modern Indonesia Since c. 1200. 4th ed. Basingstoke: Palgrave Macmillan.

[26] Elson, R.E. (1997). The End of the Peasantry in SoutheastAsia: A Social and Economic History of Peasant Livelihood, 1800–1990s. Basingstoke: Macmillan.

[27] Dick, H., Houben, V., Lindblad, J.T., & Wie, T.K. (2002). The Emergence of a National Economy: An Economic History of Indonesia, 1800–2000. Honolulu: University of Hawaii Press.

currency was unbacked by any financial reserves, meaning it was essentially fiat money printed at will by the military authorities. The occupation government engaged in excessive currency issuance to finance its military operations, leading to severe inflation and the rapid depreciation of purchasing power. The Japanese also centralized financial operations under military command, ensuring that all banking activities were subject to direct control by occupation forces. The economy was restructured into a command system, where the military dictated which industries received financial support. Major economic sectors, particularly plantation agriculture, mining, and transportation, were converted into Japanese-run enterprises, with profits directed toward the war effort.[28] Financial institutions under military oversight were prohibited from issuing credit to businesses that did not directly contribute to Japan's wartime production, effectively crippling private enterprise and dismantling the capitalist banking structures that had existed under Dutch rule.[29] As the war progressed and Japanese military needs grew, financial repression intensified, with forced contributions and direct economic extraction becoming more severe. The occupation government forced Indonesians to purchase Japanese war bonds, even though these bonds had no long-term financial security.[30] Local populations were subjected to forced labour policies, with wages paid in rapidly depreciating military currency, further exacerbating economic instability.[31] The Japanese also confiscated gold, silver, and other valuables from Indonesian citizens to supplement their wartime financial reserves, demonstrating the extent to which military authorities controlled financial transactions. By the time of Japan's surrender in August 1945, Indonesia's financial system was in a state of collapse. The excessive printing of Japanese military currency had led to hyperinflation, with prices skyrocketing due to the oversupply of paper money

[28] Lindblad, J.T. (2008). Bridges to New Business: The Economic Decolonization of Indonesia. Leiden: KITLV Press.

[29] Booth, A. (1998). The Indonesian Economy in the Nineteenth and Twentieth Centuries: A History of Missed Opportunities. London: Macmillan.

[30] Ricklefs, M.C. (2008). A History of Modern Indonesia Since c. 1200. 4th ed. Basingstoke: Palgrave Macmillan.

[31] Elson, R.E. (1997). The End of the Peasantry in SoutheastAsia: A Social and Economic History of Peasant Livelihood, 1800–1990s. Basingstoke: Macmillan.

and the severe scarcity of goods.[32] The pre-war financial infrastructure had been completely dismantled, and with the liquidation of Dutch banking institutions, there was no functioning financial system to facilitate post-war economic recovery. This financial vacuum created immediate challenges for the newly declared Republic of Indonesia, which struggled to establish a stable monetary system while still contending with Dutch attempts to reimpose colonial financial institutions in the early years of independence.[33]

After the Japanese surrender, both the Dutch and the Indonesian republic sought to assert control over financial institutions, leading to monetary disarray. The Indonesian government introduced its own currency, the Oeang Republik Indonesia (ORI), in 1946, but it faced widespread rejection in international trade and circulation was largely restricted to republican-held areas.[34] The Dutch continued to issue their own currency, leading to a chaotic dual-currency economy where ORI, Dutch-issued money, and remnants of Japanese occupation currency coexisted without regulation.[35] The lack of a unified banking system, coupled with the absence of an independent central monetary authority, left Indonesia unable to implement effective fiscal policies, worsening the financial instability. The continued Dutch control over De Javasche Bank meant that monetary policy remained largely outside the republic's control until its eventual nationalization in 1951.[36] Hyperinflation further deepened the economic crisis, driven by excessive money printing, war-related supply shortages, and collapsing production. The Japanese occupation had already triggered inflation by flooding the economy with

[32] Dick, H., Houben, V., Lindblad, J.T., & Wie, T.K. (2002). The Emergence of a National Economy: An Economic History of Indonesia, 1800–2000. Honolulu: University of Hawaii Press.

[33] Lindblad, J.T. (2008). Bridges to New Business: The Economic Decolonization of Indonesia. Leiden: KITLV Press.

[34] Kahin, G.M. (1952). Nationalism and Revolution in Indonesia. Ithaca, NY: Cornell University Press.

[35] Dick, H., Houben, V., Lindblad, J.T., & Wie, T.K. (2002). The Emergence of a National Economy: An Economic History of Indonesia, 1800–2000. Honolulu: University of Hawaii Press.

[36] Ricklefs, M.C. (2008). A History of Modern Indonesia Since c. 1200. 4th ed. Basingstoke: Palgrave Macmillan.

military-issued currency, and after independence, the republican government was forced to continue printing ORI to finance the war effort.[37] This rapid expansion of the money supply, combined with disruptions to trade and production, eroded the purchasing power of the currency. Essential goods, particularly rice and textiles, became scarce, leading to dramatic price increases that disproportionately affected urban populations.[38] The Dutch naval blockade further exacerbated the situation by cutting off Indonesia's access to international markets, making it difficult to import necessities and worsening the inflationary spiral.[39] Efforts to impose price controls proved largely ineffective, as black-market activities flourished in response to supply shortages, further destabilizing the economy.[40] The lack of monetary stability forced many transactions to shift toward barter trade or reliance on foreign currencies, undermining confidence in the ORI and delaying efforts to establish a functional post-war economy. By the time formal independence was recognized in 1949, Indonesia's economic foundations were in ruins. The government faced an overwhelming debt burden, a fragmented and unregulated financial system, and an inflation crisis that stifled growth and investment. The economic devastation shaped Indonesia's early post-independence policies, pushing the state toward interventionist economic strategies, including the nationalization of banks and key industries.[41] The long-term consequences of this crisis extended well beyond the immediate post-war period, influencing economic policy decisions in the 1950s and laying the groundwork for later economic instability under Sukarno's Guided Democracy. Indeed, upon gaining independence in 1949, Indonesia inherited a devastated economic system with weak state

[37] Booth, A. (1998). The Indonesian Economy in the Nineteenth and Twentieth Centuries: A History of Missed Opportunities. London: Macmillan.

[38] Elson, R.E. (1997). The End of the Peasantry in SoutheastAsia: A Social and Economic History of Peasant Livelihood, 1800–1990s. Basingstoke: Macmillan.

[39] Lindblad, J.T. (2008). Bridges to New Business: The Economic Decolonization of Indonesia. Leiden: KITLV Press.

[40] Dick, H., Houben, V., Lindblad, J.T., & Wie, T.K. (2002). The Emergence of a National Economy: An Economic History of Indonesia, 1800–2000. Honolulu: University of Hawaii Press.

[41] Ricklefs, M.C. (2008). A History of Modern Indonesia Since c. 1200. 4th ed. Basingstoke: Palgrave Macmillan.

capacity and a lack of effective financial institutions.[42] The economic vacuum left by the dismantling of Dutch banking structures and the severe monetary instability caused by the over issuance of Japanese military currency made it difficult for the new government to restore confidence in the financial system. The continued existence of multiple competing currencies (Dutch-issued money, the Japanese occupation rupiah, and the Oeang Republik Indonesia, or ORI) made it challenging to stabilize the monetary system.[43] Sukarno's government, struggling to consolidate control, resorted to expansionary fiscal policies, including excessive money printing to finance development projects, worsening inflationary pressures. The economic instability caused by the war also led to an interventionist economic model, as nationalist leaders, including Sukarno, were sceptical of foreign capitalist influences. In the early 1950s, the government nationalized Dutch-owned assets, particularly in the plantation, oil, and banking sectors, to assert economic independence.[44] However, the lack of skilled Indonesian managers and bureaucratic inefficiencies led to state mismanagement of key industries, reducing productivity and exacerbating fiscal deficits.[45] These policies foreshadowed the economic instability that defined Guided Democracy, where state control over the economy intensified, but without effective planning mechanisms to ensure economic stability. One of the most critical economic challenges that carried over into the Guided Democracy period (1959–1965) was chronic inflation. By the late 1950s, the economic turmoil of the independence era had not been resolved, and inflation surged due to unchecked government spending, poor revenue collection, and an over-reliance on deficit financing.[46] The government printed money excessively to finance Sukarno's ambitious state-led development

[42] Lindblad, J.T. (2008). Bridges to New Business: The Economic Decolonization of Indonesia. Leiden: KITLV Press.

[43] Booth, A. (1998). The Indonesian Economy in the Nineteenth and Twentieth Centuries: A History of Missed Opportunities. London: Macmillan.

[44] Ricklefs, M.C. (2008). A History of Modern Indonesia Since c. 1200. 4th ed. Basingstoke: Palgrave Macmillan.

[45] Dick, H., Houben, V., Lindblad, J.T., & Wie, T.K. (2002). The Emergence of a National Economy: An Economic History of Indonesia, 1800–2000. Honolulu: University of Hawaii Press.

[46] Lindblad, J.T. (2015). Economic Globalization and Indonesian Economy since the Late Nineteenth Century. Singapore: ISEAS-Yusof Ishak Institute.

projects, such as large-scale infrastructure programs and industrialization initiatives. However, these projects were often politically motivated rather than economically viable, leading to inefficient resource allocation and worsening budget deficits. Inflation rates skyrocketed to over 600% by 1965, eroding real wages and leading to widespread economic hardship.[47] The weak institutional foundations inherited from the 1940s also contributed to corruption, rent-seeking behaviour, and economic inefficiencies under Guided Democracy. The absence of a strong, independent central bank meant that monetary policy was dictated by political needs rather than economic stability. The government frequently intervened in banking operations, forcing credit expansion to fund politically driven projects, further fuelling inflation and economic distortions.[48] The lack of a coherent industrial policy, combined with import restrictions and inefficient state enterprises, contributed to economic stagnation and rising black-market activity.[49] Another consequence of the post-independence economic crisis was the growing reliance on bartering trade agreements and bilateral economic deals with communist and non-aligned countries during the Cold War period. As Indonesia's foreign exchange reserves dwindled, the government turned to Soviet and Chinese aid to finance state-led industrialization.[50] These economic partnerships prioritized ideological alignment over sustainable economic policies, leading to distorted trade relations and further economic inefficiencies. The term "distorted trade relations" refers to the fact that Indonesia's trade agreements with the Soviet Union and China were not structured around comparative advantage or market-driven trade patterns but were instead dictated by Cold War geopolitical interests.[51] Rather than engaging in mutually beneficial free trade, Indonesia entered into barter-based trade

[47] Booth, A. (1998). The Indonesian Economy in the Nineteenth and Twentieth Centuries: A History of Missed Opportunities. London: Macmillan.

[48] Ricklefs, M.C. (2008). A History of Modern Indonesia Since c. 1200. 4th ed. Basingstoke: Palgrave Macmillan.

[49] Dick, H., Houben, V., Lindblad, J.T., & Wie, T.K. (2002). The Emergence of a National Economy: An Economic History of Indonesia, 1800–2000. Honolulu: University of Hawaii Press.

[50] Lindblad, J.T. (2008). Bridges to New Business: The Economic Decolonization of Indonesia. Leiden: KITLV Press.

[51] Lindblad, J.T. (2008). Bridges to New Business: The Economic Decolonization of Indonesia. Leiden: KITLV Press.

deals that prioritized political alliances over economic efficiency.[52] For example, Indonesia agreed to export raw materials, such as rubber and petroleum, to the Soviet Union and China at artificially low prices, often receiving military equipment, industrial machinery, and infrastructure projects in return.[53] These agreements favoured political loyalty over market dynamics, meaning that Indonesia often received goods and machinery unsuited to its actual economic needs, leading to waste and inefficiency.[54] A key example of this distorted trade was the Soviet-financed "Projects of Guided Democracy," a series of large-scale industrial and infrastructure projects promoted by Sukarno to showcase national development. Many of these projects, such as the Hotel Indonesia, the Senayan sports complex, and the Monas (National Monument), were prestige-driven rather than economically productive.[55] These projects absorbed significant financial resources but did not generate the economic output needed to sustain Indonesia's fragile economy. Furthermore, Soviet and Chinese machinery and industrial equipment were often technically incompatible with Indonesian infrastructure and workforce skills, leading to additional inefficiencies as the government struggled to maintain and utilize these investments effectively.[56] The phrase "further economic inefficiencies" refers to the misallocation of resources, fiscal mismanagement, and inflationary pressures that resulted from these trade policies. Because Indonesia was exporting primary commodities at below-market prices while importing non-productive goods and military supplies, the country suffered from a worsening balance-of-payments crisis.[57] The government printed more money to cover its expenses,

[52] Booth, A. (1998). The Indonesian Economy in the Nineteenth and Twentieth Centuries: A History of Missed Opportunities. London: Macmillan.

[53] Ricklefs, M.C. (2008). A History of Modern Indonesia Since c. 1200. 4th ed. Basingstoke: Palgrave Macmillan.

[54] Dick, H., Houben, V., Lindblad, J.T., & Wie, T.K. (2002). The Emergence of a National Economy: An Economic History of Indonesia, 1800–2000. Honolulu: University of Hawaii Press.

[55] Lindblad, J.T. (2015). Economic Globalization and Indonesian Economy since the Late Nineteenth Century. Singapore: ISEAS-Yusof Ishak Institute.

[56] Booth, A. (1998). The Indonesian Economy in the Nineteenth and Twentieth Centuries: A History of Missed Opportunities. London: Macmillan.

[57] Dick, H., Houben, V., Lindblad, J.T., & Wie, T.K. (2002). The Emergence of a National Economy: An Economic History of Indonesia, 1800–2000. Honolulu: University of Hawaii Press.

leading to hyperinflation that exceeded 600% by 1965.[58] This monetary instability further reduced investment in productive industries and drove more economic activity into the black market, where goods were often traded at significantly higher prices than official government rates.[59] Additionally, the reliance on barter trade agreements with China and the Soviet Union made it difficult for Indonesia to engage in international trade with Western and non-aligned nations. Many of Indonesia's traditional trading partners, such as the United States, Britain, and the Netherlands, reduced their economic engagement with Indonesia due to its increasingly socialist-aligned economic policies.[60] This narrowed Indonesia's trade network and limited its ability to diversify exports, making the economy more vulnerable to commodity price fluctuations and external shocks.[61] By the mid-1960s, the economic inefficiencies caused by these trade distortions had reached a breaking point. The government's failure to maintain fiscal discipline, combined with politically motivated industrial projects and deteriorating trade balances, contributed to severe economic stagnation. The lack of hard currency reserves, coupled with an unmanageable foreign debt burden, left Indonesia in a state of economic collapse by 1965, setting the stage for the fall of Sukarno and the rise of Suharto's New Order regime.[62] By the mid-1960s, Indonesia's economic instability under Guided Democracy had reached a breaking point, characterized by hyperinflation, falling investment, and growing external debts. The economic turmoil contributed to widespread political unrest, culminating in Sukarno's eventual downfall in 1965. The policies implemented in response to the economic crisis of the 1940s had laid the groundwork for systemic weaknesses, which were exacerbated by Sukarno's interventionist and inflationary economic policies. The transition to Suharto's

[58] Ricklefs, M.C. (2008). A History of Modern Indonesia Since c. 1200. 4th ed. Basingstoke: Palgrave Macmillan.

[59] Lindblad, J.T. (2008). Bridges to New Business: The Economic Decolonization of Indonesia. Leiden: KITLV Press.

[60] Booth, A. (1998). The Indonesian Economy in the Nineteenth and Twentieth Centuries: A History of Missed Opportunities. London: Macmillan.

[61] Lindblad, J.T. (2015). Economic Globalization and Indonesian Economy since the Late Nineteenth Century. Singapore: ISEAS-Yusof Ishak Institute.

[62] Ricklefs, M.C. (2008). A History of Modern Indonesia Since c. 1200. 4th ed. Basingstoke: Palgrave Macmillan.

New Order regime (1966–1998) marked a shift toward economic liberalization, stabilization policies, and foreign investment, as a corrective response to the economic failures of Guided Democracy.[63]

The war had not only secured political independence but also forced Indonesia into an era of economic uncertainty that would take decades to overcome. These challenges shaped Indonesia's early post-colonial economic policies, leading to state intervention in key industries and a long-term dependence on foreign aid and international loans to finance reconstruction efforts.[64] One of the most significant economic strains was the diversion of government funds and revenue toward military expenditures. The nascent Indonesian government, under President Sukarno, had extremely limited financial resources, as much of the country's formal economy and banking system had been under Dutch control before the occupation. Following the Japanese surrender in 1945, the Dutch sought to reclaim Indonesia, leading to a protracted conflict that forced the new republic to allocate whatever funds it could muster to arm and supply nationalist forces. This left little for rebuilding infrastructure, stabilizing food supplies, or developing public services. Additionally, taxation was weak, as the Indonesian government lacked an effective administrative system to collect revenue, further deepening fiscal constraints.[65] The war also disrupted agriculture and food production, exacerbating the food shortages that had already been severe due to the Japanese occupation. Many farmers, particularly in Java and Sumatra, abandoned their fields either to join guerrilla forces or because conflict made agricultural work too dangerous. Key rice-growing regions were affected by military operations, while transportation networks critical for moving food supplies were damaged or inaccessible. The destruction of irrigation systems and storage facilities further reduced yields, leading to periodic food crises and widespread malnutrition.[66] Labour shortages and economic dislocation compounded the crisis. The armed struggle required the mobilization

[63] Ricklefs, M.C. (2008). A History of Modern Indonesia Since c. 1200. 4th ed. Basingstoke: Palgrave Macmillan.

[64] Ricklefs, M.C. (2008). A History of Modern Indonesia Since c. 1200. 4th ed. Basingstoke: Palgrave Macmillan.

[65] Booth, A. (1998). The Indonesian Economy in the Nineteenth and Twentieth Centuries: A History of Missed Opportunities. London: Macmillan.

[66] Ricklefs, M.C. (2008). A History of Modern Indonesia Since c. 1200. 4th ed. Basingstoke: Palgrave Macmillan.

of large sections of the male workforce, diverting skilled and unskilled labour from productive sectors like industry, mining, and transportation into military service. The lack of labourers in key industries caused production levels to drop sharply. In urban areas, economic activity was further disrupted as businesses closed or operated at reduced capacity due to insecurity and logistical difficulties. As the war intensified, many labourers left their jobs to join the nationalist forces, either as soldiers or in support roles such as logistics and supply. This mass mobilization reduced the workforce available for key industries, leading to a sharp decline in production across multiple sectors, including agriculture, mining, and manufacturing.[67]

The plantation sector, historically a cornerstone of the colonial economy, was among the hardest hit. Under Dutch rule, Indonesia had been a major global supplier of commodities such as rubber, coffee, and sugar. However, during the independence war, many plantations were abandoned, occupied by nationalist forces, or destroyed in the fighting. The exodus of workers, combined with supply chain disruptions, caused output to plummet. The rubber industry, which had been one of the Dutch East Indies' primary exports, suffered particularly severe declines. By 1948, production levels had fallen to a fraction of their pre-war output, affecting Indonesia's ability to generate much-needed foreign exchange.[68] In the oil sector, another crucial pillar of Indonesia's economy, the war resulted in extensive damage to infrastructure. Oil refineries in Sumatra and Kalimantan, which had been critical for Dutch economic interests, became strategic targets for both Indonesian nationalists and Dutch forces. The destruction of oil storage facilities and transport networks further crippled production. This decline had broader economic repercussions, as oil revenues had historically financed public infrastructure and government operations. Without stable oil production, the newly

[67] Reid, A. (1974). The Indonesian National Revolution 1945–1950. Hawthorn, Australia: Longman.

[68] Booth, A. (1998). The Indonesian Economy in the Nineteenth and Twentieth Centuries: A History of Missed Opportunities. London: Macmillan.

established republican government struggled to fund essential services, deepening the economic crisis.[69]

Urban areas faced additional economic challenges as commerce and industry ground to a halt. In major cities such as Jakarta, Surabaya, and Bandung, businesses struggled to remain open amid the conflict. The war created widespread insecurity, as Dutch military operations and nationalist guerrilla tactics disrupted trade routes, making the transportation of goods and raw materials difficult. Additionally, many urban businesses suffered from a lack of investment and credit, as banking institutions were either shut down or operated with extreme restrictions. The financial uncertainty, combined with hyperinflation, further discouraged business activity.[70] Logistical challenges also played a critical role in undermining urban economies. Indonesia's transportation infrastructure, already weakened by the destruction caused during the Japanese occupation, deteriorated further during the war. Railways and bridges were frequently sabotaged by nationalist forces seeking to hinder Dutch military movements. Meanwhile, Dutch forces targeted key transport hubs to weaken the independence movement. As a result, the distribution of goods became highly inefficient, leading to shortages of essential supplies such as rice, textiles, and fuel in urban centres. This not only increased living costs but also forced many businesses to scale down or cease operations altogether.[71]

The combination of labour shortages, industrial collapse, and logistical breakdowns left the Indonesian economy in a state of severe disarray by the time formal independence was achieved in 1949. The prolonged conflict not only delayed economic recovery but also entrenched regional disparities, as some areas were able to sustain limited economic activity while others were entirely devastated. The post-war government faced enormous challenges in rebuilding industries, restoring infrastructure, and reintegrating the displaced workforce into productive sectors. This economic dislocation contributed to the difficulties of state-building in

[69] Lindblad, J.T. (2008). Bridges to New Business: The Economic Decolonization of Indonesia. Leiden: KITLV Press.

[70] Dick, H., Houben, V., Lindblad, J.T., & Wie, T.K. (2002). The Emergence of a National Economy: An Economic History of Indonesia, 1800–2000. Honolulu: University of Hawaii Press.

[71] Kahin, G.M. (1952). Nationalism and Revolution in Indonesia. Ithaca, NY: Cornell University Press.

the early years of independence, shaping Indonesia's economic trajectory for decades to come.[72] The conflict also led to large-scale population displacement, as civilians fled areas of heavy fighting, further undermining economic productivity and stability.[73] Furthermore, the destruction of infrastructure had lasting economic consequences. Railways, bridges, and ports were frequent targets of sabotage by nationalist forces attempting to disrupt Dutch supply lines. In retaliation, Dutch forces often destroyed key economic assets to weaken Indonesian resistance. By the end of the war in 1949, much of Indonesia's transportation and communication networks were either heavily damaged or non-functional, further impeding economic recovery in the early years of independence. The destruction of oil installations, particularly in Sumatra, deprived the new republic of a vital revenue source, as Indonesia's oil industry had historically been a major contributor to the economy.[74] Trade and commerce were also deeply affected, as the war disrupted domestic and international trade networks. The Dutch navy-imposed blockades on key ports, preventing the export of essential commodities such as rubber, coffee, and sugar—historically major sources of revenue. The inability to engage in international trade deprived Indonesia of foreign exchange, which was crucial for purchasing necessary imports such as machinery, industrial goods, and medicines. This economic isolation further weakened the republic's ability to sustain its population and rebuild after the war.[75] By the time the Netherlands officially recognized Indonesia's independence in 1949, the country faced an economy in ruins. The war had not only exhausted financial and material resources but had also entrenched economic fragmentation, as different regions experienced varying levels of devastation and control. The long-term effects of this wartime economic strain would shape Indonesia's early economic policies, as the government struggled to balance military spending, industrialization, and social welfare in the post-independence era. These conditions led to widespread

[72] Lindblad, J.T. (2008). Bridges to New Business: The Economic Decolonization of Indonesia. Leiden: KITLV Press.

[73] Kahin, G.M. (1952). Nationalism and Revolution in Indonesia. Ithaca, NY: Cornell University Press.

[74] Furnivall, J.S. (1948). Colonial Policy and Practice: A Comparative Study of Burma and NetherlandsIndia. Cambridge: Cambridge University Press.

[75] Elson, R.E. (1997). The End of the Peasantry in SoutheastAsia: A Social and Economic History of Peasant Livelihood, 1800–1990s. Basingstoke: Macmillan.

shortages of food, fuel, and essential goods, exacerbating the socio-economic hardships faced by the population and creating significant obstacles for the nascent government.[76]

Politically, the post-independence period was characterized by efforts to establish a cohesive and effective government amid immense challenges. The republic faced regional fragmentation, as diverse ethnic and cultural groups navigated the shift from colonial rule to national unity. Administrative capacities were limited, with many civil servants lacking experience in governance or technical expertise. Furthermore, the Dutch, backed by Western powers, mounted sustained military and diplomatic campaigns to reassert control over Indonesia, leading to protracted conflicts such as the Indonesian National Revolution. These confrontations forced the government to focus on military resistance, delaying critical economic and social reforms. At the same time, the economic policies pursued by the republic reflected a mix of pragmatism and idealism, as leaders sought to assert economic sovereignty while addressing the immediate crises of poverty and famine. Nationalization of key industries and plantations symbolized a decisive break from colonial domination but often fell short in practice due to inadequate resources and governance frameworks.[77]

The social fabric of post-independence Indonesia was deeply shaped by the collective mobilization and sacrifices of the nationalist movement. Experiences of forced labour, famine, and economic hardship under both Dutch and Japanese rule had fostered a sense of shared identity and purpose among Indonesians. This unity became a critical source of resilience during the early years of independence, as communities rallied together to support the republic's survival. However, this solidarity was evaluated by post-war realities. Political factionalism, regional disparities, and competing visions for Indonesia's future created tensions that complicated efforts to create an inclusive and equitable framework for governance and development. The armed struggle against the Dutch further diverted resources from reconstruction, prolonging economic instability

[76] Elson, R. E. (2009). The Idea of Indonesia: A History. Cambridge: Cambridge University Press.

[77] Bosma, U. (2013). The Sugar Plantation in Indiaand Indonesia: Industrial Production, 1770–2010. Cambridge: Cambridge University Press.

and social dislocation.[78] The international context also presented significant challenges to Indonesia's recovery. Western powers, particularly the Netherlands, sought to regain control of Indonesia, isolating the republic diplomatically and limiting access to foreign aid. This lack of international recognition and support hampered the government's ability to stabilize the economy and rebuild infrastructure. Instead, Indonesia relied heavily on grassroots support, local ingenuity, and the solidarity forged during the independence struggle to sustain itself. Despite these limitations, the resilience of the Indonesian people and the determination of its leaders laid the groundwork for eventual sovereignty and state-building. These efforts also highlighted the enduring legacy of colonial exploitation, as the republic struggled to overcome the systemic inequalities and dependencies entrenched by centuries of foreign domination.[79]

The proclamation of independence and its immediate aftermath revealed both the immense challenges and the extraordinary resilience that defined Indonesia's transition to nationhood. The republic's economic and political struggles underscored the deep scars left by colonial and wartime exploitation, but they also demonstrated the power of collective action and nationalist resolve. The period laid the foundation for Indonesia's eventual consolidation as a sovereign state, while also highlighting the complexities of achieving true economic independence and social cohesion in the face of entrenched structural inequalities.

Economic Challenges of the Revolutionary Government

The revolutionary government of Indonesia, established after the proclamation of independence on August 17, 1945, faced a complex array of economic challenges as it sought to build a sovereign state amidst a backdrop of war, political instability, and colonial economic legacies. The economy inherited by the fledgling republic was one ravaged by decades of Dutch exploitation and the devastation of the Japanese occupation. Agricultural productivity was in decline, industries were crippled, and infrastructure was severely damaged. Hyperinflation plagued the

[78] Cribb, R. (1994). Gangsters and Revolutionaries: The Jakarta People's Militia and the Indonesian Revolution, 1945–1949. Honolulu: University of Hawai'i Press.

[79] Elson, R. E. (2009). The Idea of Indonesia: A History. Cambridge: Cambridge University Press.

economy as Japanese-issued currency flooded the market, while food shortages and the collapse of trade networks exacerbated widespread poverty and famine.,[80,81] These challenges underscored the monumental task of creating an economic framework capable of supporting the revolutionary struggle while laying the groundwork for post-war recovery. One of the revolutionary government's most pressing challenges was the establishment of economic sovereignty. To break free from colonial economic structures, the government embarked on nationalization efforts, targeting Dutch-owned enterprises and assets. This move symbolized Indonesia's rejection of colonial dominance and its commitment to control its resources. However, nationalization was fraught with difficulties, as the government lacked the administrative and technical expertise to manage these enterprises effectively. Additionally, resistance from Dutch businesses and international stakeholders further complicated these efforts.[82] The introduction of a national currency, the Oeang Republik Indonesia (ORI), in 1946 was another critical step toward economic independence. While it aimed to stabilize the economy and assert national legitimacy, the ORI faced challenges from competing currencies, including Japanese wartime notes and Dutch-issued guldens, leading to confusion and economic instability.[83]

The war for independence (1945–1949) imposed immense financial and logistical pressures on the revolutionary government. Resources were diverted to support the armed struggle, leaving little for development or social welfare. The government relied heavily on grassroots mobilization and local ingenuity to sustain the economy during this period. Villages and communities were encouraged to adopt self-sufficiency, producing food and essential goods to support the military and civilian population. This spirit of gotong royong (mutual cooperation) became a hallmark of the independence movement, reflecting the resilience of Indonesian

[80] Elson, R. E. (2009). The Idea of Indonesia: A History. Cambridge: Cambridge University Press.

[81] Ricklefs, M. C. (2008). A History of Modern Indonesia Since c.1200. 4th ed. Basingstoke: Palgrave Macmillan.

[82] Feith, H. (1962). The Decline of Constitutional Democracy in Indonesia. Ithaca: Cornell University Press.

[83] Reid, A. (1974). The Indonesian National Revolution, 1945–1950. Hawthorn: Longman Australia.

society in the face of adversity.[84] However, the burden of war also exposed the limitations of this approach, as many regions faced shortages of basic necessities, exacerbating socio-economic inequalities and fuelling internal discontent. International isolation further compounded Indonesia's economic challenges. The Netherlands, supported by Western powers, sought to regain control of the archipelago, using military force and diplomatic pressure to undermine the revolutionary government. Indonesia's limited access to foreign aid and resources forced the government to rely on unconventional methods to fund its operations. This included leveraging informal trade networks, negotiating with local elites, and tapping into the illegal market. While these strategies sustained the independence struggle, they also entrenched informal economic practices that would persist into the post-colonial era.[85] The revolutionary government's efforts to negotiate foreign recognition and aid, including engaging the United Nations and other international bodies, highlighted the intertwined nature of economic survival and political legitimacy. Despite these challenges, the economic strategies of the revolutionary government laid the foundations for Indonesia's post-colonial development. The emphasis on nationalization and self-sufficiency reflected a broader vision of economic sovereignty that would shape the policies of subsequent governments. The economic strategies implemented by Indonesia's revolutionary government during the struggle for independence between 1945 and 1950, though constrained by war and limited resources, played a crucial role in shaping the trajectory of post-colonial development. These strategies were informed by the nationalist movement's long-standing critique of the exploitative colonial economy, which had prioritized the extraction of resources for foreign benefit while neglecting the welfare of the Indonesian population. The revolutionary government, therefore, sought to redefine the nation's economic structure to achieve sovereignty and self-sufficiency, which would become key pillars of Indonesia's post-colonial policies.[86] Nationalization was a principal component of this strategy, reflecting

[84] Anderson, B. R. O. G. (1972). Java in a Time of Revolution: Occupation and Resistance, 1944–1946. Ithaca: Cornell University Press.

[85] Kahin, G. M. (1952). Nationalism and Revolution in Indonesia. Ithaca: Cornell University Press.

[86] Elson, R. E. (2009). The Idea of Indonesia: A History. Cambridge: Cambridge University Press.

the government's determination to break free from colonial dominance. Dutch-owned enterprises, particularly in key sectors such as plantations, manufacturing, and banking, were targeted for nationalization. This move was both symbolic and pragmatic, as it asserted the republic's control over its economy while attempting to redirect resources to support the independence struggle. Although the nationalization efforts were fraught with challenges—including a lack of technical expertise, resistance from Dutch companies, and limited administrative capacity—they signalled a decisive break from the colonial model. The principle of state control over critical industries became a cornerstone of economic policy in the post-colonial period, influencing subsequent governments' approaches to industrialization and resource management.[87] The emphasis on self-sufficiency, or swadeshi in nationalist discourse, was equally significant. Faced with international isolation and a lack of external support, the revolutionary government turned to grassroots initiatives to sustain the economy. Local communities were encouraged to produce food, clothing, and other essentials, fostering a spirit of resilience and cooperation. This approach not only supported the immediate needs of the revolutionary struggle but also planted the seeds for future policies that sought to reduce dependency on foreign imports and promote domestic production. The idea of self-sufficiency resonated deeply within the nationalist ideology and would later influence policies such as import substitution industrialization and agricultural reform during the Sukarno and Suharto eras.[88] Rooted in the rejection of exploitative colonial systems that prioritized exports for foreign benefit, self-sufficiency represented a broader vision of economic sovereignty and resilience. This ideology resonated powerfully with both political leaders and the general population, becoming a guiding principle for key economic strategies in the Sukarno and Suharto eras. Under Sukarno's leadership in the 1950s and 1960s, self-sufficiency took the form of import substitution industrialization (ISI), which aimed to reduce Indonesia's dependency on foreign imports by developing domestic industries. The strategy reflected a desire to break free from the colonial economic structure, which had left Indonesia reliant on exporting raw materials while importing finished goods. Policies such as protective

[87] Feith, H. (1962). The Decline of Constitutional Democracy in Indonesia. Ithaca: Cornell University Press.

[88] Ricklefs, M. C. (2008). A History of Modern Indonesia Since c.1200. 4th ed. Basingstoke: Palgrave Macmillan.

tariffs, subsidies for local industries, and state-led industrial development sought to nurture domestic production capabilities, particularly in sectors like textiles, cement, and consumer goods. Sukarno's Guided Democracy emphasized economic independence as a cornerstone of national identity, with self-sufficiency presented as a means of asserting Indonesia's autonomy on the global stage. However, the ISI strategy faced significant challenges, including inefficiencies in state-run enterprises, limited technical expertise, and a lack of capital, which hindered its long-term sustainability.[89]

During Suharto's New Order regime (1966–1998), the commitment to self-sufficiency persisted but was adapted to align with the regime's developmentalist agenda. Agricultural reform became a central focus, particularly the drive for self-sufficiency in rice production, a staple crop and a symbol of national security. The government implemented extensive programs to modernize agriculture, including the introduction of high-yield varieties, subsidies for fertilizers and pesticides, and investments in irrigation infrastructure. These efforts culminated in Indonesia achieving self-sufficiency in rice by the mid-1980s, an accomplishment celebrated as a major milestone in the nation's development. However, this success came with environmental and social costs, such as soil degradation from intensive farming practices and the marginalization of small-scale farmers unable to compete with larger, more mechanized operations.[90] Beyond agriculture, Suharto's economic policies sought to balance self-sufficiency with engagement in global markets. While the regime promoted domestic industries, it also embraced foreign investment in key sectors like oil and gas, recognizing the limitations of isolationist strategies. The "limitations of isolationist strategies" in Indonesia's economic policy under Suharto's New Order regime highlight the practical constraints and inefficiencies of pursuing economic self-reliance without integrating into the global economy. While the nationalist emphasis on self-sufficiency sought to reduce dependency on foreign powers, isolationist strategies often struggled to address the complexities of a modern, interconnected global

[89] Elson, R. E. (2009). The Idea of Indonesia: A History. Cambridge: Cambridge University Press.

[90] Ricklefs, M. C. (2008). A History of Modern Indonesia Since c.1200. 4th ed. Basingstoke: Palgrave Macmillan.

economy. One major limitation was the lack of access to capital and technology, which were essential for industrialization and infrastructure development. Domestic industries, particularly in their initial stages, lacked the financial resources and technical expertise needed to expand and modernize. Without foreign investment, many sectors faced stagnation, as local capabilities could not meet the demands of large-scale development.[91] Additionally, the domestic market, though sizeable, was insufficient to sustain industrial growth. Many industries required economies of scale to become profitable, which necessitated access to international markets. Isolationist strategies constrained Indonesia's ability to engage in export-led growth, limiting the country's potential to earn foreign exchange and integrate its industries into global supply chains. Compounding these issues were inefficiencies in state-led enterprises, which were often the focus of isolationist policies. These enterprises, shielded from foreign competition, frequently suffered from mismanagement, corruption, and a lack of innovation, becoming a drain on public resources rather than a driver of economic progress.[92] Isolationist strategies also left Indonesia dependent on imports for critical goods, such as machinery, technology, and specialized raw materials. Efforts to promote domestic production often fell short of meeting these needs, leading to trade imbalances and vulnerabilities in key sectors. Moreover, the rise of economic globalization during the late twentieth century rendered isolationist approaches increasingly untenable. Countries that embraced international trade and investment were better positioned to access technological advancements, attract foreign direct investment, and participate in global economic growth. Indonesia's attempts to remain economically insular risked leaving the country marginalized in a rapidly integrating world economy.[93] Recognizing these limitations, Suharto's regime adopted a more pragmatic approach, selectively opening key sectors such as oil, gas, and mining to foreign investment. This shift allowed Indonesia to benefit from external capital and expertise while maintaining state control over strategic industries. This balance reflected

[91] Booth, A. (1998). The Indonesian Economy in the Nineteenth and Twentieth Centuries: A History of Missed Opportunities. London: Macmillan Press.

[92] Ricklefs, M. C. (2008). A History of Modern Indonesia Since c.1200. 4th ed. Basingstoke: Palgrave Macmillan.

[93] Elson, R. E. (2009). The Idea of Indonesia: A History. Cambridge: Cambridge University Press.

an acknowledgment that complete economic isolation was neither feasible nor beneficial for achieving long-term development. The integration of foreign investment into Indonesia's development strategy demonstrated a nuanced understanding of the need to leverage global opportunities while preserving national interests, illustrating the complexities of balancing self-sufficiency with economic engagement.

The original pragmatic approach reflected an evolution of the nationalist ideology, prioritizing economic stability and growth over strict adherence to self-sufficiency. Yet, the emphasis on state-led development and centralized control often resulted in corruption, inefficiency, and uneven distribution of benefits, reinforcing regional and social inequalities.[94] The enduring appeal of self-sufficiency as an economic principle highlights its symbolic significance in Indonesia's post-colonial identity. It represented not just economic independence but also a rejection of foreign dominance and an aspiration for national dignity. While the practical outcomes of self-sufficiency policies were mixed, their influence on Indonesia's development trajectory underscores the complex interplay between ideology and economic strategy in the country's efforts to forge a sustainable and equitable post-colonial economy. Post-independence economic strategies underscored a broader vision of economic sovereignty, which sought to place control of Indonesia's resources and industries firmly in the hands of Indonesians. This vision extended beyond immediate economic concerns to encompass political and cultural independence, rejecting the paternalistic structures of colonial rule. The revolutionary government's efforts to establish a national currency, the Oeang Republik Indonesia (ORI), exemplified this commitment to sovereignty. Although the ORI faced significant challenges, such as hyperinflation and competition from other currencies, it represented a critical step toward asserting Indonesia's economic autonomy and national identity.[95] The legacy of these strategies was profound. Nationalization and self-sufficiency became enduring themes in Indonesia's economic policies, shaping debates about the role of the state, the management of natural resources, and the balance between domestic development and global engagement. However, the limitations and contradictions of these early efforts also highlighted the

[94] Booth, A. (1998). The Indonesian Economy in the Nineteenth and Twentieth Centuries: A History of Missed Opportunities. London: Macmillan Press.

[95] Reid, A. (1974). The Indonesian National Revolution, 1945–1950. Hawthorn: Longman Australia.

difficulties of achieving economic sovereignty in a post-colonial context. The lack of institutional capacity and skilled labour, combined with the pressures of rebuilding a war-torn economy, meant that many of the revolutionary government's goals were only partially realized. Nevertheless, the foundations laid during this period provided a framework for Indonesia's subsequent economic development, demonstrating the transformative potential of aligning economic policies with nationalist aspirations. The revolutionary period also revealed the enduring legacies of colonial exploitation and the structural weaknesses of Indonesia's economy, which would continue to pose challenges in the years to come. The combination of resilience, innovation, and ideological commitment demonstrated during this era underscored the transformative potential of the independence struggle, even as it highlighted the complexity of achieving sustainable economic development in the aftermath of colonial rule.

The Role of International Support and Recognition

International support and recognition played a pivotal role in shaping Indonesia's struggle for independence and its eventual transition to sovereignty during the period between 1945 and 1950. The revolutionary government, established after the Proclamation of Independence on August 17, 1945, faced significant challenges in gaining legitimacy on the global stage. Dutch efforts to reclaim control of Indonesia were bolstered by support from Western powers, particularly the United States and Britain, who viewed Indonesia through the lens of their geopolitical interests in the early Cold War period. Despite these obstacles, Indonesia's leaders skilfully leveraged diplomatic channels, international alliances, and public opinion to advance their cause for independence and secure vital economic and political support.[96] One of the critical strategies employed by Indonesia was the internationalization of its independence struggle. Recognizing the limitations of armed resistance alone, Indonesian leaders sought to appeal to global organizations, such as the United Nations, to gain broader support. The diplomatic efforts

[96] Kahin, G. M. (1952). Nationalism and Revolution in Indonesia. Ithaca: Cornell University Press.

of figures like Sutan Sjahrir and Mohammad Hatta were instrumental in presenting Indonesia's case to the international community. These leaders framed the independence movement as part of the broader wave of decolonization and self-determination sweeping across Asia and Africa, aligning Indonesia with global anti-colonial sentiments. The Linggadjati Agreement of 1946 and subsequent negotiations underscored Indonesia's willingness to engage diplomatically, even as Dutch military campaigns continued to destabilize the region.[97]

Economic support from neighbouring countries and sympathetic states also played a crucial role in sustaining the revolutionary government. Informal trade networks and aid from nations such as India and Egypt helped Indonesia circumvent the Dutch blockade, providing essential supplies and funding to maintain the independence movement. These connections highlighted the importance of regional solidarity, as other newly independent or decolonizing nations rallied to Indonesia's cause. Additionally, Indonesia's strategic importance as a resource-rich archipelago made its independence struggle a focal point in global political discourse, further emphasizing the need for international recognition.[98]

The role of public opinion, particularly in the United States and Europe, cannot be understated. Indonesian leaders capitalized on the growing awareness of colonial injustices and the post-World War II emphasis on human rights and self-determination. High-profile atrocities committed during Dutch military campaigns, such as the Rawagede massacre, were widely publicized and drew international condemnation. The massacre had significant economic and political repercussions that shaped Indonesia's post-independence economic development. These atrocities, widely publicized and condemned by the international community, not only strengthened Indonesia's nationalist movement but also influenced the economic policies of both Indonesia and the Netherlands in the following years. The Rawagede massacre, which occurred on December 9, 1947, in West Java, was one of the most infamous war crimes committed by Dutch forces during the Indonesian War of Independence (1945–1949). Dutch troops executed 431 unarmed villagers

[97] Feith, H. (1962). The Decline of Constitutional Democracy in Indonesia. Ithaca: Cornell University Press.

[98] Elson, R. E. (2009). The Idea of Indonesia: A History. Cambridge: Cambridge University Press.

to suppress nationalist resistance and capture a key revolutionary leader. The mass killing, part of broader counterinsurgency efforts, was emblematic of the harsh tactics employed by Dutch forces as they attempted to reclaim control over Indonesia's valuable economic assets, particularly its plantations, oil fields, and trade networks.[99,100]

The international backlash against such atrocities had profound economic consequences for the Netherlands. The Dutch government, which had initially relied on post-World War II Marshall Plan funds from the United States to finance military operations in Indonesia, came under increasing pressure to cease hostilities. The United States, viewing the Dutch attempt to reclaim Indonesia as an obstacle to regional stability and economic recovery, threatened to withdraw financial support unless the Netherlands agreed to negotiate Indonesian independence. The mounting diplomatic and financial pressure, coupled with domestic anti-war sentiment in the Netherlands, forced the Dutch to reconsider their colonial ambitions.[101] For Indonesia, these atrocities reinforced nationalist resistance and shaped early economic policies. The Rawagede massacre and similar events intensified popular support for a self-sufficient economic model, as Dutch economic dominance had become synonymous with colonial oppression. Following independence, Indonesia pursued policies aimed at reducing foreign economic influence, including the nationalization of Dutch-owned enterprises in the 1950s. The expropriation of Dutch businesses, particularly in the plantation, oil, and banking sectors, was partly justified as a response to colonial-era violence and economic exploitation.[102] Additionally, the economic impact of the Dutch military campaigns extended beyond Indonesia's independence in 1949. The destruction of infrastructure, including bridges, railways, and factories, significantly hampered post-war reconstruction efforts. The Dutch, in their attempt to weaken nationalist forces, often targeted economic assets, leaving Indonesia with a severely damaged

[99] Kahin, G.M. (1952). Nationalism and Revolution in Indonesia. Ithaca, NY: Cornell University Press.

[100] Ricklefs, M.C. (2008). A History of Modern Indonesia Since c. 1200. 4th ed. Basingstoke: Palgrave Macmillan.

[101] Lindblad, J.T. (2008). Bridges to New Business: The Economic Decolonization of Indonesia. Leiden: KITLV Press.

[102] Booth, A. (1998). The Indonesian Economy in the Nineteenth and Twentieth Centuries: A History of Missed Opportunities. London: Macmillan.

industrial and transportation sector. The cost of rebuilding these critical economic structures placed further strain on Indonesia's early development efforts, contributing to inflation, economic instability, and an increased reliance on foreign aid in the early years of independence.[103] The Rawagede massacre, alongside other acts of Dutch military repression, thus had long-term implications for Indonesia's economic trajectory. It strengthened anti-colonial sentiment, justified policies of economic nationalism, and contributed to the severing of Dutch economic ties, reshaping Indonesia's trade relationships and industrial policies in the post-independence era. Moreover, these incidents weakened Dutch moral authority and increased pressure on the Netherlands to negotiate a resolution. By skilfully managing both diplomatic efforts and public relations campaigns, Indonesia succeeded in framing its struggle not only as a national issue but as a global imperative for justice and equality.[104] The eventual transfer of sovereignty in December 1949, formalized through the Dutch Indonesian Round Table Conference, marked the culmination of these efforts. While the agreement retained certain economic and political ties between Indonesia and the Netherlands, it represented a significant victory for the revolutionary government. The international recognition of Indonesia's independence underscored the power of diplomatic engagement and the necessity of global support in achieving decolonization. However, the terms of the agreement also reflected the enduring economic challenges Indonesia would face in its post-colonial era, as Dutch enterprises retained significant influence over key sectors of the economy, and the burden of wartime debts further complicated the republic's efforts to assert full economic sovereignty.[105] International support and recognition were integral to Indonesia's path to independence, providing diplomatic leverage, economic resources, and moral authority. The revolutionary government's ability to navigate complex international dynamics while maintaining grassroots support at home

[103] Dick, H., Houben, V., Lindblad, J.T., & Wie, T.K. (2002). The Emergence of a National Economy: An Economic History of Indonesia, 1800–2000. Honolulu: University of Hawaii Press.

[104] Cribb, R. and Brown, C. (1995). Modern Indonesia: A History Since 1945. London: Longman.

[105] Ricklefs, M. C. (2008). A History of Modern Indonesia Since c.1200. 4th ed. Basingstoke: Palgrave Macmillan.

exemplified the interconnected nature of political and economic struggles in the decolonization era. These efforts not only secured Indonesia's sovereignty but also laid the foundation for its role as a leader in the post-colonial world order.

Nationalization and Economic Sovereignty

The struggle for Indonesia's independence was not solely a political battle but also an economic one, as the revolutionary government sought to establish control over key resources and industries to assert economic sovereignty. Nationalization emerged as a central strategy in this effort, reflecting a broader ambition to dismantle the exploitative colonial structures that had prioritized Dutch interests at the expense of local development. The nationalization of Dutch-owned enterprises, particularly in sectors such as plantations, banking, and infrastructure, symbolized Indonesia's rejection of colonial domination and its commitment to economic self-determination. However, these efforts were fraught with challenges. The lack of technical expertise, administrative capacity, and capital to effectively manage these enterprises often limited their productivity and profitability, while resistance from Dutch stakeholders and international entities added further complications.[106] The economic policies of the revolutionary government also sought to address the immediate needs of a population grappling with widespread poverty, famine, and displacement caused by years of war and occupation. Nationalization efforts were accompanied by measures aimed at stabilizing the economy, such as the introduction of the Oeang Republik Indonesia (ORI) as a national currency. This move was intended to establish financial independence and reduce reliance on colonial-era currencies, but it faced significant challenges, including inflation and a lack of public trust in the new monetary system. Additionally, the government's efforts to assert control over key industries often encountered logistical hurdles, as many enterprises had been damaged or neglected during the Japanese occupation and the subsequent war for independence.[107]

[106] Feith, H. (1962). The Decline of Constitutional Democracy in Indonesia. Ithaca: Cornell University Press.

[107] Elson, R. E. (2009). The Idea of Indonesia: A History. Cambridge: Cambridge University Press.

The emphasis on economic sovereignty was deeply tied to the broader nationalist ideology that underpinned Indonesia's independence movement. Leaders such as Sukarno and Hatta viewed economic independence as inseparable from political freedom, arguing that true sovereignty could only be achieved by breaking free from the structures of dependency established under colonial rule. This vision extended beyond the nationalization of assets to encompass a commitment to self-sufficiency and equitable development. The revolutionary government encouraged grassroots initiatives to promote local production and resource management, reflecting the spirit of gotong royong (mutual cooperation) that had been a cornerstone of the independence movement. However, these efforts often fell short of addressing the structural inequalities and systemic inefficiencies inherited from the colonial economy, underscoring the complexity of achieving economic sovereignty in a post-colonial context.[108]

The nationalization policies of the revolutionary period also had significant implications for Indonesia's post-independence economic trajectory. By establishing state control over strategic industries, the government laid the foundation for the centralized economic policies that would dominate the early years of the republic. However, the limitations of these efforts—exacerbated by war, resource scarcity, and international isolation—highlighted the challenges of transitioning from a colonial economy to a self-reliant one. The revolutionary government's focus on economic sovereignty set an enduring precedent, influencing debates about the role of the state, foreign investment, and resource management in Indonesia's development for decades to come.[109]

The quest for nationalization and economic sovereignty during the revolutionary period was not without its contradictions. While it underscored the importance of breaking free from colonial exploitation, it also revealed the vulnerabilities of a nation emerging from years of conflict and systemic underdevelopment. The revolutionary government's policies reflected a bold vision of independence that sought to empower Indonesians economically, yet they also demonstrated the inherent difficulties of implementing such a vision in the face of practical and structural

[108] Ricklefs, M. C. (2008). A History of Modern Indonesia Since c.1200. 4th ed. Basingstoke: Palgrave Macmillan.

[109] Booth, A. (1998). The Indonesian Economy in the Nineteenth and Twentieth Centuries: A History of Missed Opportunities. London: Macmillan Press.

constraints. This tension between aspiration and reality would continue to shape Indonesia's economic policies and development path in the post-independence era.

Social Mobilization and the Struggle for Unity

Social mobilization and the struggle for unity were central to Indonesia's independence movement during the revolutionary period from 1945 to 1950. The revolutionary government and nationalist leaders faced the dual challenge of galvanizing a diverse and fragmented population while building a cohesive national identity. Indonesia's archipelagic geography, combined with its ethnic, cultural, and religious diversity, had long been a barrier to political and social unity. The independence struggle provided an opportunity to foster solidarity by framing the fight against colonialism as a shared national cause. This mobilization was deeply rooted in nationalist rhetoric, which emphasized anti-colonialism, economic sovereignty, and the concept of gotong royong (cooperation) as foundational values.[110] Mass organizations played a critical role in uniting Indonesians across regional and class divides. Groups such as the Indonesian National Party (PNI) and Sarekat Islam, along with trade unions and peasant associations, helped to channel economic grievances into collective action. These organizations not only supported the revolutionary government's efforts to resist Dutch reoccupation but also facilitated grassroots engagement in the broader struggle for independence. Mobilization efforts extended to rural areas, where the majority of Indonesians lived, by promoting the idea that independence would bring economic justice and an end to colonial exploitation. These campaigns were vital in ensuring widespread participation in the independence movement, even as regional disparities and local loyalties sometimes complicated efforts to achieve national unity.[111]

The revolutionary government also employed cultural and linguistic tools to foster a sense of shared identity. The promotion of the Indonesian language as the lingua franca was a significant step in breaking down regional divisions and establishing a common national identity.

[110] Anderson, B. R. O. G. (1972). Java in a Time of Revolution: Occupation and Resistance, 1944–1946. Ithaca: Cornell University Press.

[111] Kahin, G. M. (1952). Nationalism and Revolution in Indonesia. Ithaca: Cornell University Press.

Educational initiatives and propaganda campaigns emphasized the ideals of unity and self-determination, using symbols such as the national flag and anthem to rally diverse groups under a single banner. These efforts were particularly effective in urban areas, where nationalist leaders such as Sukarno and Hatta articulated visions of a united Indonesia that resonated across ethnic and social boundaries.[112] However, the struggle for unity was not without its challenges. Regionalism and localism often clashed with the centralizing tendencies of the revolutionary government. Some regions, such as Aceh and parts of Sulawesi, expressed dissatisfaction with Jakarta's leadership, viewing it as overly Javanese-centric. These tensions were exacerbated by the economic hardships of the period, as food shortages, hyperinflation, and resource scarcity fuelled discontent among the population. The revolutionary government's reliance on grassroots mobilization sometimes led to conflicts between local leaders and central authorities, highlighting the difficulties of balancing national unity with regional autonomy.[113] Despite these challenges, the shared experiences of hardship and resistance during the independence struggle played a critical role in forging a collective identity. The mobilization of women, youth, and workers brought previously marginalized groups into the national movement, broadening the base of support for the republic. Organizations such as PETA (Defenders of the Homeland) and youth groups like Pemuda Indonesia provided not only military and logistical support but also platforms for social and political engagement. These efforts underscored the transformative nature of the independence movement, which not only sought to end colonial rule but also to lay the foundations for an inclusive and equitable national framework.[114] The social mobilization of the revolutionary period laid the groundwork for Indonesia's post-independence efforts to build a unified state. The emphasis on collective action and shared purpose helped to mitigate, though not eliminate, the centrifugal forces that threatened to undermine national cohesion. By framing the struggle for independence as a unifying cause, the revolutionary government succeeded in rallying diverse populations under the

[112] Ricklefs, M. C. (2008). A History of Modern Indonesia Since c.1200. 4th ed. Basingstoke: Palgrave Macmillan.

[113] Elson, R. E. (2009). The Idea of Indonesia: A History. Cambridge: Cambridge University Press.

[114] Cribb, R. and Brown, C. (1995). Modern Indonesia: A History Since 1945. London: Longman.

banner of an independent Indonesia, even as the legacies of colonial exploitation and regional inequalities continued to present challenges for the young republic.

Conclusion

The period from 1945 to 1950 was a defining moment in Indonesia's journey toward sovereignty, marked by the complex dual challenge of asserting independence and laying the foundations of a functional state. The Proclamation of Independence on August 17, 1945, led by Sukarno and Hatta, was a powerful declaration of self-determination, signalling a break from colonial domination. However, the years that followed exposed the monumental difficulties of transforming a colonially subjugated and war-torn territory into a unified, independent nation. The revolutionary government inherited an economy ravaged by decades of extractive colonialism, exacerbated by the devastation of the Japanese occupation and subsequent conflict with Dutch forces. Systemic poverty, hyperinflation, infrastructure collapse, and deep regional disparities left the fledgling republic with limited capacity to govern effectively, underscoring the fragility of the economic and political structures inherited from colonial rule.[115]

Economic strategies during this period reflected the aspirations of the nationalist movement for sovereignty and self-reliance. Nationalization efforts targeted Dutch-owned enterprises in key sectors such as plantations, banking, and transportation, symbolizing a rejection of colonial economic dominance. Similarly, the introduction of the Oeang Republik Indonesia (ORI) as the national currency represented an assertion of financial independence. Yet, these initiatives were fraught with challenges. The lack of technical expertise and administrative capacity undermined the effectiveness of nationalized enterprises, while the fledgling government struggled to manage inflation and gain public trust in the new currency. The war for independence further diverted scarce resources, leaving critical sectors of the economy underdeveloped and amplifying economic instability.[116] Grassroots initiatives, such as the promotion

[115] Ricklefs, M. C. (2008). A History of Modern Indonesia Since c.1200. 4th ed. Basingstoke: Palgrave Macmillan.

[116] Elson, R. E. (2009). The Idea of Indonesia: A History. Cambridge: Cambridge University Press.

of gotong royong (mutual cooperation), showcased the resilience and ingenuity of the Indonesian people during this period. Local communities mobilized to produce food, rebuild infrastructure, and support the revolutionary cause, reflecting a deep-seated commitment to collective action. However, these efforts highlighted the broader systemic weaknesses inherited from the colonial economy, which had prioritized resource extraction over local development. The collapse of the plantation economy, coupled with food shortages and hyperinflation, underscored the enormity of the task facing the revolutionary government. These challenges revealed the limits of idealistic visions of self-sufficiency and demonstrated the need for pragmatic solutions to achieve economic stability and growth.[117]

Socially, the revolutionary period was characterized by both unity and fragmentation. The shared experiences of exploitation under colonialism and hardship during the Japanese occupation fostered a powerful sense of collective identity. Nationalist leaders effectively framed the independence movement as a unifying struggle, transcending regional, ethnic, and class divides. Yet, this unity was often fragile, as political factions and regional loyalties complicated efforts to build an inclusive national framework. The revolutionary government's mobilization of the population for military and economic purposes showcased the interconnected nature of these objectives but also exposed the tensions between national priorities and local realities. Regional disparities and resistance to central authority in areas such as Aceh and South Sulawesi highlighted the difficulties of achieving a cohesive and equitable national vision.[118]

The role of international dynamics during this period further shaped the trajectory of the independence struggle. The lack of immediate global recognition, coupled with Dutch-backed military campaigns, left Indonesia diplomatically and economically isolated. Leaders like Sutan Sjahrir and Mohammad Hatta skilfully leveraged the growing global anti-colonial sentiment to secure international support, aligning Indonesia's struggle with the broader decolonization movement. Diplomatic breakthroughs, such as the Linggadjati Agreement, demonstrated the strategic importance of engaging the global community. Yet,

[117] Feith, H. (1962). The Decline of Constitutional Democracy in Indonesia. Ithaca: Cornell University Press.

[118] Anderson, B. R. O. G. (1972). Java in a Time of Revolution: Occupation and Resistance, 1944–1946. Ithaca: Cornell University Press.

these efforts often required compromises that underscored the tension between asserting sovereignty and navigating the realities of international power dynamics.[119] The revolutionary period laid the ideological and institutional foundations for Indonesia's post-colonial development. The emphasis on economic sovereignty, nationalization, and collective resilience represented a profound rejection of colonial hierarchies and an aspiration for economic justice. However, the limitations of these strategies, rooted in the structural deficiencies of the colonial economy and exacerbated by the demands of the independence struggle, highlighted the enduring challenges of nation-building. This period revealed the inherent tension between the idealism of self-reliance and the pragmatism required to address immediate economic and political crises. As Indonesia emerged from this transformative era, the experiences of collective struggle and resilience became integral to its national identity. The triumphs and challenges of the revolutionary period provided critical lessons for subsequent leaders, shaping debates on economic development, political unity, and social equity. The legacies of this time, both constructive and cautionary, underscored the interconnectedness of economic and political sovereignty, laying the foundation for Indonesia's ongoing journey as a sovereign state.

References

Anderson, B. R. O'G. (1972) Java in a Time of Revolution: Occupation and Resistance, 1944-1946. Ithaca, NY: Cornell University Press.

Booth, A. (1998). The Indonesian Economy in the Nineteenth and Twentieth Centuries: A History of Missed Opportunities. London: Macmillan Press.

Bosma, U. (2013). The Sugar Plantation in India and Indonesia: Industrial Production, 1770–2010. Cambridge: Cambridge University Press.

Cribb, R. (1994). Gangsters and Revolutionaries: The Jakarta People's Militia and the Indonesian Revolution, 1945–1949. Honolulu: University of Hawai'i Press.

Cribb, R., and Brown, C. (1995) Modern Indonesia: A History Since 1945. London: Longman.

Dick, H., Houben, V., Lindblad, J.T., & Wie, T.K. (2002). The Emergence of a National Economy: An Economic History of Indonesia, 1800-2000. Honolulu: University of Hawaii Press.

[119] Kahin, G. M. (1952). Nationalism and Revolution in Indonesia. Ithaca: Cornell University Press.

Elson, R. E. (2009) The Idea of Indonesia: A History. Cambridge: Cambridge University Press.

Feith, H. (1962) The Decline of Constitutional Democracy in Indonesia. Ithaca, NY: Cornell University Press.

Kahin, G. M. (1952) Nationalism and Revolution in Indonesia. Ithaca, NY: Cornell University Press.

Lindblad, J.T. (2008). Bridges to New Business: The Economic Decolonization of Indonesia. Leiden: KITLV Press.

Lindblad, J.T. (2015). Economic Globalization and Indonesian Economy since the Late Nineteenth Century. Singapore: ISEAS-Yusof Ishak Institute.

Reid, A. (1974) The Indonesian National Revolution, 1945–1950. Hawthorn, VIC: Longman Australia.

Ricklefs, M. C. (2008) A History of Modern Indonesia Since c.1200. 4th edn. Stanford, CA: Stanford University Press.

Van der Eng, P. (2008). "Food Supply in Java during War and Decolonisation, 1940–1950." Australian Economic History Review, 48(1), 62–95.

Vickers, A. (2005) A History of Modern Indonesia. Cambridge: Cambridge University Press.

CHAPTER 9

Guided Democracy and Economic Nationalism (1950–1965)

Introduction

The period from 1950 to 1965 in Indonesia was marked by significant political and economic shifts as the newly independent nation sought to define its identity and chart a course for development. This era, dominated by the policies of Guided Democracy under President Sukarno, was characterized by a strong emphasis on economic nationalism and state control over the economy. Chapter 8: Guided Democracy and Economic Nationalism (1950–1965) explored the interplay between political ideology and economic policy during this transformative period, highlighting the successes and challenges that shaped Indonesia's economic trajectory. Following the turbulent years of revolution and the struggle for independence, Indonesia faced the formidable task of economic reconstruction and development. President Sukarno, envisioning a new path for the nation, introduced the concept of Guided Democracy in 1957, which aimed to consolidate political power and steer the country toward a more centralized and state-controlled economic model.,[1,2] Guided Democracy was closely linked to the broader

[1] Feith, H. (1962) The Decline of Constitutional Democracy in Indonesia. Ithaca, NY: Cornell University Press.

[2] Ricklefs, M. C. (2008) A History of Modern Indonesia Since c.1200. 4th edn. Stanford, CA: Stanford University Press.

S. Ramesh, *The Political Economy of Indonesia's Economic Development, Volume I*, https://doi.org/10.1007/978-3-031-94350-8_9

ideology of economic nationalism, which sought to reduce foreign influence and promote self-sufficiency by prioritizing domestic industries and resources.[3] During this period, the Indonesian government pursued a series of policies aimed at nationalizing key industries, including those previously owned by Dutch and other foreign interests. This move was seen as a necessary step toward achieving economic independence and breaking free from the remnants of colonial exploitation.[4] However, these policies also led to significant economic challenges, including inefficiencies in state-owned enterprises, inflation, and a decline in foreign investment.[5] This chapter will examine the impact of these economic policies on the broader population. While Sukarno's vision of economic nationalism resonated with many Indonesians, particularly in the context of anti-colonial sentiment, the realities of economic management under Guided Democracy were complex and often problematic. The emphasis on political unity and centralization frequently came at the expense of economic pragmatism, leading to economic stagnation and widespread poverty by the mid-1960s.[6] In addition to economic policies, this period was marked by significant political developments, including the increasing influence of the military and the Communist Party of Indonesia (PKI) in national affairs. The tension between these groups and the eventual shift toward authoritarianism under Sukarno set the stage for the dramatic political changes that would follow in the late 1960s.[7,8]

[3] McVey, R. T. (1965) The Rise of Indonesian Communism. Ithaca, NY: Cornell University Press.

[4] Glassburner, B. (1971) 'Economic Policy-Making in Indonesia, 1950–1957', Economic Development and Cultural Change, 19(3), pp. 289–308.

[5] Booth, A. (1998) The Indonesian Economy in the Nineteenth and Twentieth Centuries: A History of Missed Opportunities. London: Macmillan.

[6] Robison, R. (1986) Indonesia: The Rise of Capital. Sydney: Allen & Unwin.

[7] Lev, D. S. (1966) The Transition to Guided Democracy: Indonesian Politics, 1957–1959. Ithaca, NY: Modern IndonesiaProject, Cornell University.

[8] Ricklefs, M. C. (2008) A History of Modern Indonesia Since c.1200. 4th edn. Stanford, CA: Stanford University Press.

The Emergence of Guided Democracy

The emergence of Guided Democracy in Indonesia during the period from 1950 to 1965 marked a pivotal shift in the nation's political and economic trajectory, reflecting the tensions between nationalist aspirations and the practical challenges of state-building in a newly independent nation. Guided Democracy, introduced by President Sukarno in 1957, was a direct response to the growing political instability and economic discontent that threatened the unity and viability of the young republic. Sukarno envisioned a centralized system capable of overcoming the centrifugal forces of regionalism, ideological divisions, and external pressures. Rooted in ideals of anti-colonialism and national development, Guided Democracy sought to establish a uniquely Indonesian model of governance and economic management, rejecting Western democratic frameworks as incompatible with the country's cultural and historical context.[9]

A defining feature of Guided Democracy was its emphasis on economic nationalism, exemplified by the nationalization of Dutch-owned enterprises. This policy aimed to sever Indonesia's economic dependence on its former colonial ruler and redirect resources toward national development. Industries such as plantations, mining, and transportation were brought under state control, symbolizing a decisive break from colonial economic structures. However, the execution of these policies exposed significant limitations. The lack of technical expertise, bureaucratic inefficiency, and widespread corruption undermined the productivity of nationalized enterprises. Furthermore, tensions between Jakarta and regional leaders over the control and distribution of resources exacerbated existing regional inequalities, fuelling dissatisfaction and resistance in provinces such as Aceh and South Sulawesi.[10] While nationalization embodied the aspiration for economic sovereignty, it also highlighted the challenges of transitioning from an extractive colonial economy to a self-reliant system.

Guided Democracy sought to address the socio-economic grievances of marginalized groups, including workers and peasants, by encouraging their participation in the political process. Populist measures such as

[9] Feith, H. (1962). The decline of constitutional democracy in Indonesia. Cornell University Press.

[10] Ricklefs, M. C. (2008). A history of modern Indonesia since c. 1200 (4th ed.). Palgrave Macmillan.

land reform and wage increases were intended to promote social equity and secure grassroots support. However, these initiatives often failed to achieve their objectives due to weak implementation and opposition from entrenched elites. The uneven application of land reforms, for example, left many rural communities without meaningful relief, further deepening economic disparities and fostering discontent. The disconnect between the government's rhetoric and the lived experiences of the population underscored the limitations of Guided Democracy's socio-economic agenda.[11]

Politically, Guided Democracy was characterized by Sukarno's effort to balance competing ideologies—nationalism, communism, and political Islam—within a centralized system. Sukarno's vision was to transcend party-based democracy, which he perceived as divisive and alien to Indonesia's cultural traditions. By centralizing decision-making under his leadership, Sukarno aimed to foster national unity and streamline governance. However, this concentration of power marginalized dissenting voices, eroded political pluralism, and paved the way for authoritarian tendencies. The suppression of opposition parties and the increasing dominance of Sukarno's rhetoric over substantive policy discussions weakened the institutional foundations of governance, leaving Indonesia vulnerable to political instability and elite domination.[12]

On the international stage, Guided Democracy reflected Indonesia's ambitions to assert its sovereignty through an independent foreign policy. As a leader of the Non-Aligned Movement, Sukarno sought to position Indonesia as a champion of anti-imperialism and a mediator between the Cold War blocs. This assertive stance reinforced Sukarno's vision of Indonesia as a self-reliant and sovereign nation. However, the economic costs of pursuing an ambitious foreign policy, including military campaigns in regions such as West Papua, placed additional strain on Indonesia's fragile economy. Domestic mismanagement compounded these challenges, with inflation spiralling out of control, infrastructure development stagnating, and public dissatisfaction with unmet economic promises intensifying.[13]

[11] Elson, R. E. (2009). The idea of Indonesia: A history. Cambridge University Press.

[12] Anderson, B. R. O. G. (1972). Java in a time of revolution: Occupation and resistance, 1944–1946. Cornell University Press.

[13] Booth, A. (1998). The Indonesian economy in the nineteenth and twentieth centuries: A history of missed opportunities Macmillan Press.

The legacy of Guided Democracy is one of ambition tempered by the realities of governance in a post-colonial context. Sukarno's efforts to chart a uniquely Indonesian path to development reflected a bold vision of economic nationalism and political unity. However, the limitations of state control, inefficiencies in implementation, and the failure to fully address regional and socio-economic disparities revealed the practical challenges of translating nationalist ideals into effective policy. At the same time, Guided Democracy fostered a sense of national pride and solidarity, resonating deeply with the masses despite its shortcomings.

As Indonesia transitioned to the New Order under Suharto, the lessons of Guided Democracy—both its achievements and its failures—remained a critical reference point. The emphasis on state-led development and the balance between economic sovereignty and international engagement continued to shape the nation's policies. Guided Democracy's legacy underscores the enduring tension between idealism and pragmatism in nation-building, offering valuable insights into the complexities of achieving sustainable development and political cohesion in a diverse and dynamic society.

Economic Nationalism and State Control

During the period from 1950 to 1965, Indonesia's policy of economic nationalism and state control under President Sukarno's Guided Democracy represented a bold attempt to assert sovereignty and dismantle colonial economic structures. The nationalization of Dutch-owned enterprises in the late 1950s was central to this strategy, with approximately 246 companies taken over and restructured as state-owned enterprises (SOEs).[14] This policy was driven by both political and economic motivations, aiming to sever ties with colonial influences and establish economic self-reliance. The transition to state control, however, exposed significant operational and managerial challenges. Many nationalized enterprises suffered from inefficiencies due to a lack of expertise and bureaucratic mismanagement. For instance, Pertamina, the state oil company formed from nationalized Dutch assets, expanded rapidly into areas like shipping

[14] Ricklefs, M.C. (2008) A History of Modern Indonesia Since c. 1200. 4th ed. Basingstoke: Palgrave Macmillan.

and construction but was plagued by corruption and financial mismanagement, undermining its effectiveness.[15] These issues were emblematic of the broader limitations of centralized economic control during this period. In addition to nationalization, the government implemented measures such as the Foreign Exchange Certificate System (FECS) to manage currency transactions and regulate trade. While these policies were intended to enhance economic sovereignty, they often resulted in unintended consequences, including the emergence of black markets and difficulties for import-dependent businesses.[16] This highlighted the challenges of balancing state intervention with market dynamics in a rapidly changing economic landscape.

Socially, the emphasis on economic nationalism also led to significant demographic and cultural shifts. Presidential Directive No. 10 of 1959, for example, restricted the commercial activities of foreign nationals in rural areas, disproportionately affecting ethnic Chinese traders. This policy not only altered the socio-economic composition of Indonesia's rural economy but also fuelled tensions between the ethnic Chinese community and the broader population, illustrating the complexities of implementing nationalist policies in a diverse society.[17] Despite these challenges, the rhetoric of economic nationalism resonated deeply with the population, fostering a sense of pride and unity. Sukarno's emphasis on self-reliance and anti-colonialism aligned with the broader aspirations of a newly independent nation. However, the practical outcomes of these policies often fell short, with inflationary pressures, stagnating infrastructure development, and uneven regional economic growth undermining the broader objectives of Guided Democracy.[18]

Indonesia's pursuit of economic nationalism and state control during the Guided Democracy era reflected an ambitious attempt to redefine its economic and political trajectory. While the policies succeeded in asserting sovereignty and fostering national pride, they also revealed the inherent

[15] Booth, A. (1998) The Indonesian Economy in the Nineteenth and Twentieth Centuries: A History of Missed Opportunities. Basingstoke: Macmillan.

[16] Feith, H. (1962) The Decline of Constitutional Democracy in Indonesia. Ithaca, NY: Cornell University Press.

[17] Elson, R.E. (2009) The Idea of Indonesia: A History. Cambridge: Cambridge University Press.

[18] Anderson, B.R.O.G. (1972) Java in a Time of Revolution: Occupation and Resistance, 1944–1946. Ithaca, NY: Cornell University Press.

challenges of transitioning from a colonial to a self-reliant economy. The mixed legacy of this period underscores the need for robust institutional frameworks and a balanced approach to state intervention in post-colonial nation-building.

Nationalization of Foreign Enterprises

The nationalization of foreign enterprises in Indonesia during the Guided Democracy period (1950–1965) was a cornerstone of Sukarno's economic nationalism. This policy aimed to assert sovereignty and reduce the economic dominance of colonial powers, particularly the Netherlands. The process began in earnest in 1957 when the Indonesian government expropriated approximately 246 Dutch-owned enterprises following the breakdown of diplomatic relations over the West Irian issue.[19] These enterprises, which spanned sectors such as plantations, mining, and transportation, were brought under state control to redirect resources toward national development and to foster economic independence.

While nationalization was politically popular, its economic implementation faced numerous challenges. The takeover of Dutch enterprises often occurred without adequate planning, resulting in operational inefficiencies. For instance, the lack of skilled personnel to manage the newly acquired industries led to declines in productivity. Pertamina, the state oil company formed from the nationalization of Dutch oil assets, exemplifies both the potential and pitfalls of this policy. While it symbolized Indonesia's ambition for resource sovereignty, its operations were hampered by corruption and financial mismanagement, limiting its effectiveness.[20] Moreover, nationalization was not limited to Dutch-owned firms. Foreign companies from other nations, including British and American enterprises, were affected to varying degrees. For example, in the plantation sector, the government's acquisition of estates was celebrated as a step toward economic justice, but many of these estates suffered from deteriorating infrastructure and declining output post-nationalization due

[19] Ricklefs, M.C. (2008) A History of Modern Indonesia Since c. 1200. 4th ed. Basingstoke: Palgrave Macmillan.

[20] Booth, A. (1998) The Indonesian Economy in the Nineteenth and Twentieth Centuries: A History of Missed Opportunities. Basingstoke: Macmillan.

to insufficient reinvestment and expertise.[21] This highlighted the challenges of transitioning from private ownership to state control in the absence of robust institutional frameworks.

The nationalization process also had significant sociopolitical ramifications. Presidential Directive No. 10 of 1959, which restricted rural commerce by foreign nationals, targeted ethnic Chinese traders. This policy, while framed as a nationalist measure, exacerbated ethnic tensions and displaced many Chinese Indonesians from their traditional roles in the economy (Elson, 2009). The subsequent urban migration of these traders reshaped Indonesia's socio-economic landscape and contributed to long-term inequalities between ethnic groups. Additionally, the nationalization of foreign enterprises created new regional disparities. Provinces like Aceh and West Sumatra, which housed significant natural resources, often felt marginalized as Jakarta exerted centralized control over nationalized industries. The failure to equitably distribute resources and development benefits fostered resentment and sporadic uprisings in these regions.[22] This underscored the limitations of the centralized economic model promoted during Guided Democracy. Critically, while the nationalization of foreign enterprises aimed to dismantle colonial economic legacies, it often reinforced structural inefficiencies. The absence of strategic reinvestment in state-controlled industries, combined with bureaucratic mismanagement, undermined the broader goals of economic nationalism. Inflation soared during this period, and infrastructure development stagnated, further highlighting the gap between nationalist rhetoric and practical outcomes.[23] Despite its shortcomings, the nationalization policy contributed to fostering a sense of national pride and economic sovereignty among Indonesians. It resonated with the broader anti-colonial sentiment of the era and reinforced Indonesia's leadership role in the Non-Aligned Movement, as Sukarno sought to position the country as a champion of Third World solidarity and self-reliance.[24].

[21] Feith, H. (1962) The Decline of Constitutional Democracy in Indonesia. Ithaca, NY: Cornell University Press.

[22] Ricklefs, M.C. (2008) A History of Modern Indonesia Since c. 1200. 4th ed. Basingstoke: Palgrave Macmillan.

[23] Anderson, B.R.O.G. (1972) Java in a Time of Revolution: Occupation and Resistance, 1944–1946. Ithaca, NY: Cornell University Press.

[24] Booth, A. (1998) The Indonesian Economy in the Nineteenth and Twentieth Centuries: A History of Missed Opportunities. Basingstoke: Macmillan.

The nationalization of foreign enterprises in Indonesia during the Guided Democracy period was a bold yet flawed attempt to assert economic independence and promote national development. While it achieved symbolic victories against colonial dominance, the practical challenges of managing nationalized industries and addressing regional inequalities revealed the complexities of post-colonial nation-building. The legacy of this policy continues to offer lessons on the balance between sovereignty, efficiency, and equity in economic governance.

Challenges and Consequences of Economic Policies

The economic policies implemented during Indonesia's Guided Democracy era (1950–1965) under President Sukarno were ambitious, aiming to assert national sovereignty and reduce reliance on foreign powers. However, these policies were fraught with challenges and yielded significant and often unintended consequences for the nation's economic development. A primary economic challenge was the inefficiency and mismanagement of nationalized enterprises. As part of the broader strategy of economic nationalism, the government expropriated Dutch-owned companies in sectors such as plantations, mining, and transportation.[25] These enterprises were transformed into state-owned entities, but the lack of skilled managers and financial expertise often led to operational inefficiencies. For instance, the state oil company Pertamina, though symbolically important, became a hotbed of corruption and poor financial management, undermining its potential to contribute effectively to economic development.[26]

Inflation emerged as a significant consequence of the Guided Economy. By centralizing economic planning and prioritizing state-led industrialization, the government resorted to monetary expansion to finance its ambitious projects. Inflation rates spiralled, with estimates reaching over 600% in the early 1960s.[27] This eroded purchasing power

[25] Ricklefs, M.C. (2008) A History of Modern Indonesia Since c. 1200. 4th ed. Basingstoke: Palgrave Macmillan.

[26] Booth, A. (1998) The Indonesian Economy in the Nineteenth and Twentieth Centuries: A History of Missed Opportunities. Basingstoke: Macmillan.

[27] Feith, H. (1962) The Decline of Constitutional Democracy in Indonesia. Ithaca, NY: Cornell University Press.

and heightened economic instability, particularly affecting the lower-income population, who faced skyrocketing prices for basic goods. The policies also deepened regional disparities. The central government's control over resources created tensions between Jakarta and resource-rich provinces such as Aceh, West Sumatra, and South Kalimantan. These regions felt marginalized as revenues from resource extraction were disproportionately allocated to fund national programs or Sukarno's ambitious infrastructure projects, such as the construction of Jakarta's iconic Monas monument.[28] This fuelled resentment and occasional uprisings, exposing the challenges of centralized economic control in a geographically and culturally diverse nation. Socially, the policies of Guided Democracy exacerbated inequalities and social tensions. For instance, restrictions on rural commerce through policies like Presidential Directive No. 10 of 1959 disproportionately targeted ethnic Chinese traders, many of whom were forced to relocate to urban centres or emigrate.[29] This not only disrupted local economies but also increased ethnic tensions, as the directive was perceived as discriminatory.

The emphasis on industrialization and state control came at the expense of agricultural development, further compounding socio-economic challenges. While Sukarno's government prioritized industrial projects, the agricultural sector, which employed the majority of the population, suffered from underinvestment. This neglect led to stagnating productivity and rural poverty, fuelling discontent among peasants who were promised land reforms that were poorly implemented.[30] Internationally, Indonesia's assertive foreign policy under Sukarno, including military campaigns in West Papua and an aggressive stance against Malaysia during the Konfrontasi, placed additional strain on the fragile economy. These actions were intended to bolster national pride and sovereignty but required significant financial resources, diverting funds from critical domestic needs. Moreover, Indonesia's withdrawal from

[28] Anderson, B.R.O.G. (1972) Java in a Time of Revolution: Occupation and Resistance, 1944–1946. Ithaca, NY: Cornell University Press.

[29] Elson, R.E. (2009) The Idea of Indonesia: A History. Cambridge: Cambridge University Press.

[30] Ricklefs, M.C. (2008) A History of Modern Indonesia Since c. 1200. 4th ed. Basingstoke: Palgrave Macmillan.

the United Nations in 1965 further isolated the country from international economic cooperation, compounding its economic woes.[31] While the economic policies of Guided Democracy were rooted in aspirations for sovereignty, self-reliance, and social equity, their implementation revealed significant challenges. Inflation, inefficiencies in state enterprises, regional disparities, and social tensions highlighted the complexities of transitioning from a colonial economy to a self-reliant system. These challenges, coupled with the economic strains of Sukarno's ambitious political agenda, left Indonesia vulnerable to economic stagnation and instability. The Guided Democracy era thus serves as a cautionary tale about the risks of centralized economic planning and the importance of balancing political ambitions with sound economic management.

Political Dynamics and Economic Impacts

The Guided Democracy era in Indonesia (1950–1965) under President Sukarno was shaped by intricate political dynamics that deeply influenced the nation's economic trajectory. Sukarno's leadership sought to centralize power and balance the competing forces of nationalism, communism, and political Islam to create a unified vision for the nation. However, these political strategies had profound and often destabilizing economic consequences.

Politically, Sukarno's Guided Democracy aimed to transcend Western-style pluralism, which he viewed as alien to Indonesia's cultural and historical context.[32] Instead, he advocated for a system that placed decision-making in the hands of a centralized leadership, ostensibly to foster national unity. However, this concentration of power marginalized political opposition, eroded democratic institutions, and paved the way for authoritarian tendencies. The marginalization of opposition parties, such as the Masjumi (Modernist Muslim Party), alienated significant sections of the population, exacerbating political polarization.[33] Economically, this centralization of power translated into state-led development

[31] Booth, A. (1998) The Indonesian Economy in the Nineteenth and Twentieth Centuries: A History of Missed Opportunities. Basingstoke: Macmillan.

[32] Feith, H. (1962) The Decline of Constitutional Democracy in Indonesia. Ithaca, NY: Cornell University Press.

[33] Ricklefs, M.C. (2008) A History of Modern Indonesia Since c. 1200. 4th ed. Basingstoke: Palgrave Macmillan.

policies. Sukarno prioritized grand infrastructure projects, such as the construction of Jakarta's Monas monument and the Bung Karno Sports Stadium, as symbols of national pride.[34] While these projects were politically significant, they drained public finances and diverted resources away from critical sectors like agriculture and education. Furthermore, the politicization of economic decision-making often resulted in policies driven by ideology rather than pragmatic economic considerations.[35] The alignment of political ideologies with economic strategies also had significant consequences. Sukarno's balancing act between the Indonesian Communist Party (PKI) and other political factions influenced the allocation of resources. For example, the PKI's push for land reform led to sporadic attempts at redistributing land to the rural poor. However, these initiatives were poorly implemented and often met with resistance from landowners and local elites, exacerbating rural inequalities.[36] The failure to fully address socio-economic grievances contributed to the growing tensions between rural and urban populations.

The regional dimensions of political dynamics further complicated the economic impacts of Sukarno's policies. Regions rich in natural resources, such as Aceh and West Sumatra, felt marginalized by Jakarta's centralized control over revenue distribution. The dissatisfaction among these regions manifested in rebellion and unrest, such as the PRRI (Revolutionary Government of the Republic of Indonesia) movement in Sumatra.[37] The central government's suppression of these movements drained resources and highlighted the fragility of Indonesia's political and economic cohesion during this period. On the international stage, Sukarno's political ambitions were intertwined with economic policies. His leadership in the Non-Aligned Movement and assertive foreign policy, including the confrontation with Malaysia (Konfrontasi), placed significant financial strain in Indonesia. The military campaigns and diplomatic isolation that accompanied these policies diverted funds from domestic

[34] Anderson, B.R.O.G. (1972) Java in a Time of Revolution: Occupation and Resistance, 1944–1946. Ithaca, NY: Cornell University Press.

[35] Booth, A. (1998) The Indonesian Economy in the Nineteenth and Twentieth Centuries: A History of Missed Opportunities. Basingstoke: Macmillan.

[36] Elson, R.E. (2009) The Idea of Indonesia: A History. Cambridge: Cambridge University Press.

[37] Ricklefs, M.C. (2008) A History of Modern Indonesia Since c. 1200. 4th ed. Basingstoke: Palgrave Macmillan.

development and exacerbated economic instability. By 1965, inflation had reached catastrophic levels, exceeding 600%, as the government struggled to finance its political and military ambitions.[38] The interplay between political dynamics and economic impacts was further complicated by the government's inability to manage state-owned enterprises effectively. Many of these enterprises, created through the nationalization of Dutch assets, became arenas for political patronage rather than economic efficiency. Corruption and mismanagement plagued these entities, undermining their contribution to economic growth.[39] The political dynamics of the Guided Democracy era were marked by Sukarno's efforts to centralize power and navigate ideological divisions. While these strategies aimed to foster unity and national pride, their economic impacts were often detrimental. The prioritization of political symbolism over pragmatic policy, coupled with the challenges of managing regional and ideological tensions, left Indonesia economically strained and politically fragmented. This period serves as a critical case study in understanding the complex relationship between political ambitions and economic realities in post-colonial nation-building.

Conclusion

The Guided Democracy era in Indonesia (1950–1965) represents a transformative yet tumultuous chapter in the nation's post-independence development. Under Sukarno's leadership, the nation pursued a bold vision of centralized governance, economic nationalism, and cultural self-determination. However, while this vision aimed to address the socio-economic and political legacies of colonialism, its implementation revealed significant limitations and contradictions.

Economically, the policies of Guided Democracy were deeply rooted in the ideals of sovereignty and self-reliance. The nationalization of foreign enterprises, particularly those owned by Dutch interests, symbolized Indonesia's break from colonial dependency and its aspirations for economic independence. Yet, the transition to state ownership often exposed deficiencies in management expertise and institutional

[38] Booth, A. (1998) The Indonesian Economy in the Nineteenth and Twentieth Centuries: A History of Missed Opportunities. Basingstoke: Macmillan.

[39] Feith, H. (1962) The Decline of Constitutional Democracy in Indonesia. Ithaca, NY: Cornell University Press.

capacity. State-owned enterprises became mired in inefficiency, corruption, and bureaucratic mismanagement, undermining their potential to drive sustainable development.[40]+[41] The failure to equitably distribute the benefits of nationalization further exacerbated regional disparities, fuelling discontent and resistance in resource-rich provinces such as Aceh and West Sumatra.

Politically, Guided Democracy sought to create a unified national identity by centralizing authority and balancing competing ideologies—nationalism, communism, and political Islam. Sukarno's vision of a uniquely Indonesian governance model, however, came at the expense of political pluralism and institutional stability. The suppression of opposition parties and the growing influence of the Indonesian Communist Party (PKI) created tensions that destabilized the political landscape.[42] This authoritarian drift eroded the democratic foundations of governance, leaving the country vulnerable to political and economic fragmentation.

Socially, the emphasis on economic nationalism led to demographic and cultural shifts, particularly in the treatment of ethnic Chinese communities. Policies such as Presidential Directive No. 10 of 1959 disrupted rural commerce and heightened ethnic tensions, demonstrating the unintended social consequences of nationalist policies.[43] Presidential Directive No. 10 of 1959 significantly disrupted rural commerce in Indonesia and heightened ethnic tensions, illustrating the unintended social consequences of nationalist policies. The directive sought to limit the influence of ethnic Chinese traders in rural areas by mandating their relocation to urban centres. This policy was part of broader efforts to empower Indigenous (pribumi) Indonesians in the economy and reduce dependency on foreign-dominated sectors. However, the directive disrupted established trade networks and created economic inefficiencies. Ethnic Chinese traders were integral intermediaries in rural economies, linking producers to markets and providing goods and services. Their removal

[40] Booth, A. (1998). The Indonesian Economy in the Nineteenth and Twentieth Centuries: A History of Missed Opportunities. London: Palgrave Macmillan.

[41] Ricklefs, M.C. (2008). A History of Modern Indonesia Since c.1200. 4th edn. Basingstoke: Palgrave Macmillan.

[42] Feith, H. (1962). The Decline of Constitutional Democracy in Indonesia. Ithaca, NY: Cornell University Press.

[43] Elson, R.E. (2009). The Idea of Indonesia: A History. Cambridge: Cambridge University Press.

left a vacuum that Indigenous traders were ill-equipped to fill, leading to supply chain disruptions and a decline in rural economic activity.[44,45]

The policy also exacerbated ethnic tensions by institutionalizing discrimination against the Chinese community, portraying them as obstacles to national economic sovereignty. This reinforced nationalist narratives that framed ethnic Chinese as economic exploiters and alienated them from the broader social fabric of Indonesia. The directive's impact extended beyond economic displacement, fuelling social hostility and legitimizing anti-Chinese sentiment. Many ethnic Chinese, who were long-term residents or citizens, faced increased social marginalization.[46] The policy's implementation demonstrated a lack of adequate preparation or support for Indigenous traders to take over economic roles effectively. The resulting vacuum in rural commerce highlighted the gap between nationalist rhetoric and practical outcomes, as the policy prioritized symbolic assertions of sovereignty over economic pragmatism.[47] In addition to economic and social ramifications, the directive undermined efforts to foster national unity. Instead of integrating diverse communities into a cohesive national identity, it deepened societal divides. It has been noted how the exclusionary approach of such policies alienated ethnic minorities, contributing to long-term sociopolitical tensions.[48] By disrupting rural economies and fostering ethnic resentment, the policy weakened the social cohesion necessary for sustainable development. The broader lesson from this period is the importance of balancing ideological objectives with pragmatic governance. The directive reflects the challenges faced by post-colonial nations in addressing economic disparities while navigating the complexities of social and cultural diversity.

The case of Presidential Directive No. 10 of 1959 underscores the risks of implementing nationalist policies without sufficient institutional capacity or consideration for unintended consequences. While

[44] Coppel, C.A. (1983). Indonesian Chinese in Crisis. Oxford: Oxford University Press.

[45] Booth, A. (1998). The Indonesian Economy in the Nineteenth and Twentieth Centuries: A History of Missed Opportunities. London: Palgrave Macmillan.

[46] Suryadinata, L. (1992). Pribumi Indonesians, the Chinese Minority, and China: A Study of Perceptions and Policies Singapore: Marshall Cavendish.

[47] Mackie, J.A.C. (1976). Konfrontasi: The Indonesia-Malaysia Dispute, 1963–1966. Kuala Lumpur: Oxford University Press.

[48] Elson, R.E. (2009). The Idea of Indonesia: A History. Cambridge: Cambridge University Press.

it aimed to empower indigenous Indonesians economically, its flawed execution resulted in economic stagnation and deepened ethnic divisions, illustrating the limitations of an ideologically driven approach to governance.,[49,50,51] The failure to implement meaningful land reforms left rural populations disillusioned, further deepening socio-economic inequalities. On the international stage, Sukarno's assertive foreign policy, exemplified by Indonesia's leadership in the Non-Aligned Movement and its confrontation with Malaysia, reinforced the nation's sovereignty and anti-imperialist identity. However, these ambitions placed enormous strain on Indonesia's already fragile economy. The military campaigns and symbolic infrastructure projects drained resources, contributing to hyperinflation and economic stagnation by the mid-1960s.[52]

The legacy of Guided Democracy is both complex and instructive. While it fostered a sense of national pride and identity, it also highlighted the challenges of transitioning from colonial dependence to self-reliance in a diverse and resource-constrained context. The legacy of Guided Democracy (1957–1965) under Sukarno in Indonesia is multifaceted, reflecting both its achievements and significant limitations. It fostered national pride by emphasizing sovereignty, cultural identity, and the rejection of colonial dependency. Sukarno's vision of a centralized, uniquely Indonesian governance model was rooted in reclaiming agency from colonial powers, promoting ideals of self-reliance and economic independence. The nationalization of foreign enterprises, particularly Dutch-owned assets, symbolized a break from colonial economic control and was a bold assertion of sovereignty.[53,54] By foregrounding anti-imperialist rhetoric, Sukarno positioned Indonesia as a leader in the Non-Aligned

[49] Booth, A. (1998). The Indonesian Economy in the Nineteenth and Twentieth Centuries: A History of Missed Opportunities. London: Palgrave Macmillan.

[50] Coppel, C.A. (1983). Indonesian Chinese in Crisis. Oxford: Oxford University Press.

[51] Suryadinata, L. (1992). Pribumi Indonesians, the Chinese Minority, and China: A Study of Perceptions and Policies Singapore: Marshall Cavendish.

[52] Anderson, B. (1972). Java in a Time of Revolution: Occupation and Resistance, 1944–1946. Ithaca, NY: Cornell University Press.

[53] Feith, H. (1962). The Decline of Constitutional Democracy in Indonesia. Ithaca, NY: Cornell University Press.

[54] Ricklefs, M.C. (2008). A History of Modern Indonesia Since c.1200. 4th edn. Basingstoke: Palgrave Macmillan.

Movement, reinforcing national pride and a sense of global importance.[55] However, the era also underscored the challenges of transitioning from colonial dependence to self-reliance, especially in a resource-constrained and sociopolitically diverse context. Economically, the policies of Guided Democracy were ambitious but poorly executed. The nationalization efforts lacked the managerial expertise and institutional capacity required to transform state-owned enterprises into engines of growth. Instead, these enterprises were plagued by inefficiency, corruption, and bureaucratic mismanagement, undermining their intended developmental role.[56] Furthermore, the economic policies exacerbated regional inequalities, as resource-rich provinces like Aceh and West Sumatra resisted centralized control, leading to tensions and rebellions.[57]

The political framework of Guided Democracy aimed to balance competing ideologies—nationalism, communism, and political Islam—but at the expense of political pluralism and institutional stability. Sukarno's authoritarian tendencies marginalized opposition parties and concentrated power in his hands. The resulting political instability weakened democratic institutions and left Indonesia vulnerable to economic mismanagement and social unrest.[58] Socially, Guided Democracy's emphasis on nationalism often overlooked the complexities of Indonesia's ethnically and culturally diverse population. Policies like Presidential Directive No. 10 of 1959, which targeted ethnic Chinese traders, alienated a key segment of the population and disrupted rural economies, deepening socio-economic divisions.[59,60] The failure to implement meaningful land reforms further highlighted the gap between nationalist ideals and practical governance, leaving rural communities disillusioned and

[55] Anderson, B. (1972). Java in a Time of Revolution: Occupation and Resistance, 1944–1946. Ithaca, NY: CornelUniversity Press.

[56] Booth, A. (1998). The Indonesian Economy in the Nineteenth and Twentieth Centuries: A History of Missed Opportunities. London: Palgrave Macmillan.

[57] Feith, H. (1962). The Decline of Constitutional Democracy in Indonesia. Ithaca, NY: Cornell University Press.

[58] Ricklefs, M.C. (2008). A History of Modern Indonesia Since c.1200. 4th edn. Basingstoke: Palgrave Macmillan.

[59] Coppel, C.A. (1983). Indonesian Chinese in Crisis. Oxford: Oxford University Press.

[60] Elson, R.E. (2009). The Idea of Indonesia: A History. Cambridge: Cambridge University Press.

exacerbating inequalities.[61] The legacy of Guided Democracy serves as a critical case study of the interplay between political ideology, economic strategy, and governance in post-colonial nation-building. While the era instilled a sense of national pride and laid the groundwork for asserting sovereignty, it also revealed the importance of institutional capacity, pragmatic policy-making, and inclusive governance. The challenges faced during Guided Democracy highlighted the need for sustainable development strategies that align with the realities of sociopolitical diversity and limited resources. The era underscored the importance of balancing political ambitions with pragmatic economic governance, as the gap between nationalist rhetoric and practical outcomes left the nation economically strained and politically fragmented. As Indonesia transitioned into the New Order under Suharto, the lessons of Guided Democracy—its achievements and its failures—remained a critical reference point. The emphasis on state-led development, coupled with the need to address regional disparities and institutional inefficiencies, continued to shape the trajectory of Indonesia's economic and political evolution.

The Guided Democracy era serves as a vital case study in understanding the interplay between political ideology, economic strategy, and the realities of governance in post-colonial nation-building. The Guided Democracy era in Indonesia (1957–1965) offers a rich and instructive case study for examining how political ideology, economic strategy, and governance intersect in the context of post-colonial nation-building. This period highlights the complexities faced by newly independent states attempting to assert sovereignty, foster national identity, and achieve economic independence while contending with resource constraints, diverse populations, and fragile institutions. Guided Democracy was rooted in Sukarno's vision of a unified Indonesian identity and governance system, distinct from Western models of liberal democracy. This ideology sought to harmonize Indonesia's pluralistic society by balancing competing factions of nationalism, communism, and political Islam. Sukarno's emphasis on centralized control and charismatic leadership reflected a deliberate effort to address colonial legacies of division and dependency. However, the implementation of this ideology often undermined political pluralism and institutional development. The concentration of power in the executive weakened

[61] Booth, A. (1998). The Indonesian Economy in the Nineteenth and Twentieth Centuries: A History of Missed Opportunities. London: Palgrave Macmillan.

democratic institutions, creating a system that was ill-equipped to manage dissent and socio-economic challenges.[62,63]

Economically, the era was marked by ambitious strategies aimed at reducing dependency on foreign capital and asserting control over national resources. Policies such as the nationalization of Dutch enterprises and the creation of state-owned companies were emblematic of this drive for self-reliance. However, these strategies revealed critical weaknesses in governance and institutional capacity. Many state enterprises were poorly managed, plagued by inefficiency, and riddled with corruption, which impeded their ability to contribute to sustainable economic growth.[64] These shortcomings illustrate the challenges of aligning ideological aspirations with pragmatic economic governance.

The interplay between political ideology and economic strategy during this era also had significant social implications. For example, policies aimed at fostering economic nationalism, such as Presidential Directive No. 10 of 1959, disrupted established economic structures and exacerbated ethnic tensions. By targeting ethnic Chinese traders, the directive not only alienated a key segment of the population but also destabilized rural commerce, highlighting the risks of ideological policies that do not account for social diversity and economic realities.[65,66] The Guided Democracy era underscores the importance of institutional robustness in post-colonial governance. While its ideological goals were aimed at achieving national unity and independence, the period also demonstrated how weak institutions, and authoritarian governance could exacerbate economic inefficiencies and social divides. The failure to implement inclusive and effective policies led to regional inequalities, political instability, and economic stagnation, ultimately contributing to the regime's collapse

[62] Feith, H. (1962). The Decline of Constitutional Democracy in Indonesia. Ithaca, NY: Cornell University Press.

[63] Ricklefs, M.C. (2008). A History of Modern Indonesia Since c.1200. 4th edn. Basingstoke: Palgrave Macmillan.

[64] Booth, A. (1998). The Indonesian Economy in the Nineteenth and Twentieth Centuries: A History of Missed Opportunities. London: Palgrave Macmillan.

[65] Coppel, C.A. (1983). Indonesian Chinese in Crisis. Oxford: Oxford University Press.

[66] Elson, R.E. (2009). The Idea of Indonesia: A History. Cambridge: Cambridge University Press.

and the transition to Suharto's New Order.[67] As a case study, the Guided Democracy era offers critical lessons for other post-colonial nations. It highlights the need for a careful balance between ambitious ideological objectives and pragmatic governance strategies. The period illustrates that while political ideologies can inspire unity and assert national identity, they must be supported by strong institutions, effective economic management, and inclusive policies to achieve sustainable development.

References

Anderson, B. R. O. G. (1972). Java in a time of revolution: Occupation and resistance, 1944-1946. Cornell University Press.

Booth, A. (1998) The Indonesian Economy in the Nineteenth and Twentieth Centuries: A History of Missed Opportunities. London: Macmillan.

Coppel, C.A. (1983). Indonesian Chinese in Crisis. Oxford: Oxford University Press.

Elson, R. E. (2009). The idea of Indonesia: A history. Cambridge University Press.

Feith, H. (1962) The Decline of Constitutional Democracy in Indonesia. Ithaca, NY: Cornell University Press.

Glassburner, B. (1971) 'Economic Policy-Making in Indonesia, 1950-1957', Economic Development and Cultural Change, 19(3), pp. 289-308.

Lev, D. S. (1966) The Transition to Guided Democracy: Indonesian Politics, 1957-1959. Ithaca, NY: Modern Indonesia Project, Cornell University.

Mackie, J.A.C. (1976). Konfrontasi: The Indonesia-Malaysia Dispute, 1963–1966. Kuala Lumpur: Oxford University Press.

McVey, R. T. (1965) The Rise of Indonesian Communism. Ithaca, NY: Cornell University Press.

Ricklefs, M. C. (2008) A History of Modern Indonesia Since c.1200. 4th edn. Stanford, CA: Stanford University Press.

Robison, R. (1986) Indonesia: The Rise of Capital. Sydney: Allen & Unwin.

Suryadinata, L. (1992). Pribumi Indonesians, the Chinese Minority, and China: A Study of Perceptions and Policies. Singapore: Marshall Cavendish.

[67] Ricklefs, M.C. (2008). A History of Modern Indonesia Since c.1200. 4th edn. Basingstoke: Palgrave Macmillan.

CHAPTER 10

The New Order Era (1966–1998)

Introduction

The New Order era in Indonesia, spanning from 1966 to 1998, represents a critical phase in the country's political and economic development. Under the leadership of President Suharto, Indonesia underwent profound transformations that reshaped its economy and political landscape. Following the political and economic turmoil of the Guided Democracy period, the New Order regime emerged with a strong mandate to restore order and economic stability. Suharto's government implemented a series of economic reforms aimed at liberalizing the economy, attracting foreign investment, and promoting rapid industrialization.[1,2] The New Order's economic policies were characterized by pragmatic market-oriented strategies that significantly differed from the state-controlled economy of the previous era. These reforms led to impressive economic growth, particularly during the 1970s and 1980s, which came to be known as the "Indonesian economic miracle."[3] The New Order's economic policies under Suharto were characterized by

[1] Robison, R. (1986) Indonesia: The Rise of Capital. Sydney: Allen & Unwin.

[2] Hill, H. (2000) The Indonesian Economy since 1966: SoutheastAsia's Emerging Giant. Cambridge: Cambridge University Press.

[3] Booth, A. (1998) The Indonesian Economy in the Nineteenth and Twentieth Centuries: A History of Missed Opportunities. London: Macmillan.

S. Ramesh, *The Political Economy of Indonesia's Economic Development, Volume I*, https://doi.org/10.1007/978-3-031-94350-8_10

pragmatic, market-oriented strategies that marked a departure from the Guided Democracy era's state-controlled economy. These reforms played a pivotal role in driving Indonesia's impressive economic growth during the 1970s and 1980s, a period often referred to as the "Indonesian economic miracle." The pragmatic approach emphasized macroeconomic stability, openness to foreign investment, and export-oriented industrialization. The government focused on creating an environment conducive to economic growth by fostering market mechanisms, albeit under tight state supervision. One of the most notable reforms was the decision to stabilize the economy after the hyperinflation and economic mismanagement of the 1960s. Under the guidance of a group of Western-trained economists known as the "Berkeley Mafia," the regime implemented strict fiscal and monetary policies that successfully curbed inflation and stabilized the rupiah.[4]

Foreign investment was a cornerstone of the New Order's strategy. Suharto's government liberalized foreign investment laws and provided incentives to attract multinational corporations, particularly in the oil, gas, and manufacturing sectors. This policy helped diversify the economy and created jobs, contributing significantly to GDP growth.[5] The extent to which Indonesia's economy was diversified under Suharto's New Order regime was notable, but it remained constrained by structural dependencies and regional disparities. Structural dependencies and regional disparities highlight the limitations and inequalities in Indonesia's economic development under Suharto's New Order regime. Structural dependencies refer to the reliance on specific sectors or resources, which made the economy vulnerable to external shocks and market volatility. During the 1970s oil boom, Indonesia's growth relied heavily on oil and gas revenues, which accounted for a substantial share of government income and export earnings. These revenues funded large-scale infrastructure projects and development programs, but the economy became overly dependent on oil, reducing the urgency for diversification into other sectors. When global oil prices fell in the 1980s, the country faced fiscal deficits and economic instability, exposing the risks of this dependency. While efforts to diversify into manufacturing and

[4] Hill, H. (1996). The Indonesian Economy: Growth and Structural Change. Cambridge: Cambridge University Press.

[5] Booth, A. (1998). The Indonesian Economy in the Nineteenth and Twentieth Centuries: A History of Missed Opportunities. London: Palgrave Macmillan.

export-oriented industries were partially successful, much of the industrial base relied on low-cost labour in sectors like textiles and footwear. This reliance on low-value-added exports limited Indonesia's ability to transition into more sophisticated and competitive industries, leaving the economy vulnerable to external pressures.[6,7] The problem of structural dependency was compounded by crony capitalism, where key industries such as banking, construction, and resource extraction were dominated by elites with close ties to Suharto's regime. During Suharto's New Order regime, the problem of structural dependency was deeply intertwined with crony capitalism, as key industries such as banking, construction, and resource extraction were dominated by elites closely tied to the regime. These individuals and networks, drawn from Suharto's family, trusted business allies, and military officials, used their connections to amass significant wealth and influence, shaping Indonesia's economic landscape in ways that entrenched inequality and inefficiency. Central to this system was Suharto's own family, which wielded immense economic power. His children were at the heart of this network. Tutut Suharto (Siti Hardiyanti Rukmana) controlled toll roads and broadcasting businesses, while Tommy Suharto (Hutomo Mandala Putra) monopolized the lucrative clove trade and held large-scale logging concessions. Bambang Trihatmodjo, another of Suharto's children, became a significant player in construction and real estate. Their privileged access to government contracts and state resources epitomized the concentration of economic power within the first family.[8,9] Beyond the Suharto family, trusted allies also dominated key industries. Liem Sioe Liong, later known as Sudono Salim, was one of Suharto's closest business associates and a prime example of the mutually beneficial relationships fostered during this era. As the head of the Salim Group, Liem controlled Bank Central Asia (BCA), one of Indonesia's largest private banks, as well as interests in flour milling, cement production, and consumer goods. His success

[6] Hill, H. (1996). The Indonesian Economy: Growth and Structural Change. Cambridge: Cambridge University Press.

[7] Booth, A. (1998). The Indonesian Economy in the Nineteenth and Twentieth Centuries: A History of Missed Opportunities. London: Palgrave Macmillan.

[8] Robison, R. (1986). Indonesia: The Rise of Capital. Sydney: Allen & Unwin.

[9] Schwarz, A. (1994). A Nation in Waiting: Indonesia's Search for Stability. Boulder, CO: Westview Press.

was largely built on his relationship with Suharto, who provided preferential access to markets and government contracts in exchange for political and financial support.[10] The timber industry offers another example of crony capitalism, with figures like Bob Hasan rising to dominance. A long-time confidant of Suharto, Hasan controlled vast forestry concessions and used his influence to shape the timber and plywood industries. His privileged position allowed him to amass enormous wealth while sidelining competitors through regulatory favouritism and monopolistic practices.[11] The military also played a significant role in the economy, as senior officers leveraged their positions to control businesses and secure lucrative contracts. Figures such as General Benny Moerdani exemplified how military officials used their influence to dominate sectors like construction and logistics, blurring the lines between state authority and private enterprise.[12] This entanglement of political power and economic privilege entrenched inefficiencies within the economy. Rather than fostering competitive markets, these elite networks prioritized their own enrichment, reinforcing structural dependencies on specific industries like oil and natural resources. The broader economy suffered from stifled innovation and limited opportunities for equitable growth, with wealth concentrated among a select few at the expense of the wider population.[13] By the late 1990s, the systemic vulnerabilities created by this crony-capitalist framework became evident. The Asian Financial Crisis exposed the fragility of Indonesia's economy, as many of the industries controlled by Suharto's allies collapsed under the weight of their inefficiencies and corruption, contributing to the regime's eventual downfall. This concentration of economic power led to inefficiencies, stifled competition, and perpetuated corruption. Such practices not only undermined sustainable growth but also prevented the development of a robust and competitive private sector.[14]

[10] Robison, R. (1986). Indonesia: The Rise of Capital. Sydney: Allen & Unwin.

[11] Schwarz, A. (1994). A Nation in Waiting: Indonesia's Search for Stability. Boulder, CO: Westview Press.

[12] Crouch, H. (1978). The Army and Politics in Indonesia. Ithaca, NY: Cornell University Press.

[13] Booth, A. (1998). The Indonesian Economy in the Nineteenth and Twentieth Centuries: A History of Missed Opportunities. London: Palgrave Macmillan.

[14] Robison, R. (1986). Indonesia: The Rise of Capital. Sydney: Allen & Unwin.

Regional disparities refer to the unequal economic development across Indonesia's vast archipelago. Economic activity and investment were disproportionately concentrated in urban centres like Jakarta and resource-rich provinces such as Riau and East Kalimantan. These areas benefitted from industrialization and resource exploitation, while rural and peripheral regions, particularly in eastern Indonesia, remained underdeveloped and reliant on agriculture. Java, for instance, housed most of Indonesia's industrial and urban activities, further exacerbating rural–urban inequalities. Resource-rich regions experienced uneven development, as revenues from natural resources were often extracted by the central government or controlled by elite networks with little reinvestment in local communities. This disparity fuelled resentment in provinces like Aceh and Papua, where resource wealth coexisted with poverty and inadequate infrastructure.[15] The unequal distribution of economic benefits also had broader social and political consequences. Disparities in access to education, healthcare, and public services further entrenched inequality, leaving many regions marginalized. These inequalities undermined national cohesion and contributed to regional tensions, as communities in less developed areas perceived themselves as neglected or exploited by central authorities. Despite Indonesia's notable economic growth under the New Order, the persistence of structural dependencies and regional disparities reveals the limitations of its development model and underscores the need for more inclusive and equitable economic policies.[16,17] Nevertheless, the liberalization of foreign investment laws and the incentives provided to multinational corporations helped Indonesia transition from a predominantly agricultural economy to one with significant contributions from manufacturing, oil and gas extraction, and services.

During the 1970s, the oil and gas sectors became dominant contributors to GDP, driven by windfalls from the global oil price boom. Revenues from these sectors funded significant infrastructure development and industrialization efforts. However, this reliance on oil revenues

[15] Hadiz, V. (2010). Localising Power in Post-Authoritarian Indonesia:A SoutheastAsia Perspective. Stanford, CA: Stanford University Press.

[16] Booth, A. (1998). The Indonesian Economy in the Nineteenth and Twentieth Centuries: A History of Missed Opportunities. London: Palgrave Macmillan.

[17] Hill, H. (1996). The Indonesian Economy: Growth and Structural Change. Cambridge: Cambridge University Press.

also created a vulnerability to global market fluctuations, as seen in the economic challenges Indonesia faced when oil prices declined in the 1980s.[18] To mitigate this dependency, the government promoted export-oriented industrialization in the 1980s, encouraging diversification into manufacturing industries such as textiles, garments, electronics, and footwear. These sectors benefitted from Indonesia's large, inexpensive labour force and trade liberalization measures, which included tariff reductions and the establishment of export processing zones.[19] By the 1990s, manufacturing had overtaken agriculture as the largest sector in terms of GDP contribution, reflecting a significant shift in the economic structure.[20] Agriculture, while declining in relative GDP contribution, remained a critical part of the economy, employing a substantial portion of the population and benefitting from government initiatives such as the Green Revolution. Increased rice production, supported by investments in irrigation, fertilizers, and rural infrastructure, helped achieve self-sufficiency in rice by the mid-1980s, illustrating the partial diversification within the agricultural sector itself.[21] Despite these successes, diversification was uneven. The economy continued to rely heavily on resource extraction, particularly oil, gas, and timber, which sustained export earnings but also perpetuated regional inequalities. Resource-rich provinces like Riau and East Kalimantan benefitted disproportionately, while other regions lagged in development.[22,23] Additionally, the industrial base was concentrated in urban areas like Jakarta, exacerbating rural–urban disparities. Overall, while the New Order achieved substantial diversification compared to the pre-1966 economy, the shift was incomplete. Resource dependency, regional inequalities, and a concentration of industrial activity in certain sectors and regions left Indonesia exposed

[18] Hill, H. (1996). The Indonesian Economy: Growth and Structural Change. Cambridge: Cambridge University Press.

[19] Radelet, S., & Sachs, J.D. (1998). "The EastAsianFinancial Crisis: Diagnosis, Remedies, Prospects." Brookings Papers on Economic Activity, 1998(1), 1–90.

[20] Booth, A. (1998). The Indonesian Economy in the Nineteenth and Twentieth Centuries: A History of Missed Opportunities. London: Palgrave Macmillan.

[21] Hill, H. (1996). The Indonesian Economy: Growth and Structural Change. Cambridge: Cambridge University Press.

[22] Booth, A. (1998). The Indonesian Economy in the Nineteenth and Twentieth Centuries: A History of Missed Opportunities. London: Palgrave Macmillan.

[23] Robison, R. (1986). Indonesia: The Rise of Capital. Sydney: Allen & Unwin.

to external shocks, such as the Asian Financial Crisis, which revealed the fragility of its economic foundation.[24]

The oil boom of the 1970s provided a windfall that was invested in infrastructure, education, and health, laying the groundwork for future economic expansion. However, heavy reliance on oil revenues exposed the economy to vulnerabilities when global oil prices declined in the 1980s.[25] The government also promoted export-oriented industrialization by investing in manufacturing industries, such as textiles and electronics, which benefitted from Indonesia's abundant and inexpensive labour force. The deregulation of trade and financial markets in the mid-1980s, prompted by declining oil revenues, further bolstered Indonesia's export competitiveness. These reforms included reducing tariffs, easing import restrictions, and liberalizing the banking sector, which enhanced the flow of foreign capital and trade.[26]

The "Indonesian economic miracle" was characterized by several macroeconomic features. GDP growth averaged 7% annually during much of the 1970s and 1980s, driven by robust performance in the agricultural, manufacturing, and resource extraction sectors.[27] The agricultural sector, in particular, benefitted from the Green Revolution and government investments in rural infrastructure, leading to significant increases in rice production and rural incomes. Poverty rates declined markedly during this period, with the percentage of Indonesians living below the poverty line falling from 60% in 1970 to approximately 15% by 1990.[28] Economic stability was another hallmark of the period. Prudent fiscal policies and tight monetary controls helped maintain low inflation rates, providing a stable environment for business investment. The government's commitment to infrastructure development, including the construction of roads,

[24] Radelet, S., & Sachs, J.D. (1998). "The EastAsianFinancial Crisis: Diagnosis, Remedies, Prospects." Brookings Papers on Economic Activity, 1998(1), 1–90.

[25] Hill, H. (1996). The Indonesian Economy: Growth and Structural Change. Cambridge: Cambridge University Press.

[26] Radelet, S., & Sachs, J.D. (1998). "The EastAsianFinancial Crisis: Diagnosis, Remedies, Prospects." Brookings Papers on Economic Activity, 1998(1), 1–90.

[27] Booth, A. (1998). The Indonesian Economy in the Nineteenth and Twentieth Centuries: A History of Missed Opportunities. London: Palgrave Macmillan.

[28] Hill, H. (1996). The Indonesian Economy: Growth and Structural Change. Cambridge: Cambridge University Press.

ports, and telecommunications networks, further facilitated economic growth by improving connectivity and market access.[29]

However, the "economic miracle" also had its limitations. Economic benefits were unevenly distributed, with urban centres like Jakarta and resource-rich regions gaining disproportionately. The reliance on a centralized, state-dominated system fostered corruption and inefficiencies, while the lack of political reform meant that economic gains were not matched by progress in governance.[30] The corruption was systemic and deeply entrenched, driven by patronage networks that linked Suharto's political allies, military officials, and business elites. State-owned enterprises (SOEs), which were pivotal to the regime's economic strategy, became key sites of rent-seeking. High-ranking officials used their authority to siphon funds through inflated procurement contracts, embezzlement, and kickbacks from private contractors. For example, infrastructure projects were often awarded to companies owned by Suharto's family or close associates, regardless of their qualifications or the quality of their work.[31] These practices not only diverted resources from productive investments but also drove up costs and delayed project completion, reducing the overall efficiency of public spending. In resource-rich regions, corruption further undermined the equitable distribution of revenues. Resource extraction industries, particularly oil, gas, and timber, were tightly controlled by elites with close ties to the central government. Local communities in these regions often saw little benefit from the exploitation of their resources. Instead, royalties and profits were funnelled to Jakarta, where they were distributed among Suharto's inner circle and used to sustain patronage networks.[32] This imbalance fuelled regional grievances, particularly in provinces like Aceh and Papua, where resource wealth coexisted with widespread poverty and inadequate infrastructure.

Inefficiencies were also evident in the over-centralized management of the economy. Bureaucratic red tape and a lack of transparency slowed decision-making and discouraged private sector innovation. For instance,

[29] Booth, A. (1998). The Indonesian Economy in the Nineteenth and Twentieth Centuries: A History of Missed Opportunities. London: Palgrave Macmillan.

[30] Robison, R. (1986). Indonesia: The Rise of Capital. Sydney: Allen & Unwin.

[31] Robison, R. (1986). Indonesia: The Rise of Capital. Sydney: Allen & Unwin.

[32] Schwarz, A. (1994). A Nation in Waiting: Indonesia's Search for Stability. Boulder, CO: Westview Press.

licensing processes for businesses were cumbersome and often required bribes to expedite approvals, creating barriers for smaller entrepreneurs who lacked the connections or resources to navigate the system. This environment stifled competition and concentrated economic opportunities among politically connected firms.[33]

The agricultural sector, while crucial to employment and rural livelihoods, also suffered from inefficiencies tied to corruption and mismanagement. Fertilizer subsidies and irrigation projects, intended to support rural development, were frequently misallocated or misappropriated by local officials. As a result, many rural areas failed to see the full benefits of government programs, further widening the development gap between urban and rural regions.[34] The lack of political reform compounded these issues, as there were few checks on the misuse of power. Suharto's authoritarian governance model ensured that opposition voices were marginalized, and institutions like the judiciary and anti-corruption bodies were either weak or co-opted. This lack of accountability allowed corruption to flourish unchecked and prevented meaningful governance reforms that could have addressed these inefficiencies.[35] These weaknesses became evident during the Asian Financial Crisis, which exposed the structural vulnerabilities of the economy and brought the New Order to an end.[36] Central to the New Order's success was the regime's ability to maintain political stability through a combination of authoritarian control and the co-optation of various political and social groups. The government suppressed political dissent, tightly controlled the media, and restricted the activities of opposition parties, while simultaneously fostering a developmentalist ideology that prioritized economic growth and national

[33] Booth, A. (1998). The Indonesian Economy in the Nineteenth and Twentieth Centuries: A History of Missed Opportunities. London: Palgrave Macmillan.

[34] Hill, H. (1996). The Indonesian Economy: Growth and Structural Change. Cambridge: Cambridge University Press.

[35] Robison, R. (1986). Indonesia: The Rise of Capital. Sydney: Allen & Unwin.

[36] Radelet, S., & Sachs, J.D. (1998). "The EastAsianFinancial Crisis: Diagnosis, Remedies, Prospects." Brookings Papers on Economic Activity, 1998(1), 1–90.

unity.[37,38] This political stability was crucial in creating a conducive environment for economic development, but it also came at the cost of human rights and democratic freedoms.

The chapter will also explore the darker aspects of the New Order era, including the concentration of economic power among Suharto's inner circle, widespread corruption, and the unequal distribution of wealth.[39,40] While the New Order regime succeeded in delivering economic growth, it also entrenched crony capitalism and exacerbated income inequalities, laying the groundwork for social tensions that would eventually contribute to the regime's downfall.

The Asian financial crisis of 1997–1998 exposed the vulnerabilities of the New Order's economic model, leading to a severe economic downturn, widespread social unrest, and ultimately, the resignation of Suharto in 1998. The crisis revealed the deep-seated structural weaknesses in Indonesia's economy, including its over-reliance on foreign capital, the fragility of its financial sector, and the lack of effective governance.[41,42] This chapter will analyse how these factors contributed to the collapse of the New Order and the subsequent transition to a more democratic and decentralized political system.

Economic Reforms and Growth Strategies

The New Order Era under Suharto (1966–1998) was marked by sweeping economic reforms and growth strategies that transformed Indonesia from a largely agrarian economy into one of Southeast Asia's major emerging markets. These reforms were initially driven by the need

[37] Anderson, B. R. O'G. (1990) Language and Power: Exploring Political Cultures in Indonesia. Ithaca, NY: Cornell University Press.

[38] McLeod, R. H. (2000) 'Soeharto's Indonesia: A Better Class of Corruption', Agenda: A Journal of Policy Analysis and Reform, 7(2), pp. 99–112.

[39] MacIntyre, A. (2003) The Power of Institutions: Political Architecture and Governance. Ithaca, NY: Cornell University Press.

[40] Winters, J. A. (1996) Power in Motion: Capital Mobility and the Indonesian State. Ithaca, NY: Cornell University Press.

[41] Hill, H. (2000) The Indonesian Economy since 1966: SoutheastAsia's Emerging Giant. Cambridge: Cambridge University Press.

[42] Soesastro, H. and Basri, M. C. (1998) 'Survey of Recent Developments', Bulletin of Indonesian Economic Studies, 34(1), pp. 3–54.

to stabilize the economy after the Guided Democracy period, which had left Indonesia in a state of hyperinflation, stagnation, and severe fiscal deficits.[43] The New Order regime prioritized macroeconomic stabilization, export-led growth, and the establishment of pro-market policies, which were instrumental in fostering sustained economic growth. Key to this transformation was the government's partnership with Western economists, known as the "Berkeley Mafia," who implemented policies that curbed inflation, stabilized the rupiah, and opened the economy to foreign investment. This early focus on fiscal and monetary discipline restored confidence in Indonesia's financial markets and laid the groundwork for future growth.[44] The government adopted an export-oriented industrialization (EOI) strategy, focusing on sectors such as oil, gas, and manufacturing. Oil revenues, buoyed by the 1970s oil boom, played a critical role in funding large-scale infrastructure projects and rural development programs, including the Transmigration Program. However, the heavy reliance on oil revenues also made the economy vulnerable to fluctuations in global oil prices, a limitation the government sought to address through diversification efforts in the 1980s.[45]

Structural adjustments in the mid-1980s, prompted by declining oil revenues and external debt pressures, represented a second wave of reforms. These adjustments included deregulation of trade and investment policies, a reduction in tariff and non-tariff barriers, and financial sector liberalization.[46] These reforms encouraged foreign direct investment (FDI) in manufacturing, particularly in textiles and electronics, which became significant contributors to export earnings. By the 1990s, Indonesia had emerged as a regional hub for labour-intensive manufacturing, benefiting from a large and inexpensive labour force.[47] However, the benefits of these growth strategies were unevenly distributed. While

[43] Hill, H. (1996). The Indonesian Economy Since 1966: SoutheastAsia's Emerging Giant. Cambridge: Cambridge University Press.

[44] Booth, A. (1998). The Indonesian Economy in the Nineteenth and Twentieth Centuries: A History of Missed Opportunities. London: Palgrave Macmillan.

[45] Hill, H. (1996). The Indonesian Economy Since 1966: SoutheastAsia's Emerging Giant. Cambridge: Cambridge University Press.

[46] Pangestu, M. (1996). Economic Reforms, Deregulation, and Privatization: The Indonesian Experience. Jakarta: Centre for Strategic and International Studies.

[47] Booth, A. (1998). The Indonesian Economy in the Nineteenth and Twentieth Centuries: A History of Missed Opportunities. London: Palgrave Macmillan.

GDP growth averaged 7% annually from the late 1980s to mid-1990s, rural–urban income disparities and regional inequalities persisted.[48] The economic growth during this period was driven by export-oriented industrialization and foreign investment, significant rural–urban income disparities and regional inequalities persisted, highlighting the uneven distribution of economic benefits. This growth was concentrated in urban centres, particularly on the islands of Java and Bali, which benefitted from greater industrial activity, infrastructure investments, and access to export markets. Conversely, rural areas, particularly in the Outer Islands such as Sumatra, Kalimantan, and Papua, remained heavily reliant on agriculture and resource extraction, sectors that experienced slower productivity growth and offered lower wages.[49,50]

Government policies during the New Order era favoured urban industrial development, often at the expense of rural economies. For example, large-scale infrastructure projects and manufacturing investments were disproportionately concentrated in urban regions, perpetuating a development gap between urban and rural areas.[51] Furthermore, while Java's urban areas saw increased employment opportunities and rising incomes due to manufacturing and service sector growth, rural agricultural communities faced stagnant incomes due to limited technological advancements and declining global commodity prices for key exports like rubber and palm oil.[52] Regional inequalities also persisted as resource-rich provinces such as Aceh and East Kalimantan, despite contributing significantly to national revenues through oil and gas production, saw limited reinvestment in local infrastructure and social services. These provinces experienced growing discontent as the central government retained a

[48] Hill, H. (1996). The Indonesian Economy Since 1966: SoutheastAsia's Emerging Giant. Cambridge: Cambridge University Press.

[49] Booth, A. (1998). The Indonesian Economy in the Nineteenth and Twentieth Centuries: A History of Missed Opportunities. London: Palgrave Macmillan.

[50] Hill, H. (2000). Indonesia's Industrial Transformation. Singapore: Institute of Southeast Asian Studies.

[51] Hill, H. (2000). Indonesia's Industrial Transformation. Singapore: Institute of Southeast Asian Studies.

[52] Pangestu, M., & Habir, A.D. (1989). Indonesia's Agricultural Development: Policy and Performance. Jakarta: CSIS.

large share of their resource revenues to fund development in Java and Bali, further exacerbating regional tensions.[53,54]

This imbalance in economic development contributed to a dual economy, where the urban industrial sector thrived while rural and peripheral regions lagged behind. The regional disparities and rural–urban divide underscored the need for more inclusive development policies to ensure that the benefits of rapid economic growth were equitably distributed across Indonesia's diverse geographic and social landscape.[55] The close ties between the state and conglomerates fostered crony capitalism, leading to inefficiencies and corruption that undermined long-term economic sustainability.[56] These structural weaknesses, combined with over-reliance on short-term foreign capital, contributed to Indonesia's vulnerability during the 1997 Asian Financial Crisis. Crony capitalism became a defining feature of Indonesia's economic landscape during the Suharto-led New Order era (1966–1998). Under this system, powerful political elites and well-connected business conglomerates formed mutually beneficial relationships, wherein access to lucrative government contracts, licenses, and subsidies was often determined by personal or familial connections rather than merit or competition.[57] While this arrangement fuelled rapid economic growth for much of the New Order period, it also entrenched structural inefficiencies and created an economy heavily dependent on patronage.

The centralization of economic decision-making under Suharto allowed select conglomerates to dominate critical sectors such as banking, construction, and natural resources. Figures like Liem Sioe Liong, whose Salim Group grew into one of Indonesia's largest conglomerates, exemplified the deep interdependence between state power and private enterprise.[58] While these conglomerates generated employment and spurred industrial growth, their privileged status often stifled competition, limited

[53] Robison, R. (1986). Indonesia: The Rise of Capital. Sydney: Allen & Unwin.

[54] Hill, H. (1996). The Indonesian Economy Since 1966: SoutheastAsia's Emerging Giant. Cambridge: Cambridge University Press.

[55] Booth, A. (1998). The Indonesian Economy in the Nineteenth and Twentieth Centuries: A History of Missed Opportunities. London: Palgrave Macmillan.

[56] Robison, R. (1986). Indonesia: The Rise of Capital. Sydney: Allen & Unwin.

[57] Robison, R. (1986). Indonesia: The Rise of Capital. Allen & Unwin.

[58] Schwarz, A. (1994). A Nation in Waiting: Indonesia's Search for Stability. Westview Press.

innovation, and created monopolistic practices that hindered broader economic development. The privileged status of conglomerates like Liem Sioe Liong's Salim Group during Suharto's New Order regime stifled innovation and competition by fostering monopolistic practices and creating barriers to entry for smaller and medium-sized enterprises (SMEs). This environment allowed these large conglomerates to dominate key sectors of the economy while disincentivizing efficiency and innovation. The Salim Group, as a prime example, benefitted from Suharto's patronage and exclusive access to state resources, including preferential treatment in obtaining government contracts, credit from state-owned banks, and access to import and export licenses. Such privileges enabled the conglomerate to monopolize industries like flour milling through its company, Bogasari, and palm oil production, thereby limiting market opportunities for competitors. These monopolies discouraged new entrants by creating artificially high barriers to entry, such as controlling supply chains and lobbying for regulations that favoured large incumbents.[59]

This environment stifled competition, as smaller businesses struggled to access the same levels of capital, infrastructure, and market share. For example, preferential lending practices by state banks ensured that politically connected conglomerates received loans on favourable terms, while smaller firms were either excluded from financing or forced to borrow at higher interest rates. This unequal access to credit suppressed entrepreneurial activity, particularly in innovative industries that required significant upfront investment.[60]

Innovation was further constrained by the lack of incentives for conglomerates to improve efficiency or adopt new technologies. Protected by their close ties to the regime and shielded from competitive pressures, these businesses often focused on maintaining their monopolistic advantages rather than investing in research and development or improving productivity. For instance, the Salim Group's dominance in the flour milling sector reduced the motivation to enhance production processes or diversify product offerings, as its market position was secure due to government-imposed restrictions on imports and other

[59] Robison, R. (1986). Indonesia: The Rise of Capital. Sydney: Allen & Unwin.

[60] Schwarz, A. (1994). A Nation in Waiting: Indonesia's Search for Stability. Boulder, CO: Westview Press.

competitors.[61] Moreover, the concentration of economic power in a few conglomerates led to economic inefficiencies by discouraging market-driven resource allocation. These conglomerates often operated across multiple sectors, crowding out specialized firms that might have been more innovative or efficient. For example, the involvement of politically connected conglomerates in industries ranging from banking to real estate diluted focus and expertise, leading to suboptimal performance in many sectors.[62] The reliance on patronage networks also perpetuated corruption, further distorting the economic landscape. Conglomerates often secured their positions through bribes and political favours, which distorted market mechanisms and directed resources toward maintaining their dominance rather than fostering a dynamic and competitive economy. This reliance on rent-seeking behaviour diverted attention and resources away from innovation and productive enterprise, hampering broader economic development.[63] The conglomerates like the Salim Group exemplified how close ties between state power and private enterprise undermined competition and innovation in Indonesia. Their monopolistic practices, facilitated by political patronage, created an economic environment where efficiency and technological progress were secondary to maintaining entrenched advantages. This dynamic hindered the broader economic development necessary for a diversified and resilient economy. Furthermore, many of these conglomerates were shielded from market pressures, enabling inefficiencies and fostering an over-reliance on political connections. Corruption, a hallmark of crony capitalism, permeated Indonesia's economic institutions. Rent-seeking behaviour, where elites extracted economic rents through monopolies, inflated contracts, and kickbacks, undermined public trust and diverted resources away from productive investments. Public infrastructure projects, for example, were frequently plagued by inflated costs and substandard quality, reflecting the systemic inefficiencies of this system.[64] This environment disincentivized

[61] Hill, H. (1996). The Indonesian Economy: Growth and Structural Change. Cambridge: Cambridge University Press.

[62] Booth, A. (1998). The Indonesian Economy in the Nineteenth and Twentieth Centuries: A History of Missed Opportunities. London: Palgrave Macmillan.

[63] Robison, R., & Hadiz, V. (2004). Reorganising Power in Indonesia: The Politics of Oligarchy in an Age of Markets. London: Routledge.

[64] Booth, A. (1998). The Indonesian Economy in the Nineteenth and Twentieth Centuries: A History of Missed Opportunities. Macmillan.

foreign and domestic investment in sectors that could have fostered long-term, sustainable growth.

A key vulnerability exacerbated by this crony-capitalist framework was Indonesia's over-reliance on short-term foreign capital, particularly in the 1990s. In a bid to sustain growth and finance the deficit, the government liberalized its financial sector, encouraging a surge in foreign portfolio investments and short-term borrowing. While this influx of capital initially spurred growth, it masked underlying structural weaknesses, including a fragile banking system dominated by poorly regulated conglomerate-owned banks.[65] These banks often engaged in reckless lending practices, channelling funds to connected businesses rather than assessing the viability of projects based on sound economic principles. When the 1997 Asian Financial Crisis struck, these vulnerabilities were laid bare.

The 1997 Asian Financial Crisis starkly revealed the structural vulnerabilities embedded within Indonesia's economic system, vulnerabilities that had accumulated over decades of crony capitalism, weak financial regulation, and over-reliance on short-term foreign capital. Indonesia's economic growth during the Suharto-led New Order period appeared robust, with annual GDP growth averaging 7% in the decades leading up to the crisis.[66] However, this growth was underpinned by a governance model that heavily favoured politically connected conglomerates. State resources were routinely funnelled toward these conglomerates, often at the expense of efficiency and economic sustainability. This system of crony capitalism created an economic environment in which market competition was stifled, decision-making was driven by political favouritism, and resources were allocated to entities lacking the capacity for productive use. The dominance of politically linked conglomerates not only entrenched corruption but also inhibited broader private sector development, leaving the economy vulnerable to external shocks.[67]

Financial sector vulnerabilities further compounded these risks. In the years preceding the crisis, Indonesia liberalized its financial markets to attract foreign investment, leading to a rapid expansion of private banks. However, regulatory oversight lagged behind, allowing many banks—often owned by conglomerates—to engage in risky lending

[65] Hill, H. (2000). The Indonesian Economy. Cambridge University Press.

[66] Hill, H. (2000). The Indonesian Economy. Cambridge University Press.

[67] Robison, R. (1986). Indonesia: The Rise of Capital. Allen & Unwin.

practices. Loans were frequently directed toward affiliated businesses without adequate risk assessment, resulting in a significant accumulation of non-performing loans.[68] This fragile banking system, combined with the government's reliance on short-term foreign capital inflows, created a precarious economic foundation. By the mid-1990s, Indonesia's foreign-denominated debt had ballooned, much of it unhedged, leaving the economy overly sensitive to currency volatility. The country's managed exchange rate policy further exacerbated the problem, as the rupiah became overvalued, reducing export competitiveness and increasing reliance on external borrowing.[69]

The crisis was triggered by external shocks, beginning in Thailand with the collapse of the Thai baht in July 1997. This event set off a wave of speculative attacks and capital outflows across Southeast Asia, quickly spreading to Indonesia. The rupiah, which was initially pegged to a basket of currencies, came under severe pressure, forcing the government to float the currency in August 1997. The subsequent devaluation of the rupiah was catastrophic, with its value plummeting by over 80% within months.[70] The depreciation dramatically increased the cost of servicing foreign-denominated debt, pushing many businesses and banks into insolvency. The banking sector, already weakened by reckless lending practices, collapsed as depositors lost confidence and withdrew funds en masse, necessitating government intervention and the nationalization of failing institutions.[71] These financial disruptions severely impacted the real economy, with GDP contracting by more than 13% in 1998. The crisis also triggered widespread unemployment and a sharp increase in poverty rates, plunging millions of Indonesians into economic hardship.[72] The crisis not only exposed Indonesia's economic vulnerabilities but also highlighted the dangers of over-reliance on short-term capital flows and inadequate regulatory frameworks. The reliance on foreign portfolio investments to finance growth masked deeper structural weaknesses,

[68] Hill, H. (2000). The Indonesian Economy. Cambridge University Press.

[69] Schwarz, A. (1994). A Nation in Waiting: Indonesia's Search for Stability. Westview Press.

[70] Booth, A. (1998). The Indonesian Economy in the Nineteenth and Twentieth Centuries: A History of Missed Opportunities. Macmillan.

[71] Hill, H. (2000). The Indonesian Economy. Cambridge University Press.

[72] Booth, A. (1998). The Indonesian Economy in the Nineteenth and Twentieth Centuries: A History of Missed Opportunities. Macmillan.

including inefficient state enterprises and a lack of economic diversification.[73] Political factors further exacerbated the crisis, as Suharto's government struggled to maintain public confidence amidst growing accusations of nepotism and corruption. The economic collapse fuelled public protests, culminating in Suharto's resignation in May 1998 and the end of his three-decade rule.[74] The aftermath of the crisis prompted significant economic and political reforms in Indonesia. Under the guidance of the International Monetary Fund (IMF), the country undertook measures to improve financial regulation, reduce corruption, and enhance market transparency. While these reforms have strengthened Indonesia's economic resilience in subsequent decades, the legacy of the vulnerabilities exposed during the 1997 crisis continues to shape its development trajectory.

The Asian Financial Crisis thus serves as a critical case study in the importance of sound governance, effective regulation, and sustainable economic practices. Indonesia's experience underscores the dangers of economic models that prioritize short-term growth over long-term stability and the risks inherent in systems where economic power is concentrated in the hands of a few politically connected entities. These lessons remain highly relevant not only for Indonesia but also for other developing economies seeking to navigate the complexities of globalization and financial liberalization. The rapid withdrawal of foreign capital triggered a currency devaluation that caused debt denominated in foreign currencies to skyrocket. Conglomerates, heavily leveraged with foreign loans, faced insolvency, while the banking sector crumbled under the weight of bad debts. The crisis exposed the fragility of Indonesia's crony-capitalist system, with its lack of transparency, poor governance, and reliance on short-term capital flows. GDP contracted by over 13% in 1998, poverty rates surged, and political upheaval ensued, leading to Suharto's resignation.

The legacy of these structural weaknesses continued to shape Indonesia's post-crisis recovery and reform trajectory. The International Monetary Fund (IMF) imposed strict conditions on bailout packages,

[73] Robison, R. (1986). Indonesia: The Rise of Capital. Allen & Unwin.

[74] Schwarz, A. (1994). A Nation in Waiting: Indonesia's Search for Stability. Westview Press.

demanding reforms aimed at dismantling monopolies, improving financial regulation, and curbing corruption. While these reforms achieved varying degrees of success, the entrenched nature of state-conglomerate ties posed enduring challenges to building a transparent and competitive economic framework. The intertwining of state power and conglomerates in Indonesia not only hindered long-term economic sustainability but also amplified the nation's vulnerability to external shocks. The 1997 Asian Financial Crisis underscored the need for deep structural reforms to address systemic inefficiencies, improve governance, and reduce the economy's reliance on politically connected enterprises and volatile foreign capital. Despite the challenges, the economic reforms of the New Order era laid the foundation for Indonesia's integration into the global economy. The period serves as a critical case study in understanding the trade-offs between rapid growth, inequality, and governance in developing economies.

Political Stability and Authoritarian Control

The New Order era (1966–1998) under President Suharto was characterized by a political system that prioritized stability and authoritarian control to foster economic development. Suharto's regime, which emerged following the tumultuous aftermath of the 1965 coup and the mass killings of alleged communists, consolidated power through a combination of military dominance, centralized governance, and suppression of dissent.[75] The regime sought to create a controlled political environment that would ensure long-term stability and provide the foundation for rapid economic growth. However, this approach came with significant trade-offs, including the erosion of democratic freedoms, the marginalization of political opposition, and the entrenchment of corruption and patronage networks.

Suharto's strategy for maintaining political stability was deeply rooted in authoritarian control. The military, or Tentara Nasional Indonesia (TNI), played a central role in the political system, serving as both a governing body and a tool for suppressing dissent. Through the doctrine of dwifungsi (dual function), the military was granted both security and sociopolitical roles, effectively embedding itself in all aspects of

[75] Anderson, B. R. O. G. (1983). Old State, New Society: Indonesia's New Order in Comparative Historical Perspective. Journal of Asian Studies, 42(3), 477–496.

governance.[76] This allowed the regime to stifle opposition movements, particularly those linked to political Islam and regional separatist groups, such as the Free Aceh Movement (GAM). The suppression of regional aspirations for autonomy ensured that Jakarta maintained control over resource-rich provinces, though it often exacerbated local grievances and created long-standing tensions.[77]

The political system was further stabilized by the systematic marginalization of opposition parties. Suharto's government restricted political competition by limiting the number of parties and tightly controlling their activities. Golkar, the state-sponsored political organization, became the dominant vehicle for political participation, while opposition parties like the Indonesian Democratic Party (PDI) and the United Development Party (PPP) were co-opted or suppressed.[78] Elections, held every five years, were heavily manipulated to ensure Golkar's victory, rendering them little more than a facade of democracy. This control over political institutions allowed Suharto to project an image of stability and order, even as the regime's legitimacy was built on coercion rather than popular consent.

Economic development was central to Suharto's consolidation of power, as the regime sought to legitimize its authoritarian rule through improved living standards and national prosperity. The government's success in achieving sustained economic growth and poverty reduction during the 1970s and 1980s earned the regime considerable domestic and international support.[79] However, this growth was accompanied by the entrenchment of crony capitalism, with Suharto's family and close associates benefiting disproportionately from state resources. Corruption became systemic, as government contracts, licenses, and monopolies were awarded to politically connected conglomerates, undermining economic efficiency and creating significant vulnerabilities that would later contribute to the 1997 Asian Financial Crisis.[80] While political

[76] Crouch, H. (1978). The Army and Politics in Indonesia. Cornell University Press.

[77] Aspinall, E. (2009). Islam and Nation: Separatist Rebellion in Aceh, Indonesia. Stanford University Press.

[78] Schwarz, A. (1994). A Nation in Waiting: Indonesia's Search for Stability. Westview Press.

[79] Hill, H. (2000). The Indonesian Economy. Cambridge University Press.

[80] Robison, R. (1986). Indonesia: The Rise of Capital. Allen & Unwin.

stability under Suharto facilitated economic growth and development, it came at a significant cost to human rights and political freedoms. The regime employed repressive measures to silence dissent, including censorship, arbitrary arrests, and forced disappearances. Human rights abuses were particularly acute in regions with active separatist movements, such as Aceh, Papua, and East Timor, where military operations were used to suppress local resistance.[81] These actions highlighted the authoritarian nature of the regime and the limits of its commitment to inclusivity and justice.

The legacy of political stability under authoritarian control in the New Order era remains deeply contested. On one hand, Suharto's rule is credited with achieving relative economic stability and improving infrastructure and social welfare. On the other hand, the suppression of political freedoms, the concentration of power in the hands of a narrow elite, and the systemic corruption that characterized his regime left a legacy of inequality and institutional weakness. The eventual collapse of the New Order in 1998, amid the economic turmoil of the Asian Financial Crisis and widespread public protests, underscored the fragility of a political system built on authoritarianism and patronage rather than genuine democratic legitimacy.

Crony Capitalism and Corruption

The New Order era (1966–1998) under President Suharto was defined by a political economy heavily reliant on crony capitalism and entrenched corruption. Suharto's consolidation of power created a system in which economic resources were concentrated in the hands of his family, close allies, and a select group of politically connected conglomerates. This arrangement ensured loyalty among elites and sustained the regime's grip on power but came at the expense of economic efficiency, equitable development, and institutional integrity.

Crony capitalism in Indonesia during this period was exemplified by the dominance of Suharto's family and their associates in critical sectors of the economy. Major infrastructure projects, natural resource extraction, and banking were allocated to a small group of well-connected conglomerates, such as the Salim Group, led by Liem Sioe Liong. Liem,

[81] Aspinall, E. (2009). Islam and Nation: Separatist Rebellion in Aceh, Indonesia. Stanford University Press.

a close associate of Suharto, controlled vast portions of the economy, including food production, banking, and manufacturing, benefitting from government-backed monopolies and favourable regulations.[82] Such arrangements discouraged competition, as market access was often determined by political connections rather than merit or innovation. Corruption was systemic, permeating all levels of government and business. Public procurement contracts were frequently inflated, with large sums siphoned off to enrich officials and their networks. For instance, the Pertamina oil scandal in the 1970s exposed how state-owned enterprises were used as vehicles for corruption. Ibnu Sutowo, then-head of Pertamina, amassed substantial personal wealth while accumulating debts that ultimately burdened the national budget.[83] This example underscores how corruption not only undermined corporate governance but also diverted resources away from public investments, exacerbating social inequalities. The pervasive nature of corruption was institutionalized through practices such as kkn (korupsi, kolusi, nepotisme—corruption, collusion, and nepotism). This triad of unethical behaviours became a hallmark of the Suharto regime, with government positions and lucrative business opportunities routinely allocated to those with personal ties to the ruling elite.[84] For example, Suharto's children gained control of monopolies in sectors such as toll roads, clove distribution, and television broadcasting, consolidating their economic power at the expense of broader economic participation.[85]

Crony capitalism and corruption also distorted economic policy and weakened institutions. Decisions on resource allocation and policy implementation were often driven by the interests of Suharto's inner circle rather than by considerations of public welfare or economic sustainability. This dynamic fostered inefficiencies, as protected conglomerates lacked the incentives to innovate or improve productivity. Moreover, the diversion of public funds toward private enrichment stifled investments in critical areas such as education, healthcare, and infrastructure, further

[82] Robison, R. (1986). Indonesia: The Rise of Capital. Allen & Unwin.

[83] Schwarz, A. (1994). A Nation in Waiting: Indonesia's Search for Stability. Westview Press.

[84] Crouch, H. (1978). The Army and Politics in Indonesia. Cornell University Press.

[85] Hill, H. (1996). The Indonesian Economy: Growth and Structural Change. Cambridge: Cambridge University Press.

entrenching economic disparities.[86] The impact of this system became starkly evident during the 1997 Asian Financial Crisis, when Indonesia's economy collapsed under the weight of its structural weaknesses. The conglomerates that had thrived under Suharto's patronage were heavily indebted in foreign currencies, and the sharp depreciation of the rupiah rendered many insolvent. Banks, often owned by these same conglomerates, were unable to recover loans, triggering a systemic banking crisis. Public outrage against corruption and nepotism fuelled widespread protests, culminating in Suharto's resignation in 1998.[87] The legacy of crony capitalism and corruption during the New Order remains deeply ingrained in Indonesia's political economy. While post-1998 reforms have sought to address these issues, including the establishment of the Corruption Eradication Commission (KPK), the remnants of the New Order's practices continue to influence governance and economic dynamics. The latter refers to the enduring impact of institutionalized corruption, clientelism, and crony capitalism established during Suharto's New Order era (1966–1998) on Indonesia's post-reform political and economic systems. While the fall of Suharto in 1998 marked a significant political shift, many structures and networks tied to the New Order persisted, shaping the nation's governance and economy in profound ways.

The New Order was characterized by a centralized, hierarchical system of governance in which economic and political power was concentrated among elites closely tied to Suharto. These elites included military officials, government bureaucrats, and business conglomerates, creating a tightly controlled patronage system that facilitated rent-seeking behaviour and corruption.[88] Even after Suharto's resignation, many of these networks remained intact, as members of the old regime maintained their influence through entrenched positions in politics and business.[89] One major legacy of the New Order is the persistence of oligarchic power.

[86] Booth, A. (1998). The Indonesian Economy in the Nineteenth and Twentieth Centuries: A History of Missed Opportunities. Macmillan.

[87] Hill, H. (1996). The Indonesian Economy: Growth and Structural Change. Cambridge: Cambridge University Press.

[88] Robison, R. (1986). Indonesia: The Rise of Capital. Sydney: Allen & Unwin.

[89] Hadiz, V., & Robison, R. (2005). "Neo-liberal Reforms and Illiberal Consolidations: The Indonesian Paradox." Journal of Development Studies, 41(2), 220–241.

Despite reforms intended to promote decentralization and democratization, local elites—often former New Order officials or their associates—adapted to the new political environment by leveraging their economic resources to dominate regional politics. These individuals used their wealth to influence elections, secure government contracts, and maintain their economic privileges, perpetuating inequality and inefficiency in resource distribution.[90] Decentralization granted significant fiscal and administrative autonomy to regional governments, a move intended to empower local communities and improve governance. However, it also created opportunities for these elites to consolidate their power at the regional level. Leveraging their economic resources and pre-existing patronage networks, they dominated local politics and used their influence to secure government contracts, manipulate electoral outcomes, and maintain their economic privileges, often at the expense of equitable development.[91] These elites, who frequently controlled key industries such as natural resources, construction, and agribusiness, played a pivotal role in financing political campaigns, thus ensuring loyalty from candidates and elected officials. This practice entrenched a form of "money politics," where wealth became a prerequisite for political success. Such dynamics often resulted in policy decisions that favoured elite interests over broader public welfare, perpetuating inequality in the distribution of resources and development opportunities.[92] Furthermore, the decentralization process, while democratic, often lacked adequate mechanisms for accountability and oversight. Local elites exploited this institutional weakness to entrench themselves further, using their control over regional budgets to distribute patronage and reward loyal supporters. This behaviour has been particularly pronounced in resource-rich provinces, such as Riau and East Kalimantan, where local governments have significant revenues from oil, gas, and mining but allocate disproportionately low investments in public services and infrastructure.[93] The continued

[90] Aspinall, E., & Berenschot, W. (2019). Democracy for Sale: Elections, Clientelism, and the State in Indonesia. Ithaca, NY: Cornell University Press.

[91] Aspinall, E., & Berenschot, W. (2019). Democracy for Sale: Elections, Clientelism, and the State in Indonesia. Ithaca, NY: Cornell University Press.

[92] Buehler, M. (2013). "Married with the State: Business Elites and Electoral Politics in Indonesia's Democratic Transition." Comparative Political Studies, 46(7), 912–935.

[93] Hadiz, V. (2010). Localising Power in Post-Authoritarian Indonesia:A SoutheastAsia Perspective. Stanford, CA: Stanford University Press.

dominance of these elites not only perpetuates inequality but also undermines efforts to improve governance and reduce corruption. For instance, public procurement processes and government tenders are frequently manipulated to favour companies linked to influential local figures, reducing transparency and efficiency. These practices reinforce economic inefficiencies and limit the potential for genuine grassroots participation in decision-making.[94] Despite the promises of reform, the resilience of New Order era networks demonstrates the complexity of dismantling entrenched patronage systems. While decentralization has provided some regions with greater autonomy and fostered political diversity, it has also enabled the entrenchment of local power structures that mirror the centralization and rent-seeking behaviours of the New Order era, undermining the broader goals of democratization and equitable development.[95]

Economic dynamics also continue to bear the imprint of New Order practices. State-owned enterprises (SOEs), which were often used during the New Order to distribute patronage, remain significant players in Indonesia's economy. While post-1998 reforms have aimed to improve transparency and efficiency, many SOEs are still plagued by inefficiencies and allegations of corruption. For example, political appointees with ties to influential elites continue to dominate leadership positions in SOEs, undermining efforts to professionalize their management.[96] Additionally, the extractive industries—particularly oil, gas, and mining—remain sectors where New Order-style rent-seeking and patronage thrive. Despite efforts to regulate these industries and ensure equitable distribution of revenues, they continue to serve as sources of wealth for well-connected elites, often at the expense of environmental sustainability and community welfare.[97]

The establishment of the Corruption Eradication Commission (KPK) and other reform initiatives has sought to address these entrenched practices, but their effectiveness has been limited by resistance from vested

[94] Warburton, E. (2020). "Reforming Indonesia's Anti-Corruption Institutions: The Limits of Resistance." Asian Survey, 60(2), 248–270.

[95] Aspinall, E., & Fealy, G. (2010). Soeharto's New Order and Its Legacy: Essays in Honour of Harold Crouch. Canberra: ANU Press.

[96] Buehler, M. (2013). "Married with the State: Business Elites and Electoral Politics in Indonesia's Democratic Transition." Comparative Political Studies, 46(7), 912–935.

[97] Varkkey, H. (2015). The Haze Problem in SoutheastAsia: Palm Oil and Patronage. London: Routledge.

interests within the political and economic elite. Frequent challenges to the KPK's authority and efforts to dilute its powers highlight the difficulty of dismantling the legacy of New Order corruption.[98] The remnants of the New Order's practices persist in Indonesia's governance and economic systems through entrenched networks of elites, ongoing patronage in politics and business, and the slow pace of institutional reforms. These challenges underscore the deep-rooted nature of Suharto-era structures and their enduring impact on the nation's development trajectory. Understanding this period is crucial for addressing the structural challenges that persist in Indonesia's development trajectory.

The Asian Financial Crisis and the Fall of Suharto

The 1997 Asian Financial Crisis marked a turning point in Indonesia's modern economic development, exposing deep-seated vulnerabilities in its economic and political systems and ultimately leading to the fall of President Suharto, who had ruled for over three decades. The crisis, which began in Thailand with the collapse of the Thai baht, quickly spread across Southeast Asia, with Indonesia experiencing one of the most severe economic collapses in the region. The crisis not only highlighted structural weaknesses in Indonesia's economy, such as crony capitalism, over-reliance on short-term foreign capital, and weak financial institutions, but also underscored the political fragility of the New Order regime.[99,100]

Indonesia's economy, heavily dependent on foreign loans and investments, was particularly vulnerable when investor confidence waned during the crisis. By 1997, Indonesia had accumulated significant foreign-denominated debt, much of it unhedged, exposing businesses and banks to substantial risks as the rupiah depreciated. When the currency lost more than 80% of its value within months, the cost of servicing this debt soared, driving many corporations and financial institutions into insolvency. The banking sector, already burdened with non-performing

[98] Warburton, E. (2020). "Reforming Indonesia's Anti-Corruption Institutions: The Limits of Resistance." Asian Survey, 60(2), 248–270.

[99] Hill, H. (1996). The Indonesian Economy: Growth and Structural Change. Cambridge: Cambridge University Press.

[100] Robison, R. (1986). Indonesia: The Rise of Capital. Allen & Unwin.

loans due to reckless lending practices, collapsed, necessitating a government bailout that further strained public finances.[101,102] The economic crisis quickly translated into social and political turmoil. Inflation skyrocketed, eroding purchasing power and pushing millions of Indonesians into poverty. Food prices surged, and shortages of essential goods became widespread, fuelling widespread discontent. Public protests erupted in cities across the country, with students, labour unions, and middle-class citizens demanding political reform and an end to Suharto's regime. These protests were exacerbated by long-standing grievances over corruption, nepotism, and the concentration of wealth among Suharto's family and close allies.[103]

Suharto's inability to manage the crisis further eroded his legitimacy. In a bid to stabilize the economy, the government sought assistance from the International Monetary Fund (IMF), which imposed strict structural adjustment measures. These included deregulation, privatization, and subsidy cuts, particularly on fuel and basic commodities, which disproportionately affected the poor and fuelled further unrest. The implementation of these reforms was perceived as a surrender of national sovereignty, deepening public resentment toward Suharto and his administration.[104] The culmination of these pressures came in May 1998, when massive demonstrations and riots engulfed Jakarta and other major cities. The violence, which included looting, arson, and targeted attacks on ethnic Chinese businesses, underscored the depth of societal fractures exacerbated by years of economic mismanagement and authoritarian rule. Amid mounting pressure from the public, political elites, and even segments of the military, Suharto resigned on May 21, 1998,

[101] Booth, A. (1998). The Indonesian Economy in the Nineteenth and Twentieth Centuries: A History of Missed Opportunities. Macmillan.

[102] Schwarz, A. (1994). A Nation in Waiting: Indonesia's Search for Stability. Westview Press.

[103] Crouch, H. (1978). The Army and Politics in Indonesia. Cornell University Press.

[104] Hill, H. (1996). The Indonesian Economy: Growth and Structural Change. Cambridge: Cambridge University Press.

marking the end of the New Order era.[105,106] The fall of Suharto marked a dramatic shift in Indonesia's political and economic landscape. While the immediate aftermath of his resignation was chaotic, it also paved the way for significant reforms. Indonesia transitioned to a democratic system, implemented measures to combat corruption, and introduced greater decentralization of political and fiscal power. However, the legacy of the crisis and Suharto's authoritarian rule continued to shape the country's development trajectory, leaving enduring challenges in addressing inequality, institutional weaknesses, and regional disparities.

The Asian Financial Crisis and the fall of Suharto serve as a critical case study in the intersection of economic vulnerabilities and political instability. Indonesia's experience highlights the importance of robust governance, sound economic policies, and inclusive institutions in sustaining long-term development and resilience against external shocks. Sound economic policies involve measures that foster macroeconomic stability and sustainable growth. During the New Order era, Indonesia pursued rapid industrialization and infrastructure development, funded significantly by external borrowing. While these strategies spurred growth, they were underpinned by crony capitalism and weak regulatory oversight. Government-linked firms with close ties to Suharto accumulated unsustainable debts, which became liabilities when the crisis triggered capital flight and a sharp depreciation of the rupiah.[107,108] The government's delayed and inconsistent policy responses, including ineffective foreign exchange interventions and failure to close insolvent banks promptly significantly undermined investor confidence and intensified the economic crisis in Indonesia.[109] These missteps highlighted both the structural weaknesses of Indonesia's financial system and the challenges of governance under Suharto's New Order regime. One of the government's key

[105] Aspinall, E. (2009). Islam and Nation: Separatist Rebellion in Aceh, Indonesia. Stanford University Press. Schwarz, A. (1994). A Nation in Waiting: Indonesia's Search for Stability. Westview Press.

[106] Schwarz, A. (1994). A Nation in Waiting: Indonesia's Search for Stability. Westview Press.

[107] Booth, A. (1998). The Indonesian Economy in the Nineteenth and Twentieth Centuries: A History of Missed Opportunities. London: Palgrave Macmillan.

[108] Robison, R. (1986). Indonesia: The Rise of Capital. Sydney: Allen & Unwin.

[109] Radelet, S., & Sachs, J.D. (1998). "The EastAsianFinancial Crisis: Diagnosis, Remedies, Prospects." Brookings Papers on Economic Activity, 1998(1), 1–90.

failures was its handling of the rupiah's dramatic devaluation. As speculative attacks on Southeast Asian currencies intensified in mid-1997, the Indonesian government initially resisted allowing the rupiah to float freely. Instead, it attempted to defend the currency by intervening in foreign exchange markets, using its foreign reserves to prop up the rupiah's value. However, these interventions were insufficient, as reserves were quickly depleted without stabilizing the currency.[110] By the time the government allowed the rupiah to float in August 1997, it had already lost significant value, and the delayed decision only deepened market uncertainty.

Inconsistent monetary policy compounded the problem. The government alternated between raising interest rates to stabilize the currency and lowering them to stimulate economic activity, sending mixed signals to investors. This lack of a coherent strategy eroded confidence further, as markets perceived the government as indecisive and ill-equipped to handle the crisis.[111] The banking sector, already fragile due to years of crony capitalism and weak regulation, was another major contributor to the crisis. Prior to the crisis, Indonesia's banking system had expanded rapidly following deregulation in the late 1980s, but oversight mechanisms failed to keep pace. Many banks were poorly managed and heavily exposed to non-performing loans, often issued to politically connected businesses without proper risk assessment.[112] When the crisis hit, the collapse of the rupiah increased the cost of servicing foreign-denominated debts, leading to widespread defaults. The government's response to the banking crisis was both delayed and inadequate. While other countries in the region, such as South Korea, moved quickly to recapitalize and restructure their banking sectors, Indonesia hesitated. Suharto's reluctance to close insolvent banks, many of which were owned by his allies, exacerbated the situation. For example, the closure of 16 small banks in November 1997—widely perceived as a politically motivated move—triggered panic among depositors and led to a widespread

[110] Radelet, S., & Sachs, J.D. (1998). "The EastAsianFinancial Crisis: Diagnosis, Remedies, Prospects." Brookings Papers on Economic Activity, 1998(1), 1–90.

[111] Hill, H. (1996). The Indonesian Economy: Growth and Structural Change. Cambridge: Cambridge University Press.

[112] Booth, A. (1999). "The Impact of the Crisis on Poverty and Equity." Developing Economies, 37(4), 401–418.

loss of confidence in the banking system.[113] Efforts to restore stability, such as the establishment of the Indonesian Bank Restructuring Agency (IBRA) in early 1998, were undermined by political interference and corruption. The IBRA was tasked with recapitalizing banks, recovering bad loans, and overseeing asset sales, but its effectiveness was limited by a lack of transparency and resistance from vested interests within Suharto's regime.[114] The government's failure to respond decisively and consistently to the crisis reflected deeper governance issues. The lack of coordination between monetary, fiscal, and regulatory authorities revealed institutional weaknesses, while the regime's prioritization of elite interests over systemic stability further eroded domestic and international confidence. This combination of factors transformed a currency and banking crisis into a broader economic and political collapse, culminating in Suharto's resignation in May 1998. In contrast, other nations in the region, such as Malaysia, implemented more decisive policy measures, including temporary capital controls, that mitigated the severity of the crisis's impact on their economies.[115]

Inclusive institutions are critical in ensuring broad-based participation in economic and political systems, promoting equitable distribution of resources, and reducing elite capture. During the New Order, Indonesia's institutions were predominantly extractive, concentrating wealth and power within Suharto's network of elites and business allies.[116,117] The exclusion of broader societal participation in decision-making created significant socio-economic inequalities. These disparities were evident during the crisis, as austerity measures, such as the removal of fuel subsidies under IMF recommendations, disproportionately burdened

[113] Schwarz, A. (1998). A Nation in Waiting: Indonesia's Search for Stability. Boulder, CO: Westview Press.

[114] Robison, R., & Hadiz, V. (2004). Reorganising Power in Indonesia: The Politics of Oligarchy in an Age of Markets. London: Routledge.

[115] Jomo, K. S. (2001) SoutheastAsia's Misunderstood Miracle: Industrial Policy and Economic Development in Thailand, Malaysiaand Indonesia. Boulder, CO: Westview Press.

[116] Acemoglu, D. & Robinson, J. A. (2012) Why Nations Fail: The Origins of Power, Prosperity, and Poverty. New York: Crown Publishers.

[117] Robison, R. (1986) Indonesia: The Rise of Capital. Sydney: Allen & Unwin.

low-income populations.[118] Widespread protests erupted in response, revealing the fragility of a governance system that lacked mechanisms to cushion economic shocks for vulnerable communities. Inclusive institutions that could have provided social safety nets or facilitated meaningful political engagement were absent, exacerbating the political and economic instability that culminated in Suharto's resignation.[119]

External shocks, such as the speculative attacks on Asian currencies and the sudden withdrawal of foreign capital during the Asian Financial Crisis, exposed Indonesia's structural vulnerabilities. The economy's heavy reliance on short-term foreign debt and a pegged exchange rate system rendered it particularly susceptible to external pressure.[120] Additionally, Indonesia's dependence on exports of commodities like oil and gas, which experienced volatile global prices, further weakened its economic resilience.[121] Unlike more diversified economies such as Singapore, which had shifted to high-value manufacturing and services, Indonesia's narrow economic base left it ill-prepared to withstand external disruptions.[122]

Indonesia's experience during the Asian Financial Crisis underscores the critical interplay between governance, economic policy, and institutional structures. Weak governance and crony capitalism undermined economic stability, while exclusive institutions deepened inequalities and eroded societal trust. The crisis ultimately forced Indonesia into a period of significant political and economic transformation, highlighting the necessity of robust, equitable, and forward-looking systems to sustain long-term development and resilience against future challenges.

[118] Rosser, A. (2002) The Politics of Economic Liberalization in Indonesia: State, Market and Power. Richmond: Curzon Press.

[119] Aspinall, E. & Fealy, G. (2010) Soeharto's New Order and Its Legacy: Essays in Honour of Harold Crouch. Canberra: ANU E Press.

[120] Radelet, S. & Sachs, J. (1998) The EastAsianFinancial Crisis: Diagnosis, Remedies, Prospects. Brookings Papers on Economic Activity, 1998(1), pp. 1–74.

[121] Hill, H. (2000) The Indonesian Economy since 1966: SoutheastAsia's Emerging Giant. Cambridge: Cambridge University Press.

[122] Booth, A. (1998) The Indonesian Economy in the Nineteenth and Twentieth Centuries: A History of Missed Opportunities. London: Macmillan.

Legacy of the New Order: Economic and Political Implications

The New Order era (1966–1998) under President Suharto left an indelible mark in Indonesia's economic and political landscape. While it was a period of substantial economic growth and infrastructural development, it was also characterized by deep-seated structural weaknesses, systemic corruption, and political repression. These dynamics shaped Indonesia's post-New Order trajectory, leaving a mixed legacy that continues to influence the nation's governance and development.

Economically, the New Order is often credited with achieving significant progress in poverty reduction, education, and infrastructure development. The government's focus on export-oriented industrialization and agricultural self-sufficiency, particularly through the Green Revolution, led to improvements in rice production and rural livelihoods.[123] During the 1970s and 1980s, Indonesia experienced consistent GDP growth, buoyed by oil revenues and foreign investment. Suharto's government also fostered economic stability by maintaining low inflation and implementing macroeconomic policies that were broadly effective in attracting international capital.[124] However, this economic progress came at a cost. The New Order's reliance on centralized decision-making and state-led development created an environment ripe for crony capitalism. Suharto's family and close allies were given control over key industries and lucrative monopolies, consolidating economic power within a narrow elite.[125] This entrenchment of crony capitalism stifled competition and innovation, leaving the economy vulnerable to external shocks. The systemic corruption embedded in the political and economic system further exacerbated inefficiencies, diverting resources away from productive investments and exacerbating inequality.[126] Politically, the New Order regime established a highly centralized and authoritarian state, suppressing dissent and limiting political freedoms. Through mechanisms such as dwifungsi

[123] Booth, A. (1998) The Indonesian Economy in the Nineteenth and Twentieth Centuries: A History of Missed Opportunities. London: Macmillan.

[124] Hill, H. (2000) The Indonesian Economy since 1966: SoutheastAsia's Emerging Giant. Cambridge: Cambridge University Press.

[125] Robison, R. (1986) Indonesia: The Rise of Capital. Sydney: Allen & Unwin.

[126] Schwarz, A. (1994). A Nation in Waiting: Indonesia's Search for Stability. Westview Press.

(dual function), the military maintained a dominant role in governance, ensuring Suharto's control over the political system.[127] Opposition parties were tightly controlled, with Golkar, the government's political vehicle, dominating elections. Civil society and independent media were constrained, and human rights abuses were widespread, particularly in regions with separatist movements, such as Aceh, Papua, and East Timor.[128]

The combination of economic centralization and political repression created a fragile foundation for Indonesia's long-term development. The vulnerabilities of this system became starkly apparent during the 1997 Asian Financial Crisis. The crisis exposed the structural weaknesses of Indonesia's crony-capitalist economy, including over-reliance on short-term foreign debt, a poorly regulated banking system, and a lack of transparency in business transactions. As the rupiah plummeted and the economy collapsed, public outrage over corruption and nepotism erupted into widespread protests, culminating in Suharto's resignation in 1998.[129] The fall of the New Order marked the beginning of Indonesia's Reformasi (Reform) era, characterized by efforts to democratize the political system and address the legacy of authoritarianism. Decentralization policies were introduced to empower regional governments and reduce the concentration of power in Jakarta, while anti-corruption measures, such as the establishment of the Corruption Eradication Commission (KPK), sought to tackle the systemic corruption inherited from the New Order. However, the remnants of Suharto's political and economic networks continued to exert influence, slowing the pace of reform and perpetuating challenges such as inequality and weak institutional capacity.[130]

The legacy of the New Order is thus one of contrasts. While it delivered economic growth and improved living standards for many Indonesians, it also entrenched a system of governance that prioritized stability and elite interests over inclusivity and transparency. Understanding this legacy is critical to contextualizing Indonesia's ongoing struggles with corruption,

[127] Crouch, H. (1978). The Army and Politics in Indonesia. Cornell University Press.

[128] Aspinall, E. (2009). Islam and Nation: Separatist Rebellion in Aceh, Indonesia. Stanford University Press.

[129] Hill, H. (2000) The Indonesian Economy since 1966: SoutheastAsia's Emerging Giant. Cambridge: Cambridge University Press.

[130] Aspinall, E. (2009). Islam and Nation: Separatist Rebellion in Aceh, Indonesia. Stanford University Press.

inequality, and institutional reform, as well as its successes in maintaining democratic governance in the post-New Order era.

Conclusion

The New Order era (1966–1998) under President Suharto was a transformative period in Indonesia's history, marked by significant achievements and enduring challenges. Economically, the regime's focus on macroeconomic stabilization, export-oriented industrialization, and infrastructural development propelled Indonesia into the ranks of Southeast Asia's emerging economies. Initiatives such as the Green Revolution improved agricultural productivity, leading to substantial reductions in rural poverty and increased food security.[131] The government also prioritized investments in physical infrastructure, including roads, ports, and electricity, which enhanced connectivity and supported industrial growth. These efforts resulted in sustained GDP growth and declining poverty rates, earning Indonesia recognition as a developmental success story. However, this economic growth was accompanied by deep structural imbalances. The benefits of development were disproportionately concentrated in urban centres, leaving rural areas and resource-rich provinces underdeveloped. The centralization of decision-making in Jakarta marginalized regional governments and exacerbated inequalities. For instance, provinces like Aceh and Papua, despite contributing significantly to national revenues through natural resource extraction, received inadequate reinvestment in public services and infrastructure, fuelling regional grievances and separatist movements.[132] This dual economy, characterized by thriving urban hubs and neglected peripheries, highlighted the uneven distribution of development under the New Order.

The economic successes of the New Order were also underpinned by a system of crony capitalism that concentrated wealth and power in the hands of Suharto's family and close associates. Key industries such as banking, construction, and oil and gas were dominated by politically

[131] Mackie, J. A. C. (1995). Money and Power in Indonesia: Political Economy in the New Order and Beyond. Allen & Unwin.

[132] Tirtosudarmo, R. (1995). The Politics of Population Mobility in Indonesia.GadjahMada University Press.

connected conglomerates, which benefited from monopolies, government contracts, and favourable regulations.[133] This patronage system stifled competition, discouraged innovation, and created inefficiencies that undermined the long-term sustainability of Indonesia's economic model. Moreover, corruption became deeply institutionalized, with public funds frequently diverted to enrich elites at the expense of social investments.[134] Politically, the New Order regime established an authoritarian system that suppressed dissent and centralized power in the executive. Through the doctrine of dwifungsi (dual function), the military played a dominant role in governance, serving as both a political force and a security apparatus. This arrangement allowed Suharto to maintain control over opposition groups and manage separatist challenges in regions such as East Timor and Aceh. However, these measures came at a significant cost to political freedoms and human rights. Widespread censorship, arbitrary arrests, and military operations in restive provinces left a legacy of repression and mistrust that persisted into the Reformasi period.[135]

The 1997 Asian Financial Crisis exposed the vulnerabilities of the New Order's economic model, leading to one of the most severe economic and political crises in Indonesia's history. The rapid devaluation of the rupiah, coupled with soaring inflation and the collapse of the banking sector, revealed the fragility of an economy heavily reliant on foreign capital and sustained by weak regulatory frameworks.[136] This combination of factors created a perfect storm that devastated Indonesia's financial stability and highlighted systemic flaws in its economic governance.

The rupiah, which had been managed under a loosely pegged exchange rate system, began to lose value rapidly in mid-1997 when speculative attacks targeted currencies across Southeast Asia. Indonesia, heavily reliant on foreign capital to finance its economic growth, was particularly vulnerable. Short-term foreign loans, much of which were denominated in U.S. dollars, constituted a significant portion of corporate and banking sector liabilities. When the rupiah depreciated by over 80% between July

[133] Budiman, A., Hatley, B., & Kingsbury, D. (1999). Reformasi: Crisis and Change in Indonesia. Monash Asia Institute.

[134] Winters, J. A. (1996). Power in Motion: Capital Mobility and the Indonesian State. Cornell University Press.

[135] Klinken, G. van, & Barker, J. (2009). State of Authority: The State in Society in Indonesia.Cornell SoutheastAsia Program.

[136] MacIntyre, A. (1999). Business and Politics in Indonesia. Allen & Unwin.

1997 and January 1998, these debts became unmanageable, triggering widespread defaults.[137] For example, many Indonesian companies that had borrowed in dollars but earned revenue in rupiah found themselves unable to meet their obligations, leading to bankruptcies and layoffs across the private sector. Inflation soared as the rupiah's collapse made imports drastically more expensive, particularly essential goods like food and fuel. Inflation rates exceeded 75% by mid-1998, eroding household purchasing power and exacerbating social unrest. This was particularly devastating for lower-income households, which spent a larger proportion of their income on basic necessities.[138] The government's attempts to stabilize the currency through interventions, including raising interest rates and seeking loans from the International Monetary Fund (IMF), were largely ineffective in the face of eroded investor confidence and political instability. The banking sector was one of the hardest hit, as weak regulatory frameworks failed to prevent or contain the crisis. Prior to the crisis, the banking sector had expanded rapidly, fuelled by deregulation in the late 1980s that had encouraged the proliferation of new banks without adequate oversight. Many of these banks were closely tied to Suharto's political and business cronies, and their lending practices were riddled with nepotism and corruption. Loans were often made to politically connected businesses with little regard for creditworthiness or risk assessment. When the crisis hit, a wave of defaults caused these banks' balance sheets to collapse, leading to widespread bank closures and a loss of public confidence in the financial system.[139] For example, Bank Summa, controlled by the prominent Soeryadjaya family, was among the high-profile casualties of the crisis. Efforts by the government to stabilize the banking sector, including a blanket guarantee on bank deposits and the establishment of the Indonesian Bank Restructuring Agency (IBRA), were undermined by the scale of the crisis and lingering corruption. The IBRA's mandate to recapitalize and restructure failing banks was often

[137] Radelet, S., & Sachs, J.D. (1998). "The EastAsianFinancial Crisis: Diagnosis, Remedies, Prospects." Brookings Papers on Economic Activity, 1998(1), 1–90.

[138] Booth, A. (1998). The Indonesian Economy in the Nineteenth and Twentieth Centuries: A History of Missed Opportunities. London: Palgrave Macmillan.

[139] Robison, R., & Hadiz, V. (2004). Reorganising Power in Indonesia: The Politics of Oligarchy in an Age of Markets. London: Routledge.

compromised by political interference, further delaying recovery.[140] The crisis also revealed deeper structural flaws in Indonesia's economic model. Its dependence on foreign capital, particularly short-term loans, made the economy highly vulnerable to external shocks. At the same time, the lack of effective regulation and oversight in the financial sector allowed risky practices to flourish unchecked. These weaknesses not only intensified the severity of the crisis but also contributed to the erosion of public trust in the government, culminating in Suharto's resignation in 1998 amidst widespread protests and economic collapse. Public anger over corruption, nepotism, and rising inequality fuelled mass protests, culminating in Suharto's resignation in May 1998. This marked the end of the New Order and initiated a period of democratic transition, characterized by decentralization and political reform.

The legacy of the New Order is complex and multifaceted. On one hand, the regime's economic policies laid the foundation for significant development achievements, lifting millions out of poverty and transforming Indonesia into a middle-income country. On the other hand, its authoritarian governance, entrenched corruption, and inequitable development left deep scars on the nation's political and economic fabric. Post-New Order reforms have sought to address these issues, with mixed results. While democratization and anti-corruption measures have achieved notable progress, the enduring influence of entrenched elites and the structural challenges inherited from the New Order continue to shape Indonesia's development trajectory.

In conclusion, the New Order era underscores the trade-offs between state-led development and inclusive governance. Indonesia's experience during this period provides valuable lessons on the importance of accountability, transparency, and equitable resource distribution in achieving sustainable development. As the nation moves forward, addressing the lingering effects of the New Order's legacy will remain a critical task in building a resilient and inclusive democracy.

References

Acemoglu, D. & Robinson, J. A. (2012) Why Nations Fail: The Origins of Power, Prosperity, and Poverty. New York: Crown Publishers.

[140] Hill, H. (1996). The Indonesian Economy: Growth and Structural Change. Cambridge: Cambridge University Press.

Anderson, B. R. O'G. (1990) Language and Power: Exploring Political Cultures in Indonesia. Ithaca, NY: Cornell University Press.
Aspinall, E. (2009). Islam and Nation: Separatist Rebellion in Aceh, Indonesia. Stanford University Press.
Aspinall, E., & Berenschot, W. (2019). Democracy for Sale: Elections, Clientelism, and the State in Indonesia. Ithaca, NY: Cornell University Press.
Aspinall, E., & Fealy, G. (2010). Soeharto's New Order and Its Legacy: Essays in Honour of Harold Crouch. Canberra: ANU Press.
Booth, A. (1998) The Indonesian Economy in the Nineteenth and Twentieth Centuries: A History of Missed Opportunities. London: Macmillan.
Booth, A. (1999). "The Impact of the Crisis on Poverty and Equity." Developing Economies, 37(4), 401–418.
Budiman, A., Hatley, B., & Kingsbury, D. (1999). Reformasi: Crisis and Change in Indonesia. Monash Asia Institute.
Buehler, M. (2013). "Married with the State: Business Elites and Electoral Politics in Indonesia's Democratic Transition." Comparative Political Studies, 46(7), 912–935.
Crouch, H. (1978). The Army and Politics in Indonesia. Cornell University Press.
Hadiz, V. (2010). Localising Power in Post-Authoritarian Indonesia: A Southeast Asia Perspective. Stanford, CA: Stanford University Press.
Hill, H. (1996). The Indonesian Economy Since 1966: Southeast Asia's Emerging Giant. Cambridge: Cambridge University Press.
Hill, H. (1996). The Indonesian Economy: Growth and Structural Change. Cambridge: Cambridge University Press.
Jomo, K. S. (2001) Southeast Asia's Misunderstood Miracle: Industrial Policy and Economic Development in Thailand, Malaysia and Indonesia. Boulder, CO: Westview Press.
Klinken, G. van, & Barker, J. (2009). State of Authority: The State in Society in Indonesia. Cornell Southeast Asia Program.
MacIntyre, A. (1999). Business and Politics in Indonesia. Allen & Unwin.
MacIntyre, A. (2003) The Power of Institutions: Political Architecture and Governance. Ithaca, NY: Cornell University Press
Mackie, J. A. C. (1995). Money and Power in Indonesia: Political Economy in the New Order and Beyond. Allen & Unwin.
McLeod, R. H. (2000) 'Soeharto's Indonesia: A Better Class of Corruption', Agenda, 7(2), pp. 99–112.
Pangestu, M., & Habir, A.D. (1989). Indonesia's Agricultural Development: Policy and Performance. Jakarta: CSIS.
Pangestu, M. (1996). Economic Reforms, Deregulation, and Privatization: The Indonesian Experience. Jakarta: Centre for Strategic and International Studies.

Radelet, S. & Sachs, J. (1998) The East Asian Financial Crisis: Diagnosis, Remedies, Prospects. Brookings Papers on Economic Activity, 1998(1), pp. 1–74.

Robison, R. (1986) Indonesia: The Rise of Capital. Sydney: Allen & Unwin.

Robison, R., & Hadiz, V. (2004). Reorganising Power in Indonesia: The Politics of Oligarchy in an Age of Markets. London: Routledge.

Rosser, A. (2002) The Politics of Economic Liberalization in Indonesia: State, Market and Power. Richmond: Curzon Press.

Schwarz, A. (1994). A Nation in Waiting: Indonesia's Search for Stability. Westview Press.

Soesastro, H., and Basri, M. C. (1998) 'Survey of Recent Developments', Bulletin of Indonesian Economic Studies, 34(1), pp. 3–54.

Tirtosudarmo, R. (1995). The Politics of Population Mobility in Indonesia. Gadjah Mada University Press.

Varkkey, H. (2015). The Haze Problem in Southeast Asia: Palm Oil and Patronage. London: Routledge.

Warburton, E. (2020). "Reforming Indonesia's Anti-Corruption Institutions: The Limits of Resistance." Asian Survey, 60(2), 248–270.

Winters, J. A. (1996) Power in Motion: Capital Mobility and the Indonesian State. Ithaca, NY: Cornell University Press.

CHAPTER 11

Conclusion

Introduction

Indonesia's economic development over the past four millennia has been shaped by a combination of geographical advantages, external influences, governance structures, and socio-economic transformations. From the early maritime kingdoms of Srivijaya and Majapahit to the Dutch colonial economy, post-independence nationalism, and the authoritarian industrialization of the New Order, each era has left an imprint on the country's political economy. The economic structure of Indonesia has continuously evolved, driven by both internal dynamics and global interactions. While historical legacies have influenced modern economic patterns, the country has also undergone significant shifts in response to external pressures and internal political transitions.

This chapter consolidates the main themes and patterns from previous discussions, analysing the long-term trends that have defined Indonesia's development. By examining the trajectory of trade, industrialization, external economic forces, inequality, governance, and policy-making, we gain a deeper understanding of how Indonesia has navigated the complexities of economic growth. The chapter further highlights the historical continuities, major turning points, and structural challenges that continue to shape the nation's economy. The final section outlines key lessons for the future, emphasizing sustainable and inclusive growth, institutional reform, and balanced economic development.

S. Ramesh, *The Political Economy of Indonesia's Economic Development, Volume I*, https://doi.org/10.1007/978-3-031-94350-8_11

Historical Continuities and Transformations

A fundamental feature of Indonesia's economic history is the tension between continuity and transformation. While political regimes, economic strategies, and global circumstances have changed, several enduring themes have shaped the country's trajectory. The economy has been continuously influenced by trade, external economic dependence, and patterns of industrialization. Even as Indonesia has undergone substantial political and structural changes, historical economic legacies have persisted, creating both opportunities and challenges.

The Persistence of Trade and External Orientation

Indonesia's economic development has been fundamentally shaped by its position as a maritime trading hub. The Srivijaya Empire (seventh–thirteenth centuries) leveraged its control over the Malacca Strait, positioning itself as a dominant force in regional commerce. This tradition continued under the Majapahit Empire (fourteenth–fifteenth centuries), which further expanded Indonesia's trade networks, connecting the archipelago to China, India, and the Middle East. Trade brought wealth and prosperity to early kingdoms, demonstrating the strategic role of Indonesia's geography in global commerce.

The Dutch colonial era (seventeenth–twentieth centuries) transformed the economy by integrating Indonesia into global supply chains, restructuring production to serve European markets. The Cultivation System (1830s–1870s) and subsequent plantation economies locked Indonesia into a pattern of export-oriented, resource-based dependency, where the production of cash crops such as coffee, sugar, and rubber prioritized the needs of the colonial administration rather than local economic development. Despite independence, this structural dependence persisted in different forms. Under Suharto's New Order (1966–1998), Indonesia aggressively pursued foreign direct investment (FDI) and export-led industrialization, accelerating growth but reinforcing vulnerabilities to global market fluctuations. This model boosted manufacturing and natural resource exports but also led to over-reliance on foreign capital and external demand. The 1997–1998Asian Financial Crisis exposed the fragility of this approach, triggering a financial collapse that forced Indonesia into deep economic and political reform. While the post-1998 Reformasi period saw efforts to reduce reliance on external forces,

Indonesia remains heavily dependent on commodity exports, foreign investment, and global supply chains.

Industrialization and Economic Modernization

Indonesia's transformation from an agrarian economy to an industrial economy has been uneven and marked by discontinuities. Under Dutch colonial rule, the economy remained overwhelmingly agrarian, with infrastructure projects such as railways and ports primarily serving plantation-based exports. While colonial investments in infrastructure provided long-term benefits, industrialization was delayed by an economic model that prioritized raw material extraction over local manufacturing.

Post-independence efforts at industrialization were state-driven, particularly under Sukarno's Guided Democracy (1957–1965). The government sought to nationalize industries and assert economic independence, but these efforts were poorly managed, leading to stagnation, inflation, and inefficiencies. Economic mismanagement, coupled with political instability, resulted in weak industrial progress. In contrast, Suharto's New Order (1966–1998) introduced market-oriented policies that facilitated rapid industrialization. The state promoted foreign investment, deregulation, and privatization, fostering growth in manufacturing, mining, and oil. By the late 1980s, Indonesia had become an export-driven economy, benefitting from natural resource booms and manufacturing expansion. However, the growth model relied on low labour costs, foreign capital, and resource extraction, creating structural weaknesses such as environmental degradation and economic inequality. The post-1998 Reformasi era saw an expansion of the service sector, digital economy, and regional industrialization, yet industrialization remains unevenly distributed, concentrated in Java, while many outer islands continue to lag behind.

The Role of External Influences

Indonesia's economic development cannot be understood without considering the impact of external forces. The country's economic trajectory has been shaped by pre-colonial trade networks, colonial extraction, Cold War economic policies, and contemporary globalization. External interactions have brought both opportunities and challenges, influencing economic structures, governance strategies, and resource allocation.

Pre-Colonial Trade and Cultural Exchange

Long before European colonialism, Indian and Chinese merchants played a significant role in shaping Indonesian trade networks. Indian influence introduced Hindu-Buddhist cultural and governance models, shaping the early kingdoms of Srivijaya, Majapahit, and Tarumanagara. Simultaneously, Chinese traders established commercial networks, introducing goods such as ceramics, textiles, and silver. This historical integration into global commerce laid the foundation for Indonesia's future role as a trading hub. Even today, the Chinese-Indonesian business community remains a dominant economic force, controlling major sectors such as banking, retail, and manufacturing. Despite facing political and social challenges, the ethnic Chinese business elite has been central to Indonesia's economic success. These historical trade interactions demonstrate how external influences shaped local economic structures and cultural development.

Colonialism and Economic Exploitation

The Dutch colonial period (1602–1942) radically altered Indonesia's economy, reorienting it toward resource extraction for European benefit. The Dutch East India Company (VOC) monopolized the spice trade, later replaced by direct colonial rule that imposed exploitative economic policies. Two key periods stand out:

The Cultivation System (1830s–1870s): This policy forced local farmers to produce cash crops such as coffee and sugar, benefiting the Dutch while impoverishing rural Indonesians.

The Liberal Period (1870s–1930s): Dutch policies promoted private European plantations, leading to capitalist development but also deepening rural inequality and land dispossession.

Colonialism left a legacy of economic dualism, where an elite-controlled export sector coexisted with widespread rural poverty. This structure persisted into the post-independence period, influencing economic policies and social inequalities.

Cold War, Globalization, and Neoliberalism

During the Cold War (1945–1991), Indonesia became a battleground for competing economic ideologies. Sukarno's government adopted a socialist model, emphasizing state control over resources and economic nationalism. However, this model failed to generate growth, leading to inflation, shortages, and foreign capital flight. Suharto's New Order reversed this by aligning Indonesia with Western capitalism, implementing market liberalization, privatization, and FDI incentives. While this led to high growth rates, it also encouraged corruption, elite monopolization, and environmental degradation. The post-1998 era further deepened Indonesia's integration into global markets, with strong export growth in natural resources, electronics, and palm oil. However, the reliance on foreign investment and commodity exports continues to expose Indonesia to global economic volatility, as seen in the 1997 financial crisis and the 2008 global recession.

Economic Inequality and Social Disparities

Indonesia's economic history has been characterized not just by growth and structural transformation but also by persistent inequality. Economic benefits have rarely been evenly distributed across regions, social classes, and ethnic groups, creating deep structural disparities that continue to shape modern Indonesia. While some regions have experienced rapid industrialization and infrastructure development, others remain marginalized and underdeveloped. Wealth concentration in the hands of a small elite, the dominance of Java in economic and political affairs, and the stark divide between urban and rural areas have contributed to a fragmented and unequal economic landscape.

Regional Disparities: The Java-Centric Economy

Since the Majapahit and Srivijaya periods, economic and political power has been concentrated in Java, a pattern that intensified under Dutch colonial rule. The Dutch administration centralized trade, bureaucracy, and infrastructure in Batavia (modern Jakarta), reinforcing Java's dominance while neglecting other regions. Even after independence, this Java-centric model persisted, with the island remaining the economic and administrative heart of Indonesia. Java's dominance is reflected in infrastructure development, industrialization, and government investment. The island hosts most of Indonesia's factories, universities, financial institutions, and corporate headquarters, making it the primary beneficiary of economic growth. In contrast, regions such as Papua, Maluku, and

East Nusa Tenggara remain underdeveloped and heavily dependent on resource extraction. While Java has received consistent investments in transport, digital infrastructure, and energy, the outer islands suffer from poor connectivity, limited access to markets, and underfunded public services. A stark example of this imbalance is Eastern Indonesia, which, despite its rich natural resources (gold, copper, oil, and timber), has some of the highest poverty rates in the country. The mining and plantation industries in these regions are often controlled by foreign corporations or Javanese conglomerates, meaning that local communities see little economic benefit from resource extraction. This uneven development has fuelled grievances and regional tensions, particularly in Papua, where demands for greater autonomy and economic justice remain unresolved.

Wealth Concentration and Crony Capitalism

Economic power in Indonesia has historically been concentrated in the hands of a small elite, from colonial plantation owners to modern-day business oligarchs. During Suharto's New Order (1966–1998), the government promoted rapid economic growth but also created a system of patronage capitalism, where business tycoons with personal ties to Suharto controlled key industries. Prominent figures such as Liem Sioe Liong (Salim Group), Bob Hasan (timber), and Suharto's own family accumulated vast wealth through monopolies, government contracts, and regulatory favouritism. By the 1990s, Indonesia had developed an exclusive capitalist class that dominated banking, real estate, and industry, while millions of Indonesians remained trapped in informal and low-wage employment.

The fall of Suharto in 1998 led to political liberalization but did not fundamentally restructure economic power. The same oligarchs retained control over major industries, adapting to democracy by funding political parties and influencing government policies. Palm oil conglomerates (Sinar Mas, Wilmar, Astra Agro Lestari) expanded at the expense of small farmers and Indigenous communities, while banking and finance remain concentrated among a handful of family-owned firms. The intersection between economic and political elites ensures that wealth remains in the hands of a privileged few, making meaningful economic reform difficult.

The Urban–Rural Divide

Indonesia's economic inequalities extend beyond regional disparities to the divide between urban and rural communities. Cities like Jakarta, Bandung, Surabaya, and Medan benefit from modern infrastructure, advanced education systems, and financial services, while rural areas remain underdeveloped, with low productivity and limited access to markets. Many rural communities continue to rely on subsistence agriculture, facing low crop yields, price volatility, and exploitative intermediaries.

Efforts to reduce rural poverty, such as land reform programs, rural electrification, and agricultural modernization, have had limited success due to weak enforcement and corruption. Many farmers still lack secure land tenure, making them vulnerable to land grabs by corporations and government-backed projects. Without targeted policies to bridge the rural–urban divide, millions of Indonesians will remain locked in economic precarity.

The Political Economy of Governance

Governance has played a decisive role in shaping Indonesia's economic trajectory. Throughout history, the country has oscillated between authoritarian centralization and democratic decentralization, each with distinct economic consequences. Early kingdoms such as Srivijaya and Majapahit relied on centralized control over trade routes and taxation to generate wealth. This tradition of top-down economic governance continued under Dutch colonial rule, where a highly bureaucratic system ensured that economic benefits flowed to the metropole rather than local populations.

Post-independence governance saw Indonesia experiment with multiple economic and political models. Sukarno's Guided Democracy (1957–1965) emphasized state control and nationalism, but mismanagement led to economic turmoil. In contrast, Suharto's New Order (1966–1998) introduced a mix of authoritarianism and economic liberalization, resulting in high growth but entrenched corruption and elite monopolization. The post-1998 Reformasi era marked a transition to democracy and decentralization, bringing both opportunities and new governance challenges.

Authoritarianism vs. Economic Growth: The New Order Model

The New Order (1966–1998) under Suharto is often described as a period of economic growth at the cost of political repression. Suharto's government introduced state-led industrialization, foreign investment incentives, and large-scale infrastructure projects, which resulted in sustained economic expansion. Between the 1970s and early 1990s, Indonesia's GDP grew by an average of 7% per year, making it one of the fastest-growing economies in Asia. The government focused on export-oriented industrialization, utilizing low labour costs and natural resources to attract foreign capital, particularly from Japan and the West. However, this economic success came with significant structural weaknesses. Suharto's model was based on patronage capitalism, where economic power was concentrated in the hands of military elites, political allies, and business tycoons loyal to the regime. Large conglomerates such as Salim Group, Sinar Mas, and Astra International secured monopolies over industries ranging from food production to manufacturing, ensuring that the benefits of economic growth remained restricted to a privileged elite. Meanwhile, small businesses and informal sector workers received little government support. While Suharto's policies created a more diversified economy, they also fostered deep corruption. Government contracts, licensing, and financial bailouts were distributed based on political loyalty rather than market efficiency, leading to inefficiencies and systemic economic vulnerabilities. These flaws were brutally exposed during the 1997–1998Asian Financial Crisis, when massive capital flight, a collapsing banking sector, and plummeting currency values triggered an economic meltdown. The crisis exacerbated unemployment, inflation, and social unrest, forcing Suharto to resign after three decades in power.

Post-1998: Democratic Reforms and Challenges

The fall of Suharto in 1998 marked a dramatic shift in Indonesia's governance structure, as the country embarked on a path of democratization and economic reform. The Reformasi era (1998–present) introduced key democratic reforms, including free elections, press freedom, and political decentralization. These changes created a more open political environment, allowing for greater public participation in economic policy-making. However, the transition from authoritarianism to democracy also introduced new economic governance challenges. One of the most significant reforms was decentralization (2001), which shifted power from the central government to local and regional authorities. While this allowed for more localized decision-making and resource allocation, it also led to fragmented governance, inconsistencies in economic policy, and new forms of corruption. Many local governments lacked the expertise or institutional capacity to manage economic policies effectively, leading to wasteful spending, bureaucratic inefficiencies, and rent-seeking behaviour. Moreover, Indonesia's political landscape post-1998 became heavily influenced by oligarchs and business elites, who leveraged campaign financing and media control to shape policy in their favour. Political dynasties and business tycoons increasingly dominated parliament, ensuring that economic reforms continued to serve the interests of large corporations rather than broader society. This has made efforts at land reform, labour rights protections, and anti-monopoly regulations difficult to implement.

Corruption and Weak Institutions

Despite democratic reforms, corruption remains a major impediment to Indonesia's economic progress. While institutions such as the Corruption Eradication Commission (KPK) have taken steps to prosecute high-level officials, political interference and legal loopholes often allow corrupt actors to avoid accountability. Judicial corruption remains a major issue, with businesses and political elites frequently bribing judges and regulators to secure favourable rulings. Large-scale infrastructure projects, while essential for economic growth, are often riddled with cost inflation and procurement fraud due to bribery in government contracts. The mining, logging, and palm oil industries continue to operate with minimal environmental oversight, as corrupt officials frequently overlook illegal activities in exchange for financial incentives. While civil society, independent media, and social movements have strengthened accountability, systemic corruption remains a major obstacle to achieving inclusive and sustainable economic development.

Lessons for the Future

Indonesia stands at a critical juncture in its economic development, facing both opportunities and challenges. The country has successfully transitioned from an agrarian and resource-dependent economy to a diverse and globally integrated economy. However, structural weaknesses, institutional inefficiencies, and environmental degradation threaten long-term sustainability. Moving forward, policy reforms, strategic investments, and governance improvements will be key in ensuring inclusive and resilient growth.

Balancing Global Integration with Domestic Development

Throughout its history, Indonesia has relied heavily on external trade and foreign investment, dating back to the maritime empires of Srivijaya and Majapahit. The Dutch colonial economy entrenched an export-driven structure, prioritizing raw material extraction for global markets. Post-independence policies oscillated between economic nationalism under Sukarno and global market integration under Suharto. Today, Indonesia remains highly dependent on commodity exports, including palm oil, coal, natural gas, and rubber, making the economy vulnerable to global price fluctuations and demand shocks. To mitigate this external dependency, Indonesia must diversify its industrial base and invest in high-value sectors. The government must shift from low-cost manufacturing to technology-intensive industries, such as semiconductors, digital services, electric vehicles (EVs), and pharmaceuticals. This requires substantial investment in research and development (R&D), innovation hubs, and human capital development. Countries like South Korea and Taiwan successfully transitioned from resource-based economies to high-tech economies through government-backed industrial policies, a model that Indonesia could adapt. Furthermore, trade policies must prioritize value-added exports. Instead of merely exporting raw materials like bauxite and nickel, Indonesia should develop downstream processing industries. The government's 2020 ban on unprocessed nickel exports was a step in the right direction, compelling investors to establish domestic smelters and refining facilities. Expanding similar policies to copper, palm oil, and timber industries will allow Indonesia to capture greater economic value from its natural resources. At the same time, strengthening domestic enterprises and SMEs (small and medium enterprises) is crucial. While large conglomerates dominate banking, retail, and energy, SMEs contribute 60% of GDP and employ 97% of Indonesia's workforce. Expanding access to credit, digital infrastructure, and market linkages for SMEs can boost economic competitiveness and local entrepreneurship.

Addressing Structural Inequality

Despite impressive economic growth, Indonesia faces deep structural inequality, exacerbated by regional disparities, wealth concentration, and rural–urban divides. The Java-centric economic model continues to marginalize outer islands like Sumatra, Kalimantan, Sulawesi, and Papua, where poverty rates remain significantly higher than in Jakarta and Surabaya. Without targeted policies, these inequalities will persist, fuelling regional grievances and social unrest. To promote balanced regional development, the government must implement Special Economic Zones (SEZs) outside Java, offering tax incentives, infrastructure investment, and streamlined regulations to attract industries to underdeveloped regions. Successful SEZs in Vietnam, China, and the Philippines have demonstrated how strategic regional investments can stimulate job creation and economic diversification. Additionally, improving inter-island connectivity through better ports, highways, and digital networks will help integrate regional economies into national and global supply chains. Land reform remains another critical issue in reducing inequality. The Suharto-era land distribution policies favoured large agribusinesses, logging firms, and palm oil conglomerates, often at the expense of small farmers and indigenous communities. Implementing a transparent and fair land redistribution program, coupled with legal protections for customary land rights, will empower rural populations and reduce land-related conflicts.

Expanding social protection programs is also essential in reducing income disparities. Policies such as cash transfer programs, universal healthcare expansion, and subsidized education have successfully lifted millions out of poverty in Brazil (Bolsa Familia) and China. Indonesia must scale up and modernize its welfare programs, ensuring better targeting, reduced corruption, and stronger administrative capacity.

Strengthening Institutions and Anti-Corruption Efforts.

Weak institutions and pervasive corruption continue to undermine Indonesia's long-term economic potential. While democratic reforms have strengthened civil liberties and political participation, governance challenges persist in judiciary independence, regulatory enforcement, and public administration. The Corruption Eradication Commission (KPK) has made significant strides in prosecuting high-profile cases, yet political interference and legal loopholes have often weakened its effectiveness.

One of the biggest barriers to economic progress is bureaucratic inefficiency. Investors frequently cite complex licensing procedures, regulatory uncertainty, and inconsistent law enforcement as deterrents to business expansion. Streamlining business regulations, enhancing e-governance, and strengthening legal enforcement will improve investor confidence and economic productivity. Judicial reform is another urgent priority. Many business disputes, land conflicts, and corruption cases remain unresolved due to bribery within the judiciary. Strengthening judicial integrity, ensuring transparent appointment processes, and increasing public accountability will help rebuild trust in the legal system. Political finance reform is also necessary to reduce the influence of oligarchs and corporate interests in policy-making. Campaign financing laws must be restructured to limit private donations and promote greater transparency in election spending. Without these reforms, economic policies will continue to be shaped by elite interests rather than national priorities.

Environmental Sustainability: Managing Resource Extraction

Indonesia faces severe environmental challenges due to deforestation, illegal logging, industrial pollution, and unsustainable mining practices. While natural resources have fuelled economic growth, their unchecked exploitation threatens long-term ecological and economic stability. Historically, palm oil plantations, mining operations, and timber industries have expanded with little regard for environmental impact, leading to biodiversity loss, indigenous displacement, and climate vulnerability. To ensure sustainable development, Indonesia must adopt stricter environmental regulations and enforcement mechanisms. The government should introduce carbon taxes on high-emission industries, strengthen land-use planning to protect rainforests, and incentivize eco-friendly business practices. Countries such as Norway and Costa Rica have successfully implemented green policies without sacrificing economic growth, providing valuable models for Indonesia. Investing in renewable energy is also critical. Despite being rich in geothermal, solar, and hydroelectric potential, Indonesia remains heavily reliant on coal and fossil fuels. The government must accelerate the transition to clean energy by offering subsidies for solar panel installations, expanding wind and hydroelectric projects, and phasing out coal power plants. Expanding green energy infrastructure will not only reduce carbon emissions but also create high-value jobs and attract sustainable investment. Finally, stronger legal protections for Indigenous land rights are essential. Indigenous communities have been disproportionately affected by deforestation and land seizures, often losing access to ancestral lands without adequate compensation. Strengthening legal frameworks to recognize customary land ownership will prevent corporate encroachment and promote community-led conservation efforts.

Conclusion

Indonesia's economic development has been a story of resilience, adaptation, and structural transformation, shaped by four millennia of trade, colonialism, nationalism, globalization, and governance reforms. From the early maritime empires of Srivijaya and Majapahit, which leveraged strategic geography and trade networks, to the Dutch colonial system that restructured the economy for European benefit, Indonesia's historical trajectory has been defined by external dependence, elite economic control, and struggles for self-sufficiency. The post-independence period brought efforts to break free from colonial economic legacies, but internal mismanagement, authoritarian rule, and corruption continued to shape economic policy. Despite these challenges, Indonesia has emerged as one of the largest and fastest-growing economies in Southeast Asia, transitioning from an agrarian-based economy to an industrial and service-driven one. However, despite significant progress, persistent structural weaknesses continue to hinder equitable and sustainable growth. The economy remains highly dependent on natural resource exports, making it vulnerable to global commodity price fluctuations. Wealth and industrial activity are concentrated in Java, exacerbating regional disparities and fuelling social and economic inequalities. The political economy remains dominated by oligarchic elites, who use their economic power to influence policy-making and protect monopolistic interests. Furthermore, corruption, weak institutions, and environmental degradation pose additional barriers to long-term development.

Historical Patterns and Their Modern Legacy

One of the most enduring themes in Indonesia's economic history is the tension between external dependence and efforts at self-sufficiency. The country has long been integrated into global trade networks, from pre-colonial maritime empires to Dutch colonialism and post-independence globalization. However, each phase of integration has come with significant risks and challenges. Colonial-era extraction prioritized European interests, leaving Indonesia with a resource-dependent economic structure. The New Order (1966–1998) sought to modernize the economy through foreign investment and industrialization, but this approach led to crony capitalism and economic vulnerabilities. The 1997–1998Asian Financial Crisis revealed the dangers of excessive dependence on foreign capital, forcing economic restructuring under IMF-imposed conditions. Today, Indonesia continues to struggle with balancing openness to global markets while building a resilient domestic economy. Another key historical continuity is the concentration of economic power among elites. During the Dutch era, wealth was controlled by European plantation owners and Chinese middlemen. The post-independence period saw the emergence of a state-controlled economy under Sukarno, followed by the rise of military-backed business conglomerates under Suharto. Even in the democratic era post-1998, political and business elites have retained significant control over strategic industries, infrastructure projects, and banking. As a result, Indonesia's economic policies have often been designed to protect elite interests, rather than promote broad-based, inclusive development.

Key Structural Challenges

Despite impressive growth, Indonesia faces four major structural challenges that must be addressed to ensure long-term economic sustainability:

Economic Inequality and Regional Disparities

Java remains the economic and administrative centre, while outer islands lag behind in infrastructure, industrialization, and investment.

Smallholder farmers, rural communities, and indigenous groups continue to be marginalized by large corporate monopolies, particularly in palm oil, logging, and mining.

Policies must focus on decentralizing economic growth, promoting investment in underdeveloped regions, and empowering SMEs to ensure more equitable wealth distribution.

Governance and Corruption

While democracy has brought political freedoms, weak institutions and rent-seeking behaviour continue to limit effective economic governance. Judicial corruption, regulatory inefficiencies, and opaque business practices deter foreign and domestic investment and limit economic competitiveness. Strengthening anti-corruption measures, improving regulatory transparency, and enforcing rule of law will be crucial in building investor confidence and reducing economic inefficiencies.

Environmental Sustainability and Resource Management

Deforestation, industrial pollution, and unsustainable mining practices threaten long-term agricultural productivity and biodiversity. Indonesia remains one of the world's largest carbon emitters, due to its reliance on coal and rapid deforestation for palm oil plantations. Implementing stronger environmental policies, transitioning to renewable energy, and enforcing corporate accountability will be key in ensuring sustainable growth.

Balancing Global Integration and Domestic Industrialization

Indonesia must move beyond commodity-based exports and develop value-added industries such as electronics, pharmaceuticals, and advanced manufacturing. Expanding research and development (R&D), investing in technical education, and promoting digital transformation will allow Indonesia to compete in higher-value industries. Strengthening regional trade agreements, reducing import dependencies, and enhancing domestic production capacity will improve economic resilience against global shocks.

The Path Forward: Strategic Policy Recommendations

To achieve sustained, inclusive, and equitable economic development, Indonesia must pursue a multi-pronged strategy focused on industrial diversification, institutional reform, and environmental protection. Key priorities include:

Investing in Infrastructure and Human Capital: Expanding transportation networks, digital infrastructure, and educational institutions to ensure broad-based economic participation.

Strengthening Governance and Transparency: Enhancing regulatory frameworks, empowering anti-corruption agencies, and promoting open government initiatives to attract investment and reduce inefficiencies.

Developing a Green Economy: Shifting toward renewable energy sources, implementing carbon pricing mechanisms, and promoting eco-friendly industries to mitigate climate risks.

Empowering SMEs and Local Enterprises: Providing financial support, digital access, and market linkages for small businesses to drive grassroots economic development.

Regional Economic Decentralization: Establishing Special Economic Zones (SEZs) in underdeveloped provinces, improving inter-island connectivity, and ensuring equal resource distribution.

Conclusion: Indonesia's Potential in the Twenty-First Century

Indonesia has enormous potential to become a leading economic powerhouse in the twenty-first century. As the fourth most populous nation, the largest economy in Southeast Asia, and a key member of the G20, Indonesia is well-positioned to leverage its demographic dividend, rich natural resources, and strategic geographic location. However, to fully realize this potential, bold economic reforms, institutional strengthening, and sustainable policies must be pursued. The nation's historical experience demonstrates both resilience and adaptability. While past challenges have often stemmed from colonial legacies, elite dominance, and governance weaknesses, Indonesia has also repeatedly overcome crises and reinvented its economic model. Moving forward, the country must learn from history and implement policies that prioritize long-term stability over short-term gains. Indonesia's economic transformation will depend on its ability to harness innovation, promote inclusive development, and build strong institutions. If the right policies are adopted, Indonesia can transition from a resource-dependent economy to a knowledge-based, technologically advanced, and environmentally sustainable global leader.

Final Thought

History has shown that economic success is not predetermined—it is the result of strategic choices and sound governance. The lessons of the past provide Indonesia with a blueprint for a more equitable and prosperous future. The decisions made today will determine whether Indonesia fulfils its aspiration of becoming a high-income nation or remains trapped in the middle-income dilemma. The opportunity exists—it is now up to policymakers, businesses, and society to seize it.

Index

A

S. Ramesh, *The Political Economy of Indonesia's Economic Development, Volume I*, https://doi.org/10.1007/978-3-031-94350-8

D

J

T

U

V

The manufacturer's authorised representative in the EU is Springer Nature Customer Service Centre GmbH, Europaplatz 3, 69115 Heidelberg, Germany. If you have any concerns regarding our products, please contact ProductSafety@springernature.com

Printed and bound by CPI Group (UK) Ltd, Croydon, CR0 4YY
01/10/2026
02225967-0017